ABOUT THE AUTHOR

KENDALL PRESTON, JR., is Senior Staff Scientist in the Research Department of the Perkin-Elmer Corporation where he pioneered in the development of coherent optical computers. He is the inventor of the membrane light modulator and of synthetic-aperture acoustic holography and holds more than a dozen patents, both foreign and domestic.

After receiving both his B.A. and M.S. degrees from Harvard University in the early 1950s, Mr. Preston joined the technical staff of the Bell Telephone Laboratories. There he worked on the application of new semiconductor and magnetic materials to the fabrication of logic and memory systems for a variety of industrial, military, and commercial computers. He participated in the development of memory systems for the Nike Zeus and the Bell System Data Processing programs using the memory element called the Twistor.

In the 1960s Mr. Preston joined the Perkin-Elmer Corporation as Manager of New Product Development in the Optical Group. In conjunction with a variety of military and civilian government agencies the author pioneered the development of coherent optical computers for use in radar, sonar, communications, holography, and pattern recognition. In association with a NASA program at the University of Pittsburgh, the author's group was the first to demonstrate the application of optical computation for automatically locating chromosome spreads on microscope slides. As part of a National Institutes of Health program with the University of Rochester, the author's group created the first digital computer capable of automating certain tasks in biomedical image processing, such as the counting and identification of human peripheral white blood cells.

Mr. Preston has published papers on a variety of topics in many professional journals and trade publications. He is a member of many professional societies, including the American Association for the Advancement of Science, the Biological Engineering Society (Great Britain), the Biomedical Engineering Society, the Harvard Engineers and Scientists, the Institute of Electrical and Electronics Engineers, and the New York Academy of Sciences. He has served on many committees of the IEEE, and was founder and chairman of the Connecticut Chapter of the Professional Technical Group on Electronic Computers as well as Vice-Chairman of the Connecticut Section. Recently he has served with the Engineering Foundation in organizing a series of Engineering Foundation Research Conferences on Engineering in Medicine.

Coherent
Optical
Computers

Coherent Optical Computers

Kendall Preston, Jr.

Senior Staff Scientist, The Perkin-Elmer Corporation
Formerly of Bell Telephone Laboratories

McGRAW-HILL BOOK COMPANY

New York   St. Louis   San Francisco   Düsseldorf   Johannesburg
Kuala Lumpur   London   Mexico   Montreal   New Delhi
Panama   Rio de Janeiro   Singapore   Sydney   Toronto

Library of Congress Cataloging in Publication Data

Preston, Kendall
  Coherent optical computers.

  Includes bibliographical references.
  1. Optical data processing. I. Title.
TK7895.06P74   621.3819'598   73-152008
ISBN 0-07-050785-6

1234567890MAMM765432

This book was set in Linofilm Baskerville by The European Printing Corporation Limited, and printed and bound by The Maple Press Company. The editors were Tyler G. Hicks and Lila M. Gardner. The designer was Naomi Auerbach. Teresa F. Leaden supervised production.

*To my mother and father
for their interest and encouragement
and my wife, Sally, and daughter, Louise,
for their patience*

Contents

6. Lens-system Fabrication and Test   177

7. Method of Output Detection   206

8. Digital Techniques   232

9. Applications   251

x   Contents

Preface

This book is written by an electronics systems engineer for the engineer or student who requires a broad introduction at an advanced level to the relatively new field of optical computation. It is assumed that the reader is fluent in electromagnetic theory, information theory, and quantum electronics and needs no introduction to single- and double-sideband communications. Thus this book does not provide material of a tutorial nature but does guide the reader to background literature when necessary.

Because of the important overlap between optical computer engineering and applied physics, the reader will find that the text emphasizes a fundamental physical and mathematical approach to each facet of the subject. Mathematical models are frequently developed so as to contribute to a basic understanding of such phenomena as the interaction of optical radiation with spatial light modulators, lens elements, and photodetectors.

Chapter One provides what is hoped will be an interesting historical review as well as a summary of the technological state-of-the-art in coherent optical computation. Methods of optical design which relate specifically to the coherent optical computer are surveyed in Chapter Two. Chapter Three discusses both traditional and modern light sources with particular reference to the laser. The mathematics of optical computation is the subject of Chapter Four. Chapter Five is an extensive review of methods for entering information into the optical computer by various types of spatial light modulation. Here photographic, acoustic, thermoplastic, and membrane light-modulating techniques are treated in detail. Lens fabrication as well as lens-system test and evaluation are the subject of Chapter Six. Chapter Seven deals with methods of computer output detection and treats problems in both the spatial and temporal domain. Chapter Eight deals with digital techniques. Finally, Chapter Nine discusses and illustrates most of the important modern applications.

Some chapters, such as those on light sources, optical design, and photodetection, are written as concise summaries or surveys with frequent reference to the available literature. Other chapters, such as those on the mathematics of optical computation and on spatial light modulation, are rigorous analytical treatments and are frequently accompanied by the presentation of original material. Chapter Eight on coherent digital techniques discloses entirely new and previously unpublished developments.

The reader should remember that successful optical-computer design is a complex multidisciplinary pursuit which, of necessity, requires a depth of knowledge in many fields. This provides challenge, excitement, and rewards to those who are successful in exploiting this new technology. It is hoped that this book will assist the reader in capitalizing on these possibilities.

In preparing this book the author has benefited from the assistance of many colleagues who have furnished illustrative material. Such illustrations carry the appropriate credit line. Those which do not were supplied to the author by the Perkin-Elmer Corporation for which the author is wholeheartedly indebted. James Pascucci and Grace Chew of Perkin-Elmer are to be congratulated for their accomplishments in preparing the excellent line drawings. The author also thanks Jeanne McLeod, Andrea Miller, Carol Safranek, and Leslie Whone, all of Perkin-Elmer, for the many months spent typing and retyping the manuscript, and Gennifer Austin who assisted in preparing the index. Finally Abe Offner and Joseph Vrabel, also of Perkin-Elmer, contributed useful and comprehensive reviews of Chapters Two and Four, respectively.

Kendall Preston, Jr.

**Coherent
Optical
Computers**

Chapter One

Introduction

1.00 Historical Background

The first major research and development effort in coherent-optical-computer systems was initiated in 1953 at the University of Michigan. This program was contracted with the U.S. Army Signal Corps, Fort Monmouth, New Jersey [1.1]* and the U.S. Air Force Wright Patterson Air Development Center, Dayton, Ohio [1.2]. "Project Michigan," as the program was called, without question represents one of the most successful applications of coherent optical computation. Project Michigan was stimulated by the discovery, made at the University of Michigan, of the analogy between electronic matched filtering in airborne coherent radar signal processing and the interaction between a conical lens and a coherently illuminated two-dimensional recording of the incoming radar signals (see Chap. Nine). One of the early optical computers built at Project Michigan is shown in Fig. 1.1. Since this computer was designed before the invention of the laser, it was powered

*Numbers in brackets refer to numbered references listed at the end of the chapter.

1

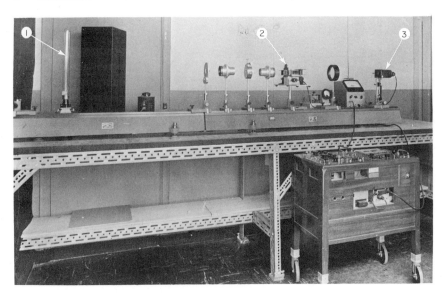

Fig. 1.1   Early optical computer used at the University of Michigan for radar signal processing. (1) Light source, (2) film transport, (3) output detector. (*University of Michigan.*)

by light generated by a mercury arc. Operation in real time was therefore impossible but a significant economic improvement over the equivalent electronic radar-signal-processing methodology was achieved. As will be discussed in more detail in Chapter Nine, this type of coherent optical computer consists of a light source; an input film transport, which carries a photographic recording of incoming radar signals through the system; and an optical system consisting of conical and spherical lenses arranged so as to form by cross correlation an image of the radar reflectivity of the ground. Specifically this optical computer continuously calculates a set of correlation functions given by the equation

$$c_i(t) = \int_A s_i(x - v_T t) r_i(x) dx \qquad (1.1)$$

where $s_i(x - v_T t)$ is the signal received from the ith range-resolution cell, v_T is the input film-transport velocity, and r_i is the so-called "reference function" for the ith range-resolution cell. The output correlation functions $c_i(t)$, or "radar map," are recorded on a moving output photographic film carried by the output film transport in synchronism with the input film. Later versions of this type of optical computer include the AN/APQ-102 designed and fabricated by the Arizona Division of the Goodyear Aerospace Corporation under contract to the McDonnell-Douglas Corporation, using lens elements produced by the Perkin–Elmer Corporation (see Fig. 1.2).

Fig. 1.2 The AN/APQ-102 optical computer for use with military coherent side-looking radars. (1) Output film transport and chemical processor, (2) input film transport. (*Goodyear Aerospace Corp.*)

Probably the most sophisticated coherent optical computer for coherent radar signal processing is the precision optical processor (POP) which is now in operation at the University of Michigan. The POP computer, shown in Fig. 1.3, which was designed and fabricated in a joint Project Michigan–Perkin-Elmer program under contract to the U.S. Air Force, is equivalent to hundreds of digital central processing units operating in parallel. In digital terms, the POP computer multiplies 100 million pairs of 5-bit words and performs an equal number of 5-bit additions each millisecond. This is equivalent to a digital processing rate of about 10^{12} bits per second. Still further increases in speed are within the state of the art.

Another coherent-optical-computer research and development

Fig. 1.3 The precision optical processor. (*University of Michigan.*)

program of significance was that undertaken by the Columbia University Electronics Research Laboratory (CUERL). This program, started in 1958, has been concerned with phased-array radar signal processing as related to Project Defender conducted by the Advanced Research Projects Agency (ARPA). Unlike the airborne coherent radar mapping systems developed under Project Michigan, which can afford to record incoming signals on photographic film, chemically develop the recording, and move it through the optical computer so as to perform calculations in "delayed real time," phased-array radar systems must operate instantaneously on received signals as they arrive. This requirement led CUERL to concentrate its efforts on developing means other than photographic film for entering data in the optical computer. The approach selected was to use an array of acoustic-delay-line light modulators (see Chap. Five). By time-multiplexing signals from the phased-array radar into the appropriate acoustic light-modulating channels, the associated optical computer could be made to model the phased array and thereby calculate target positions in real time. A photograph of a coherent optical computer used by CUERL for phased-array radar-signal-processing studies is shown in Fig. 1.4.

Fig. 1.4 An optical computer for time-multiplexed, radar array signal processing. (1) Signal simulator, (2) 24-channel light modulator, (3) integrating lens, (4) drive mechanism, (5) photomultiplier, (6) slit transport mechanism, (7) X-Y recorder, (8) drive control. (*Columbia University Electronics Research Laboratory, now Riverside Research Institute.*)

Although the major application of coherent optical computation to date has been in radar signal processing, certain other applications have been investigated. Sylvania (Buffalo), Texas Instruments (Dallas), Boeing (Seattle), and Perkin-Elmer (Norwalk) have produced coherent optical computers for use in correlation-type communication receivers. Figure 1.5 pictures an optical computer for this purpose made by

Fig. 1.5 Coherent optical matched filter for use in digital communications. (1) Light source, (2) output detector, (3) acoustic-delay-line light modulators. (*United States Air Force.*)

Sylvania under contract to the U.S. Air Force Rome Air Development Center. This computer acts as a matched filter in a digital communications system using a pseudonoise code as a carrier (see Chap. Nine).

Many organizations in addition to those mentioned above are active in the field of coherent optical computation. Included are many industrial organizations such as American Optical (Southbridge), Conductron (Ann Arbor), General Electric (Syracuse), KMS Industries (Ann Arbor), Litton (Van Nuys), Lockheed (Plainfield and Palo Alto), Magnavox (Torrance), Radio Corporation of America (Morristown and Burlington), Sperry Rand (Sudbury and Great Neck), Technical Operations (Burlington), and United Aircraft (East Hartford), to name some of the most active. The reader is referred to the references for information on programs which have been conducted [1.3 to 1.57]. Besides applications in radar and communications, coherent optical computers have been built for use in sonar signal processing, seismology, image enhancement, antenna pattern analysis, signal analysis, and pattern recognition. Guiding this effort are many U.S. Department of Defense laboratories including, besides those mentioned above, the U.S. Army Geodesy, Intelligence, and Mapping Research and Development Agency (Fort Belvoir), the Naval Electronics Laboratory (San Diego), the Naval Underwater Sound Laboratory (New London), the Naval Ordnance Test Station (China Lake and Pasadena), the Office of Naval

Research (Washington), the Applied Physics Laboratory (Silver Spring), and others.

1.10   Basic Considerations

The coherent optical computer is used primarily in areas where vast numbers of calculations must be performed per unit time with only moderate accuracy.   The 10^{12} bits per second data-processing rate of the POP computer mentioned above could not possibly be achieved economically by purely electronic methods.   However, POP, as with other coherent optical computers, achieves accuracies of merely 1 to 10 parts in 100 in its calculations.   This limits the practical application of such computers to areas where high speed is vital but high accuracy is far less important.

The basic block diagram of a typical coherent optical computer is shown in Fig. 1.6.   A source of coherent optical energy is used to power the computer.   The term *coherent* implies that the optical frequency of the light source must be phase-locked to a small fraction of a radian for a length of time characteristic of the transit-time difference between different paths from the input of the optical system to the output.   For a typical optical frequency of 3.10^{14} Hz and a transit-time difference of several picoseconds this requirement implies frequency stability or *temporal coherence* of the order of several parts per thousand.   This requirement is fairly readily met by both lasers and properly filtered spectral sources (see Chap. Three).   In addition to meeting this

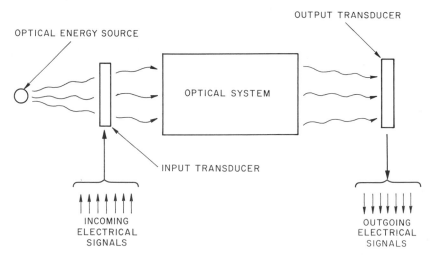

Fig. 1.6   General block diagram of a typical coherent optical computer system.

temporal-coherence requirement, the source of optical power for the coherent optical computer must exhibit *spatial coherence*. This implies that the phase of the optical frequency must be uniform across the spatial extent of the computer input plane. In other words, the computer must be illuminated from a single point source of temporally coherent light. To qualify as a point source, light illuminating the optical computer must come from a region in space whose diameter d meets the Abbe criterion [1.58], namely,

$$d = 1.22\lambda_L f_{no} \tag{1.2}$$

where λ_L is the optical wavelength and f_{no} is the f-number of the illuminating lens, i.e., the ratio of its focal length to its aperture.

At the input to the optical computer a transducer is used to both temporally and spatially modulate the illuminating light. The photographic-film-recording and acoustic-delay-line light modulators mentioned in Sec. 1.00 are typical embodiments of the input transducer. The optical system of the coherent optical computer in conjunction with the input transducer or transducers performs the required mathematical operations. Finally, an output transducer transforms the optical energy at the output of the computer into the desired set of output signals.

Mathematical calculations which may be performed by the coherent optical computer fall into five basic categories:

1. One- and two-dimensional spectrum analysis
2. Multichannel spectrum analysis
3. Frequency-plane matched filtering
4. Multichannel matched filtering
5. Multichannel correlation

Each of the above operations implies a somewhat different computer configuration. Typical examples of such configurations and a description of the method in which they perform the required calculations are treated on the following pages.

1.20   Spectrum Analysis

First consider spectrum analysis by the coherent optical computer. As is shown analytically in Chapter Four, the light amplitude distributions in the front and back focal planes of a lens have a two-dimensional Fourier-transform relationship given by the following equation:

$$E_2(\omega_x, \omega_y) = C_0 \iint E_1(x_1, y_1) e^{-j(\omega_x x_1 + \omega_y y_1)} \, dx_1 \, dy_1 \tag{1.3}$$

where E_1 and E_2 are the input and output electric field distributions, respectively.   The radian spatial frequencies ω_x and ω_y are related to the coordinates in the output plane by the expressions $\omega_x = 2\pi x_2/\lambda_L F$ and $\omega_y = 2\pi y_2/\lambda_L F$, where λ_L is the optical wavelength and F the focal length of the optical system utilized.   A coherent optical computer which takes advantage of this relationship in order to perform two-dimensional spectrum analysis is shown in Fig. 1.7.   The computer is powered by a continuous-wave gas laser consisting of a resonant cavity containing a plasma tube.   The plasma tube contains the energized gas mixture needed to generate light by stimulated emission of radiation at the required optical frequency.   An optical system is employed which expands the light beam emitted by the laser to the required aperture size.   The input transducer is placed in the front focal plane of the computer lens system and the output transducer in the back focal plane of this system.   Figure 1.7 illustrates the elementary case wherein the desired input is a simple one-dimensional sinusoid as plotted in Fig. 1.8.   A sinusoidal light amplitude input distribution can be produced (with a bias term) by recording the function shown in Fig. 1.8c on photographic film.   Since recordings on photographic film are traditionally measured in terms of light intensity transmission, the plot is the square of the desired light amplitude function.

A photograph of such an input recording is shown in Fig. 1.9. Mathematically the light intensity transmission $t_i(x_1, y_1)$ of the recording

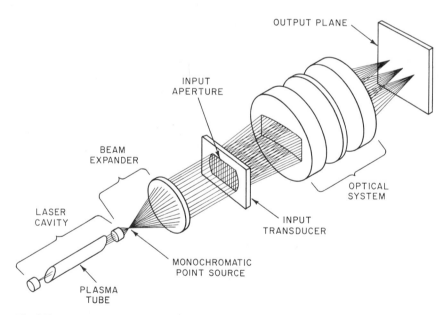

Fig. 1.7   Optical configuration for two-dimensional spectrum analysis.

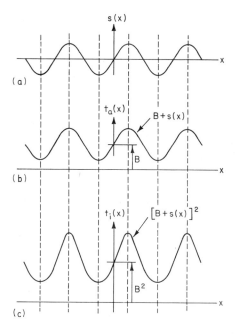

Fig. 1.8 Graph of a simple sinu-soidal-input pattern.

may be expressed by

$$t_i(x_1,y_1) = (B + \cos \omega_{x0}x_1)^2 \tag{1.4}$$

where B is called the bias term.   The light amplitude transmission $t_a(x_1,y_1)$ is therefore given by

$$t_a(x_1,y_1) = \sqrt{t_i(x_1,y_1)} = B + \cos \omega_{x0}x_1 \tag{1.5}$$

which may also be written

$$t_a(x_1,y_1) = B + \frac{e^{j\omega_{x0}x_1}}{2} + \frac{e^{-j\omega_{x0}x_1}}{2} \tag{1.6}$$

As will be discussed in Chapter Four, the term $e^{j\omega_{x0}x_1}$ represents a wave of light traveling at an angle whose sine is $\omega_{x0}\lambda_L/2\pi$ with respect to the optical axis, i.e., the axis of the optical system.   Similarly, the term $e^{-j\omega_{x0}x_1}$ represents a wave of light traveling at an angle whose sine is $-\omega_{x0}\lambda_L/2\pi$ with respect to the optical axis.   Finally, the bias term B represents a wave traveling parallel to the optical axis.   Thus the action of the sinusoidal input recording is to break up the incident light wave into three parts traveling in three different directions.   This phenomenon is called *diffraction*.

When the recording shown in Fig. 1.9 is placed in the input plane of the coherent optical computer and the output is detected by a spatial

Fig. 1.9 Photographic recording of a one-dimensional sinusoid.

square-law detector such as photographic film, the result is as shown in Fig. 1.10. Note that output is $E_2(\omega_x, \omega_y)E_2^*(\omega_x, \omega_y)$, where the asterisk represents the complex conjugate. This quantity is the power spectrum or Wiener spectrum of $E_1(x_1, y_1)$. The coordinates of the Wiener spectrum are the spatial frequency coordinates ω_x and ω_y. Light energy at the origin ($\omega_x = 0$, $\omega_y = 0$) in Fig. 1.10 represents the zero frequency or bias term present in the input recording. Light energy is also found at $\omega_x = \pm\omega_{x0}$ because of the effects of diffraction. Thus both positive and negative frequencies are symmetrically displayed in the output of the spectrum analyzer with no folding of the spectrum about the zero-frequency axis. Note also the so-called "side-lobe" structure in Fig. 1.10 which occurs in the vicinity of the points $(0,0)$, $(\omega_{x0}, 0)$, and $(-\omega_{x0}, 0)$ in the $\omega_x\omega_y$ plane. This phenomenon is analogous to time side lobes in electronics. In the coherent optical computer discussed here, the two-dimensional spatial side-lobe structure is observed because of the spatial limitations of the input aperture. In fact, as will be shown in Chapter Four, the side-lobe structure is related to the convolution of the Fourier transform of the input aperture with the Fourier transform of an infinite one-dimensional sine wave. The complete expression for the light intensity distribution $I(\omega_x, \omega_y)$ in the output plane of the coherent optical spectrum analyzer is given by

$$I(\omega_x, \omega_y) = E_2(\omega_x, \omega_y)E_2^*(\omega_x, \omega_y) = |T_a(\omega_x, \omega_y)*A(\omega_x, \omega_y)|^2 \qquad (1.7)$$

where $T_a(\omega_x, \omega_y)$ is the Fourier transform of $t_a(x_1, y_1)$ and $A(\omega_x, \omega_y)$ is the Fourier transform of the aperture. The asterisk in the expression on the right-hand side of the equation indicates convolution.

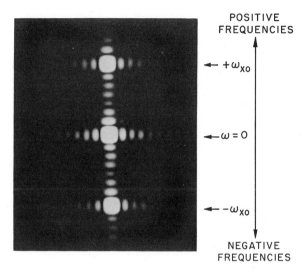

POSITIVE
FREQUENCIES

← $+\omega_{xo}$

← $\omega = 0$

← $-\omega_{xo}$

NEGATIVE
FREQUENCIES

Fig. 1.10 Photographic recording of the light intensity distribution in the output plane of a two-dimensional optical spectrum analyzer having a simple one-dimensional sinusoid of frequency ω_0 as input.

In comparison with most electronic spectrum analyzers the coherent computer has the advantage that it is "wide open," i.e., it does not scan through frequency as a function of time.   In fact the coherent optical spectrum analyzer acts as a filter bank with parallel outputs.   In order to compare the quality of a coherent optical computer used as a spectrum analyzer with its electronic counterpart, it is important to determine the time-bandwidth (TW) of the system.   The analogous quantity in optics is usually known as the space-bandwidth or SW.   The space-bandwidth of an optical spectrum analyzer can be calculated from a knowledge of the maximum number of cycles of the highest spatial frequency over which it can operate and the size of the input aperture.

Figure 1.11 shows a sinusoidal input recording placed in the front focal plane of a coherent optical spectrum analyzer as well as the corresponding output spectrum.   The angle $2\theta_1$ is called the *field angle* of the optical system, where θ_1 is the maximum diffraction angle at which the optical system will function.   This angle corresponds to the maximum spatial frequency in the recording, ω_{xm}.   The field angle can be shown to be given by the expression $2\arcsin(\omega_{xm}\lambda_L/2\pi)$.   The angle θ_2 which is half of the total angle subtended by the usable portion of the input recording is given by $\arctan(A/2F)$, where A is the physical extent of the input aperture and F is the focal length of the optical system. Equivalently, θ_2 is the $\arctan(1/2f_{no})$, where f_{no} is the f-number of the optical system.   The space-bandwidth of the optical system is defined

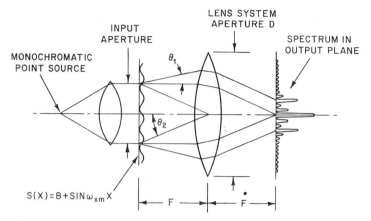

Fig. 1.11 Optical-computer schematic used to demonstrate space-band-width calculation.

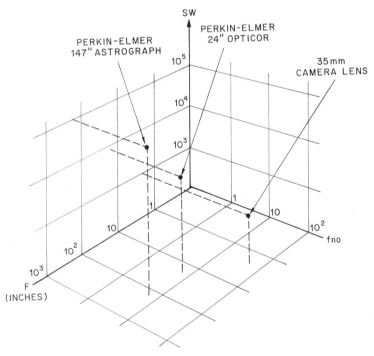

Fig. 1.12 Space-bandwidth product as a function of focal length and f-number for some typical lens systems.

as the total number of cycles of the maximum frequency over which the optical system will function.   Thus the space-bandwidth is $A\omega_{xm}/2\pi$, which is readily shown to be equal to $(F \sin \theta_1)/\lambda_L f_{no}$ or merely $F\theta_1/\lambda_L f_{no}$ when θ_1 is a small angle.

A plot of the space-bandwidth of some existing optical systems is shown in Fig. 1.12.   In some cases space-bandwidth values as high as 100,000 have been achieved in modern high-precision optical systems. Interestingly, the space-bandwidth of even an ordinary 35-mm camera lens can be as high as 1,000.   Note that the coherent f-number of such a lens is much smaller than the f-number quoted for ordinary photography.   High values of space-bandwidth provide the optical spectrum analyzer with the ability to achieve high frequency resolution in the output plane for a given input spatial frequency range or bandwidth.

1.30   Multichannel Spectrum Analysis

Figure 1.13 shows a modification of the coherent optical computer which can perform multichannel spectrum analysis.   The equation describing the performance of this computer is as follows:

$$E_2(\omega_x, y) = E_2(\omega_x, y_i) = \frac{1}{2\pi} \int E_1(x, y_i) e^{-j\omega_x x} \, dx \qquad (1.8)$$

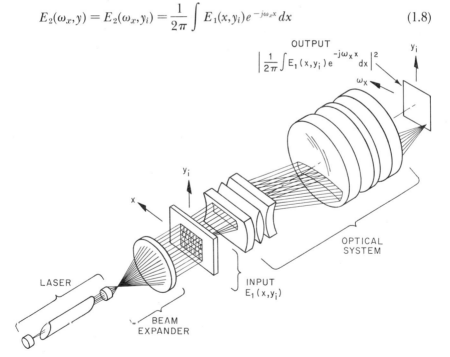

Fig. 1.13   Multichannel spectrum analyzer.

where $i = 1, 2, \ldots, N$. Here the input transducer introduces N one-dimensional signals, $E_1(x, y_i)$, in the input plane, where x is the signal variable and i is an index separating the signals in the y dimension. The design of the optical computer shown in Fig. 1.13 permits light illuminating a particular signal channel in the y dimension to be imaged upon a corresponding channel in the output plane. In the x direction, however, a Fourier transform is taken. This operation is made possible by the use of an astigmatic optical system using lenses having cylindrical surfaces. The output plane is found to contain a channel-by-channel spectrum analysis of the multichannel input function. So that the spectrum of one channel does not affect that of another, there must be spatial guard bands between channels which are wide enough to prevent spatial side lobes generated by one channel in the y direction from interfering with the adjacent channels. If the size of the guard bands required to eliminate channel-to-channel interference is excessive, spatial weighting of the input illumination, called *apodization*, can be used to cause side-lobe suppression in the y direction. The details of this technique will be discussed in Chapter Four.

1.40   Frequency-plane Matched Filtering

Figure 1.14 shows a somewhat more complex computer configuration wherein a photographic recording whose amplitude transmission is proportional to the function $H(\omega_x, \omega_y)$ is placed in the Fourier-transform plane or *spatial frequency plane* of an optical spectrum analyzer. A second Fourier transform is then taken by adding additional optics to the optical system. With this optical computer it is possible to do frequency-plane matched filtering. If the input to the computer is $E_1(x, y) = s(x, y) + n(x, y)$, where $s(x, y)$ is a signal to be located in a background of noise $n(x, y)$, the frequency-plane matched filter $H(\omega_x, \omega_y)$ may be shown [1.17] to be

$$H(\omega_x, \omega_y) = \frac{S^*(\omega_x, \omega_y)}{|N(\omega_x, \omega_y)|^2} \tag{1.9}$$

where $S^*(\omega_x, \omega_y)$ is the complex conjugate of the Fourier transform of $s(x, y)$ and $N(\omega_x, \omega_y)$ is the Fourier transform of $n(x, y)$. If $n(x, y)$ is white gaussian noise, then $N(\omega_x, \omega_y)$ is a constant and

$$H(\omega_x, \omega_y) = C_0 S^*(\omega_x, \omega_y) \tag{1.10}$$

In Fig. 1.14 a transparency whose amplitude transmission is $H(\omega_x, \omega_y)$ is placed in the spatial frequency plane with $s(x, y)$ in the input plane. The electric field distribution $E_2(\omega_x, \omega_y)$ in the spatial frequency plane is thus

$$E_2(\omega_x, \omega_y) = C_0 S(\omega_x, \omega_y) S^*(\omega_x, \omega_y) \tag{1.11}$$

The multiplication shown takes place because light passing through a transparency assumes the value of the incident light amplitude times the amplitude-transmission function of the transparency.

Finally, the electric field distribution in the output plane is the Fourier transform of $E_2(\omega_x, \omega_y)$ and is given by

$$E_3(x_3, y_3) = C_0 \iint S(\omega_x, \omega_y) S^*(\omega_x, \omega_y) e^{-j(x_3\omega_x + y_3\omega_y)} d\omega_x d\omega_y$$

$$= C_0 \iint s(x, y) s(x_3 + x, y_3 + y) \, dx \, dy \tag{1.12}$$

which is recognized as the autocorrelation function of the input signal $s(x, y)$. Formation of the autocorrelation function of the input signal in the output plane of the optical computer is characteristic of matched filtering. For further details on this process the reader is referred to Chapter Four.

When the electric field distribution $s(x, y) + n(x, y)$ appears in the input plane, the spatial frequency plane contains the electric field

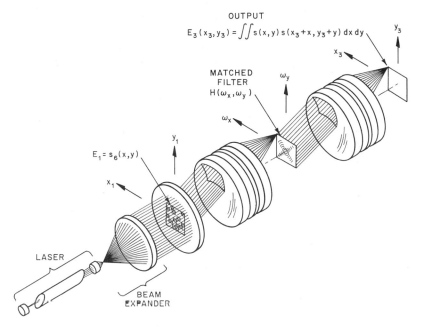

Fig. 1.14   Optical configuration required for frequency-plane matched filtering.

distribution

$$E_2(\omega_x, \omega_y) = C_0[S(\omega_x, \omega_y)S^*(\omega_x, \omega_y) + N(\omega_x, \omega_y)S^*(\omega_x, \omega_y)] \quad (1.13)$$

Again the electric field distribution in the output plane is obtained by taking the Fourier transform, resulting, in this case, in the superposition of two correlation functions, namely,

$$E_3(x_3, y_3) = C_0 \iint s(x, y)s(x_3 + x, y_3 + y) \, dx \, dy$$

$$+ C_0 \iint s(x, y)n(x_3 + x, y_3 + y) \, dx \, dy \quad (1.14)$$

Thus the desired correlation function occurs in a background of light which represents the correlation between the signal to be detected and the accompanying noise.   For white gaussian noise this may be shown to be the optimum method of signal detection [1.17].

1.50 Multichannel Frequency-plane Matched Filtering

An optical-computer configuration which permits multichannel matched filtering is shown in Fig. 1.15.   A one-dimensional signal $s(x)$ is recorded by the input transducer, and its one-dimensional Fourier transform is displayed spread across the ω_x dimension of the frequency plane independent of the orthogonal dimension.   As in the multichannel spectrum analyzer, this operation is made possible by the use of an astigmatic optical system.   Such a system permits imaging to be performed in one dimension for the purpose of multiplication while simultaneously carrying out the Fourier transform in the orthogonal dimension.   In the spatial frequency plane shown in Fig. 1.15 there is a set of one-dimensional frequency-plane matched filters $H_i(\omega_x)$.   In the output plane the light amplitude distribution is given by

$$E_3(x_3, y_i) = \int S(\omega_x)H_i(\omega_x)e^{-jx_3\omega_x} \, d\omega_x$$

$$= \int s(x)r_i(x_3 + x) \, dx \quad (1.15)$$

where the so-called "reference functions" $r_i(x)$ are the inverse Fourier transforms of $H_i^*(\omega_x)$ and $i = 1, 2, \ldots, N$.   The quantity N may be as large as the space-bandwidth product of the lens system.   Thus the multichannel frequency-plane matched filter shown in Fig. 1.15 could be used to compare simultaneously the spectrum of a single input signal with a library of from 10,000 to 100,000 reference spectra.   This feat of instantaneous parallel processing would be extremely difficult to instrument in an all-electronic system and amply illustrates the enormous data-processing capability of the coherent optical computer.

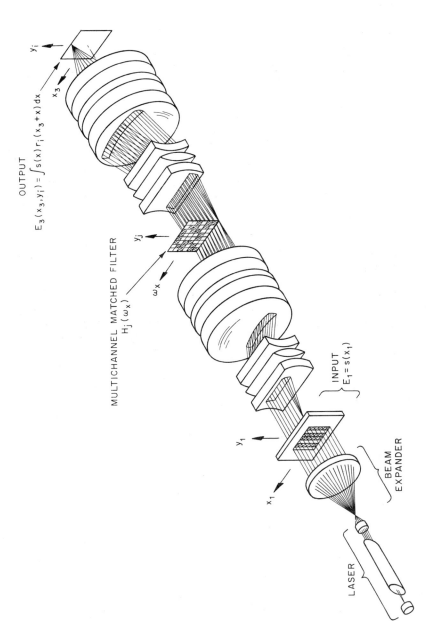

OUTPUT

$$E_3(x_3, y_i) = \int s(x) r_i(x_3 + x) dx$$

MULTICHANNEL MATCHED FILTER
$H_j(\omega_x)$

INPUT
$E_1 = s(x_1)$

BEAM
EXPANDER

LASER

Fig. 1.15 Multichannel frequency-plane matched filter.

1.60   Multichannel Optical Correlation

Spatial-frequency-plane matched filtering is not the only method of performing correlation detection with the coherent optical computer. It is also possible to perform both single and multichannel correlation in a spatial-plane correlator. Figure 1.16 shows an optical computer arranged as a multichannel spatial-plane correlator which provides results similar to the optical-computer configuration shown in Fig. 1.15. Here the input signal recording $s(x)$ is imaged directly on a multichannel photographic recording of the reference signals $r_i(x)$. This computer requires that either the input signal recording or the reference signal recordings be moved in their respective planes in order to produce the desired correlation functions. Typically the input signal is recorded on a moving medium such as photographic film having a transport velocity v_T. The light amplitude distribution in the output plane at $x_4 = 0$ is given by

$$E_4(t, y_i) = \int s(x - v_T t) r_i(x) \, dx \qquad (1.16)$$

where $i = 1, 2, \ldots, N$.

These correlation functions occur in N discrete locations along the y_4 axis as a function of time whereas in the spatial-frequency-plane matched filtering system shown in Fig. 1.15 the autocorrelation functions track the location of the signal in the input plane. Figure 1.16 shows the so-called "zero-order stop" which is used to remove the bias term occurring when the signal is recorded as $B + s(x)$. As discussed in Sec. 1.20, the bias term causes light to appear in the spatial frequency plane at $\omega_x = 0$. This light is a source of noise since its image would appear on the y_4 axis in the output plane superimposed on the desired output signals. The zero-order stop removes this source of noise from the system. The references may also be recorded with a bias as $B + r_i(x)$. Therefore, the complete expression for the light amplitude distribution in the output plane is given by

$$E_4(t, \omega_x, y_i) = \int s(x - v_T t) r_i(x) e^{-j\omega_x x} \, dx + B \int s(x - v_T t) e^{-j\omega_x x} \, dx \qquad (1.17)$$

As can be seen, the output plane is a spatial frequency plane for the x_4 dimension. Essentially all the light energy represented by the second term in eq. (1.17) appears off axis and the correlation term appears entirely at $\omega_x = 0$. Thus a set of photodetectors placed on the y_4 axis can be used to produce the desired correlation signals.

1.70   Other Computational Modes

Coherent optical computers may be used to calculate many mathematical functions which are important in spectrum analysis, matched filtering,

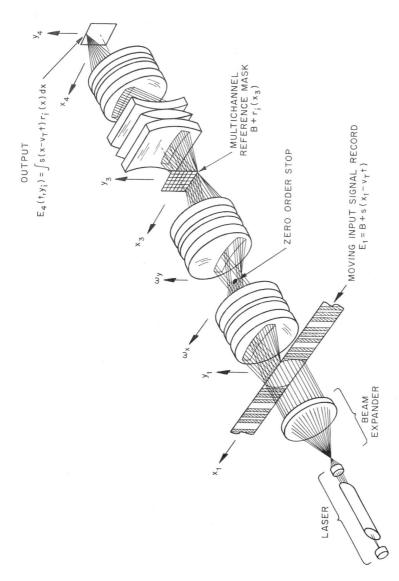

OUTPUT

$$E_4(t,y_i) = \int s(x - v_T t) r_i(x) dx$$

y_4

x_4

MULTICHANNEL
REFERENCE MASK
$B + r_i(x_3)$

y_3

x_3

ω_y

ZERO ORDER STOP

ω_x

MOVING INPUT SIGNAL RECORD
$E_1 = B + s(x_1 - v_T t)$

y_1

BEAM
EXPANDER

x_1

LASER

Fig. 1.16 Multichannel spatial-plane correlator.

and signal processing in general. Many of these functions have already been discussed in the preceding sections. In the remainder of this chapter a few additional illustrations of the utility of the coherent optical computer are furnished.

One is the use of the optical computer in calculating the ambiguity function, $\psi(\omega, \tau)$, as given by the equation below:

$$\psi(\omega, \tau) = \int f(t) f(t + \tau) e^{-j\omega t} \, dt \tag{1.18}$$

The ambiguity function may be computed optically by means of the computer configuration shown in Fig. 1.16 wherein the function $f(t)$ is recorded in the input plane as $f(x_1)$, where $x_1 = t$. The functions $f(t + \tau)$ are recorded as the reference functions in the optical system as $f(x_3 + x_i)$, where $x_3 = t$ and $x_i = \tau_i$. The desired output is produced by recording the entire light energy distribution in the output plane.

Continuing still further, eq. (1.18) can be generalized by using as reference functions the operator $k(t, \tau)$, yielding an output given by the equation

$$g(\tau) = \int f(t) k(t, \tau) \, dt \tag{1.19}$$

where $k(t, \tau)$ is the kernel function for any general linear operation. The solutions of this more general equation may also be calculated by means of coherent optical computation.

Finally, it should be mentioned that the coherent optical computer has utility in phased-array beam forming [1.22] wherein the following set of equations must be instrumented:

$$b_j(t) = \sum_{i=1}^{i=N} s_i(t - \tau_{ij}) \tag{1.20}$$

Here, $b_j(t)$ is the output of the jth beam, the $s_i(t)$ are signals arising over an N-element array, and the τ_{ij} is the time-delay matrix. An optical computer to instrument beam forming differs from those described above in that a multiple imaging lens system or hologram [1.59] is used to cause the multichannel input signal recordings to be imaged on a multiplicity of transparencies containing the time-delay information. Such an optical-computer configuration is shown in Fig. 1.17. As can be seen, an array of N detectors placed beyond the time-delay transparencies are used to form the N summations required.

1.80   Comparison with Noncoherent Optical Computational Methods

Although noncoherent methods of optical computation are not treated in this book, this section briefly discusses the methodology involved and

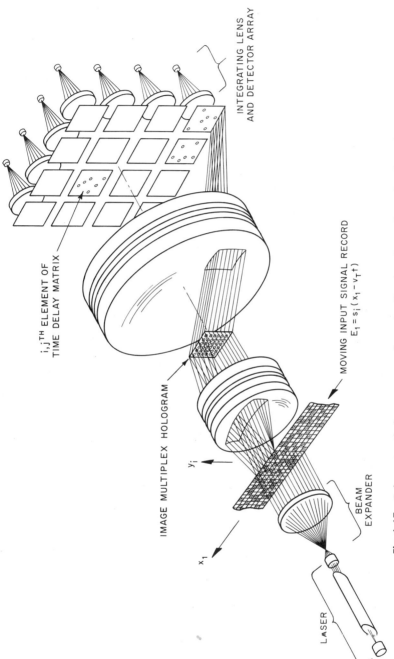

Fig. 1.17 Coherent-optical-computer configuration for phased-array beam forming using multiple time-delay matrices.

INTEGRATING LENS
AND DETECTOR ARRAY

i,j^{TH} ELEMENT OF
TIME DELAY MATRIX

IMAGE MULTIPLEX HOLOGRAM

y_i

x_1

MOVING INPUT SIGNAL RECORD
$E_1 = s_i(x_1 - v_T t)$

BEAM
EXPANDER

LASER

compares it with that of the coherent optical computer. Noncoherent optical computers are defined as those optical computers which use neither point-source nor single-frequency illumination [1.60 to 1.63]. Using an area source of multichromatic illumination, the noncoherent optical computer operates upon light intensity distributions rather than light amplitude distributions as formed in the various focal planes of the optical system. No planes exist where spatial frequencies are displayed, so that it is impossible to perform frequency-plane matched filtering with the noncoherent optical computer. Spatial-plane correlation on both a two-dimensional and multichannel basis is possible. However, bias removal cannot in general be performed, so that the output equation analogous to eq. (1.17) becomes

$$I_4(t, y_i) = B^2 \int dx + B \int r_i(x)\, dx + B \int s(x - v_T t)\, dx$$
$$+ \int s(x - v_T t) r_i(x)\, dx \quad (1.21)$$

where $I_4(t, y_i)$ is the light intensity in the output plane and $B + s(x)$ and $B + r_i(x)$ are now the light-intensity-transmission functions of the input signal and the references. As can be seen, both the signal and reference terms appear in the output of the noncoherent optical computer. The desired correlation integral which also appears in the output is accompanied by a constant bias term as well as two additional terms corresponding to the integral of the product of both signal and references with their corresponding biases. The bias terms corrupt the desired correlation-function output. For large values of B the result is to place an unusually wide dynamic-range requirement on the output transducer and to cause the accuracy of the calculation being performed to be limited by fluctuation and shot noise inherent in B. This limits the number of detectable levels in the function being calculated.

In certain special cases where $s(x)$ is essentially noise-free and of limited dynamic range, the noncoherent optical computer has the advantage that it requires an optical system which is relatively simple. This system would consist of illuminating optics, a lens system which images the input signal on the reference, and an output lens system which directs the mutually transmitted light to a detector array. However, in most applications of interest where correlation detection is required of signals in the presence of noise and where frequency-plane matched filtering and bias-removal techniques are usefully employed, the noncoherent optical computer is placed at a disadvantage.

As has been explained above, the coherent optical computer eliminates the unwanted terms in eq. (1.21) from the output. This occurs because the light energy which relates to each of the unwanted terms may be made to appear physically separated within the optical system.

and the output transducer may be located where only the desired correlation term appears. The accuracy and dynamic range of the coherent optical computer are limited primarily by the energy level obtainable from coherent light sources, the quality of the optical system, and the noise of the output transducer or photodetector. Before the invention of the laser it was difficult to obtain a coherent light source of sufficient brilliance. With the advent of the laser, light-flux availability no longer limits the dynamic range of coherent optical computers. Measurements of actual computer performance have shown that existing lasers permit dynamic ranges of from 40 to 60 dB in coherent optical computer systems for input signals having space-bandwidth products of at least 10,000.

Therefore, although in certain special cases the noncoherent optical computer may have worthwhile application, the treatment developed in this book is limited to what is felt to be the more useful methodology, i.e., that of coherent optical computation.

REFERENCES

1.1 U.S. Army Contract DA-36-039-SC-78801.

1.2 U.S. Air Force Contract AF33 (600)-38019.

1.3 Elias, P.: Optics and Communication Theory, *J. Opt. Soc. Amer.*, **43**: 229 (1953).

1.4 Cheatham, T. P., Jr., and A. Kohlenberg: Optical Filters: Their Equivalence to and Differences from Electrical Networks, *IRE Conv. Rec.*, (4): 6 (1954).

1.5 O'Neill, E. L.: Spatial Filtering in Optics, *IRE Trans. Inform. Theory*, **IT-2**: 56 (1956).

1.6 Cutrona, L. J., et al.: Filtering Operations Using Coherent Optics, *Proc. Nat. Elec. Conf.* (October, 1959).

1.7 Lambert, L., M. Arm, and I. Weissman: A Radar Technique Using an Electro-optical Two-dimensional Filter, *Nat. Conv. Mil. Electron.* (1960).

1.8 Cutrona, L. J., E. N. Leith, C. J. Palermo and L. J. Porcello: Optical Data Processing and Filtering Systems, *IRE Trans. Inform. Theory*, **IT-6**: 386 (1960).

1.9 Reich, A., and L. Slobodin: Optical Pulse Expansion/Compression, *Nat. Aerospace Electron. Conf.* (1961).

1.10 Leith, E. N., and J. Upatnieks: Reconstructed Wavefronts and Communications Theory, *J. Opt. Soc. Amer.*, **52**: 1123 (1962).

1.11 Hoefer, W. G.: Optical Processing of Simulated IF Pulse Doppler Signals, *IRE Trans. Mil. Electron.*, **MIL-6**: 174 (1962).

1.12 Lambert, L. B.: Wideband Instantaneous Spectrum Analyzers Employing Delay Line Light Modulators, *IRE Conv. Rec.*, (6): 69 (1962).

1.13 Slobodin, L.: Optical Correlation Techniques, *Proc. IEEE (Corresp.)*, **51**: 1782 (1963).

1.14 Arm, M., et al.: Optical Correlation Technique for Radar Pulse Compression, *Proc. IEEE (Corresp.)*, **52**: 842 (1964).

1.15 Gerig, J. S., and H. Montague: A Simple Optical Filter for Chirp Radar, *Proc. IEEE (Corresp.)*, **52**: 1753 (1964).

1.16 Williams, R. E.: The Panchromatic Principle in Optical Filtering, *IEEE Trans. Inform. Theory*, **IT-10**: 227 (1964).

1.17 Vander Lugt, A.: Signal Detection by Complex Spatial Filtering, *IEEE Trans. Inform. Theory*, **IT-10**: 139 (1964).

1.18   Preston, K., Jr.: Use of the Fourier Transformable Properties of Lenses for Signal Spectrum Analysis, "Optical and Electro-optical Information Processing," chap. 4, M.I.T., Cambridge, Mass., 1965.

1.19   Williams, R. E.: Partially Coherent Processing by Optical Means, *IEEE Trans. Inform. Theory,* **IT-11**: 449 (1965).

1.20   Izzo, N. F.: Optical Correlation Technique Using a Variable Reference Function, *Proc. IEEE (Corresp.),* **53**: 1740 (1965).

1.21   Leith, E. N., et al.: Coherent Optical Systems for Data Processing, Spatial Filtering, and Wavefront Reconstruction, "Optical and Electro-optical Information Processing," chap. 8, M.I.T., Cambridge, Mass., 1965.

1.22   Beste, D. C., and E. N. Leith: An Optical Technique for Simultaneous Beam Forming and Cross-correlation, *IEEE Conv. Rec.,* (4): 177 (1965).

1.23   Kozma, A. and D. L. Kelly: Spatial Filtering for Detection of Signals Submerged in Noise, *Appl. Opt.,* **4**: 387 (1965).

1.24   Preston, K., Jr.: Computing at the Speed of Light, *Electronics,* 72 (Sept. 6, 1965).

1.25   Ingalls, A. L., et al.: Velocity and Frequency Filtering of Seismic Data Using Laser Light, *Geophysics,* **30**: 1144 (1965).

1.26   Lambert, L. B., et al.: Electro-optical Signal Processors for Phased Array Antennas, "Optical and Electro-optical Information Processing," chap. 38, M.I.T., Cambridge, Mass., 1965.

1.27   Lambert, L. B.: Optical Correlation, "Modern Radar," Wiley, New York, 1965.

1.28   Thomas, C. E.: Optical Spectrum Analysis of Large Space Bandwidth Signals, *Appl. Opt.,* **5**: 1782 (1966).

1.29   Cutrona, L. J., et al.: On the Application of Coherent Optical Processing Technique to Synthetic-aperture Radar, *Proc. IEEE,* **54**: 1026 (1966).

1.30   Vander Lugt, A.: Practical Considerations for the Use of Spatial Carrier Frequency Filters, *Appl. Opt.,* **5**: 1760 (1966).

1.31   King, M., et al.: Real-time Electro-optical Signal Processors with Coherent Detection, *Appl. Opt.,* **6**: 1367 (1967).

1.32   McMahon, D. H.: Wideband Pulse Compression via Brillouin Scattering in the Bragg Limit, *Proc. IEEE,* **55**: 1602 (1967).

1.33   Collins, J. H., et al.: Optical Signal Processing at Microwave Frequencies, *IEEE Sonics and Ultrasonics Symp.* (1967).

1.34   Allen, J. B., and C. R. Jones: Optical Processing of Flight Test Data, *IEEE J. Quantum Electron.,* **QE-3**: 503 (1967).

1.35   Schulz, M. B., et al.: Optical Pulse Compression Using Bragg Scattering by Ultrasonic Waves, *Appl. Phys. Lett.,* **11**: 237 (1967).

1.36   Offner, A.: Design and Specification Criteria for Optical Data Processors, *Appl. Opt.,* **7**: 2285 (1968).

1.37   Atzeni, C., and L. Pantani: Una Esperienza Espanzione/Compressione di Impulsi Mediante Correlatore Ottice, *Alta Freq. (Corresp.),* **37**: 687 (1968).

1.38   Jernigan, J. L.: Correlation Technique Using Microwaves, *Proc. IEEE (Corresp.),* **58**: 374 (1968).

1.39   Preston, K., Jr.: An Array Optical Spatial Phase Modulator, *Digest of Technical Papers, Int. Solid State Circuits Conf.,* 100 (1968).

1.40   Carleton, H. R., et al: A Simplified Coherent Optical Correlator, *Appl. Opt.,* **7**: 105 (1968).

1.41   Dobrin, M. B.: Optical Processing in the Earth Sciences, *IEEE Spectrum,* **6**: 59 (September, 1968).

1.42   Collins, J. H., et al.; Recent Advances in Signal Processing Techniques Using Light Diffraction by Sound at Microwave Frequencies, *Rec. New England Regional Electron. Meeting,* 154 (1968).

1.43 Leith, E. N., and A. L. Ingalls: Synthetic Data Processing by Wavefront Reconstruction, *Appl. Opt.*, **7**: 539 (1968).

1.44 Leith, E. N.: Optical Processing Techniques for Simultaneous Pulse Compression and Beam Sharpening, *IEEE Trans. Aerospace and Electron. Syst.*, **AES-4**: 879 (1968).

1.45 Maloney, W. T.: Acousto-optical Approaches to Radar Signal Processing, *IEEE Int. Conv. Digest*, 72 (1969).

1.46 Atzeni, C., and L. Pantani: A Simplified Optical Correlator for Radar Signal Processing, *Proc. IEEE (Corresp.)*, **57**: 344 (1969).

1.47 Carleton, H. R., et al.: Collinear Heterodyning in Optical Processors, *Proc. IEEE*, **57**: 769 (1969).

1.48 Stark, H., et al.: Linear Spatial Filtering with Crossed Ultrasonic Light Modulators, *Proc. IEEE (Corresp.)*, **57**: 1455 (1969).

1.49 Parks, J. K.: An Acousto-optic Receiver and Fast Spectrum Analyzer for Electromagnetic Signals in the VHF-UHF Range, *IEEE Trans. Commun. Tech.*, **COM-17**: 686 (1969).

1.50 Brown, W. M., and L. J. Porcello: An Introduction to Synthetic Aperture Radar, *IEEE Spectrum*, **6**: 52 (September, 1969).

1.51 Watkins, L. S.: Inspection of Integrated Circuit Photomasks with Intensity Spatial Filters, *Proc. IEEE*, **57**: 1634 (1969).

1.52 Maloney, W. T.: Acousto-optical Approaches to Radar Signal Processing, *IEEE Spectrum*, **6**: 40 (October, 1969).

1.53 Squire, W. D., et al.: Linear Signal Processing and Ultrasonic Transversal Filters, *IEEE Trans. Microwave Theory and Tech.*, **MTT-17**: 1020 (1969).

1.54 Preston, K., Jr.: A Coherent Optical Computer System Using the Membrane Light Modulator, *IEEE Trans. Aerospace and Electron. Syst.*, **AES-6**: 458 (1970).

1.55 Atzeni, C., and L. Pantani: Optical Signal Processing Through Dual-channel Ultrasonic Light Modulators, *Proc. IEEE (Corresp.)*, **58**: 501 (1970).

1.56 Anderson, W. L., and R. L. Everett: Electroencephalographic and Electrocardiographic Data Reduction by Coherent Optical Techniques, *SWIEECO Conf. Rec.*, (1970).

1.57 Lendaris, G. C., and G. L. Stanley: Diffraction Pattern Sampling for Automatic Pattern Recognition, *Proc. IEEE*, **58**: 198 (1970).

1.58 Abbe, E.: *Archiv. Mikroskop.*, **9**: 413 (1873).

1.59 Sun, L.: Generating Multiple Images for Integrated Circuits by Fourier-transform Hologram, *Proc. IEEE (Corresp.)*, **56**: 116 (1968).

1.60 Kovaszkay, L. S. G., and A. Arman: Optical Autocorrelation of Two Dimensional Patterns, *Rev. Sci. Inst.*, **28**: 793 (1957).

1.61 Howell, B. J.: Optical Analog Computers, *J. Opt. Soc. Amer.*, **49**: 1012 (1959).

1.62 McLachlan, D., Jr.: The Role of Optics in Applying Correlation Functions to Pattern Recognition, *J. Opt. Soc. Amer.*, **52**: 454 (1962).

1.63 Talamini, A. J., and E. C. Farnett: New Target for Radar: Sharper Vision with Optics, *Electronics*, 58 (Dec. 27, 1965).

Chapter Two

Lens-system Design

2.00   Introduction and Historical Background

The optical-computer engineer need not be an accomplished lens-system designer any more than the digital-computer engineer need be capable of the detailed design of integrated circuitry.   However, in both cases, the engineer must be able to make his requirements clear to the actual designer.   He must also be able to appreciate the general design trade-offs which are available.   Finally, he must be able to interpret the results of the design and relate its characteristics to those of other components of the optical-computer system.   It is the purpose of this chapter to provide the reader with a basic knowledge of lens-system design methods so that he may more accurately and reasonably specify lens-system requirements and thus assure desired performance.

Lens systems are currently designed by methods based on Snell's law of refraction and simple analytic geometry.   These methods were developed to a large extent in the nineteenth century. In addition, a method called *ray tracing* is employed; in this method the designer determines the performance of the lens system by calculating the paths taken by light as they pass through the lenses which constitute the lens system. Before the recent advent of large-scale digital computers ray tracing was an extremely laborious procedure. Now, use of computers has revolutionized lens-system design and permits much greater sophistication in the approach taken to design optimization. This chapter introduces the reader to ray-tracing fundamentals in order to permit him to grasp the foundations on which the ray-tracing formalism is built. No effort is made to discuss all the subtleties and fine points of this method, since not only is there an extensive literature on the subject but also almost as many approaches to design optimization using ray tracing as there are qualified optical designers. In fact, sophisticated optical design is as much an art as a science and relies to a large extent on the experience and skill of the individual designer. To design successfully the lens system of any coherent optical computer, especially those computers requiring cylindrical lens elements, it is necessary to enlist the assistance of qualified members of the optical design community.

Most coherent optical computers require that wavefronts produced by diffraction in the input plane be focused to points in the succeeding Fourier-transform plane. Simultaneously points in the input plane must be mapped into corresponding wavefronts in the Fourier plane. These wavefronts are in turn mapped into points in the plane defined by the next Fourier transform and so on until they finally emerge in the output plane.

Historically the fundamental treatment of the operation performed by a general optical system on an input wavefront was first dealt with by Hamilton [2.1] in the early nineteenth century. The interested reader may wish to review an excellent discussion of Hamilton's work by Synge [2.2]. More recently Goldstein [2.3] effectively related classic mechanics to geometrical optics and also demonstrated the relationship between Hamilton's characteristic equation of geometrical optics and the Schrödinger equation of wave mechanics. Basically, Hamilton recognized that every optical system has a "characteristic function" V which is a function of the cartesian coordinates of both the input and output spaces of the system. Thus, V is given more completely by the expression

$$V = (x_1, y_1, z_1, x_n, y_n, z_n) \tag{2.1}$$

where the origin of the input space is at $x_1 = y_1 = z_1 = 0$ and of the output space at $x_n = y_n = z_n = 0$. A specific value of the characteristic function is the optical path length between a specified point in the input space and another point in the output space. Hamilton demonstrated the existence of the characteristic function using Fermat's principle that optical path length is an extremal so that, unless (x_1, y_1, z_1) and (x_n, y_n, z_n)

are object and image points, there is only one ray through (x_1, y_1, z_1) which will reach (x_n, y_n, z_n). Hamilton showed that the characteristic function may be used to determine the output wavefront for any input wavefront, where the term "wavefront" refers to a surface of constant optical phase. Since ray trajectories are everywhere perpendicular to the wavefront, it may be demonstrated that it is possible to calculate the direction cosines of a ray both where it enters the optical system and where it exits from the optical system, as follows:

$$l_1 = \frac{\partial V}{\partial x_1} \qquad l_n = \frac{\partial V}{\partial x_n}$$

$$m_1 = \frac{\partial V}{\partial y_1} \qquad m_n = \frac{\partial V}{\partial y_n} \qquad (2.2)$$

$$n_1 = \frac{\partial V}{\partial z_1} \qquad n_n = \frac{\partial V}{\partial z_n}$$

where l_1, m_1, n_1 and l_n, m_n, n_n are direction cosines in the input and output spaces, respectively.

Although Hamilton's work is of great value conceptually, it is difficult to calculate the characteristic function for all but the most trivial optical systems. In practice, therefore, it is usual to determine the relationship of entrance and exit points by means of tracing individual rays.

2.10 Definition of Terms

Before proceeding with a description of the methodology of ray tracing it is essential to present definitions of the terms utilized by the optical designer. Start with the term *lens element*. This term refers to a single piece of material (usually glass) bounded by appropriately curved surfaces (usually spherical). Lens elements usually appear in clusters which are physically supported in the same mechanical mounting or *lens cell*. The term *lens* is defined here as referring to such a cluster (this definition is not universal). Finally a *lens system* comprises a multiplicity of lenses each of which may be constructed of several lens elements. A description of the characteristics of a complete lens system specifically designed for use in coherent optical computation will be presented in Sec. 2.30.

Figure 2.1 shows a typical lens element. Its axis of symmetry is called the *optical axis*. This axis usually takes the direction of the z axis in a cartesian coordinate system. The lens element itself consists of a medium in which the velocity of light is lower than the velocity of light in air. The reciprocal of the ratio of the velocity of light in the medium to the velocity of light in air is called the *optical index*. The physical dimensions of the lens element as well as the optical index of the material from which it is fabricated determine its effect on an impinging optical wavefront. These physical dimensions are the radii of the two surfaces as well as the thickness of the lens element. A surface which curves to the right, i.e., the left-hand surface in Fig. 2.1, is said to have a positive radius of curvature. A surface with curvature to the left is therefore taken as having a negative radius of curvature.

The *vertices* of the lens element occur where the surfaces of the lens intersect the optical axis. There are both a left and a right vertex for every lens element. These vertices are often called "front" and "back" vertices, respectively. In Fig. 2.1 the front vertex is labeled V_1 and the back vertex V_2. The distance between the vertices of a lens element is called the *axial thickness*. If a ray of light which is parallel to the optical axis enters the lens element from a point on the left (point A in Fig. 2.1, for example) and is refracted so as to intersect the optical axis, the point of intersection is called the *principal back focus* of the lens (point F_2 in Fig. 2.1). Similarly, if a ray which is parallel to the optical axis enters the lens element in the reverse direction from a point such as B in Fig. 2.1, it will intersect the optical axis at the *principal front focus*, F_1. As will be seen later, the exact points of intersection will depend upon the distances of the initial rays from the optical axis.

If the ray which intersects the optical axis at F_2 is extended back through the lens element (without regard to refraction by the surface of the lens element) to the point where it would intersect the ray parallel to the optical axis through point A, the locus of the points of intersection (as a function of the distance of A from the optical axis) is called the *back principal surface* of the lens element. If a ray through F_1 is similarly extended to the point where it intersects the ray parallel to the optical axis through point B, the locus of points of intersection is called the

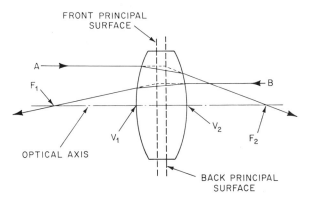

Fig. 2.1   Schematic of a typical lens element.

front principal surface of the lens element. The intersection of the front principal surface with the optical axis is defined as the *front principal point* of the lens element. Similarly, the *back principal point* of a lens element is defined as the point of intersection of the back principal surface with the optical axis. Note that the back principal surface is to the right of the centerline of the lens element shown in Fig. 2.1. Similarly, the front principal surface is to the left of the centerline. The radii of curvature of the lens element, its axial thickness, and the optical index determine where the principal surfaces occur. Note that the principal surfaces do not always fall within the lens element itself. In the case of a lens element having surfaces with extreme curvature, as is shown in Fig. 2.2, it is possible for the principal surfaces to lie entirely outside the lens element.

The distance from F_2 to the back principal point is called the *equivalent back focal length* (EBFL) of the lens element, and the distance from F_1 to the front principal point is called the *equivalent front focal length* (EFFL) of the lens element. Finally, the distance from the vertex V_2 to the principal back focus F_2 is called the *back focal length* (BFL) of the lens element, and the distance from V_1 to F_1 is called the *front focal length* (FFL) of the lens element. The terms EBFL, EFFL, BFL, and FFL may also be used with reference to an assembly of lens elements or even to a lens system. In this case the vertices used are those of the first and last elements in the lens or lens system.

The *power* of a lens element is defined as the reciprocal of the equivalent focal length and is given by the following expression which is derived in Sec. 2.20:

$$P = (n-1)\left[C_1 - C_2 + C_1 C_2 (\text{a.t.})\,\frac{n-1}{n}\right] \tag{2.3}$$

where n is the optical index of the lens-element material, C_1 and C_2 are the curvatures of the front and back surfaces, respectively, and (a.t.) is

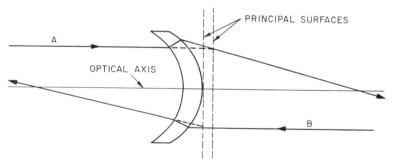

Fig. 2.2   Lens element with exterior principal surfaces.

the axial thickness.   When the approximation C_1C_2(a.t.) $\ll 1$ holds true, the power is given by

$$P = (n-1)(C_1 - C_2) \tag{2.4}$$

In this case, called the *thin-lens approximation*, the back focal length and equivalent back focal length are equal.

A lens element having positive power causes rays passing through it from left to right to converge.   The unit of lens-element power in the mks system is the *diopter*.   Since C_1 and C_2 are usually of opposite sign, it is clear from eq. (2.4) that, if the curvatures of the two surfaces are incremented by equal amounts of opposite sign, then the power of the lens remains constant.   Frequently such an alteration in curvature without changing power is important in lens design as part of an iterative procedure for correcting the aberrations of the lens or lens system. This operation, where power is left constant when the surface radii are changed, is called *lens bending*.

Another feature of a lens element is the *node*.   The nodes of a lens element are defined with reference to Fig. 2.3.   This illustration shows a particular ray through a point A, which, when geometrically traced through the lens element, exits through a point B in a direction which is parallel to its direction at entrance.   When the lines through points A and B are extended to the optical axis, the points of intersection are defined as the nodes of the lens element.   The nodes have the following interesting property: If the lens element is rotated about the *front principal node*, i.e., the node closest to A, the ray through A and this node always exits parallel to its entrance direction.   It can be shown that, for a lens element in air, the nodal points are at the intersection of the principal surfaces with the optical axis.

The following relatively obvious points should be made relating to certain practical limitations which must be placed on lens-system design.

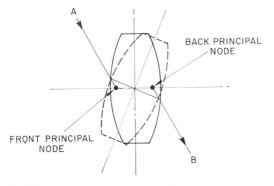

Fig. 2.3   Principal nodes of a lens element.

Firstly, the lens element itself is made physically larger than is required by wavefronts propagating through the lens system.   This is because it must be supported at its periphery by the mechanical structure of the lens cell.   The optical designer must indicate the maximum height at which rays will pass through the lens.   The region of each lens through which rays pass in the working optical system is called its *clear aperture*. Regions outside the clear aperture are not utilized and may be obscured by the mechanical supports of the lens element itself.   Secondly, the optical designer must be sure that he avoids choosing an axial thickness and radii of curvature which would cause the lens element to taper to zero thickness within the diameter required for mounting.   The thickness to which the lens element tapers at its outer diameter is called the *edge thickness*.   The above practical restrictions must be entered into the lens-design calculations to prevent a physically unrealizable design from occurring.

Since the lens system for a coherent optical computer consists of many elements, it is worth studying some of the characteristics of a multi-element lens.   Take, for example, the two-element lens shown in Fig. 2.4.   A ray entering this lens from the left through point A and parallel to the optical axis finally intersects the optical axis at the point F_{12}.   As will be shown in Sec. 2.20 the power of the lens comprised of these two lens elements is given by the following formula when the thin-lens approximation is utilized:

$$P_{12} = P_1 + P_2 - dP_1P_2 \tag{2.5}$$

where P_1 and P_2 are the individual powers of the lens elements and the distance d is the separation between the lens elements.   When thick lens elements are dealt with, P_1 and P_2 are computed from eq. (2.3) and d becomes the distance between the back principal point of the first lens element and the front principal point of the second lens element.   As can be seen in Fig. 2.4, there is a back principal surface for the two lens

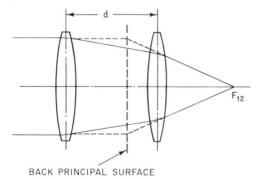

BACK PRINCIPAL SURFACE

Fig. 2.4 Lens consisting of two lens elements.

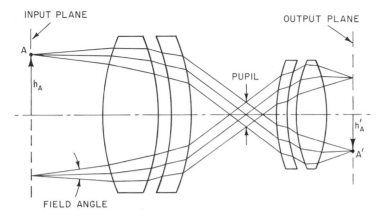

INPUT PLANE

OUTPUT PLANE

A

h_A

PUPIL

h'_A

A'

FIELD ANGLE

Fig. 2.5 Two-lens coherent-optical-computer system for taking successive Fourier transforms.

elements in combination which is located in distance $1/P_{12}$ from the back principal focus at F_{12}.

Lenses made up of lens elements may be combined into a lens system as shown in Fig. 2.5. The particular system illustrated is one of great importance in coherent optical computation because it may be used to calculate two successive Fourier transforms. The spacing between the two lenses is equal to the sum of the equivalent back focal length of one and the equivalent front focal length of the other. This implies that a ray which enters from the left at a height h_A and is parallel to the optical axis is mapped into a ray which exits from the second lens parallel to the optical axis at height h'_A. Such a lens system is called *telescopic*. If point *A* is positioned so that it also lies in the front focal plane of the first lens and *A'* lies in the back focal plane of the second lens positioned so that all rays through *A* arrive at *A'*, then points *A* and *A'* are called *conjugate points*.

Figure 2.5 shows what is called a *fan* of rays traced from point *A* to point *A'*. At point *A* the angular spread of the fan over which the lens system must function is called the *divergence angle* of the lens system. At point *A'* the angular spread is called the *convergence angle*. The *input field* or *object field* is defined by the maximum value of h_A over which the lens system must operate. Similarly, the *output field* or *image field* is defined by the maximum value of h'_A. The dimensions of the fields define the limits of what are called the *input aperture* and the *output aperture*. The *lateral magnification* of the lens system shown in Fig. 2.5 is the ratio h'_A/h_A. The *angular magnification* of a lens system is defined as the ratio of the angle with respect to the optical axis of an incoming ray to the angle of the corresponding outgoing ray. All fans of rays having equal angular spread arising from within the input aperture become *bundles* of parallel rays which intersect between the two lenses in what is called the *pupil.* The central ray in such a bundle is called the *chief ray.*

2.20 Ray Tracing

Section 2.10 has introduced the reader to the basic vocabulary of optical design. The balance of this chapter deals with methods relating to the design and evaluation of lens systems for use in coherent optical computers. The optical system shown in Fig. 2.5 is an optical computer with an input plane at A, an output plane at A', and a Fourier plane at the common intermediate focal point or pupil. If the computer is to work ideally, the following requirements should be fulfilled:

1. Ideally the first lens should bring bundles of parallel rays which arise within the input aperture to a perfect focus in its back focal plane over a region defined by the pupil. Also, this lens should cause fans of rays originating at any point in the input aperture to become parallel bundles of rays over the same region.

2. Ideally the second lens should bring parallel bundles of rays passing through the pupil to a perfect focus in the output plane and at the same time cause fans of rays originating at any point in the pupil to become parallel bundles of rays over a region defined by the output aperture.

It may be demonstrated analytically that it is not possible to fulfill both requirements simultaneously over the full field and full pupil. In practice, therefore, it is necessary to examine the effects of various possible design compromises in regard to the particular application being considered.

In designing lenses for coherent optical computers it is necessary to remove aberrations so as to optimize their focusing properties in both front and back focal planes. In the nineteenth century, originating with Petzval and Seidel, methods were devised for using ray tracing to remove lens-systems aberrations. To understand their methods, the elements of geometrical ray tracing are now reviewed. Figure 2.6 shows the general ray-tracing geometry. A boundary of radius R_i is shown which separates two media of optical indices n_i and n'_i. A ray from point A at an angle γ_i with the optical axis (z axis) is shown arriving at this boundary at a point whose distance from the z axis is x_i. Assume that the ray lies in the xz plane. Such a ray is called a *meridional ray.* The radius vector R_i is perpendicular to the boundary. The angle between it and the arriving ray is the angle of incidence I_i. It is possible to solve for the angle of incidence by using the equation

$$I_i = \gamma_i + \arcsin \frac{x_i}{R_i} \qquad (2.6)$$

The angle of refraction I'_i may be calculated from Snell's law as follows:

$$\sin I'_i = \frac{n_i}{n'_i} \sin I_i \tag{2.7}$$

Finally, it is clear that

$$\gamma'_i = \gamma_i + (I'_i - I_i) \tag{2.8}$$

Now that γ'_i has been determined, the ray may be extrapolated in a straight line to the next boundary and the calculations given by eqs. (2.6) to (2.8) repeated, noting that $n_{i+1} = n'_i$ and $\gamma_{i+1} = \gamma'_i$.

The above equations are readily programmed on a digital computer. However, their nonlinear nature makes hand calculation difficult. A method called *paraxial ray tracing* has been devised to make rapid hand calculations possible. In paraxial ray tracing all angles are assumed to be small so that the usual small-angle approximations may be made. When this is done, eqs. (2.6) to (2.8) become

$$I_i = \gamma_i + \frac{x_i}{R_i}$$

$$I'_i = \frac{n_i}{n'_i} I_i \tag{2.9}$$

$$\gamma'_i = \gamma_i + (I'_i - I_i)$$

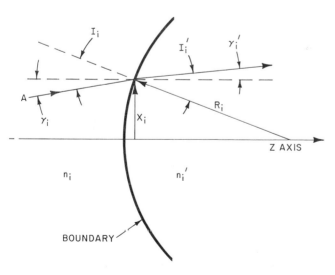

Fig. 2.6   Ray-tracing geometry.

Equations (2.9) may readily be combined to yield an equation for the output angle γ_i' in terms of all other variables, namely,

$$\gamma_i' = \frac{n_i}{n_i'}\gamma_i + \frac{n_i - n_i'}{n_i' R_i}x_i \qquad (2.10)$$

Equation (2.10) is often rewritten in a form which uses the so-called "optical direction angles" $\boldsymbol{\gamma}_i' = n_i'\gamma_i'$ and $\boldsymbol{\gamma}_i = n_i\gamma_i$ as follows:

$$\boldsymbol{\gamma}_i' = \boldsymbol{\gamma}_i + \frac{n_i - n_i'}{R_i}x_i \qquad (2.11)$$

The *power P_i* of the surface is just equal to $(n_i - n_i')/R_i$ so that it can be written that

$$\boldsymbol{\gamma}_i' = \boldsymbol{\gamma}_i - P_i x_i \qquad (2.12)$$

This may also be placed in matrix form as follows:

$$\begin{bmatrix} \boldsymbol{\gamma}_i' \\ x_i' \end{bmatrix} = \begin{bmatrix} 1 & -P_i \\ 0 & 1 \end{bmatrix} \begin{bmatrix} \boldsymbol{\gamma}_i \\ x_i \end{bmatrix} \qquad (2.13)$$

where the matrix shown is called the *refraction matrix*. The operation performed by this matrix may be combined with the matrix form of the translation operation where the ray is extrapolated to the next surface. If d_{i+1} is the distance to the next surface, then x_{i+1} is given by

$$x_{i+1} = x_i + \mathbf{d}_{i+1}\gamma_i \qquad (2.14)$$

where $\mathbf{d}_{i+1}$ is the optical distance d_{i+1}/n_i'. In matrix form this becomes

$$\begin{bmatrix} \boldsymbol{\gamma}_{i+1} \\ x_{i+1} \end{bmatrix} = \begin{bmatrix} 1 & 0 \\ \mathbf{d}_{i+1} & 1 \end{bmatrix} \begin{bmatrix} \boldsymbol{\gamma}_i \\ x_i \end{bmatrix} \qquad (2.15)$$

where the above matrix is called the *translation matrix*. The convenience of matrix notation is that paraxial ray tracing of an entire lens system may be done in one step using a system matrix which is a product of all the refraction and translation matrices.

Consider a simple example which leads to a proof of eq. (2.3). Let a lens element consist of two surfaces of radii R_1 and R_2, have an axial thickness (a.t.), and be made of material of optical index n. The system matrix $\mathbf{S}$ is then given by

$$\begin{aligned} \mathbf{S} &= \begin{bmatrix} 1 & -P_1 \\ 0 & 1 \end{bmatrix} \begin{bmatrix} 1 & 0 \\ (\mathbf{a.t.}) & 1 \end{bmatrix} \begin{bmatrix} 1 & -P_2 \\ 0 & 1 \end{bmatrix} \\ &= \begin{bmatrix} 1 - (\mathbf{a.t.})P_1 & -P_1 - P_2 + (\mathbf{a.t.})P_1 P_2 \\ (\mathbf{a.t.}) & 1 - (\mathbf{a.t.})P_2 \end{bmatrix} \end{aligned} \qquad (2.16)$$

where $(\mathbf{a.t.}) = (\text{a.t.})/n$. Now, in this particular example, $P_1 = (n-1)/R_1$ and $P_2 = (1-n)/R_2$. The power term in eq. (2.16) is $P_1 + P_2 - (\mathbf{a.t.})P_1 P_2$

which with the above values for P_1, P_2, and (**a.t.**) may be readily converted into eq. (2.3). In a similar manner eq. (2.5) may be verified.

However convenient paraxial ray tracing may be, it must be supported by further computations in order to be useful in detailed design. For example, refer to Fig. 2.7 which shows a bundle of rays distributed over the input aperture and parallel to the optical axis. If these rays are traced to the back focus F_2, using eqs. (2.6) to (2.8) rather than the paraxial approximation, it will be found that rays from near the center of the input aperture come to a different point of intersection with the optical axis than rays traced through the outer portions of the input aperture. This fact is representative of a type of aberration called *spherical aberration*. The plot shown in Fig. 2.7 describes this situation more clearly. The coordinates are the distance of a member of the bundle from the optical axis h_A plotted against the amount Δz by which the points of intersection depart from the paraxial focal point. Spherical aberration may be of either sign, depending upon surface curvature and optical index. By constructing the lens of several elements made of materials of different optical indices and of appropriate curvature it is possible to balance negative and positive spherical aberrations so as to produce a system free from spherical aberration.

Figure 2.8 illustrates an additional optical design problem. Bundles of meridional rays which are not parallel to the optical axis are shown traced through the input aperture. Off-axis foci may be calculated for various angles to the optical axis. The locus of these focal points

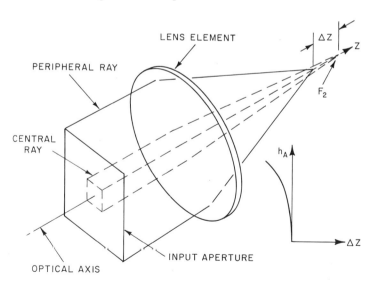

Fig. 2.7 Geometry for demonstrating spherical aberration.

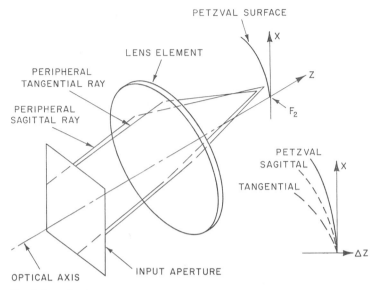

Fig. 2.8 Off-axis geometry illustrating field curvature, coma, and astigmatism.

forms a toroidal surface. The curvature of this surface represents an aberration which is called *field curvature*. Not only is the back focal surface curved but rays from the periphery of the input aperture at a particular angle focus away from paraxial rays for that angle. Typically, it is found that the focal points for these peripheral rays lie below the paraxial focus. This effect is another aberration which is known by the name of *coma*.

Another aberration is *astigmatism*. It is found that tangential rays (see Fig. 2.8), i.e., meridional rays in a plane which contains the optical axis and the image point, and sagittal rays, i.e., "skew" rays in a plane perpendicular to the tangential plane not containing the optical axis, do not focus in the same plane. This aberration is astigmatism. When this aberration is corrected, the common focal surface for tangential and sagittal rays is called the *Petzval surface*. It is found theoretically that the rate of the departure of the focus for the tangential rays from the Petzval surface to that of the sagittal rays is approximately $3:1$ (see Fig. 2.8).

Still another aberration is *distortion*. Distortion refers to the fact that, as the distance between a ray and the optical axis in the object plane is linearly increased, the distance between the intersection of this ray and the optical axis in the image plane does not increase linearly. When this nonlinearity is less than unity, the distortion is called positive; when greater than unity, it is called negative. In an imaging system positive and negative distortions are frequently referred to by the more common terms of "barrel" and "pincushion" distortion, respectively.

The above aberrations (spherical, field curvature, coma, astigmatism, and distortion) are referred to as the *Seidel aberrations.* In addition to the Seidel aberrations, the optical-computer engineer must be aware of the existence of certain unique aberrations which occur primarily in coherent optical computers used for matched filtering (see Chaps. One and Four). The matched filter in such coherent optical computers may be thought of as a special kind of hologram (see Chaps. Four and Eight). When rays are traced through the lens system of such a computer, they must be traced through the hologram in the appropriate Fourier-transform plane or pupil. An analysis of ray tracing through holograms has been made by Offner [2.4]. Offner found that, in certain cases, the hologram itself creates additional aberrations which do not usually occur in optical systems. These aberrations are characteristic of those which are found when rays are traced through a "grating," i.e., a transparency having equally spaced opaque and transparent lines. A grating diffracts light at a characteristic angle whose sine is $f_s\lambda_L$, where f_s is the number of lines in the grating per unit length and λ_L is the wavelength of the incident light. In ray tracing through holograms where f_s may be determined as a function of position, eqs. (2.6) to (2.8) are therefore replaced by

$$\gamma_i' = \gamma_i \pm \arcsin f_s(x_i) \lambda_L \tag{2.17}$$

Note that two diffracted rays are created for each incident ray. Furthermore the incident ray is maintained in the rays traced as representing the undiffracted light energy. A grating introduces aberrations in a fan of rays incident upon it. These aberrations may be determined by ordinary ray-tracing technique and may also be compensated for as with the Seidel aberrations.

In coherent optical computers the requirements of the lens-system design are so stringent that geometric aberrations must essentially be removed entirely, i.e., reduced to a small fraction of the optical wavelength. When a design has reached this point of perfection, its ability to focus is limited primarily by the physical optics phenomenon of diffraction (see Chap. Four). One method for evaluating diffraction-limited optical systems is to determine how closely the output wavefront converging to a focal point approaches a perfectly spherical wavefront. A worthwhile reference to this method, which is also one of the earlier works describing this technique, is that by Hopkins [2.5]. Figure 2.9 shows the usual configuration of an input plane at A with a bundle of off-axis meridional rays traced to the paraxial focus F_2. A fictive reference sphere with its center at the point F_2 is created. The

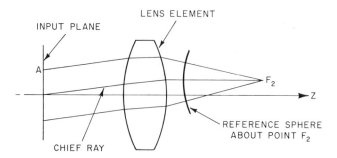

Fig. 2.9 Use of a reference sphere to determine optical path differences.

optical path lengths from points on a plane wavefront perpendicular to the chief ray in the input plane to this reference sphere are determined. Using the optical path length for the chief ray as a reference, optical path differences (OPD) are calculated and recorded in terms of fractions of an optical wavelength. This so-called OPD function is used to define a phase function across the input wavefront given by the equation

$$\phi(x_1, y_1, \alpha, \beta) = 2\pi \, \text{OPD}(x_1, y_1, \alpha, \beta) \tag{2.18}$$

where x_1 and y_1 are the coordinates of the origin of each ray in the input plane. Note that ϕ is also a function of α and β, that is, the direction angles of the chief ray where it passes through the input aperture. Thus a multivariate function exists which may be used in describing the performance of a diffraction-limited lens. If the lens were perfect, the function ϕ would be zero for all x_1, y_1, α, and β. In general this is not true, and ϕ may be utilized in conjunction with the Fourier-transformable properties of lens systems (see Chap. Four) to determine the effect of the lens system on the performance of the coherent optical computer. For example, as shown in Chapter Four, an input function in the input plane may be expanded in a Fourier series. Each term of the Fourier series has related to it a diffraction angle corresponding to specific values of α and β. Thus, in calculating the light distribution in the back focal plane of the lens shown in Fig. 2.9, eq. (4.33) which expresses the transform relationship is modified as follows:

$$F(\cos \alpha, \cos \beta) = C \int\limits_{-\infty}^{+\infty} \int\limits_{-\infty}^{+\infty} f(x_1, y_1) e^{-j[\phi(x_1, y_1, \alpha, \beta) + (2\pi/\lambda_L)(\cos \alpha \, x_1 + \cos \beta \, y_1)]} \, dx_1 \, dy_1$$

$$\tag{2.19}$$

The following section provides an example of the use of eq. (2.19) in an actual design.

2.30   Lens-system Optimization

As is mentioned in Sec. 2.00, high-speed automatic digital computers have had a significant impact on the design of lens systems for use in both coherent optical computers and for many other applications [2.6]. The first extensive study of the use of large computers in lens-system design was commenced in the early 1950s under the leadership of Baker [2.7] who at that time was associated with the Perkin-Elmer Corporation of Norwalk, Connecticut. The purpose of this study was to find out how methods of hand calculation could be replaced by automatic computation without causing the optical designer to lose touch with the particular lens-design problem during the progress of its solution. The reader must remember that it is as much the skill of the designer in guiding the computer as it is the speed of the computer that produces optimum results. Programs were written by Baker and his group, using the Mark IV computer at Harvard University, for the purpose of designing diffraction-limited lens systems. These early programs (which more recently have been significantly expanded and revised) calculated distortion and optical path differences to reference spheres centered at appropriate points in the output plane while varying system parameters but, at the same time, holding the design within practical limitations on edge thickness and other tolerances of the various lens elements. A merit of function or "objective" function was computed whose value was based on wavefront aberrations, i.e., based upon the ϕ function described in Sec. 2.20. Minimization of the objective function was accomplished by many methods including practically all those which later were independently developed by other investigators. However, the small memory and slow speed of the Mark IV computer limited the practicality of the results thus obtained.

More recently other workers [2.8 to 2.14] have rediscovered and extended Baker's techniques. Other approaches to the minimization problem have been developed. In all these approaches advantage is taken of the fact that the total of the Seidel aberrations for the entire lens system is equal to the sum of the aberrations for the individual lens elements. Since the Seidel aberrations may be selected to be either positive or negative, a cancellation can be effected. However, because of the basic nonlinearities of optical-design equations and of typical objective functions themselves, it is still not theoretically possible to determine whether a local minimum or the global minimum has been discovered as one iterates through the minimization process.

Typical of today's optimization procedures is that due to Meiron [2.15]. In his procedure, $f_1, f_2, \ldots, f_m$ are taken as aberrations and/or physical restrictions upon the design, and $u_1, u_2, \ldots, u_n$ are defined as the design parameters.   Forming the vector

$$\Delta f_i = \sum_{j=1}^{j=n} A_{ij} \Delta u_j \tag{2.20}$$

where the A_{ij} matrix is given by

$$A_{ij} = \frac{\partial f_i}{\partial u_j} \tag{2.21}$$

the Δu_j are selected so as to minimize the merit function given by

$$M = \sum_{i=1}^{i=m} a_i (\Delta f_i)^2 \tag{2.22}$$

where the a_i are factors chosen by the optical designer to weight those aberrations which he feels that it is most important to eliminate.

Such an operation was conducted recently in designing a typical optical-computer system.   In this lens system it was required that a 4×4 mm input aperture containing the input spatial light modulator be imaged onto a plane containing a spatial filter while simultaneously forming the Fourier transform in the back focal plane of the imaging lens as well as in the output plane.   This produced the Fourier transform both in its original form and in a form modified by the spatial filter.   The field angle at the input plane was ± 0.04 rad corresponding to a spatial frequency of 63 cycles/mm at the operating optical wavelength of 6328 Å.   This implied a linear space-bandwidth product of about 250 or an area space-bandwidth of 6.4×10^4.   These rather lenient requirements led to a reasonably simple optical system where no lens required more than two elements.   The resultant design is given in Table 2.1.   This design tabulation is typical of that usually produced by the optical designer.   It lists the number of each surface (starting with

TABLE 2.1

Surface no.	Radius, mm	Spacing, mm	Optical index	Clear aperture, mm
Input	....	252.5	1.0	
1	+ 105.5	3.5	1.52	15.0
2	− 43.8	0.9	1.0	15.0
3	− 42.4	2.5	1.62	15.0
4	− 108.0	375.4	1.0	
5	+ 105.5	3.5	1.52	15.0
6	− 43.8	0.9	1.0	15.0
7	− 42.4	2.5	1.62	15.0
8	− 108.0	249.7	1.0	

zero at the input plane), the radius, the thickness, i.e., the distance to the next vertex, and the optical index over this distance.

In order to evaluate the performance of the lens system before manufacture, bundles of rays were traced through the 4×4 mm aperture in the input plane to the corresponding focal points in the output plane, and OPD functions were measured as a function of field angle.   These functions were then plotted as three-dimensional models.   Photographs of these models are shown in Figs. 2.10 to 2.13.   Figure 2.10 shows the OPD function for a reference sphere about the principal back focus. As can be seen, the system is essentially perfect with all phase aberrations lying well below one one-thousandth of the optical wavelength.   Figure 2.11 is a plot of the OPD function when rays are traced through the input aperture at an angle of 0.04 rad, corresponding to the lowest practical energy value in the Fourier transforms to be calculated by the computer. The OPD function is considerably different for this case, with a maximum OPD of 0.03 wavelength.   If the lens system is now recalculated for a new back focus so as to optimize performance at a 0.04-rad angle of the chief ray, then the OPD function shown in Fig. 2.12 results.   If this focal condition is maintained and the on-axis performance is now calculated, the OPD function shown in Fig. 2.13 results.   This is the worst case, with a maximum OPD of 0.04 wavelength.   The effect of this OPD function on the performance of the computer may be calculated by means of eq. (2.18).   Figure 2.14 shows the solution using $f(x_1, y_1) = C$. In comparison with a perfect optical system there is a small (1 percent)

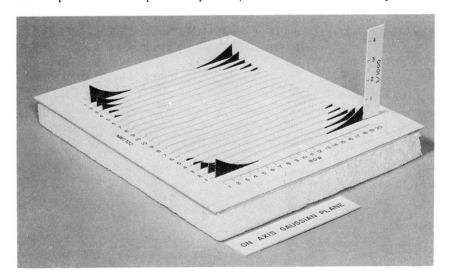

Fig. 2.10 Optical-path-difference model for a reference sphere taken on axis at the paraxial focus (black indicates negative OPD; white, positive OPD).

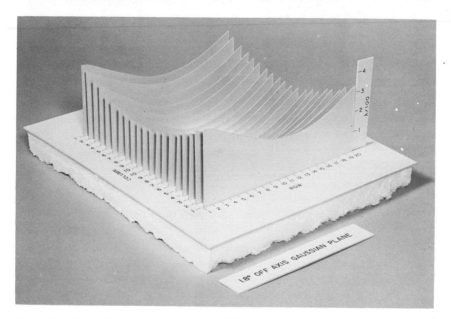

Fig. 2.11 Three-dimensional optical-path-difference model with the reference sphere taken 1.8° off axis in the paraxial plane.

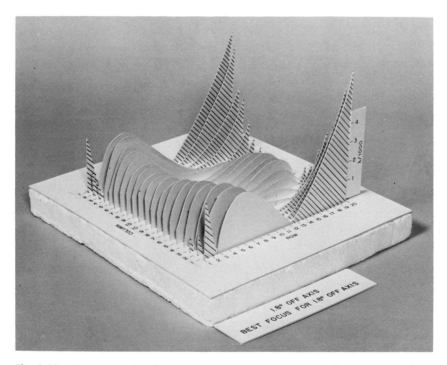

Fig. 2.12 Three-dimensional optical-path-difference model with the reference sphere at the best focus for the 1.8° off-axis position (cross-hatching indicates negative OPD; white, positive OPD).

44

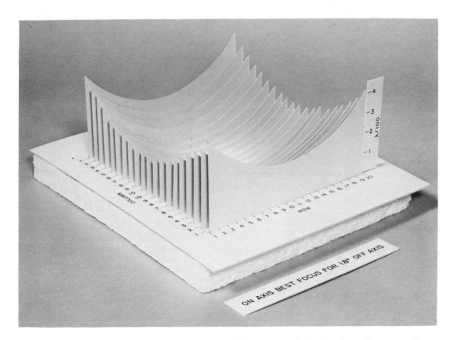

Fig. 2.13 Three-dimensional optical-path-difference model with the reference sphere taken on axis in the plane of best focus for 1.8° off axis.

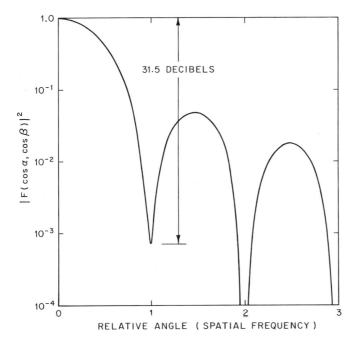

Fig. 2.14 Light intensity distribution on axis in the plane of best focus at 1.8° off axis.

45

drop in the peak value of the square of the modulus of the Fourier transform.   The most obvious effect is that the nulls are filled in with the first minimum occurring at a level 31.5 dB below the peak value of the output.

The optical system discussed in this design example was designed to work at a maximum field angle of 0.04 rad over a 4.0 × 4.0 mm aperture. Once such an optical-computer lens system has been designed and built, the question often arises whether it may be used with other combinations of aperture size and field angle.   It can be anticipated, for example, that, with a reduced aperture, the lens system might operate at a larger field angle and vice versa.   To answer this question a set of characteristic curves may be calculated for the coherent-optical-computer lens system. An example of such a set of characteristic curves is shown in Fig. 2.15. This figure plots aperture size on the ordinate and the spatial frequency corresponding to the maximum field angle on the abscissa.   Hyperbolas which are loci of constant space-bandwidth product are used as an overlay.   The operating curves of the lens are calculated for various levels of the rms optical path difference to a reference sphere taken in the worst-case position in the aperture.   Figure 2.15 shows the set of characteristic curves for an optical-computer lens system designed to work at an aperture of 60 mm up to a field angle corresponding to a spatial frequency of 80 cycles/mm at the design wavelength of 6328 Å.

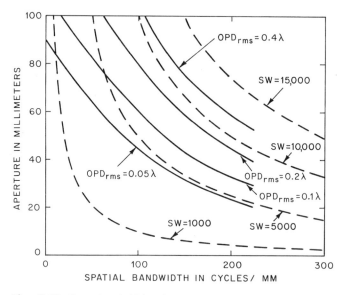

Fig. 2.15 Space-bandwidth characteristic curves for a typical coherent-optical-computer lens system.

As can be seen, this optical-computer lens system is capable of working over a wide range of aperture sizes and of spatial frequencies. The set of characteristic curves illustrated by Fig. 2.15 is extremely useful in evaluating an existing optical-computer lens system for potential use in fulfilling new optical-computer requirements.

REFERENCES

2.1 Hamilton, W. R.: Theory of Systems of Rays, *Trans. Roy. Irish Acad.*, **15**:69 (1828).

2.2 Synge, J. L.: Hamilton's Method in Geometrical Optics, *J. Opt. Soc. Amer.*, **27**:75 (1937).

2.3 Goldstein, H.: "Classical Mechanics," Addison-Wesley, Reading, Mass., 1951.

2.4 Offner, A.: Ray Tracing through a Holographic System, *J. Opt. Soc. Amer.*, **56**:1509 (1966).

2.5 Hopkins, H. H.: "Wave Theory of Aberrations," Oxford University Press, New York, 1950.

2.6 Stavroudis, O. N.: Automatic Optical Design, "Advances in Computers," Academic, New York, 1964.

2.7 Baker, J. G.: The Utilization of Automatic Calculating Machinery in the Field of Optical Design, *Perkin-Elmer Eng. Reps.* 111 (1951); 174, 204, 205, (1952); 227, 241, 255, 264 (1953); 380, 402–404 (1955).

2.8 Black, G.: Use of Electronic Computers in Optical Design, *Nature*, **175**: 164 (1955).

2.9 Wayne, C. G.: Lens Designing by Electronic Digital Computers, *Proc. Phys. Soc. (London)*, **73**:777 (1959).

2.10 Feder, D. P.: Automatic Lens Design with High Speed Computer, *J. Opt. Soc. Amer.*, **52**: 177 (1962).

2.11 Hertzberger, M.: "Modern Geometrical Optics," Interscience, New York, 1958.

2.12 "Handbook of Optical Design," U.S. Military Handbook, MIL-HDBK-140.

2.13 Kingslake, R.: "Applied Optics and Optical Engineering," vols. I and III, Academic, New York, 1965.

2.14 Smith, W. J.: "Modern Optical Engineering," McGraw-Hill, New York, 1967.

2.15 Meiron, J.: Automatic Lens Design by the Least Squares Method, *J. Opt. Soc. Amer.*, **49**: 293 (1959).

Chapter Three

Sources of Optical Power

3.00 Introduction

In general, the continuous-wave laser is the best source of optical power for use with coherent optical computers. In some cases, however, when complete spatial and/or temporal coherence is not required, other sources of illumination may be attractive. In this chapter, after a short review of the more traditional light sources and the principles of photometry, both gaseous and solid-state lasers are discussed. A concluding section compares various types of optical-power sources. As in other chapters of this book which cover areas where more rigorous treatments are available elsewhere, the approach taken is that of a survey with frequent reference to the pertinent literature.

Sources of optical power are classified as either thermal, spectral, or resonant. The thermal source is essentially a blackbody radiator whose temperature is elevated to a level which is sufficiently high to cause a significant fraction of the radiant flux to lie in the visible spectrum, i.e., in the optical electromagnetic spectrum. Figure 3.1 gives the traditional blackbody-radiance curves for reference. Typical of thermal sources is the incandescent lamp where the temperature of the filament is elevated by the electric current flowing through it.   Filaments are chosen primarily for their capability to withstand high temperatures and exhibit long life at these temperatures.   Lifetime is determined not only by the material of the filament itself but also by the ambient in which the filament is encapsulated.   Typical of modern filamentary sources, which are capable of withstanding high temperatures, is the tungsten iodide

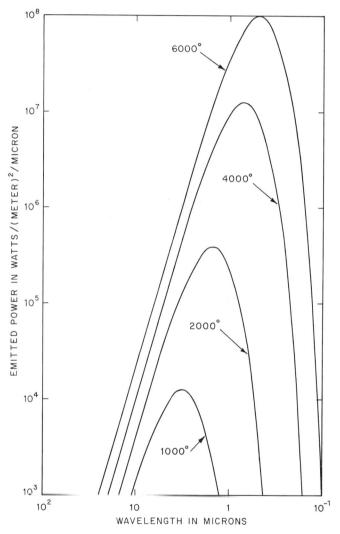

Fig. 3.1   Emissivity characteristics of blackbody radiation.

lamp which may be operated at blackbody temperatures as high as 3100° with a life of hundreds of hours.

The spectral source usually consists of an ionized or atomized gas whose temperature has been elevated by participating in either a corona or gas discharge. The result is the emission of electromagnetic energy in the optical spectrum by means of the radiative transitions of excited electrons which fall from high energy levels to lower energy levels. Because quantum effects limit these transitions to specific energy bands, the radiant flux falls only in certain energy ranges. Figure 3.2 shows an example of the typical line structure of the emission spectrum of a spectral source. Accompanying the radiance at specific spectral lines is the usual random thermal emission due to the temperature of the gas itself.

In both thermal and spectral sources the radiation is both spatially and temporally noncoherent; i.e., the relationship of both the direction and energy of photoemission from point to point in the radiating medium is random. An exception is the narrow spectral line structure of some spectral sources which can be thought of as an indication of a weak temporal coherence. If, however, an ionized or atomized medium is placed in a cavity designed to resonate at a frequency which is equal to one of the naturally emitted spectral lines, it is possible by stimulated emission of radiation to increase significantly the spatial and temporal coherence of the source. This action is commonly known as *laser* action or *l*ight *a*mplification by *s*timulated *e*mission of *r*adiation. As mentioned in Chapter One, the spatial coherence and, to a lesser degree, the tem-

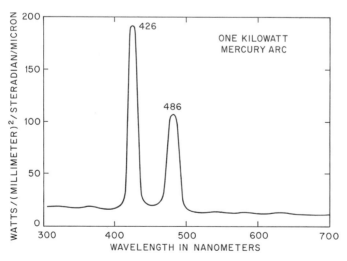

Fig. 3.2   Line spectrum of a mercury arc.

poral coherence of the laser are of particular importance to the utility and simplicity of coherent optical computers.

3.10   Principles of Photometry*

All too often the power output of the traditional thermal and spectral sources is measured in terms of *luminous flux*.   Luminous flux is output power related to the spectral sensitivity of the human eye.   A more useful measure is *radiant flux* which is the total energy as a function of wavelength irrespective of the sensitivity of the human eye at that wavelength.   Because of this anachronism and because of the importance of proper photometric calculations in designing the optical computer, it is worthwhile clarifying both classic and modern photometric terminology at this point.

The luminosity curve, i.e., the spectral-sensitivity curve of the human eye, is shown in Fig. 3.3.   Luminous flux is equal to the integral of the radiant flux of the optical-power source taken over all wavelengths as weighted by the luminosity curve.   Luminous flux is measured in *lumens*. One lumen is equivalent to approximately 1.46 mW of radiant flux having a wavelength of 5550 Å.   Note that 5550 Å is the wavelength at which the luminosity curve reaches its maximum.

Another quantity of classic importance is *luminous intensity* which is a measure of luminous flux per steradian.   The unit of luminous intensity is the *candle*.   For an extended source, classic photometry defines *luminance* as the intensity per unit of emitting area.   The unit of

---

*Strictly speaking, the term *photometry* should be used to refer to luminous flux; the term *radiometry* when referring to radiant flux.

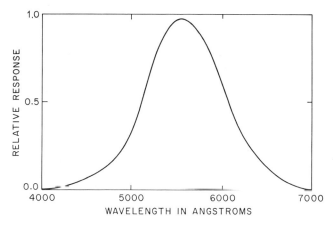

Fig. 3.3   Spectral-sensitivity curve of the human eye.

luminance is candles per unit area or, alternatively, footlamberts when area is measured in square feet.   The luminance of an extended source is also called *brightness*.   For completeness, it probably should also be noted that *illuminance* is defined as the incident luminous flux per unit area and is given traditionally in *footcandles*.   Lastly, the *color temperature* of a thermal source is equal to the temperature to which a blackbody radiator must be raised in order to produce a total visual sensation equivalent to that of the source in question.

As can be seen from the above, classic photometry leaves great room for confusion.   For example, a source emitting electromagnetic radiation outside the sensitivity of the human eye has a brightness of zero in the strict sense of the above definitions.   Attempts are currently being made to rate all sources of optical power not only in terms of luminous intensity but also in terms of watts (radiant flux) or watts per steradian (radiant intensity) as a function of wavelength.   However, this approach is not being universally followed so that at present the optical computer engineer must be familiar and able to deal with classic terminology.   Also, with the partial introduction of the metric system into photometry, further confusion arises.   Table 3.1 may be used as an aid in converting between the various units now in use.

TABLE 3.1

Luminous flux (luminous emittance)	Lumens
Luminous intensity	Lumens/steradian (candles)
Luminance (brightness)	Lumens/steradian/square foot (footlamberts)
Illuminance	Lumens/square foot (footcandles)
Radiant flux (radiant emittance)	Watts
Radiant intensity	Watts/steradian
Radiance	Watts/steradian/square meter
Irradiance	Watts/square meter

A few of the basic photometric equations are discussed in the balance of this section.   First is the equation relating the intensity I to the flux emitted from a point source given by

$$I_l = \frac{d\mathscr{F}_l}{d\Omega}$$

$$I_r = \frac{d\mathscr{F}_r}{d\Omega} \tag{3.1}$$

where I_l and I_r are luminous and radiant intensity, $\mathscr{F}_l$ and $\mathscr{F}_r$ are the luminous and radiant flux, and Ω is the angle in steradians.   The light flux incident upon a surface due to a point source is given by the equation

$$d\mathcal{F} = \frac{I\,dA}{r^2} \tag{3.2}$$

where dA is the differential area of the surface and r is the perpendicular distance from the point source to the differential surface area. For a surface illuminated from an extended source, eq. (3.2) becomes

$$d\mathcal{F} = \frac{B\,dS\,dA}{r^2} \tag{3.3}$$

where B is the brightness of the extended source and dS is its differential surface area. In general, if the plane of the source makes an angle θ with the axis connecting the source and the illuminated surface and the plane of the illuminated surface makes an angle ϕ with the same axis, eq. (3.3) is rewritten as

$$d\mathcal{F} = \frac{B\,dS\,dA \cos\phi \cos\theta}{r^2} \tag{3.4}$$

The total flux is given by integrating eq. (3.4) as follows:

$$\mathcal{F} = \int_A \int_S \int_\lambda \frac{B\cos\phi\cos\theta}{r^2}\,dA\,dS\,d\lambda \tag{3.5}$$

The differential illuminance $d\epsilon$ in the plane of the surface being illuminated is given by

$$d\epsilon = \frac{d\mathcal{F}}{dA} = \frac{B\,dS\cos\phi\cos\theta}{r^2} \tag{3.6}$$

Integrating eq. (3.6) yields the illuminance Σ as follows:

$$\Sigma = \int_S \int_\lambda \frac{B\cos\phi\cos\theta}{r^2}\,dS\,d\lambda \tag{3.7}$$

The illuminance may also be determined by multiplying the brightness of the extended source by the solid angle which the extended source subtends from the illuminated surface. Thus eq. (3.7) may be replaced by

$$\Sigma = B\Omega \tag{3.8}$$

where Ω is the solid angle subtended by the extended source.

Now consider the formulation of the brightness of the image of an extended source formed by a lens of aperture A. Let F_1 and F_2 be the conjugate distances of the source and its image, respectively, as shown in Fig. 3.4. Letting dA be an element in the aperture of the lens, it can be written that

$$d\mathcal{F}_A = \frac{B_s\,ds}{F_1^2} = \frac{B_i\,di}{F_2^2} \tag{3.9}$$

Note that the elementary areas ds and di are related by the equation

$$\frac{ds}{di} = \frac{F_1^2}{F_2^2} \tag{3.10}$$

Equations (3.9) and (3.10) may be combined to demonstrate that $B_s = B_i$; that is, the image and source brightness are identical.

The above equations are based upon the assumption that the flux entering the lens aperture and the flux exiting from it over any elementary area are identical. For actual lens systems a certain percentage of the light is absorbed. This effect must be taken into account by multiplying by the transmission of the lens elements themselves. Since transmission may vary as a function of both aperture position and angle of incidence, a calculation of the effect of lens-system transmission is difficult to formulate exactly. For making order-of-magnitude calculations, a rule of thumb is to allow for a light loss of 1 or 2 per

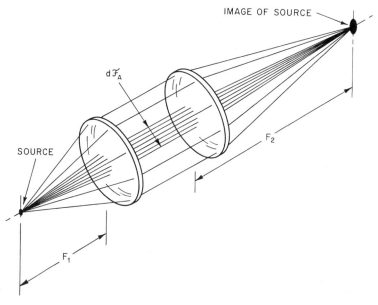

Fig. 3.4 Optical schematic for determining source and image brightness.

cent per surface in the lens system. When more exact calculations are required, ray-tracing programs must be utilized to determine the effect quantitatively. The efficiency of each lens surface is calculated as a function of wavelength and angle of incidence so as to determine the exact losses in the lens system for a particular lens design configuration. Both the characteristics of the materials used for the lens elements and those used for coating the surfaces of these elements must be known and taken into account.

In order to calculate the illuminance in the image plane of the light source, one must take into account the solid angle subtended by the lens aperture. This solid angle is given by the equation

$$\Omega = 2\pi(1 - \cos\gamma) \tag{3.11}$$

where γ is the half angle from the image point to the edge of the lens aperture A. For the small-angle approximation, $\gamma \ll 1$, eq. (3.11) may be rewritten as

$$\Omega = \frac{\pi A^2}{4F_2^2} \tag{3.12}$$

and, from eq. (3.8), the illuminance is then given by

$$\Sigma = \frac{\pi B A^2}{4F_2^2} = \frac{\pi B}{4f_{no}^2} \tag{3.13}$$

where f_{no} is the f-number of the lens in the image plane.

Additional information on traditional light sources and photometry may be obtained from Refs. [3.1] through [3.3].

3.20   Gas-laser Light Sources

The laser consists of a resonant cavity filled with an amplifying medium. The amplifying medium may be the atomic or ionic gas in a gaseous discharge tube, the electron gas formed by ions in a host crystal, or the electron gas in a p-n junction. Because the continuous-wave gas laser is presently more frequently used for powering coherent optical computers than any other source of optical power, this particular laser embodiment is treated first. The following section treats crystal and p-n-junction lasers.

Consider, for example, the well-known helium-neon laser. Pertinent energy levels are diagramed in Fig. 3.5. Light emission is due to the presence of the neon atom. However, before electrons associated with these atoms can radiate, they must be excited or "pumped" by some mechanism. This mechanism is provided by means of the collision between metastable helium $2S$ electrons and neon atoms producing $3S$

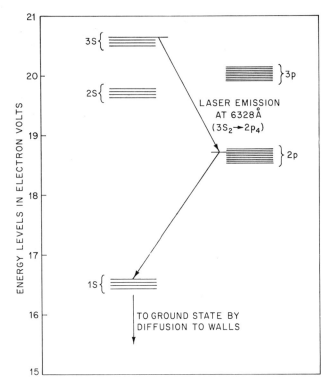

Fig. 3.5 Helium-neon-laser energy transitions.

neon electrons.   When $3S$ neon electrons decay to the $2p$ level, emission is produced at 6328 Å.   In order for this emission to occur, the lifetime of the electrons at the lower level must be considerably smaller than that associated with the electrons at the higher level.   To maintain this situation, called *population inversion*, a mechanism must be provided for returning the $2p$ electrons to the ground state.   For the commonly used helium-neon laser operating at 6328 Å, $2p$ electrons decay to the $1S$ level and thence to the ground state by collisions with the walls of the laser cavity.   The rate at which the population of $1S$ electrons must decay thus determines the allowable dimensions of the bore of the laser.   It is found for this type of laser that gain is proportional to the reciprocal of the bore diameter.

In general, to design a gas laser for high efficiency, it is desirable to use an amplifying gas medium having a narrow spectral emission line in the region where laser action is desired.   Also, the gas should have a low absorptivity (long photon lifetime) at the wavelength desired. Finally, it is useful to have the lower of the two electron levels between which the radiative transition occurs far from the ground state; i.e., the energy of the electron at this level should be considerably greater than kT, where k is Boltzmann's constant and T is temperature in degrees Kelvin.

The resonant cavity of the gas laser may have one of three basic optical configurations, all of which are shown in Fig. 3.6. These configurations have become known as the concentric, confocal, and hemispheric types. In order to increase efficiency the end windows of the gas tube are usually arranged at Brewster's angle so that no reflection occurs for electromagnetic waves whose electric vector is in a plane perpendicular to their surface. Thus, the output of such lasers is always linearly polarized.

Equations describing the structure of the electric field in such a resonant cavity have been developed by Fox, Li, and others [3.4 to 3.10] under the following simplifying assumptions:

1. The distance between end mirrors is large in comparison with the mirror diameter.

2. The resonant cavity is large with respect to the optical wavelength.

3. The field within the cavity is substantially transverse electromagnetic (TEM).

In the derivation it is assumed that the TEM wave is reflected back and forth between the end mirrors. Using Kogelnik's notation [3.12] the equations relating the fields at the two end-mirror surfaces are as follows:

$$\gamma^{(1)} E^{(1)}(s_1) = \int_{S_2} K^{(2)}(s_1, s_2) E^{(2)}(s_2) \, dS_2$$

$$\gamma^{(2)} E^{(2)}(s_2) = \int_{S_1} K^{(1)}(s_2, s_1) E^{(1)}(s_1) \, dS_1$$

(3.14)

CONCENTRIC

CONFOCAL

HEMISPHERICAL

Fig. 3.6 Basic laser-cavity configurations.

where $E^{(1)}$ and $E^{(2)}$ are the electric field distributions at the two mirror surfaces S_1 and S_2 at either end of the cavity.   The quantities s_1 and s_2 symbolize the transverse coordinates on the two mirror surfaces.   The factors $\gamma^{(1)}$ and $\gamma^{(2)}$ represent the attenuation and phase shift which take place in transit between the two surfaces.   The kernel functions $K^{(1)}$ and $K^{(2)}$ are operators which depend upon the mirror geometry and the distance between the mirrors.

As pointed out by Kogelnik, the kernel functions are equal, that is, $K^{(1)} = K^{(2)}$, but in general they are not symmetric.   One of eqs. (3.14) may be substituted in the other in order to obtain the "round-trip" equality.   When the kernels are symmetric, it can be demonstrated that the electric field distributions corresponding to different cavity modes are orthogonal over the surfaces of the end mirrors, i.e.,

$$\int_{S_1} E_m^{(1)}(s_1) E_n^{(1)}(s_1)\, dS_1 = 0$$

$$\int_{S_2} E_m^{(2)}(s_2) E_n^{(2)}(s_2)\, dS_2 = 0$$

(3.15)

where m and n correspond to the different transverse electromagnetic mode orders, i.e., the TEM_{mn}.

Solutions of eqs. (3.14) and (3.15) which are of particular interest are those which occur in the radially symmetric case when the mirrors are circular.   In this case the kernel K is given by

$$K_l(r_1, r_2) = \frac{j^{l+1}}{d} J_l \frac{2\pi r_1 r_2}{\lambda_L d} \sqrt{r_1 r_2}\, e^{(-j\pi/\lambda_L d)(g_1 r_1^2 + g_2 r_2^2)}$$

(3.16)

where J_l is a Bessel function of the first kind and the lth order, r_1 and r_2 are radial coordinates on the two mirror surfaces, $g_1 = 1 - d/R_1$ and $g_2 = 1 - d/R_2$, where d is the spacing and R_1 and R_2 are the radii of curvature of the mirrors.   The three special cases of interest are $g_1 = g_2 = 0$, $g_1 = g_2 = -1$, and $g_1 = 0$, $g_2 = -1$ which correspond to the confocal resonator, the concentric resonator, and the hemispherical resonator, respectively.

As shown in Refs. [3.11] and [3.12], the electric field distributions for circular mirrors are Laguerre-Gaussian functions whose modes are usually designated TEM_{pl}.   Of particular interest is the TEM_{00} mode for the confocal resonator whose radially symmetrical amplitude distribution is shown in Fig. 3.7.   As can be seen, the amplitude distribution is approximately gaussian across the end mirror of the cavity.   It should be noted that phase is essentially constant across the surface of the end mirror.   In designing coherent optical computers powered by

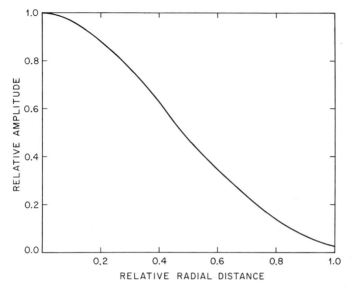

Fig. 3.7 Amplitude characteristic of the TEM_{00} laser-cavity mode. (*After Fox and Li.*)

resonant-cavity light sources, mixed-mode structures are to be avoided because the various modes will resonate at different phases. This contributes to a lowering of the efficiency of the computer and a general loss in computing accuracy. Since the TEM_{00} mode has the lowest losses, it is the first mode to occur as the gain is increased in the resonant cavity to the point where laser action occurs. Therefore, an understanding of the TEM_{00} mode is important in adjusting the computer power source to a point where efficiency is greatest. The reader is referred to Heinemann and Redlien [3.14] who discuss methods for measuring mode impurity with a high degree of sensitivity, based on the Fourier-transformable properties of optics.

Longitudinal modes may also exist in the resonator cavity. If the spectral line width of the gaseous medium is greater than $2d/\lambda_L$, it is possible for more than one longitudinal mode to be present in the cavity at the same time. Each longitudinal mode will have essentially the same transverse mode distribution but will exhibit a different resonant frequency. This is sometimes disadvantageous in coherent optical computers which are used in processing wide-bandwidth electronic signals because beat frequencies between longitudinal modes may occur as noise in the electronic output bandwidth of interest. For example, the spectral line width of fluorescing neon is approximately 1700 MHz. Therefore, in order to prevent more than one longitudinal mode from occurring, the value for d must be less than 15 cm in a helium-neon laser.   The disadvantage of a low d value is that the total power output is smaller, because of the reduction in the volume of the amplifying medium in the resonant cavity.   One advantage to the lower d value is a higher Fresnel number for a given mirror diameter, meaning that the end mirrors are well within the near-field region of each other.

For a more detailed review of laser resonator theory the interested reader is referred to the excellent survey papers by Yariv and Gordon [3.15] and Kogelnik and Li [3.16].

Helium-neon lasers of reasonably convenient size are available with output powers up to a few hundred milliwatts.   The more powerful units typically have a 200-cm resonator cavity and require input power of a thousand times the output obtained.   Although operating in a fundamental transverse mode they also operate simultaneously in many longitudinal modes.   If the cavity length is reduced to the point where only a single longitudinal mode occurs, then output power drops to between 0.1 and 1 mW with an input of between 10 and 100 W.

In order to achieve output power in the 1- to 10-W range it is necessary to use ionized-gas lasers of which the argon laser is typical.   Since the spectral line width of this gas is approximately twice that of neon, it is necessary to use a still shorter resonant cavity to obtain resonance at a single longitudinal mode.   Tube lengths for such lasers are typically 5 cm.   Two spectral lines, one in the green at 5145 Å and one in the blue at 4880 Å, may be used to produce laser action.   With longer tubes, of the order of 50 cm in length, power outputs of several watts may be obtained.   As with the helium-neon laser, efficiency is low and input power of a few kilowatts is typical.   The advantage of the ion laser is that not only is its ionization energy higher than that of the neutral-atom helium-neon laser but also energy gaps for stimulated radiative transitions are higher, ranging between 2 to 5 eV. This permits many transitions in the visible portion of the electromagnetic spectrum.   Also, whereas in neutral-atom lasers output power cannot be increased by increasing the bore diameter, because of radiation trapping (the inability to return to the ground state by collisions with the gas tube wall, as mentioned above), it is possible in the ion laser to increase power in this manner.   On the other hand, since the ion laser is best operated at a high current density in the gas discharge, bore diameter may be reduced for this reason or a magnetic field may be applied along the resonator axis to confine the discharge.   High current densities imply high plasma temperatures and the inherent danger of filling the lower energy states by thermal excitation.   However, in the ion laser the energy levels reached by the radiation transitions are farther away from the ground state than in the neutral-atom lasers.   Thus thermal repopulation of these levels is not a problem even at elevated plasma temperatures.

Fig. 3.8   A 5-W argon laser.

Another problem decidedly associated with high current density and high plasma temperature in the ion laser is erosion of the walls of the plasma tube itself.   Ion bombardment in the gas discharge causes sputtering of the walls and eventual destruction of the tube.   A solution to this problem and others associated with heating of the tube has been to use high-temperature ceramic materials for the tube.   Alumina is especially attractive since it not only has high-temperature stamina but also is a good heat conductor and can remove rapidly heat generated in the plasma.   A photograph of a modern ion laser designed for long-term operation in a rugged environment is shown in Fig. 3.8.   Useful reviews of problems associated with ion lasers have been written by

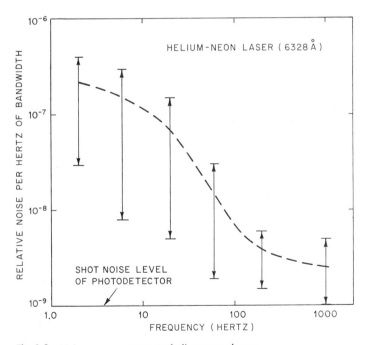

Fig. 3.9   Noise measurements on helium-neon lasers.

Labuda [3.17], Rigden [3.18], and Bell [3.19]. The latter proposes a method for reducing the plasma-tube erosion problem by the use of radio-frequency rather than direct-current excitation.

To close this section, sources of noise in the output of gas lasers are briefly mentioned. Severe noise problems may occur at very low frequencies in the single-longitudinal-mode laser, because of the gradual thermal lengthening of the cavity. One hundred percent modulation is typical at frequencies of a few tenths of a cycle per second until dimensional stabilization has been reached. This may be partially corrected by driving one of the end mirrors piezoelectrically to maintain a constant tube length and thus a constant output. Other sources of noise characteristic of direct-current excitation are caused by fluctuations in the plasma density. This type of noise is not as prevalent in the radio-frequency-excited lasers as in the direct-current lasers and can in some cases be decreased or removed from the direct-current version by keeping gas pressures to a minimum. An experimental plot of noise output as a function of frequency for both direct-current and radio-frequency-excited helium-neon lasers is shown in Fig. 3.9. Further information on this subject has been published by Bailey [3.20] and Bellisio et al. [3.21].

3.30   Solid-state Light Sources

There are two major categories of solid-state light sources: (1) crystal and glass lasers and (2) semiconductor lasers.

Lasers made from crystalline material and/or glass are similar in their action to the gas-laser light sources described in Sec. 3.20. The crystalline or glassy host material is selected so that it may be doped with an impurity atom whose ion has an appropriate energy-level structure. In such lasers excitation, or "pumping," is carried out optically rather than electrically. The host must be relatively transparent to the pump radiation whereas the impurity ion must absorb. The impurity ion must also be capable, because of the relative decay times for electrons in certain energy levels, of supporting an electron-population inversion so as to permit laser action at the desired wavelength.

An example of a crystal laser is provided when sapphire is used as a host and is doped with chromium to form ruby ($Al_2O_3:Cr$). Another example is neodymium used as a dopant in yttrium aluminum garnet ($Y_3Al_5O_{12}:Nd$). The former lases in the red; the latter, in the near infrared. Neodymium has also been used as a dopant in various glasses to form the well-known neodymium-glass lasers. The advantage of using rare-earth atoms as dopants is that in their ionized state they are strongly absorbent at typical pumping wavelengths across the infrared spectrum. This leads to efficient operation. In fact, efficiencies as high as 5 percent have been reported by Johnson et al. [3.22] using a YAG host multiple doped with the rare earths Er, Tm, and Yb, for high absorptivity in the infrared and the capability of transferring their energy to a fourth dopant, Ho, for the purpose of producing laser action at an emission wavelength of 2.1 μm.   In this case, 10 to 20 W of output power was obtained, with the disadvantage that the laser required cooling to liquid-nitrogen temperatures.   The pumping source was a tungsten filamentary lamp operating at 300 W.

Gas discharge lamps are also frequently used to pump such lasers and frequently have their emission spectrum shaped by additives so as to match the absorption spectrum of the dopant(s).

In the crystal and glass lasers the solid host material itself forms the resonant "cavity."   The material is usually shaped into a resonant structure a few centimeters long and less than a centimeter in diameter. The ends of the structure are carefully polished and coated for the required resonant condition.   The pumping lamp is then built around this structure and usually there is a mirror system designed to focus the pumping radiation on the laser material.

The advantages of such lasers are their compact size in comparison with gas lasers of equivalent output power. However, continuous-wave operation at high output power at room temperature is hard to achieve, and the high concentration of heat in the resonant structure causes mechanical distortion which makes single-mode resonance difficult to obtain.   Thus the gas laser is still utilized more frequently than the crystal or glass lasers in powering coherent optical computers.

The other type of solid-state laser which is treated in this section is the semiconductor laser.   Both gallium arsenide and gallium phosphide p-n junctions (either at liquid–gas temperatures or, in some cases, at room temperature) have been made to radiate light by the transition of injected electrons or holes between the lower levels of the conduction band and the upper levels of the valence band.   The emitted wavelength is determined primarily by the band-gap energy.   The semiconductor material is transparent at the emitted wavelength.   This is true because the electron levels below the gap on the p side are empty and on the n side in the conduction band they are full.   Thus, photons having an energy equal to the gap energy cannot be absorbed.

A typical energy-level diagram for a p-n junction is shown in Fig. 3.10a. Electrons from donor atoms in the n region have partially filled the conduction band, and holes from acceptor atoms in the p region have caused the valence band in that region to become depleted of electrons. Thus a voltage barrier exists which prevents electrons from flowing across the junction from left to right.   If a strong forward bias of sufficient magnitude is supplied across the junction, it will cause the situation diagramed in Fig. 3.10*b* to occur where electrons injected into the junction may take part in a direct transition to the valence band. The resultant energy loss results in the emission of a photon having an energy equal to the gap energy E_g. Ordinarily, therefore, light is emitted from a narrow region, namely, the *p-n* junction itself.

Alternatively, an intrinsic layer may be built between the *n* region and the *p* region. A plasma may be formed in this high-resistivity region, thus widening the zone in which light emission may take place. If the light-emitting region is contained in a resonant "cavity," laser action may be produced if a gain greater than unity is created. Frequently the resonant structure is formed merely by polishing the sides of the block of semiconductor which contains the *p-n* junction. The polished walls are made perpendicular to the plane of the *p-n* junction. It should also be mentioned that, besides pumping by electron current, it is possible to pump a semiconductor laser directly by creating electron-hole pairs, using an electron beam as described by Nicol [3.23]. For example, a 20-kV electron beam can create 10^4 electron pairs per incident electron which, when they reach the conduction and valence band edges, may form an inverted population. By polishing appropriate reflecting surfaces so as to form a cavity, laser action may be produced. Optically pumped semiconductor lasers are also possible as discussed, for example, by Melngailis [3.24].

In general, *p-n*-junction lasers are formed by many combinations of the III-V compounds. Typical of these compounds are gallium arsenide, gallium antimonide, gallium phosphide, indium antimonide, etc. Many other compounds such as the zinc and lead sulfides, tellurides, and selenides have exhibited lasing action, as well as the sulfides, selenides, and tellurides of cadmium. Combined arsenides and phosphides of gallium have been used to cover the near infrared. Cadmium sulfide has been utilized to produce radiation in the blue-green at 4950 Å. Zinc sulfide has been utilized to produce radiation in the

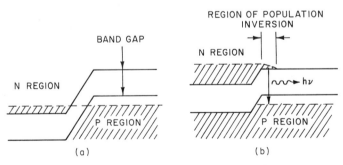

Fig. 3.10   Energy-band configurations for *p-n*-junction laser.

ultraviolet.   In terms of output power, several watts have been obtained with units cooled to liquid-nitrogen temperatures, as described, for example, by Marriance [3.25].

The advantage of the semiconductor laser is that quantum efficiency is high and the device itself is small.   One disadvantage is that there are few wavelengths available in the visible.   Also, cooling to low temperatures is often necessary for continuous-wave operation since very high current densities are required (10^5 A/cm^2 is typical).   Output power at room temperature is less than that available from other types of lasers. Also, single-mode operation is difficult to achieve, and emission angles are often as great as 10 or 20°.

3.40   Conclusion

Table 3.2 lists the radiance for typical continuous-wave neutral-atom, ion, and solid-state lasers as well as for the most traditional thermal and spectral sources.   As can be seen, the radiance of the gas laser is far greater than that of the semiconductor laser.   However, in some instances, the optical computer engineer may prefer the longer life, higher reliability, and compactness of the semiconductor optical-power sources to the more powerful gas, crystal, and glass laser systems.   This assumes, of course, that the semiconductor laser may be operated at room temperature.   Operation at room temperature often requires a large heat sink which negates the above-mentioned size advantage.

As has been mentioned previously, one major difference between the newer resonant or laser sources of optical power and the more traditional thermal and spectral sources involves considerations of both temporal and spatial coherence.   In concluding this chapter, the question of coherence is examined in more detail.

The temporal-coherence function at the point (x, y) for the electric

TABLE 3.2

Light source	Wavelength, nm	Total output, W	Efficiency, %	Radiance, W/srn/mm^2
Tungsten filament	Visible range	2–20	2–4	0.5–2.0
Mercury arc	Visible range	10–100	5–10	2–10
Helium-neon laser	633	10^{-2}–10^{-1}	< 1	10^4–10^5
Helium-cadmium laser	442	10^{-2}–10^{-1}	< 1	10^4–10^5
YAG laser	1,064	10–10^2	1–3	10^6–10^8
GaAs p-n junction	905	10^{-1}–1.0	30–70	10^{-1}–1.0

field distribution $E(x, y, t)$ is given by the equation

$$\Gamma(\tau) = \langle E(x, y, t) E^*(x, y, t - \tau) \rangle \tag{3.17}$$

where the brackets indicate a time average. Equation (3.17) is an autocorrelation function of $E(x, y, t)$ taken at the same point in space but separated by a variable time τ. Clearly if $E(x, y, t)$ consists of a single sinusoidal frequency, then the peak value attained by the temporal-coherence function will not decrease with τ. In general, however, if $E(x, y, t)$ has a finite spectral bandwidth, the coherence function will be a decreasing function of τ. The so-called "coherence time" of the electric field distribution at the point (x, y) is defined as the value of τ for which the coherence function falls to $1/e$ of its initial value. Single-longitudinal-mode gas lasers may have coherence times of the order of milliseconds in comparison with picosecond coherence time of typical spectral sources.

The parallel definition for spatial coherence is given as follows:

$$\Gamma(\xi, \eta) = \langle E(x, y, t) E^*(x + \xi, y + \eta, t) \rangle \tag{3.18}$$

where again a long time average of the correlation function of the electric field is taken. In this instance the function is dependent upon the distance between two separate points in space which are located perpendicular to the direction of optical propagation. Thus the spatial-coherence function relates to lateral coherence, whereas the temporal-coherence function relates to longitudinal coherence, i.e., coherence parallel to the direction of propagation.

In terms of coherent-optical-computer design, temporal coherence in the source of optical power is important for three reasons: (1) to permit the calculation of Fourier transforms with an accuracy which is independent of spatial frequency, (2) to permit heterodyne detection in the output plane, and (3) to take advantage of the simplicity of optical systems designed for use with monochromatic light. Spatial coherence is important in the calculation of both Fourier transforms and correlation functions at any spatial frequency. Without spatial coherence the diffraction theorem (Sec. 4.20) no longer holds since the input to the optical computer is no longer a single wavefront but instead is a multiplicity of independent or partially independent wavefronts. This destroys both the Fourier-transform relationship (Sec. 4.30) and by the same token invalidates the Wiener-Khintchine theorem (Sec. 4.40) which is often used in coherent optical computers in the process of calculating correlation functions. Without temporal coherence the phase non-uniformity across the diffracted wavefronts at the input to the optical computer causes the value of the Fourier transform being calculated to degrade with increasing spatial frequency. In this case eq. (4.34) would be rewritten

$$F(\omega_x, \omega_y) = C \iint \mathbf{f}(x_1, y_1) \gamma(\tau) \, dx_1 \, dy_1 \tag{3.19}$$

where $\tau = (x_1 \cos \alpha + y_1 \cos \beta)/c$, where α and β are the direction angles with respect to the x_1 and y_1 axes, respectively, and c is the velocity of optical propagation. Also recall that $\omega_x = (2\pi \cos \alpha)/\lambda_L$ and $\omega_y = (2\pi \cos \beta)/\lambda_L$. Finally, the quantity $\gamma(\tau)$ is the degree of coherence as given by

$$\gamma(\tau) = \frac{\Gamma(\tau)}{E(x, y, t)E^*(x, y, t)} \tag{3.20}$$

The interested reader is referred to Born and Wolf [3.26] and O'Neill [3.27] for further discussions on coherence.

There is one special configuration in coherent optical computers which is an exception to the above remarks on coherence requirements. This is the homodyne correlator (see Chap. Nine) which requires neither spatial nor temporal coherence in calculating correlation functions but which is incapable of calculating Fourier transforms or of Fourier-plane matched filtering. Except for the homodyne correlator, a lack of temporal and/or spatial coherence implies a loss of accuracy in the operation of the optical computer. The implications of this statement are made clearer by reference to the other chapters of this book.

Finally, it should be noted that the spatial coherence of even thermal, spectral, or multimode resonant sources may be improved by using an

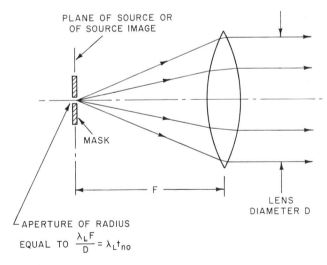

Fig. 3.11 Use of an aperture mask for achieving spatial coherence.

aperture of radius $\lambda_L f_{no}$ in the image plane of the source in order to select a single plane (or spherical) wave from the energy emitted by the source (see Fig. 3.11).   Here f_{no} is the f-number of the optical system beyond the aperture.   This, however, has the effect of removing what may be a significant fraction of the available power from the optical system.   The power reduction factor may be estimated from the quantity $1 - \pi (\lambda_L f_{no})^2 / S$, where S is the radiating area of the source. This expression for power reduction assumes that $S > \lambda_L f_{no}$ and that the source produces radiant flux over a solid angle at least equal to $\pi/4 f_{no}^2$.

REFERENCES

3.1   Levi, L.: "Applied Optics," Wiley, New York, 1968.

3.2   Brown, E. B.: "Modern Optics," Reinhold, New York, 1965.

3.3   Kingslake, R.: "Applied Optics and Optical Engineering," vol. 1, Academic, New York, 1965.

3.4   Fox, A. G., and T. Li: Resonant Modes in an Optical Maser, *Proc. IRE*, **48**: 1904 (1960).

3.5   Fox, A. G., and T. Li: Resonant Modes in a Maser Interferometer, *Bell Syst. Tech. J.*, **40**: 453 (1961).

3.6   Fox, A. G., and T. Li: Effect of Gain Saturation on the Oscillating Modes of Optical Masers, *IEEE J. Quantum Electron.*, **QE-2**: 774 (December, 1966).

3.7   Newman, D. J., and S. P. Morgan: Existence of Eigenvalues of a Class of Integral Equations Arising in Laser Theory, *Bell Syst. Tech. J.*, **43**: 113 (1964).

3.8   Cochran, J. A.: The Existence of Eigenvalues for the Integral Equations of Laser Theory, *Bell Syst. Tech. J.*, **44**: 77 (1965).

3.9   Hochstadt, H.: On the Eigenvalue of a Class of Integral Equations Arising in Laser Theory, *Soc. Ind. & Appl. Math. Rev.*, **8**: 62 (January, 1966).

3.10 Li, T.: Diffraction Loss and Selection of Modes in Maser Resonators with Circular Mirrors, *Bell Syst. Tech. J.*, **44**: 917 (1965).

3.11 Heurtley, J. C., and W. Streifer: Optical Resonator Modes-Circular Reflectors of Spherical Curvature, *J. Opt. Soc. Amer.*, **55**: 1472 (1965).

3.12 Boyd, G. D., and H. Kogelnik: Generalized Confocal Resonator Theory, *Bell Syst. Tech. J.*, **41**: 1347 (1962).

3.13 Goubau, G., and F. Schwering: On the Guided Propagation of Electromagnetic Wave Beams, *IRE Trans. Antennas & Propagation*, **AP-9**: 248 (1961).

3.14 Heinemann, H. M., and H. W. Redlien, Jr.: Observation of Mode Impurity in Gas Lasers Apparently Resonating in the TEM_{00} Mode, *Proc. IEEE*, **53**: 77 (1965).

3.15 Yariv, A., and J. P. Gordon: The Laser, *Proc. IEEE*, **51**: 4 (1963).

3.16 Kogelnik, H., and T. Li, Laser Beams and Resonators, *Proc. IEEE*, **54**: 1312 (1966).

3.17 Labuda, E. F.: Continuous Duty Argon Ion Lasers, *IEEE J. Quantum Electron.*, **QE-1**: 273 (1965).

3.18 Rigden, J. D.: A Metallic Plasma Tube for Ion Lasers, *IEEE J. Quantum Electron.*, **QE-1**: 221 (1965).

3.19 Bell, W. E.: Ring Discharge Excitation of Gas Ion Lasers, *Appl. Phys. Lett.*, **7**: 190 (1965).

3.20 Bailey, R. L., and J. H. Sanders: The Amplitude Fluctuations of Optical Maser Light, *Phys. Lett.*, **10**: 295 (1964).

3.21 Bellisio, J. A., et al.: Noise Measurements on He-Ne Laser Oscillations, *Appl. Phys. Lett.*, **4**:5 (1964).

3.22 Johnson, L. F., et al.: Efficient High-power Coherent Emission from Ho Ions in Yttrium Aluminum Garnet Assisted by Energy Transfer, *Appl. Phys. Lett.*, **8**:200 (1966).

3.23 Nicol, F. H.: Ultraviolet ZnO Laser Pumped by an Electron Beam, *Appl. Phys. Lett.*, **9**:13 (1966).

3.24 Melngailis, I.: Optically Pumped Indium Arsenide Laser, *IEEE J. Quantum Electron.*, **QE-1**:104 (1965).

3.25 Marriance, J. C.: High Power CW Operation of GaAs Injection Lasers at 77°K, *IBM J. Res. Develop.*, **8**:543 (1964).

3.26 Born, M., and E. Wolf: "Principles of Optics," Pergamon, New York, 1959.

3.27 O'Neill, E. L.: "Introduction to Statistical Optics," Addison-Wesley, Reading, Mass., 1963.

Chapter Four

The Mathematics
of Optical Computation

4.00   Introduction

In this chapter both amplitude and phase modulation of coherent optical radiation are discussed and analyzed in order to provide the mathematical background necessary for understanding the accompanying chapters.   The interaction between a plane wave of light and a two-dimensional spatial light modulator is used to introduce the Fourier-transform relationship in coherent optical spectrum analysis.   This relationship is then used to demonstrate the effects of diffraction.   The convolution and correlation integrals are then covered and related to coherent optical computation.   Next, diffraction is discussed from the Fresnel-Kirchhoff point of view.   The Wiener spectrum is defined and certain elementary examples are demonstrated.   Finally, some practical limitations are discussed in Sec. 4.70 entitled "Sources of Noise."

4.10   Modulation Techniques

Signals are introduced into the coherent optical computer by means of spatial light modulation.   This section assumes that this operation takes place in the xy plane with optical propagation of the incident light in the z direction.

4.11 Amplitude Modulation

Amplitude modulation of coherent light may be accomplished by passing a light wave through a thin film which selectively attenuates the light amplitude (either by absorption or reflection) without altering phase.   Let us represent the incident light wave as a plane wave in the $x_1 y_1$ plane with the amplitude of the electric field in that plane given by

$$E_0(x_1, y_1) = E_m e^{-j\omega_L t} \qquad \begin{array}{c} -\infty < x_1 < +\infty \\ -\infty < y_1 < +\infty \end{array} \qquad (4.1)$$

where $j = \sqrt{-1}$.   Equation (4.1) implies that the phase of the plane wave in the $x_1 y_1$ plane is dependent only upon time and upon the optical frequency ω_L, and not upon the spatial variables x_1 and y_1.   It also implies that the electric field is spatially constant in the plane and everywhere of equal peak amplitude, E_m.   The direction of propagation is, of course, perpendicular to the $x_1 y_1$ plane.   This direction defines what will be called the *optical axis* or z axis.

The effect of amplitude modulation on the incident light wave is to alter the uniform electric field distribution in the $x_1 y_1$ plane so as to create a new electric field distribution which can be described as follows:

$$E(x_1, y_1) = E_m f(x_1, y_1) e^{-j\omega_L t} \qquad (4.2)$$

where the expression $f(x_1, y_1)$ is a positive real function of the variables x_1 and y_1 only.   The effect of $f(x_1, y_1)$ upon the incident light wave is to cause a variation of light amplitude to take place in the $x_1 y_1$ plane with no accompanying variation in phase.

The fact that $f(x_1, y_1)$ is constrained to be a positive real function places a restriction upon the use of spatial light amplitude modulation. In many cases it is desired to perform two-dimensional light amplitude modulation with an arbitrary amplitude function $a(x, y)$ having both positive and negative values.   If this is the case, $f(x_1, y_1)$ is constructed as follows:

$$f(x_1, y_1) = B + a(x_1, y_1) \qquad (4.3)$$

so that

$$E(x_1, y_1) = E_m e^{-j\omega_L t}[B + a(x_1, y_1)] \qquad (4.4)$$

In the above equation B is a positive number equal in magnitude to the most negative value of $a(x, y)$.   The quantity B is referred to as the *bias term* and has the effect of preventing $f(x_1, y_1)$ from becoming negative. Another method of solving the negative-value problem is outlined in Sec. 4.13.

4.12 Phase Modulation   The above analysis may readily be extended to include pure phase modulation. Phase modulation of the incident light wave in the $x_1 y_1$ plane takes place when the incident wave passes through a thin nonabsorbing film which exhibits point-to-point differences in optical velocity (or *optical index*). The result can be described by

$$E(x_1, y_1) = E_m e^{j[-\omega_L t + \phi(x_1, y_1)]} \tag{4.5}$$

where $\phi(x_1, y_1)$ is the spatial phase-modulating function.

As will be discussed in Chapter Five, a special case of considerable interest occurs when all values of $\phi(x_1, y_1)$ are significantly less than 1 rad. In this case

$$E(x_1, y_1) \approx E_m e^{-j\omega_L t}[1 + j\phi(x_1, y_1)] \tag{4.6}$$

This situation can be seen to be much like that of spatial amplitude modulation with a strong bias term except that, here, the spatially modulated light is in temporal phase quadrature with the incident light.

4.13 Simultaneous Amplitude and Phase Modulation   In general, both amplitude and phase modulation will be produced by typical spatial light modulators. By combining the results of the above two sections a complex spatial light-modulating function may be defined as follows:

$$\mathbf{f}(x_1, y_1) = f(x_1, y_1) e^{j\phi(x_1, y_1)} \tag{4.7}$$

so that

$$E(x_1, y_1) = E_m \mathbf{f}(x_1, y_1) e^{-j\omega_L t}$$
$$= E_m f(x_1, y_1) e^{j[-\omega_L t + \phi(x_1, y_1)]} \tag{4.8}$$

The function $\mathbf{f}(x_1, y_1)$ still operates only in the $x_1 y_1$ plane within all the above-mentioned restrictions but can be seen to cause both amplitude and phase modulation simultaneously.

A special case of $\mathbf{f}(x_1, y_1)$ is of interest. Assume that it is desired to spatially amplitude-modulate light by means of the function $a(x, y)$ described above without the addition of the bias term B. This may be accomplished as follows: Define the set of points in the $x_1 y_1$ plane, where $a(x_1, y_1)$ is negative, as the set S_N. Similarly, the set S_P encompasses all points in the $x_1 y_1$ plane where $a(x_1, y_1)$ is positive or zero. Next define a spatial phase-modulating function $\phi_a(x_1, y_1)$ such that

$$\phi_a(x_1, y_1) = \begin{cases} \pi & (x_1, y_1) \in S_N \\ 0 & (x_1, y_1) \in S_P \end{cases} \tag{4.9}$$

The function f_a given below will provide spatial light modulation of the incident light in such a way that both the negative and positive values of $a(x, y)$ are realized:

$$f_a(x_1, y_1) = a(x_1, y_1)e^{j\phi_a(x_1, y_1)} \tag{4.10}$$

4.14 Polarization Effects   So far it has been assumed for simplicity that the spatial light modulators discussed are isotropic in terms of the polarization of the incident light.   In certain cases of interest the optical spatial light modulator is anisotropic, and optical amplitude and index become a function of polarization.   When this is true, the incident light must be expressed in terms of its components in the $x_1 y_1$ plane and each component treated separately.

Defining the positive z direction as the direction of light propagation and utilizing the x_1 and y_1 axes in the usual right-handed sense, the incident light wave may be represented in terms of its x_1 and y_1 components by a column vector **E**.   Following Jones' notation [4.1] **E** is expressed as follows:

$$\mathbf{E} = \begin{bmatrix} \mathbf{E}_x(x_1, y_1) \\ \mathbf{E}_y(x_1, y_1) \end{bmatrix} \tag{4.11}$$

In general, the components of **E** are complex; i.e., they have temporal components which are both in phase and in quadrature.

Following the notation used by O'Neill [4.2], the action of a spatial light modulator is specified by means of a Jones matrix, **L**, given by

$$\mathbf{L} = \begin{bmatrix} \mathbf{f}_{11}(x_1, y_1) & \mathbf{f}_{12}(x_1, y_1) \\ \mathbf{f}_{21}(x_1, y_1) & \mathbf{f}_{22}(x_1, y_1) \end{bmatrix} \tag{4.12}$$

where the elements of **L** are complex and are functions of x_1 and y_1.

The action of the spatial light modulator upon **E** is then described by the matrix multiplication

$$\mathbf{E}(x_1, y_1) = \mathbf{LE} \tag{4.13}$$

For an incident light wave which is linearly polarized parallel to the x_1 axis **E** becomes

$$\mathbf{E} = E_m e^{-j\omega_L t} \begin{bmatrix} 1 \\ 0 \end{bmatrix} \tag{4.14}$$

Other cases of interest are

1. Polarization at an angle θ to the x_1 axis

$$\mathbf{E} = E_m e^{-j\omega_L t} \begin{bmatrix} \cos\theta \\ \sin\theta \end{bmatrix} \tag{4.15}$$

2. Right circularly polarized

$$\mathbf{E} = \frac{E_m}{2} e^{-j\omega_L t} \begin{bmatrix} 1 \\ -j \end{bmatrix} \tag{4.16}$$

3. Left circularly polarized

$$\mathbf{E} = \frac{E_m}{2} e^{-j\omega_L t} \begin{bmatrix} 1 \\ j \end{bmatrix} \tag{4.17}$$

For isotropic pure amplitude modulation the **L** matrix is given by

$$\mathbf{L} = \begin{bmatrix} f(x_1, y_1) & 0 \\ 0 & f(x_1, y_1) \end{bmatrix} \tag{4.18}$$

Similarly, for isotropic pure phase modulation the **L** matrix is

$$\mathbf{L} = \begin{bmatrix} e^{j\phi(x_1, y_1)} & 0 \\ 0 & e^{j\phi(x_1, y_1)} \end{bmatrix} \tag{4.19}$$

In general, when isotropy prevails, the **L** matrix can be written

$$\mathbf{L} = \begin{bmatrix} \mathbf{f}(x_1, y_1) & 0 \\ 0 & \mathbf{f}(x_1, y_1) \end{bmatrix} \tag{4.20}$$

where, as before, $\mathbf{f}(x_1, y_1) = f(x_1 \ y_1) e^{j\phi(x_1, y_1)}$

For the anisotropic case, when there is no mixing of the x_1 and y_1 components of the incident light wave, the **L** matrix is given by

$$\mathbf{L} = \begin{bmatrix} \mathbf{f}_{11}(x_1, y_1) & 0 \\ 0 & \mathbf{f}_{22}(x_1, y_1) \end{bmatrix} \tag{4.21}$$

For the general case, eq. (4.12) must be utilized.

4.20   The Diffraction Theorem

Once the incident light wave has been spatially modulated, the effect of propagation beyond the $x_1 y_1$ plane must be determined. This action is best illustrated by recourse to Fourier analysis. At first assume that the extent of $\mathbf{f}(x_1, y_1)$ is limited to a square aperture of lateral extent, A, in the $x_1 y_1$ plane. In this case $\mathbf{f}(x_1, y_1)$ may be expanded in terms of a two-dimensional Fourier series as follows:

$$\mathbf{f}(x_1, y_1) = a_0 + \sum_{k=1}^{k=\infty} \sum_{l=1}^{l=\infty} \left[b_{kl} \cos \left(\frac{2\pi k x_1}{A} + \frac{2\pi l y_1}{A} \right) \right.$$

$$\left. + c_{kl} \sin \left(\frac{2\pi k x_1}{A} + \frac{2\pi l y_1}{A} \right) \right] \tag{4.22}$$

where the indices k and l are positive integers.   The Fourier coefficients a_0, b_{kl}, and c_{kl} are given by

$$a_0 = \frac{1}{A^2} \int\limits_{-A/2}^{+A/2} \int\limits_{-A/2}^{+A/2} \mathbf{f}(x_1, y_1) \, dx_1 \, dy_1$$

$$b_{kl} = \frac{4}{A^2} \int\limits_{-A/2}^{+A/2} \int\limits_{-A/2}^{+A/2} \mathbf{f}(x_1, y_1) \cos\left(\frac{2\pi k x_1}{A} + \frac{2\pi l y_1}{A}\right) dx_1 \, dy_1 \qquad (4.23)$$

$$c_{kl} = \frac{4}{A^2} \int\limits_{-A/2}^{+A/2} \int\limits_{-A/2}^{+A/2} \mathbf{f}(x_1, y_1) \sin\left(\frac{2\pi k x_1}{A} + \frac{2\pi l y_1}{A}\right) dx_1 \, dy_1$$

Equation (4.22) can be rewritten as follows, using the imaginary exponential notation:

$$\mathbf{f}(x_1, y_1) = a_0 + \tfrac{1}{2} \sum_{k=1}^{k=\infty} \sum_{l=1}^{l=\infty} \left[(b_{kl} - jc_{kl}) e^{j(2\pi k x_1/A + 2\pi l y_1/A)} \right.$$

$$\left. + (b_{kl} + jc_{kl}) e^{-j(2\pi k x_1/A + 2\pi l y_1/A)} \right] \qquad (4.24)$$

Combining eq. (4.24) with eq. (4.8) yields the electric field distribution in the $x_1 y_1$ plane:

$$\mathbf{E}(x_1, y_1) = a_0 E_m e^{-j\omega_L t} + \frac{E_m}{2} e^{-j\omega_L t} \sum_{k=1}^{k=\infty} \sum_{l=1}^{l=\infty} \left[(b_{kl} - jc_{kl}) \right.$$

$$\times e^{j(2\pi k x_1/A + 2\pi l y_1/A)} + (b_{kl} + jc_{kl}) e^{-j(2\pi k x_1/A + 2\pi l y_1/A)} \right] \qquad (4.25)$$

The expression

$$a_0 E_m e^{-j\omega_L t} \qquad (4.26)$$

represents a plane light wave of maximum electric field $a_0 E_m$ and radian temporal frequency ω_L traveling along the optical axis, i.e., in the positive z direction.   The expression

$$E_m e^{-j\omega_L t}(b_{kl} - jc_{kl}) e^{j(2\pi k x_1/A + 2\pi l y_1/A)} \qquad (4.27)$$

represents an infinity of new plane waves of light, each having the same radian temporal frequency as the wave traveling along the z axis but of complex amplitudes $E_m(b_{kl} - jc_{kl})$.   Note that the $k/$th wave is phase-shifted by $2\pi k$ rad across the extent A of the aperture in the x_1 direction and $2\pi l$ rad in the y_1 direction.   Since a negative phase shift implies an advance in time, those portions of the klth wave having negative values of x_1 and y_1 are ahead of the wave at the origin.   This implies that the wave in question is advanced in the third quadrant.   Since a phase shift of $2\pi k$ rad is equivalent to an advance of k wavelengths, the normal to the new plane wave has direction cosines given by

$$\cos \alpha = \frac{k\lambda_L}{A} \qquad \cos \beta = \frac{l\lambda_L}{A} \tag{4.28}$$

where α and β are the direction angles with respect to the x_1 and y_1 axes, respectively, and λ_L is the wavelength of light.

Similarly, the expression

$$E_m e^{-j\omega_L t}(b_{kl} + jc_{kl}) e^{-j(2\pi k x_1/A + 2\pi l y_1/A)} \tag{4.29}$$

represents an infinity of new plane waves of light of radian temporal frequency ω_L having complex amplitudes equal to $E_m(b_{kl} + jc_{kl})$ which are advanced in the first quadrant with respect to the origin.   The direction cosines of the normal to these plane waves are given by the equations

$$\cos \alpha = -\frac{k\lambda_L}{A} \qquad \cos \beta = -\frac{l\lambda_L}{A} \tag{4.30}$$

It is now clear that the effect of the spatial-light-modulating function $\mathbf{f}(x_1, y_1)$, acting in the $x_1 y_1$ plane, is to divide the incident plane wave of light into an infinity of new plane waves whose complex amplitudes are related to the complex Fourier coefficients of the function $\mathbf{f}(x_1, y_1)$ and whose directions of propagation are determined by the corresponding direction cosines.   This statement is an expression of what we shall call the "diffraction theorem."

The diffraction theorem provides a convenient visualization of the effect of spatial light modulation; i.e., it is convenient to think of an infinity of new plane waves propagating in the space beyond the spatial light modulator.   This is especially true in determining the effect of a lens system on each of these waves.   However, the diffraction theorem must be used with caution.   So far, at least, it has been assumed that the new plane waves caused by spatial light modulation are infinite in number but discrete in direction.   Their directions, in fact, are specified by the indices k and l which are integers.   In reality, k and l specify only physically distinguishable directions limited by the assumption that $f(x_1, y_1)$ is confined to a square aperture of dimension A in the $x_1 y_1$ plane.   As A tends to infinity, eqs. (4.28) and (4.30) indicate that the angles between distinguishable directions tend toward zero and a continuum of new plane waves results.

4.30   The Fourier-transform Relationship

In order to treat the effect of spatial light modulation of infinite extent rewrite eqs. (4.23) so as to obtain the complex Fourier coefficients as follows:

$$b_{kl} - jc_{kl} = \frac{4}{A^2} \int_{-A/2}^{+A/2} \int_{-A/2}^{+A/2} \mathbf{f}(x_1, y_1) e^{-j(2\pi/A)(kx_1 + ly_1)} dx_1 dy_1$$

$$b_{kl} + jc_{kl} = \frac{4}{A^2} \int_{-A/2}^{+A/2} \int_{-A/2}^{+A/2} \mathbf{f}(x_1, y_1) e^{j(2\pi/A)(kx_1 + ly_1)} dx_1 dy_1 \qquad (4.31)$$

where, as before, k and l are positive integers.   Since eqs. (4.31) are complex conjugates of one another, they may be expressed in a single equation as follows:

$$d_{kl} = \frac{4}{A^2} \int_{-A/2}^{+A/2} \int_{-A/2}^{+A/2} \mathbf{f}(x_1, y_1) e^{-j(2\pi/A)(kx_1 + ly_1)} dx_1 dy_1 \qquad (4.32)$$

where d_{kl} are the complex Fourier coefficients and the indices k and l take on both positive and negative integral values.   Letting A become infinite, so that the quantities k/A and l/A become infinitesimals, leads to the two-dimensional Fourier transform of $\mathbf{f}(x_1, y_1)$.   Using the expressions for the direction cosines given in eqs. (4.28) and (4.30) the two-dimensional Fourier transform $F(\cos \alpha, \cos \beta)$ is given by

$$F(\cos \alpha, \cos \beta) = C \int_{-\infty}^{+\infty} \int_{-\infty}^{+\infty} f(x_1, y_1) e^{-j(2\pi/\lambda_L)(\cos \alpha \, x_1 + \cos \beta \, y_1)} dx_1 dy_1 \quad (4.33)$$

where C is a constant of proportionality.

As is shown next in this section, lens systems in coherent optical computers cause *successive* two-dimensional Fourier transforms to be calculated in contrast to Fourier transforms allowed by inverse Fourier transforms.   Therefore, the logical choice for the value of C is $\lambda_L/2\pi$. The quantities $(2\pi \cos \alpha)/\lambda_L$ and $(2\pi \cos \beta)/\lambda_L$ in eq. (4.33) are frequently called the "radian spatial frequencies" ω_x and ω_y, and eq. (4.33) is written in the form

$$F(\omega_x, \omega_y) = C \int\!\!\int \mathbf{f}(x_1, y_1) e^{-j(\omega_x x_1 + \omega_y y_1)} dx_1 dy_1 \qquad (4.34)$$

Note that ω_x and ω_y are in radian cycles per unit length.   The corresponding spatial frequencies in cycles per unit length are $f_x = \omega_x/2\pi$ and $f_y = \omega_y/2\pi$.

In general, of course, polarization effects and the amplitude of the incident plane wave must be taken into account and eq. (4.34) written in its general form

$$F_x(\omega_x, \omega_y) = \frac{\lambda_L}{2\pi} e^{-j\omega_L t} \int\int [E_x \mathbf{f}_{11}(x_1, y_1) + E_y \mathbf{f}_{12}(x_1, y_1)]$$
$$\times e^{-j(\omega_x x_1 + \omega_y y_1)} dx_1 dy_1$$

$$F_y(\omega_x, \omega_y) = \frac{\lambda_L}{2\pi} e^{-j\omega_L t} \int\int [E_x \mathbf{f}_{21}(x_1, y_1) + E_y \mathbf{f}_{22}(x_1, y_1)]$$
$$\times e^{-j(\omega_x x_1 + \omega_y y_1)} dx_1 dy_1 \quad (4.35)$$

where E_x and E_y are the complex components of the incident field E. Clearly, a complete generalization requires that the incident light wave itself be a function of x and y. This situation, called *apodization*, will be discussed in Sec. 4.70.

Note carefully that the sign of the exponent in eq. (4.34) is negative. The exponential therefore represents a unit vector which rotates clockwise for increasing positive values of x_1 and y_1. To demonstrate the significance of this fact, take a simple example where $\mathbf{f}(x_1, y_1)$ is a function which causes the incident plane wave of light in the $x_1 y_1$ plane to be redirected into a single new plane wave traveling at an angle to the z axis. In this case $\mathbf{f}(x_1, y_1)$ may be expressed by

$$\mathbf{f}(x_1, y_1) = e^{j(a_1 x_1 + b_1 y_1)} \quad (4.36)$$

If a_1 and b_1 are positive then the new plane wave is advanced in phase in the third quadrant and should have positive direction cosines as shown in Fig. 4.1. To test this statement, combine eqs. (4.33) and (4.36) to yield the following result:

$$F(\cos \alpha, \cos \beta) = \frac{\lambda_L}{2\pi} \int\int e^{j\{[a_1 - (2\pi/\lambda_L)\cos \alpha] x_1 + [b_1 - (2\pi/\lambda_L)\cos \beta] y_1\}} dx_1 dy_1$$
$$= \delta\left(\cos \alpha - \frac{\lambda_L a_1}{2\pi}, \cos \beta - \frac{\lambda_L b_1}{2\pi}\right) \quad (4.37)$$

where δ represents the Dirac delta function. As can be seen, the desired result is obtained; i.e., a single new plane wave results, with positive direction cosines given by

$$\cos \alpha = \frac{\lambda_L a_1}{2\pi} \qquad \cos \beta = \frac{\lambda_L b_1}{2\pi} \quad (4.38)$$

When this plane wave of light passes through the lens system L_1, shown in Fig. 4.1, it will come to a focus in the back focal plane of L_1. If this plane is called the $x_2 y_2$ plane, the coordinates of the focal point are

$$x_2 = F \cos \alpha / \cos \gamma \qquad y_2 = F \cos \beta / \cos \gamma \quad (4.39)$$

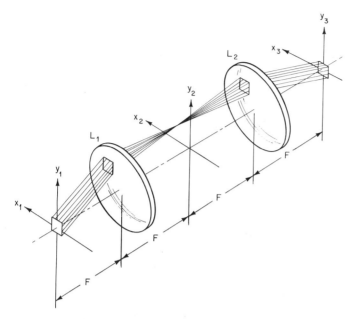

Fig. 4.1 Optical schematic showing the geometrical convention for use in calculating the performance of a coherent optical computer.

where F is the back focal length of L_1.   Note that the focal point lies in the first quadrant.   If the light now continues beyond the x_2y_2 plane through lens system L_2 and the x_2y_2 plane is in the front focal plane of L_2, a combination of eqs. (4.33) and (4.39) yields for the back focal plane of L_2 the equation

$$\mathbf{f}(x_3, y_3) = e^{-j(a_1 x_3 + b_1 y_3)} \tag{4.40}$$

Thus, instead of returning to the function given by eq. (4.36), the two successive Fourier transforms have yielded, as expected, $\mathbf{f}(-x_3, -y_3)$.

4.40   Convolution and Correlation

For convenience a table of successive Fourier transforms is given in Table 4.1.   By using this table, certain results of interest can be obtained when one considers the situation where a spatial light modulator is placed in the x_2y_2 plane as well as in the x_1y_1 plane.

Let $f_1(x_1, y_1)$ and $f_2(x_2, y_2)$ be these two light-modulating functions, respectively.   Assuming an incident plane wave in the x_1y_1 plane, the electric field distribution in the x_2y_2 plane is given by

$$E(x_2, y_2) = E_m e^{-j\omega L't} F_1(\omega_x, \omega_y) f_2(x_2, y_2) \tag{4.41}$$

where $F_1(\omega_x, \omega_y)$ is the Fourier transform of $f_1(x_1, y_1)$. The Wiener-Khintchine theorem yields the electric field distribution in the $x_3 y_3$ plane as

$$E(x_3, y_3) = E_m e^{-j\omega_L t} \iint f_1(x', y') F_2^{-1}(x_3 - x', y_3 - y') \, dx' \, dy' \tag{4.42}$$

where $F_2^{-1}(x, y)$ is the inverse Fourier transform of $f_2(x, y)$. Equation (4.42) is a convolution integral which has particular significance when the spatial-light-modulating function $f_2(x_2, y_2)$ is itself a Fourier transform. For example, let

$$f_2(x_2, y_2) = F_1(\omega_x, \omega_y) \tag{4.43}$$

The electric field distribution given by eq. (4.42) becomes

$$E(x_3, y_3) = E_m e^{-j\omega t} \iint f_1(x', y') f_1(x_3 - x', y_3 - y') \, dx' \, dy' \tag{4.44}$$

which is the convolution of $f_1(x, y)$. Now if

$$f_2(x_2, y_2) = F_1^*(\omega_x, \omega_y) \tag{4.45}$$

the electric field distribution given by eq. (4.42) becomes

$$E(x_1, y_1) = E_m e^{-j\omega_L t} \iint f_1(x', y') f_1^*(x_3 + x', y_3 + y') \, dx' \, dy' \tag{4.46}$$

which is the autocorrelation function of $f_1(x, y)$. Similarly, the cross correlation of $f_1(x, y)$ with any desired two-dimensional function may be generated in the $x_3 y_3$ plane by inserting the complex conjugate of the Fourier transform of that function in the $x_2 y_2$ plane.

Sometimes it is difficult to realize the complex conjugate of the Fourier transform of the desired function in that the spatial light modulator required is difficult to fabricate. This occurs because a thin film is needed whose optical index and optical amplitude transmission both must be varied from point to point according to the phase and amplitude

TABLE 4.1

Function	Fourier transform	Successive Fourier transform
$f(x, y)$	$F(\omega_x, \omega_y)$	$f(-x, -y)$
$f^*(x, y)$	$F^*(-\omega_x, -\omega_y)$	$f^*(-x, -y)$
$f(-x, -y)$	$F(-\omega_x, -\omega_y)$	$f(x, y)$
$f^*(-x, -y)$	$F^*(\omega_x, \omega_y)$	$f^*(x, y)$
$f(x - x_0, y - y_0)$	$e^{-j(x_0 \omega_x + y_0 \omega_y)} F(\omega_x, \omega_y)$	$f(-x - x_0, -y - y_0)$
$f^*(x - x_0, y - y_0)$	$e^{j(x_0 \omega_x + y_0 \omega_y)} F^*(-\omega_x, -\omega_y)$	$f^*(-x - x_0, -y - y_0)$
$f(-x - x_0, -y - y_0)$	$e^{-j(x_0 \omega_x + y_0 \omega_y)} F(-\omega_x, -\omega_y)$	$f(x - x_0, y - y_0)$
$f^*(-x - x_0, -y - y_0)$	$e^{j(x_0 \omega_x + y_0 \omega_y)} F^*(\omega_x, \omega_y)$	$f^*(x - x_0, y - y_0)$

of the desired function.   A common method of avoiding this difficulty
is to form a somewhat modified spatial light modulator using holographic
techniques [4.3].   To form the spatial light modulator required, a flat
sheet of unexposed photographic emulsion is placed in the x_2y_2 plane.
The function of $f_0(x,y)$ whose Fourier transform is to be recorded is
placed in the x_1y_1 plane and illuminated by a plane wave of light.   Also, a
point source of light is placed in the x_1y_1 plane at a point (x_r, y_r) some
distance away from $f_0(x_1, y_1)$.
Thus the electric field distribution in the x_1y_1 plane is given by

$$E(x_1, y_1) = E_m e^{-j\omega_L t} [f_0(x_1, y_1) + \delta(x_1 - x_r, y_1 - y_r)] \tag{4.47}$$

In the x_2y_2 plane the electric field distribution is given by the Fourier
transform of eq. (4.47), namely,

$$E(x_2, y_2) = E_m e^{-j\omega_L t} [F_0(\omega_x, \omega_y) + e^{-j(\omega_x x_r + \omega_y y_r)}] \tag{4.48}$$

As will be discussed in more detail in Sec. 5.10, the sheet of photographic
emulsion in the x_2y_2 plane records the light intensity distribution in that
plane given by

$$I(x_2, y_2) = E(x_2, y_2)E^*(x_2, y_2)$$

$$= E_m^2 [1 + F_0(\omega_x, \omega_y)F_0^*(\omega_x, \omega_y) + F_0(\omega_x, \omega_y)e^{j(\omega_x x_r + \omega_y y_r)}$$

$$+ F_0^*(\omega_x, \omega_y)e^{-j(\omega_x x_r + \omega_y y_r)}] \tag{4.49}$$

Note that the final term in eq. (4.49) contains the desired complex
conjugate of the Fourier transform of the function $f_0(x, y)$ except that it
is multiplied by the Fourier transform of the point source $\delta(x_1 - x_r,$
$y_1 - y_r)$.
   In order to generate the cross correlation between a function $f_1(x, y)$
and $f_0(x, y)$, a spatial-light-modulating function $f_1(x_1, y_1)$ is placed in the
x_1y_1 plane and the photographic recording or so-called "Fourier hologram" is placed in the x_2y_2 plane.   In the x_3y_3 plane the resultant electric field distribution is given by

$$E(x_3, y_3) = F[F_1(\omega_{x2}, \omega_{y2})I(x_2, y_2)]$$

$$= f_1(-x_3 - y_3) + \iint f_1(x', y')f_{00}(-x_3 - x', -y_3 - y') \, dx' \, dy'$$

$$+ \iint f_1(x', y')f_0(-x_3 + x_r - x', -y_3 + y_r - y') \, dx' \, dy'$$

$$+ \iint f_1(x', y') f_0^*(x_3 + x_r + x', y_3 + y_r + y') \, dx' \, dy' \tag{4.50}$$

where f_{00} is the inverse Fourier transform of $F_0 F_0^*$ and terms in E_m and
$e^{j\omega_L t}$ have been omitted.   As can be seen, the final term in eq. (4.50) is the
desired correlation function which is displaced into the third quadrant

of the x_3y_3 plane if it is assumed that both x_r and y_r are positive. For sufficiently large values of x_r and y_r the spatial displacement of the desired correlation function may be made great enough to separate it completely from the other terms in eq. (4.50). It is also interesting to note that the holographic method also generates the convolution in the first quadrant of the x_3y_3 plane.

4.50   Spatial-frequency Dispersion and the Fresnel-Kirchhoff Formulation

As mentioned in Chapter Three, an understanding of the energy distribution within the optical system of a coherent optical computer is necessary if the lens systems are to be designed with apertures sufficiently large to prevent vignetting. Returning to eq. (4.27), note that the Fourier-transform relationship yields the distribution in amplitude, phase, and direction of all new plane waves caused by spatial light modulation in the x_1y_1 plane. Each new plane wave which has traveled a distance R as shown in Fig. 4.2 experiences a lateral displacement Δr given by

$$\Delta r = R \sin \gamma$$

$$= R\sqrt{\cos^2 \alpha + \cos^2 \beta} \tag{4.51}$$

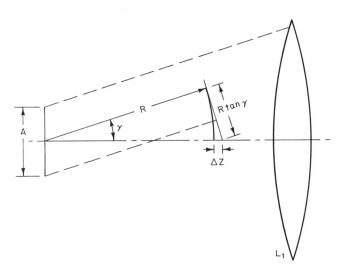

Fig. 4.2 Geometry of a plane wave which has traveled a distance R from the input aperture with a direction cosine γ with respect to the optical axis.

The components of Δr in the x and y direction are given by

$$\Delta x = R \cos \alpha \qquad \Delta y = R \cos \beta \tag{4.52}$$

The aperture of the lens system L_1 must be large enough to accept all new plane waves whose energy is significant in the performance of the required computations.   In the case of a finite aperture, the energy of a particular wave is proportional to $d_{kl} d_{kl}^*$ from eq. (4.32).

If k_{max} and l_{max} are the values of the indices k and l beyond which $d_{kl} d_{kl}^*$ is negligible, the effective diameter of L_1 is given by

$$D = \sqrt{(A + \theta_k F)^2 + (A + \theta_l F)^2} \tag{4.53}$$

where F is the front focal length and θ_k and θ_l are the field angles of the lens system, namely,

$$\theta_k = \frac{2k_{max}\lambda_L}{A} \qquad \theta_l = \frac{2l_{max}\lambda_L}{A} \tag{4.54}$$

At the same time that each new plane wave of light caused by spatial light modulation in the $x_1 y_1$ plane is undergoing a lateral displacement it is also dispersed; i.e., it is phase-shifted with respect to the undiffracted light which travels along the z axis.   Referring to Fig. 4.2 note that, if a plane wave of light has traveled a distance R along the z axis, the z-axis intercept of another plane wave traveling at an angle γ to the z-axis has advanced beyond the wave traveling along the axis by the amount given by

$$\Delta_z = \sqrt{R^2 + R^2 \tan^2 \gamma} - R \tag{4.55}$$

In most cases of interest where γ is small, the radical in eq. (4.55) may be expanded in a Taylor series and $\sin \gamma$ set equal to $\tan \gamma$ with the resultant simplification

$$\Delta z = \frac{R \sin^2 \gamma}{2}$$

$$= \frac{R}{2}(\cos^2 \alpha + \cos^2 \beta) \tag{4.56}$$

Thus the advance in phase of the diffracted plane wave over the undiffracted plane wave is given by

$$\Delta \phi = \frac{2\pi \Delta z}{\lambda_L} - \frac{\pi R}{\lambda_L}(\cos^2 \alpha + \cos^2 \beta) \tag{4.57}$$

Similar results to the above treatment of dispersion may be obtained by use of the Fresnel-Kirchhoff formulation rather than by the diffraction theorem.   First note that the response of free space to a delta function at the origin of the $x_1 y_1$ plane is given by

$$G(x_1, y_1, z) = \frac{j}{\lambda_L z} e^{j(2\pi/\lambda_L)\sqrt{x_1^2 + y_1^2 + z^2}} \tag{4.58}$$

where the multiplicative factor $j/\lambda_L z$ is used so that the integral of $G(x_1, y_1, z)$ is normalized to unity.   Applying Green's theorem to obtain the response to a general spatial-light-modulating function $f(x_1, y_1)$ yields the Fresnel-Kirchhoff integral

$$f(x, y, z) = \frac{j}{\lambda_L z} \int\limits_{-\infty}^{+\infty} \int\limits_{-\infty}^{+\infty} f(x_1, y_1) e^{j(2\pi/\lambda_L)\sqrt{(x - x_1)^2 + (y - y_1)^2 + z^2}} \, dx_1 \, dy_1 \tag{4.59}$$

Following an analysis by Leith [4.4], make the small-angle approximation

$$x - x_1 \ll z \qquad y - y_1 \ll z \tag{4.60}$$

and expand the radical in the exponent by means of the binomial theorem (neglecting terms beyond the second order) to obtain

$$f(x, y, z) = \frac{j}{\lambda_L z} e^{j(2\pi/\lambda_L)} \int\limits_{-\infty}^{+\infty} \int\limits_{-\infty}^{+\infty} f(x_1, y_1) e^{j(\pi/\lambda_L z)[(x - x_1)^2 + (y - y_1)^2]} \, dx_1 \, dy_1 \tag{4.61}$$

The phase factor $e^{j(2\pi z/\lambda_L)}$ represents a constant phase shift dependent only upon distance along the optical axis.   The balance of eq. (4.61) is the convolution of $f(x_1, y_1)$ with the function

$$f_0(x_1, y_1) = \frac{j}{\lambda_L z} e^{j(\pi/\lambda_L z)[(x - x_1)^2 + (y - y_1)^2]} \tag{4.62}$$

Applying the convolution theorem yields

$$f(x, y, z) = F[F_1(\cos \alpha, \cos \beta) F_0(\cos \alpha, \cos \beta)] \tag{4.63}$$

where $F_0(\cos \alpha, \cos \beta)$ is the Fourier transform of $f_0(x_1, y_1)$ and is given by

$$F_0(\cos \alpha, \cos \beta) = e^{-j(\pi z/\lambda_L)(\cos^2 \alpha + \cos^2 \beta)} \tag{4.64}$$

The exponent in eq. (4.64) is just the phase function given by eq. (4.57) when it is recognized that for small angles $z \approx R$.

Using the definition of the radian spatial frequencies ω_x and ω_y given by eq. (4.34), rewrite the exponent in eq. (4.64) as the phase function

$$\phi(\omega_x, \omega_y) = \frac{\lambda_L z}{4\pi} (\omega_x^2 + \omega_y^2) \tag{4.65}$$

Note again that the effect of propagation of a spatially light-modulated wave beyond the $x_1 y_1$ plane is one of dispersion.   Leith [4.4] defines the spatial-frequency dispersion factors by partial differentiation of eq. (4.65) with respect to both ω_x and ω_y as follows:

$$\frac{\partial \phi}{\partial \omega_x} = \frac{\lambda_L z}{2\pi}\,\omega_x \qquad \frac{\partial \phi}{\partial \omega_y} = \frac{\lambda_L z}{2\pi}\,\omega_y \qquad (4.66)$$

As can be seen, there is no dispersion for zero frequency, but other spatial frequencies are increasingly dispersed the larger the spatial frequency and the greater the distance of propagation. The fact that the dispersion factors are positive indicates that the phase velocity of the dispersed spatial frequencies is greater than that of the zero spatial frequencies.

4.60   Wiener Spectra

In most cases of interest the Fourier transform as such is not observable in coherent optical computers because of the present lack of direct methods of measuring the amplitude, phase, and polarity of the electric field at optical frequencies. What is measured is light intensity. Returning to the Jones vector, $\mathbf{E}$, for the electric field, the intensity $I(x,y)$ is given by

$$I(x,y) = \mathbf{E}^T \mathbf{E}^* = E_x E_x^* + E_y E_y^* \qquad (4.67)$$

where T indicates transpose and * complex conjugate. Returning to the complete expression for the Fourier transform given in eq. (4.35), the spatial-light-intensity function which is called the *Wiener spectrum* is given by

$$W(\omega_x, \omega_y) = \left| \iint [E_x \mathbf{f}_{11}(x,y) + E_y \mathbf{f}_{12}(x,y)] e^{-j(\omega_x x + \omega_y y)}\, dx\, dy \right|^2$$
$$+ \left| \iint [E_x \mathbf{f}_{21}(x,y) + E_y \mathbf{f}_{22}(x,y)] e^{-j(\omega_x x + \omega_y y)}\, dx\, dy \right|^2 \qquad (4.68)$$

If the Wiener spectrum is detected through a polarizer parallel to the x axis, only the first term of eq. (4.48) is obtained; when parallel to the y axis, the second term only is obtained.

It should be mentioned that from individual measurements of the intensity of the x and y components the so-called "Stokes' parameters" of the field may be obtained. These parameters are defined by the equations

$$S_0 = E_x^2 + E_y^2$$
$$S_1 - E_x^2 - E_y^2 \qquad (4.69)$$
$$S_2 = 2E_x E_y \cos\theta$$
$$S_3 = 2E_x E_y \sin\theta$$

where E_x and E_y are the amplitudes of the x and y components of the field and θ is the phase angle between the x and y components (usually taken as positive if the x component leads the y component). Although the Stokes' parameters completely specify the field, matrix manipulation of them requires a knowledge of the 4×4 Mueller matrix and is therefore computationally more complicated than the Jones matrix method introduced in Sec. 4.14. The advantage of the Stokes-Mueller approach is that all vector and matrix elements are real. A detailed treatment is available in O'Neill [4.2].

In this section a few simple examples of Wiener spectra are given. Take as the first example the Wiener spectrum of the aperture A in the $x_1 y_1$ plane. This aperture is, by definition, the region in the front focal plane over which the integral of eq. (4.35) is taken. There are two cases of general interest: (1) A is circular and (2) A is square or rectangular.

Again assuming for simplicity that the incident light is linearly polarized in the x direction, letting the amplitude of the electric field equal unity, and omitting the constant terms in front of the integral in eq. (4.35), the Wiener spectrum for case 1 can be expressed as follows:

$$W(\omega_x, \omega_y) = \left| \int\int_R e^{-j(\omega_x x_1 + \omega_y y_1)} \, dx_1 \, dy_1 \right|^2 \tag{4.70}$$

where the integration is taken over the circular aperture of radius R. Since A is circular, $W(\omega_x, \omega_y)$ is most readily evaluated by using the usual small-angle approximation and making the substitutions

$$
\begin{aligned}
x_1 &= r_1 \cos \theta_1 \\
y_1 &= r_1 \sin \theta_1 \\
\omega_x &= 2\pi r_2 \cos \theta_2 / \lambda_L F \\
\omega_y &= 2\pi r_2 \sin \theta_2 / \lambda_L F
\end{aligned}
\tag{4.71}
$$

where (r_1, θ_1) are polar coordinates in the $x_1 y_1$ plane and (r_2, θ_2) are polar coordinates in the $x_2 y_2$ plane. The result is

$$W(\omega_r) = \left| \int_0^R \int_0^{2\pi} e^{-j\omega_r r_1 \cos(\theta_1 - \theta_2)} r_1 \, dr_1 \, d\theta_1 \right|^2 \tag{4.72}$$

where $\omega_r = 2\pi r_2 / \lambda_L F$. Integrating with respect to θ_1 yields

$$W(\omega_r) = \left| 2\pi \int_0^R J_0(\omega_r r_1) r_1 \, dr_1 \right|^2 \tag{4.73}$$

The result of the second integration is

$$W(\omega_r) = \left| 2\pi R^2 \frac{J_1(\omega_r R)}{\omega_r R} \right|^2 \tag{4.74}$$

where $J_1(\omega_r R)$ is the first-order Bessel function. An example of this Wiener spectrum is shown in Fig. 4.3.

The function described by eq. (4.74) and shown in Fig. 4.3 is the famous Airy disk of classic physical optics. It is frequently used in the evaluation of lens systems as discussed in Chapter Six. Three plots of this spatial-light-intensity function are given in Fig. 4.4. The first plot uses a linear scale, the second a log-linear scale, and the third a log-log scale. The abscissa is normalized in terms of spatial cycles across the diameter $2R$. Although the linear scale provides the best "feel" for the light intensity variation as a function of ω_r, the log-linear form is most useful in the evaluation and understanding of coherent optical computers. This form is used most frequently elsewhere in this book. The log-log form finds widest use when large ranges of the argument are dealt with and also most clearly demonstrates the linear log-log falloff of light intensity with ω_r for $\omega_r \gg 1$.

In treating case 2 above (a square or rectangular aperture) use is made of the usual cartesian coordinate system. It turns out that in most coherent-optical-computer applications, A is, in fact, rectangular. Once more assuming linear polarization of the incident light in the x direction and dropping constant terms in front of the integral, the Wiener spectrum for this case is given by

$$W(\omega_x, \omega_y) = \left| \int_{-A_x/2}^{+A_x/2} \int_{-A_y/2}^{+A_y/2} e^{-j(\omega_x x_1 + \omega_y y_1)} \, dx_1 \, dy_1 \right|^2 \tag{4.75}$$

where A_x is the width of A in the x direction and A_y in the y direction. Integration of eq. (4.75) yields

$$W(\omega_x, \omega_y) = 16 \frac{\sin^2 (\omega_x A_x/2) \sin^2 (\omega_y A_y/2)}{\omega_x^2 \omega_y^2} \tag{4.76}$$

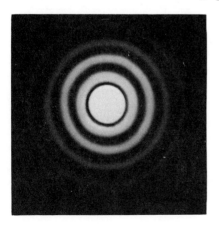

Fig. 4.3 Airy disk or Wiener spectrum of a circular aperture.

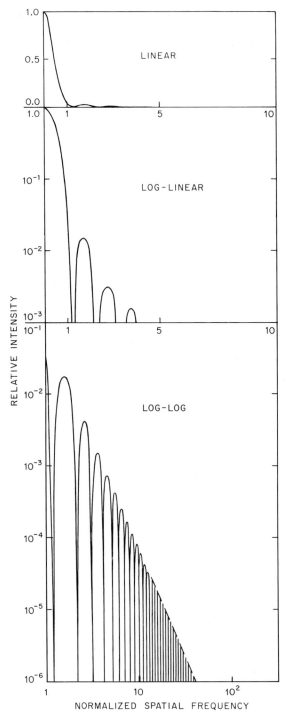

Fig. 4.4 Linear, log-linear, and log-log plots of the light intensity distribution in the Airy disk.

or, using Woodward's sinc notation [4.5], where sinc $(a) = (\sin \pi a)/\pi a$, eq. (4.76) can be written

$$W(f_x, f_y) = [A_x A_y \operatorname{sinc}(f_x A_x) \operatorname{sinc}(f_y A_y)]^2 \qquad (4.77)$$

This type of Wiener spectrum is shown in Fig. 4.5 for the case where $A_x = A_y$, that is, a square aperture, and in Fig. 4.6 for the case where $A_x = 2A_y$, that is, a rectangular aperture with an aspect ratio of 2. It should be noted that the nulls of the above function occur at points in the $x_2 y_2$ plane given by

$$x_2/F = n_x \lambda_L/A_x \qquad y_2/F = n_y \lambda_1/A_y \qquad (4.78)$$

where n_x and n_y are integers. Thus, the smaller the width of A_x or A_y, the longer is the distance between nulls. Furthermore, since x_2/F and y_2/F are the direction angles (in radians) subtended by the nulls, this indicates that these angles are directly related to the ratio of the wavelength of the radiation incident in the $x_1 y_1$ plane and the size of the aperture. Normalized linear, log-linear, and log–log plots of the square of the sinc function are given in Fig. 4.7 for the purpose of comparison with Fig. 4.4.

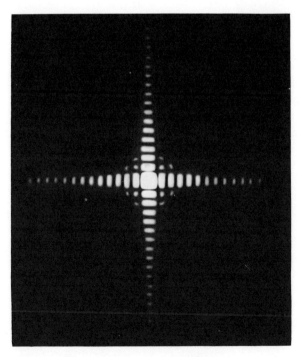

Fig. 4.5 Wiener spectrum of a square aperture.

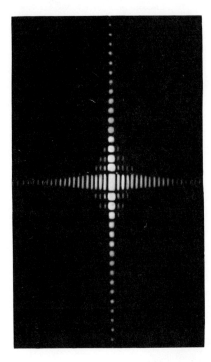

Fig. 4.6 Wiener spectrum of a rectangular aperture with a 2:1 aspect ratio.

At this point it is worthwhile considering another example of a Wiener spectrum, namely, that of a simple one-dimensional sinusoid across the aperture A.   In this case a rectangular rather than a circular aperture is assumed for the reason given above, i.e., this form of aperture is almost always encountered in coherent optical computers.   As a first example, a sinusoidal-intensity-transmission function will be treated as given by

$$t_i(x_1, y_1) = \tfrac{1}{2}(1 + m \cos \omega_0 x_1) \quad \begin{array}{l} -A_x/2 \leq x \leq A_x/2 \\ -A_y/2 \leq y \leq A_y/2 \end{array} \qquad (4.79)$$

where ω_0 is the radian spatial frequency of the sinusoidal transmission and m is called the *modulation*.   The intensity transmission, when multiplied by the intensity of the incident light, yields the intensity of the spatially modulated light.

The spatial-modulation function given in eq. (4.79) is the well-known "sine-wave test target" of noncoherent optics [4.6].   It modulates the incident light intensity.   Since the Wiener spectrum is always given by the square of the magnitude of the Fourier transform of the light amplitude, the desired Wiener spectrum is given by

$$W(\omega_x, \omega_y) = \tfrac{1}{2} \left| \int_{-A_x/2}^{+A_x/2} \int_{-A_y/2}^{+A_y/2} (1 + m \cos \omega_0 x_1)^{1/2} e^{-j(\omega_x x_1 + \omega_y y_1)} \, dx_1 \, dy_1 \right|^2$$

$$(4.80)$$

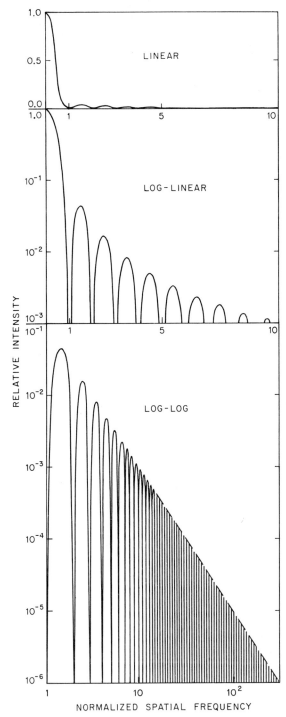

Fig. 4.7 Plot showing the light intensity distribution of a square aperture.

again making the usual simplifying assumptions.   The solution of eq.
(4.80) depends strongly upon the value of the modulation m.   Two
special cases are treated here; the solution of the general case is left to
the interested reader.   First consider the case of 100 percent modulation,   that   is, $m = 1$.   Using   the   trigonometric   identity $\cos^2 ax$
$= (1 + \cos 2ax)/2$ and taking the positive value of the square root in eq.
(4.80), the Wiener spectrum is given by

$$W(\omega_x, \omega_y) = \left| \int_{-A_x/2}^{+A_x/2} \int_{-A_y/2}^{+A_y/2} \left| \cos \frac{\omega_0}{2} x_1 \right| e^{-j(\omega_x x_1 + \omega_y y_1)} \, dx_1 \, dy_1 \right|^2 \tag{4.81}$$

The effect of the half frequency emerges more clearly when the integration in eq. (4.81) is completed.

As with many similar integrations required in the analysis of the
performance of coherent optical computers, eq. (4.81) may be solved by
using the following basic technique.   Note that the function $f(x_1)$
$= |\cos(\omega_0 x_1/2)|$ is repetitive in intervals of $2\pi/\omega_0$.   Thus, using Woodward's notation [4.5], this function may be written as $\text{rep}_{2\pi/\omega_0} f(x_1)$,
where x_1 is limited to the interval $-\pi \leq \omega_0 x_1 \leq +\pi$ and $\text{rep}_{2\pi/\omega_0}$ is a series
of delta functions over the interval A_x on the x_1 axis with a spacing of
$2\pi/\omega_0$.   The quantity $\text{rep}_{2\pi/\omega_0} f(x_1)$ is a convolution in the x_1 plane so that
application of the convolution theorem to eq. (4.81) yields

$$W(\omega_x, \omega_y) = \left| \frac{2 \sin(\omega_y A_y/2)}{\omega_y} \frac{\sin[\pi\omega_x(2N+1)/\omega_0]}{\sin(\pi\omega_x/\omega_0)} F\left(\cos \frac{\omega_0 x_1}{2}\right) \right|^2$$

$$= \left| \frac{2 \sin(\omega_y A_y/2)}{\omega_y} \frac{\sin[\pi\omega_x(2N+1)/\omega_0]}{\sin(\pi\omega_x/\omega_0)} \right.$$

$$\left. \times \left\{ \frac{\sin[\pi(2\omega_x - \omega_0)/\omega_0]}{(2\omega_x - \omega_0)/2} + \frac{\sin[\pi(2\omega_x + \omega_0)/\omega_0]}{(2\omega_x + \omega_0)/2} \right\} \right|^2 \tag{4.82}$$

where $\{\sin[\pi\omega_x(2N+1)/\omega_0]\}/\{\sin(\pi\omega_x/\omega_0)\}$ is the Fourier transform
of $\text{rep}_{2\pi/x_0}$ and $2N = A_x\omega_0/2\pi$.

A normalized plot of the result is shown in Fig. 4.8 for the case of
20π rad across the aperture, i.e., 10 spatial cycles.   Figure 4.9 shows a
photograph of the resultant Wiener spectrum.   It is seen that the half
frequency raises the side-lobe intensity, as would be anticipated, because
of distortion.   Also the intensity of the signal lobe is decreased.

The second case to be considered in discussing the sinusoidal-
intensity-transmission function is that which occurs when the modulation m is small.   For modulation less than about 20 percent ($m \leq 0.2$) we

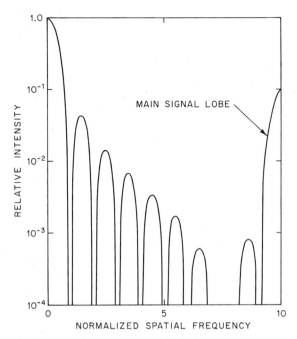

Fig. 4.8 Graph of the Wiener spectrum of a square aperture containing 10 cycles of a light intensity sine wave with 100 percent modulation.

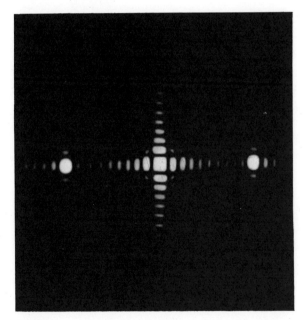

Fig. 4.9 Photograph of the Wiener spectrum of a square aperture containing 10 cycles of a 100 percent modulation light intensity sine wave.

can apply the approximation $(1+\alpha)^n \approx (1+n\alpha)$ to eq. (4.80), reducing it to

$$W(\omega_x, \omega_y) = \frac{1}{2} \left| \int_{-A_x/2}^{+A_x/2} \int_{-A_y/2}^{+A_y/2} \left(1 + \frac{m}{2} \cos \omega_0 x_1\right) e^{-j(\omega_x x_1 + \omega_y y_1)} \, dx_1 \, dy_1 \right|^2$$

(4.83)

Integration yields

$$W(\omega_x, \omega_y) = \frac{1}{2} \left| \frac{2\sin(\omega_y A_y/2)}{\omega_y} \left\{ \frac{2\sin(\omega_x A_x/2)}{\omega_x} \right. \right.$$

$$\left. \left. + \frac{m\sin[(\omega_x - \omega_0)A_x/2]}{2(\omega_x - \omega_0)} + \frac{m\sin[(\omega_x + \omega_0)A_x/2]}{2(\omega_x + \omega_0)} \right\} \right|^2 \quad (4.84)$$

A plot of eq. (4.84) is shown in Fig. 4.10 for $m = 0.2$, again corresponding to 10 spatial cycles across the aperture. The maxima at a normalized radian spatial frequency of 20π occur at the tenth aperture null. Figure 4.11 shows the corresponding photograph. It should be pointed out that the three cross-product terms in eq. (4.84) may be neglected for large values of ω_0 and the following approximation utilized:

$$W(f_x, f_y) = \frac{1}{2}[A_x A_y \operatorname{sinc}(f_x A_x) \operatorname{sinc}(f_y A_y)]^2$$

$$+ \frac{m^2}{32}\{A_x A_y \operatorname{sinc}[(f_x - f_0)A_x] \operatorname{sinc}(f_y A_y)\}^2$$

$$+ \frac{m^2}{32}\{A_x A_y \operatorname{sinc}[(f_x + f_0)A_x] \operatorname{sinc}(f_y A_y)\}^2 \quad (4.85)$$

At this point it should be obvious that the traditional sine-wave test target has a Wiener spectrum which is strongly dependent upon its modulation. Thus when spatial-light-modulation functions are introduced into an optical computer by means of an intensity transmission modulator, all Fourier components of the signal should be introduced at a modulation low enough to prevent frequency distortion in the Wiener spectrum. Another alternative is to square the signal before recording. This has the potential disadvantage of risking the introduction of intermodulation products due to nonlinearities (see Sec. 4.70).

The Wiener spectrum of an input which is a squared sine wave in intensity transmission is next calculated for purposes of comparison. The analytic expression for such a function is

$$t_i(x,y) = \frac{(1 + m\cos\omega_0 x)^2}{4} \quad (4.86)$$

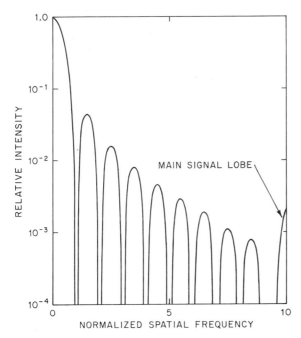

Fig. 4.10 Graph of the Wiener spectrum of a square aperture containing a light intensity sine wave of 20 percent modulation.

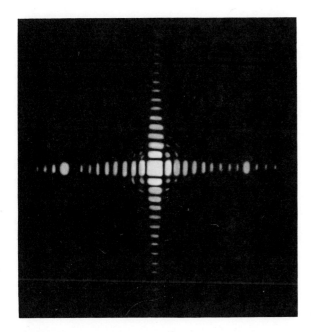

Fig. 4.11 Photograph of the Wiener spectrum of a square aperture containing 10 cycles of a light intensity sine wave of 20 percent modulation.

Note that a bias is added to prevent rectification of the signal and the creation thereby of higher-order spatial-frequency components. A divisor is used which causes the maximum value to be unity as in eq. (4.79) for $m = 1$. The Wiener spectrum is given by

$$W(\omega_x, \omega_y) = \left| \int\limits_{-A_x/2}^{+A_x/2} \int\limits_{-A_y/2}^{+A_y/2} \tfrac{1}{2}(1 + m \cos \omega_0 x_1) e^{-j(\omega_x x_1 + \omega_y y_1)} \, dx_1 \, dy \right|^2 \quad (4.87)$$

which is readily integrated to yield

$$W(\omega_x, \omega_y) = \left| \frac{2 \sin (\omega_y A_y/2)}{\omega_y} \left\{ \frac{\sin (\omega_x A_x/2)}{\omega_x} \right. \right.$$

$$\left. \left. + \frac{m \sin [(\omega_x + \omega_0) A_x/2]}{2(\omega_x + \omega_0)} + \frac{m \sin [(\omega_x - \omega_0) A_x/2]}{2(\omega_x - \omega_0)} \right\} \right|^2 \quad (4.88)$$

A plot of eq. (4.88) is shown in Fig. 4.12 for $m = 1$ and $m = 0.2$ for the case of 10 cycles across the input aperture. Comparison with Figs. 4.8 and 4.10 makes clear the increase in intensity of the Wiener spectrum at $\omega_x = \pm \omega_0$ in this case. As before, for a larger number of cycles across the aperture the three cross-product terms in eq. (4.88) can be dropped and an approximation written as follows:

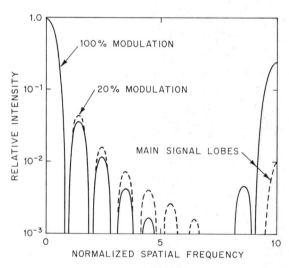

Fig. 4.12 Plot showing the Wiener spectrum of a square aperture containing 10 cycles of a light amplitude sine wave.

$$W = \tfrac{1}{4}[A_x A_y \operatorname{sinc}(f_x A_x) \operatorname{sinc}(f_y A_y)]^2$$

$$+ \frac{m^2}{16}\{\operatorname{sinc}[(f_x - f_0)A_x]\operatorname{sinc}(f_y A_y)\}^2$$

$$+ \frac{m^2}{16}\{\operatorname{sinc}[(f_x + f_0)A_x]\operatorname{sinc}(f_y A_y)\}^2 \quad (4.89)$$

Finally consider the Wiener spectrum of a simple sinusoidal phase modulator. Again, for simplicity, let us assume that the incident coherent light is linearly polarized in the x direction. The modulation function required is given by

$$\phi(x_1, y_1) = \phi_m \sin \omega_0 x_1 \quad (4.90)$$

where ϕ_m is the maximum phase modulation. It is assumed that modulation occurs in the x_1 direction only. The complex spatial-light-modulating function is given by

$$f(x_1, y_1) = e^{j\phi_m \sin \omega_0 x_1} \quad (4.91)$$

The Wiener spectrum of this function can most readily be evaluated by first expressing eq. (4.91) as a Bessel series expansion, namely,

$$f(x_1, y_1) = \sum_{n=-\infty}^{n=+\infty} J_n(\phi_m) e^{jn\omega_0 x_1} \quad (4.92)$$

The Wiener spectrum is then given by

$$W(\omega_x, \omega_y) = \left| \sum_{n=-\infty}^{n=+\infty} J_n(\phi_m) \int_{-A_x/2}^{+A_x/2} \int_{-A_y/2}^{+A_y/2} e^{-j[(\omega_x - n\omega_0)x_1 + \omega_y y_1]} \, dx_1 \, dy_1 \right|^2 \quad (4.93)$$

$$W(\omega_x, \omega_y) = \left| \frac{2\sin(\omega_y A_y/2)}{\omega_y} \sum_{n=-\infty}^{n=+\infty} J_n(\phi_m) \frac{2\sin[(\omega_x - n\omega_0)A_x/2]}{\omega_x - n\omega_0} \right|^2 \quad (4.94)$$

Plots of this expression are shown in Fig. 4.13 for the case where there are 10 spatial cycles across the input aperture for several values of ϕ_m (showing the first five harmonics). Note that the lower harmonics predominate for small values of ϕ_m whereas all are significant for the higher values.

As in the above examples, when there are many radian cycles of ω_0 across the input aperture, a good approximation to the Wiener spectrum becomes

$$W(f_x, f_y) = A_x^2 A_y^2 \sum_{n=-\infty}^{n=+\infty} [J_n^2(\phi_m)]\{\operatorname{sinc}(f_y A_y)\operatorname{sinc}[(f_x - nf_0)A_x]\}^2 \quad (4.95)$$

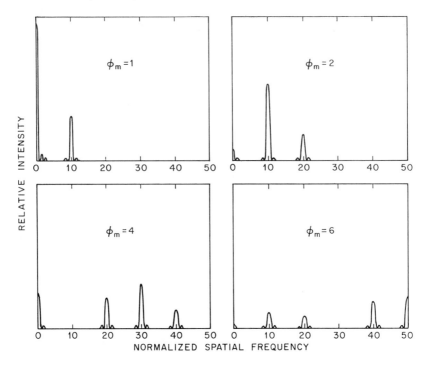

Fig. 4.13 Plot of the Wiener spectrum of a square aperture containing 10 cycles of a phase sine wave for four different modulations.

Two further approximations are useful.   One holds true for values of ϕ_m less than about 0.2 rad and is given by

$$W(f_x, f_y) = A_x^2 A_y^2 \sum_{n=-\infty}^{n=+\infty} \left(\frac{\phi_m^n}{2^n n!}\right)^2 \{\text{sinc}\,(f_y A_y)\,\text{sinc}\,[(f_x - nf_0)A_x]\}^2$$

$$(4.96)$$

The other approximation holds for large values of ϕ_m as follows:

$$W(f_x, f_y) = A_x^2 A_y^2 \sum_{n=-\infty}^{n=+\infty} \frac{2}{\pi\phi_m}\left\{\cos\left[\phi_m - \frac{\pi}{2}\,(n+1)\right]\text{sinc}\,(f_y A_y)\right.$$

$$\left. \times \text{sinc}\,[(f_x - nf_0)A_x]\right\}^2 \quad (4.97)$$

The reader familiar with **FM** communications theory will probably see many parallels between theoretical work in that field and the above expression describing the action of optical spatial phase modulation and the associated Wiener spectra.

4.70   Sources of Noise

So far it has been assumed that the spatial light modulator was an ideal thin film in that the signal recording process was completely homogeneous and the recording itself was linear. In practice, actual light modulators may be inhomogeneous; i.e., their response to a given constant input signal may vary as a function of surface position. Furthermore, light modulators may not be linear; i.e., they may distort the signal which they record. Both inhomogeneity and nonlinearity of the light modulator must be considered as sources of noise, i.e., as mechanisms which introduce error terms in the recorded signal. Since such error terms impair or alter the function of the coherent optical computer, their effect must be understood and analyzed appropriately.

The spatial light modulator is not the only source of noise in the coherent optical computer. Temporal fluctuations and spatial non-uniformities in the source of optical illumination produce noise. The lens system itself causes computations to be degraded in several ways. Also, the means for detection of optical energy in the final output plane may be noisy. It is the purpose of this section to tabulate and define some of the more common sources of noise and treat two special cases in detail.

In general, the more common forms of noise may be listed as follows:
Illumination noise
   Random temporal fluctuations
   Periodic temporal fluctuations
   Spatial nonuniformity
Spatial-light-modulator noise
   Nonlinear spatial responsivity
   Quantum noise or "grain noise"
   Random and/or periodic spatial nonuniformity
   Temporal instability or "fading"
Optical-system noise
   Random scatter from optical surfaces
   Random scatter from bulk nonuniformities
   Optical aberrations
   Secondary foci or "ghosts"
   Spatial side lobes of the zero order
Output detection noise
   Quantum noise or "shot noise"
   Nonuniform spatial responsivity
   Nonlinearities
   Temporal variation of responsivity

A treatment of illumination noise is given in Chapter Three. Chapter Five discusses grain noise, especially in regard to photographic emulsions, as well as nonlinearities and intermodulation products especially in connection with acoustic-delay-line light modulators. Temporal instability will also be treated in Chapter Five in connection with photochromic light modulators.   Optical-system noise will be discussed in Chapter Six except for the suppression of spatial side lobes which is treated in this section.   Finally, noise problems as related to output detection methods will be treated in Chapter Seven.

Consider the problem of spatial side lobes.   Spatial side lobes are defined as spurious energy in the output plane of the computer, caused by the fact that the computer aperture is not infinite.   These side lobes may cause energy to appear in regions of the output plane where signals of interest are to be detected.   Figures 4.4 and 4.7 show the side-lobe structure of both circular and square apertures.   As can be seen, the light intensity falls off as the inverse cube or square of the spatial dimension, respectively.   When a signal is introduced into the computer, the side lobes of the aperture are superimposed upon the value of the signal itself, as is seen, for example, by an analysis of eq. (4.88) and the associated plots in Fig. 4.12.   In Fig. 4.12 the strength of the signal is $0.25m^2$ times the strength of the peak of the undiffracted light passing through the aperture.   Therefore, the signal-to-side-lobe noise ratio is given by

$$\frac{S}{N} = \frac{\text{sinc}\left[(f_x - f_0)A_x\right]}{\text{sinc}\left(f_x A_x\right)} \tag{4.98}$$

The envelope of this function is given by

$$\frac{S}{N} = 0.25(m\pi f_0 A_x)^2 \tag{4.99}$$

which is plotted in terms of normalized radian spatial frequency in Fig. 4.14 for several values of m.   This plot represents a fundamental limitation on output signal to noise.

One solution to the problem of side-lobe noise is to illuminate the input aperture in a nonuniform manner designed to suppress the side lobes of the aperture.   This operation is apodization.   One useful apodizing function is the gaussian which is given by

$$f(x_1, y_1) = e^{\left[(x_1^2 + y_1^2)/(2\sigma^2)\right]} \tag{4.100}$$

The Fourier transform of the gaussian may be shown to be given by

$$F(\omega_x, \omega_y) = \sigma e^{(-\sigma^2/2)(\omega_x^2 + \omega_y^2)} \tag{4.101}$$

Hence the Wiener spectrum is given by

$$W(\omega_x, \omega_y) = \sigma^2 e^{-\sigma^2(\omega_x^2 + \omega_y^2)} \tag{4.102}$$

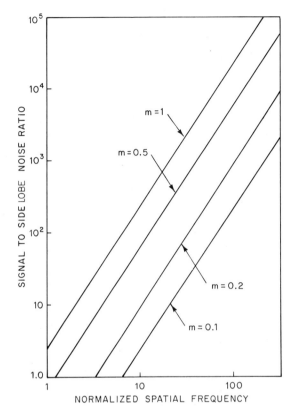

Fig. 4.14 Signal-to-side-lobe ratio for a coherent optical computer having a square aperture for various values of light amplitude modulation (m).

which is plotted in Fig. 4.15 and compared with the square of the sinc function under the assumption that $2\sigma = A_x/2 = A_y/2$; that is, the majority of the apodized illuminating light passes through the aperture. Clearly, apodization of this type leads to an increase in the ratio of signal energy in the output plane to the noise energy produced by the side lobes of the aperture.

Next, consider noise introduced by nonlinearity in the recording of the input signal on the spatial light modulator. In the ideal one-dimensional case the recorded signal $s(x)$ is a replica of the input signal $s(t)$ except for the necessary introduction of the bias B. Following the notation of Davenport and Root [4.7] the transfer function $\gamma(x)$ of a typical nonlinear recording medium has the form

$$\gamma(x) = ax^{\nu} \qquad x \geqslant 0 \tag{4.103}$$

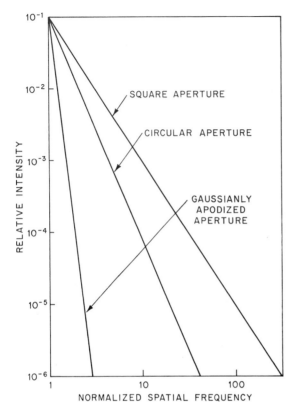

Fig. 4.15 Relative side-lobe intensity loci for square, circular, and gaussianly apodized apertures.

Using Laplace-transform methods and assuming that the spatial band-width of $s(x)$ is small with respect to the average frequency it is demonstrated in Ref. [4.7] that, if $s(x)$ is written in the form

$$s(x) = v(x) \cos [\omega_x x + \phi(x)] \qquad (4.104)$$

the recorded signal takes the form

$$f(x) = \sum_{m=0}^{m=\infty} C(\nu, m) v^\nu(x) \cos [m\omega_x x + m\phi(x)] \qquad (4.105)$$

where the coefficients $C(\nu, m)$ are given by

$$C(\nu, m) = \frac{a\epsilon_m \Gamma(\nu + 1)}{2^{\nu+1} \Gamma[1 - (m - \nu)/2] \Gamma[1 + (m + \nu)/2]} \qquad (4.106)$$

where ϵ_m is the Neumann factor which equals 1 when $m = 0$ and 2 otherwise. The gamma function, $\Gamma(n)$, is given by

$$\Gamma(n) = \int_0^\infty x^{n-1} e^{-x} dx \tag{4.107}$$

Thus the effect of a nonlinear recording process whose effect can be expressed in the form of the transfer function given in eq. (4.103) is to corrupt the input to the optical computer with a multiplicity of harmonic terms each multiplied by the νth order of the amplitude-modulating function $v(x)$ and having phase modulation m times that of the fundamental. Further discussion of the effect of recording nonlinearities in certain other cases appears in Ref. [4.8].

REFERENCES

4.1 Jones, R. C.: New Calculus for the Treatment of Optical Systems, VIII, Electromagnetic Theory, *J. Opt. Soc. Amer.*, **46**:126 (1956).

4.2 O'Neill, E. L.: "Introduction to Statistical Optics," Addison-Wesley, Reading, Mass., 1963.

4.3 Vander Lugt, A.: Signal Detection by Complex Spatial Filtering, *IEEE Trans. Inform. Theory*, **IT-10**(2):139 (April, 1964).

4.4 Leith, E. N.: Reconstructed Wavefronts and Communication Theory, *J. Opt. Soc. Amer.*, **52**(10):1123 (1962).

4.5 Woodward, P. M.: "Probability and Information Theory with Applications to Radar," Pergamon, New York, 1955.

4.6 Scott, R. M., et al.: The Practical Application of Modulation Transfer Functions, *Photogr. Sci. Eng.*, **9**:235 (1965).

4.7 Davenport, W. B., Jr., and W. L. Root: "An Introduction to the Theory of Random Signals and Noise," McGraw-Hill, New York, 1958.

4.8 Leith, E. N., et al.: Investigation of Hologram Techniques, U.S. Dept. of Commerce Clearinghouse Report AD 476267, December, 1965.

Chapter Five

Spatial
Light Modulators

5.00 Introduction

This chapter treats a variety of physical effects and devices which can be utilized to produce optical spatial amplitude and/or spatial phase modulation. These effects are discussed in terms of energy requirements, self-noise, dynamic range, information storage density, activation and decay times, as well as with regard to certain pragmatic limitations relating to uniformity, life, and reliability. Because of the rapid development of new types of spatial light modulators, some of the material presented inevitably does not represent the present state of the art. However, this survey of spatial light modulation provides a general orientation essential to understanding the problems and limitations of signal introduction in coherent optical computers.

5.10 Silver Halide Emulsions

The standard photographic emulsion is one of the most commonly used media for recording signals to be processed by coherent optical computers. Despite the inherent disadvantage of the requisite chemical development of the latent image and the nonreusability of the silver halide emulsion, this material has found extensive use in recording signals in many fields where optical computation finds application. The primary reason for its use are low recording energy, high information storage density, permanency of the recorded signals, ready availability, convenience of use, and well-calibrated properties over a wide range of characteristic variables.

There are many excellent references which treat the photographic recording process in detail [5.1 to 5.3]. Basically, this process is dependent upon two phenomena:

1. The decomposition of molecules of silver halide into silver atoms and halogen atoms by incident photons

2. The catalytic growth, during chemical development of the emulsion, of metallic silver grains nucleated by silver atoms produced from photodecomposed silver halide molecules.

It is important to understand the physics of signal recording in using silver halide emulsions. Such emulsions are composed of silver halide crystals in a gelatin matrix as shown in Fig. 5.1. The silver halide crystal is face-centered cubic with each silver ion having six nearest-neighbor halogen ions and vice versa. Both the silver and halogen ions are mobile within the crystal lattice. Current theories assume that an incident photon oxidizes a halogen ion to a halogen atom. The photoelectron so created moves through the lattice until it combines with a silver ion so as to reduce it to a silver atom. Reduction of silver ions must take place at some positively charged site, or "trap," to which the photoelectron is attracted. Lattice dislocations provide such a trap.

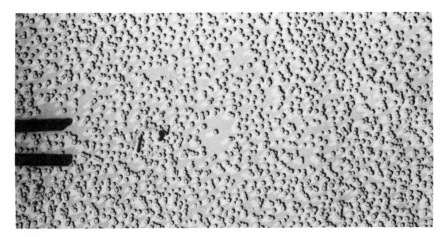

Fig. 5.1 Crystals of silver halide in a photographic emulsion. (*From C. E. K. Mees and T. H. James* [5.3], *copyright Macmillan, 1966.*)

However, if recombination takes place within the normal crystal lattice structure the resultant silver atom has a high probability of redissociating thermally into an electron and silver ion. This is true because an isolated silver atom is not stable in the normal silver halide crystal. There is also a probability that the photoelectron will recombine with the photohole created by the incident photon. Once a single stable silver atom is formed within a silver halide crystal, the crystal is capable of being chemically developed; i.e., it is "developable." Additional photoelectrons produced by incident photons may produce additional stable silver atoms within the grain but do not make the grain any more developable.

The quantum efficiency of a particular silver halide system is the probability that an incident photon will produce a stable atom of silver. Quantum efficiencies for typical silver halide systems have been found to run from a high of about 0.3 to as low as 10^{-4}. Note that within a single emulsion there may exist a range in quantum efficiency due to variations from crystal to crystal.

The theory of chemical development of silver halide emulsions is not yet complete. Basically, it can be said that any silver atom formed within the crystal by photoreduction acts as a catalyst which permits the chemical developer to reduce all the silver ions within the crystal to a metallic silver "grain." The halide ions which are left after the silver has been chemically reduced go into solution in the developer. Maximum grain size is directly proportional to crystal size. However, various grain sizes and configurations can result, as is illustrated in Fig. 5.2. Note that there is no direct relationship between the location of silver atoms in the grain and their prior location as silver ions in the crystal. The grain appears to nucleate near the surface of the crystal but forms

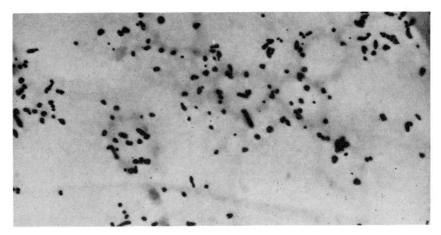

Fig. 5.2 Photographic emulsion after development, showing grains of metallic silver. (*From C. E. K. Mees and T. H. James* [5.3], *copyright Macmillan, 1966.*)

outside, rather than within, the crystal.   As discussed by James [5.4], what is called "solution-physical development" sometimes takes place where silver ions from one crystal go into solution in the developer, migrate to a site of grain nucleation, and through reduction at that site become part of that grain.   In this case, a grain may contain more silver atoms than the original crystal.   The "gain" or "amplification" of a silver halide emulsion, defined as the number of silver atoms in the resultant grains compared with the number of silver atoms which were originally photoreduced, may be as high as 10^9.

From the above discussion it is apparent that emulsion sensitivity is related to both crystal size and quantum efficiency.   It is possible to make a very sensitive or "fast" emulsion merely by fabricating it of large crystals.   This makes the cross section to arriving photons large and increases the probability of a hit for a given number of photons arriving per unit area.   Conversely, a "slow" emulsion may be created by forming relatively small silver halide crystals.   Again, sensitivity can be varied in emulsions having the same crystal size by altering the quantum efficiency.

Two types of characteristic curves for photographic emulsions are shown in Figs. 5.3 and 5.4.   Figure 5.3 shows the usual H-D (Hurter-Driffield) curves for two selected emulsions covering the range from a

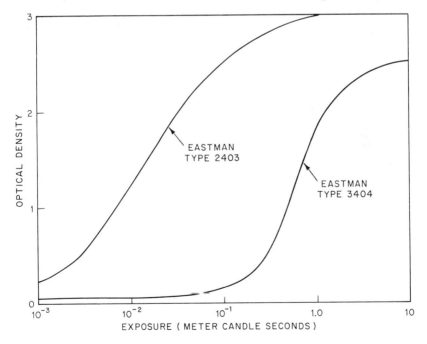

Fig. 5.3   Hurter-Driffield curves for Eastman Kodak types 2403 and 3404 emulsions exposed by a 6000°K thermal source and developed in D-19 developer for 8 min at 68°F.

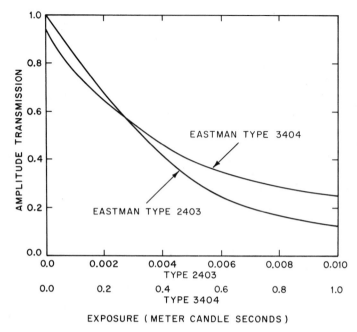

Fig. 5.4 Light-amplitude-transmission characteristics for Eastman Kodak types 2403 and 3404 emulsions.

slow, small-grained emulsion (type 3404) to a fast, large-grained emulsion (type 2403). The H-D curve is a plot of the logarithm of the light intensity absorption versus recorded energy. A more useful curve from the point of view of coherent optical computation plots light amplitude transmission versus recorded energy. Two such curves are shown in Fig. 5.4 corresponding to the two emulsions whose H-D curves are given in Fig. 5.3. It should be noted that the most usable, i.e., the most linear, portion of the light-amplitude-transmission curve occurs well below the "knee" of the H-D curve. Thus input photographic recordings for coherent optical computers lie in the range of what would ordinarily be considered "low contrast" in conventional photography. This fact is also advantageous because a high level of unmodulated light is transmitted, thus providing the high-bias, low-modulation recording which was shown in Chapter Four to combat nonlinearities. The disadvantage of the high-bias level is to make zero-order side-lobe suppression difficult and to decrease modulation efficiency.

5.11 Information Storage Density and Dynamic Range in Silver Halide Emulsions
The value of photographic film as a spatial light modulator is due to its capacity for high information storage density as

well as to its sensitivity. Clearly, the unit of information storage is the grain, which, in terms of the illuminating light in the optical computer, is basically a binary storage element; i.e., it is either present or not present. Assuming a monolayer of close-packed silver halide crystals which are capable of producing a close-packed monolayer of essentially circular grains, the maximum storage capacity of such an emulsion is given by

$$n_{b\,\text{max}} \approx \frac{1}{4\bar{r}_g^2} \tag{5.1}$$

where $n_{b_{\text{max}}}$ is the maximum number of bits which may be stored per unit area, on an average, and $2\bar{r}_g$ is the average grain diameter. To produce one silver atom and thus to record one bit, $1/\bar{\eta}$ photon is required per grain, on an average, where $\bar{\eta}$ is the average quantum efficiency. However, to record one bit with 98 percent confidence requires $4/\bar{\eta}$ photons if it is assumed that the uncertainty in the quantum efficiency can be described by Poisson statistics. Thus, the incident light flux, expressed in photons per unit area, required to achieve the above-mentioned confidence level is given by

$$n_{p_{\text{max}}} \approx \frac{1}{\bar{\eta}\bar{r}_g^2} \tag{5.2}$$

The energy required per unit area is given by $h\nu/\eta r_g^2$, where h is Planck's constant at the frequency of light, ν, at which η is measured.

The above discussion applies only to the recording of binary signals; i.e., it states that, if the number of photons given by eq. (5.2) arrive per unit area, then at least 98 percent of the crystals in that area will be made developable. The developed emulsion will be essentially opaque. When analog recording is required, the average rather than the maximum number of grains per unit area is considered. The average number of grains n_g is given by

$$\bar{n}_g = n_p\bar{\eta} \tag{5.3}$$

where n_p is the number of photons incident per unit area and $\bar{\eta}$ is the average quantum efficiency. Let n_l be the number of detectable levels to be recorded per unit area, where a detectable level is defined as that level which, on an average, is two standard deviations away from the next level. For large n_l, the number of detectable levels per unit area is given by

$$n_l = \tfrac{1}{2}\sqrt{\bar{n}_g} = \tfrac{1}{2}\sqrt{n_p\bar{\eta}} \tag{5.4}$$

where it is assumed that one standard deviation is equal to the square root of the mean. The number of bits recorded per unit area is then

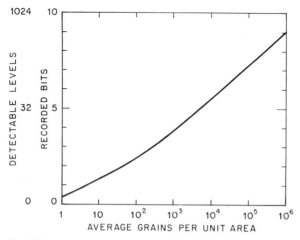

Fig. 5.5 Information-storage characteristic as a function of developed grains.

given by

$$n_b = \log_2 n_l = \tfrac{1}{2}(\log_2 \bar{n}_g - 2) \tag{5.5}$$

This relationship is plotted in Fig. 5.5.   For low values of $\bar{n}_g$, Poisson statistics must be used to determine the number of detectable levels per unit area.   For example, for there to be one detectable level per unit area, the probability of at least one or more grains being recorded must be large.   If 98 percent confidence is required, then $\bar{n}_g = 4$ is the necessary value, as shown in Fig. 5.5.

If the average grain diameter is known for a particular emulsion, it is possible to predict the number of detectable levels as a function of recorded area.   Figure 5.6 shows such a graph for the same emulsions whose characteristic curves are given in Figs. 5.3 and 5.4.   The number of detectable levels is determined by the statistical uncertainty of the recording process and is bounded at one extreme by the situation of low recording light input where no signal is recorded and at the other extreme by the situation where all grains are developed.   Thus the number of detectable levels is directly related to dynamic range.

5.12   Sources of Noise in Silver Halide Emulsions   There are two
primary sources of noise in silver halide emulsions:

1. Noise due to the random properties of the grain structure of the developed emulsion

2. Noise due to mechanical distortion of the emulsion and/or substrate

Because of the random nature of the photographic recording process

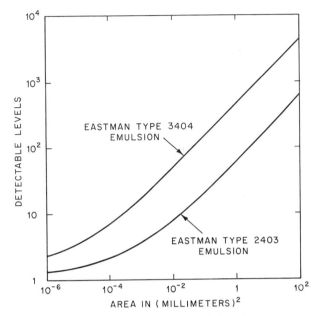

Fig. 5.6 Information-storage characteristic of Eastman Kodak types 2403 and 3404 emulsions.

and because the recorded signal appears as discrete opaque grains rather than in the form of a continuous tone recording, photographic film will create spatial noise when used in a coherent optical computer. To treat this noise problem properly, the distribution of the size of the recorded grains must be taken into account. The analysis of this problem given here follows that of O'Neill [5.5].

To determine the expected value of transmission at a point (x, y) in the emulsion, let A equal the area of an annular ring about (x, y) having radius r and width dr. To calculate the probability that a grain having its center in the annulus reaches to the point (x, y), define $p(r)$ as the probability that a grain has a radius smaller than r. The probability that the light intensity transmission t_i at (x, y) is zero, when only the grains centered in the annulus are considered, is given by

$$p(t_i = 0) = P(0) + P(1)p(r) + P(2)p^2(r) + \cdots + P(n_g A)p^{n_g A}(r) + \cdots \tag{5.6}$$

where $P(n_g A)$ is the Poisson probability that there are $n_g A$ grains in the area of the annulus, A. Recall that the Poisson probability is given by

$$P(n_g A) = \frac{(\bar{n}_g A)^{n_g A} e^{-\bar{n}_g A}}{(n_g A)!} \tag{5.7}$$

where $\bar{n}_g A$ and $n_g A$ are integers.   Combining eqs. (5.6) and (5.7) yields

$$p(t_i = 0) = e^{-\bar{n}_g A} \sum \frac{(\bar{n}_g A)^{n_g A}}{(n_g A)!} p^{n_g A}(r) = e^{-\bar{n}_g A[1-p(r)]} \tag{5.8}$$

To determine the overall light intensity transmission requires a multiplication of probabilities for all r, that is, an integration in the exponent of eq. (5.8).   Integrating the exponent over r and recalling that $A = 2\pi r\, dr$ yields the overall average light intensity transmission corresponding to an average number of grains per unit area, $\bar{n}_g$,

$$\bar{t}_i(\bar{n}_g) = e^{-2\pi \bar{n}_g \int_0^{\infty} [1-p(r)] r\, dr} \tag{5.9}$$

Take, for example, a simple case where all grains have the same radius, r_g.   In this case, $p(r)$ is given by

$$p(r) = \begin{cases} 0 & r \leqslant r_g \\ 1 & r > r_g \end{cases} \tag{5.10}$$

A combination of eqs. (5.9) and (5.10) yields for the average light intensity transmission

$$\bar{t}_i(\bar{n}_g) = e^{-\pi r_g^2 \bar{n}_g} \tag{5.11}$$

and for the average light amplitude transmission

$$\bar{t}_a(\bar{n}_g) = e^{-\pi r_g^2 \bar{n}_g/2} \tag{5.12}$$

Curves of the form given by eq. (5.12) are plotted in Fig. 5.7 superimposed on the actual curves presented in Fig. 5.4.   It is worth noting that the negative slope of the light-intensity- and light-amplitude-transmission curves means that a signal $B + s(x,y)$ is recorded as $B' - s(x,y)$.   The sign reversal must be taken into account in the design of the associated coherent optical computer when used for correlation and/or matched filtering, although in some cases, such as spectrum analysis, the sign reversal is of no importance.

In order to calculate the effect of grain noise on the performance of a coherent optical computer, the Wiener spectrum is calculated. Advantage is taken of the Wiener-Khintchine theorem which states that the Wiener spectrum is given by the inverse Fourier transform of the autocorrelation function.   Note that the autocorrelation function of the light amplitude transmission is just the probability that values of the light amplitude transmission measured at two points r and $r-r'$ are simultaneously zero.   Again following O'Neill [5.5], eq. (5.9) is utilized to write the simultaneous probability.   The integration is performed by dividing all space into two half planes by means of a perpendicular bisector to the line joining r and $r-r'$.   The probability

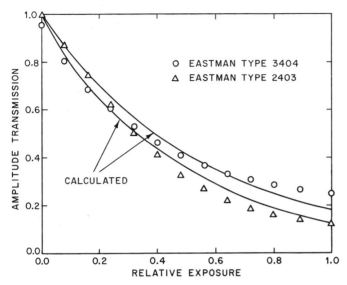

Fig. 5.7 Comparison of actual and theoretical light-amplitude-transmission characteristics.

that the light amplitude transmission is zero at r, considering grains whose centers are contained in annuli centered upon r and limited by the half plane occupied by r, is given by

$$p[t_a(r') = 0] = e^{-\bar{n}_g\{\pi \int_0^{r'/2} [1-p(r)]r\,dr + \int_{r'/2}^{\infty} \int_{\cos^{-1}r'/2r}^{\pi} [1-p(r)]r\,dr\,d\theta\}} \qquad (5.13)$$

The expression for $p[t_a(r-r') = 0]$ is essentially identical to eq. (5.13) so that the simultaneous probability or autocorrelation function, $C_{t_a}(r')$, is given by

$$C_{t_a}(r') = e^{-2\bar{n}_g\{\pi \int_0^{r'/2} [1-p(r)]r\,dr + \int_{r'/2}^{\infty} \int_{\cos^{-1}r'/2r}^{\pi} [1-p(r)]r\,dr\}} \qquad (5.14)$$

Again taking the simple case of constant grain diameter, $2r_g$, the integrals in the exponent may be completed to yield

$$C_{t_a}(r') = e^{-\pi r_g^2 \bar{n}_g[1-\psi(r')]} = t_a^{\,2[1-\psi(r')]} \qquad (5.15)$$

where

$$\psi(r') = \frac{1}{\pi}\left[\cos^{-1}\frac{r'}{2r_g} - \frac{r'}{2r_g}\sqrt{1-\left(\frac{r'}{2r_g}\right)^2}\right]$$

Plots of the light-amplitude-transmission autocorrelation function for various values of light amplitude transmission are given in Fig. 5.8 and the corresponding Wiener spectra in Fig. 5.9. All plots are in terms of

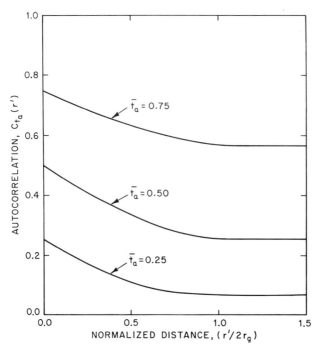

Fig. 5.8 Autocorrelation functions of photographic grain based on the assumption of constant grain diameter (r_g).

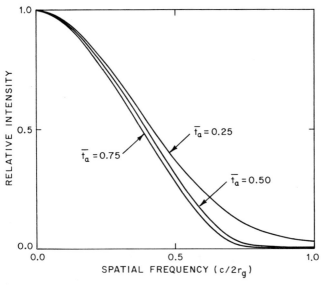

Fig. 5.9 Wiener spectra of photographic grain based upon the assumption of constant grain diameter. Abscissa is given in spatial cycles across the average grain diameter ($2r_g$).

the normalized coordinate $(r'/2r_g)$ and the corresponding normalized spatial frequency, assuming throughout that the aperture size is much greater than $r'/2r_g$. For a discussion of techniques for measuring grain noise in silver halide emulsions and results on certain specific materials the reader is referred to Stark [5.6].

Returning to eq. (5.11) which gives the average light intensity transmission $\bar{t}_i$, it should be recognized that, since $\bar{n}_g$ is the average value of a random process, there will be a variance in t_i. This variance is called *granularity* and is shown by O'Neill [5.5] to be given by

$$\sigma_{\bar{t}_i}^2 = \bar{t}_i \, (1 - \bar{t}_i) \tag{5.16}$$

Equation (5.16) is plotted in Fig. 5.10. This equation has an important bearing on the analysis of the interaction between grain noise and the recorded signal. As has been mentioned in Sec. 5.10, it is advantageous to record an input signal where the derivative, $d\bar{t}_a/d\bar{n}_g$, is a maximum, as this is the most linear portion of the characteristic curve of the emulsion. However, in this region the granularity curve has a maximum slope. For recordings in or near this region the input signal modulates the noise multiplicatively. The Wiener spectrum of the recorded signal is therefore the convolution of the noise and signal spectra. By the convolution theorem,

$$W(\omega_x) = \left| \int s(x) n(x) e^{-j\omega_x x} \, dx \right|^2 = \left| \int S(\omega_x') N(\omega_x - \omega_x') \, d\omega_x' \right|^2 \tag{5.17}$$

where $s(x)$ is the signal, $n(x)$ is the noise, and $S(\omega_x)$ and $N(\omega_x)$ are their Fourier transforms, respectively. Thus noise sidebands are added to the signal.

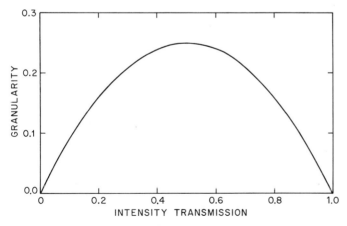

Fig. 5.10   Granularity characteristic of photographic emulsions.

On the other hand, if the input signal is of relatively small modulation and is recorded in or near the region where the slope of the granularity curve is zero, the signal and noise are additive.   In this case the Wiener spectrum is given by

$$W(\omega_x) = \left| \int [s(x) + n(x)]e^{-j\omega_x x} dx \right|^2 = |S(\omega_x)|^2 + |N(\omega_x)|^2 \qquad (5.18)$$

The user of silver halide emulsions for spatial light modulation must compromise between the desire to avoid multiplicative noise and the desire to maximize modulation efficiency and linearity.   For additional information on granularity the reader is referred to Linfoot [5.7].

As mentioned at the beginning of this section, the other primary source of noise in silver halide emulsions is that due to mechanical distortion of the emulsion and/or substrate.   Mechanical distortion may occur as lateral strains due to stretching of the emulsion or substrate or as longitudinal thickness variations.   Both types of distortion usually occur during chemical development although lateral strain may also occur as a function of storage time, temperature, and humidity.

Extensive studies of lateral strain are reported in Refs. [5.8] and [5.9]. It has been found empirically that such strains may be held in the range of 10^{-3} to 10^{-5} rms values when proper care is exercised in handling typical silver halide materials.   Best performance is obtained when the emulsion is mounted on a glass substrate.   The effect of such strain is, of course, to alter the recorded signal.   This effect may be expressed mathematically as

$$s'(x,y) = s(x - \Delta x, y - \Delta y) \qquad (5.19)$$

where $s(x,y)$ is the input signal, $s'(x,y)$ is the recorded signal after development, and $\Delta x = d_x(x,y)$, $\Delta y = d_y(x,y)$, where $d_x(x,y)$ and $d_y(x,y)$ are the lateral-distortion functions.   In coherent optical systems having large space-bandwidths careful control of lateral distortion is imperative.

Longitudinal distortion due to thickness variations has also received careful attention.   See, for example, measurements reported by Ingalls [5.10].   Such distortion is found to be due to the manufacturing process and also due to nonuniform thickness expansion of the emulsion during development.   In the latter case the distortion is correlated with the signal.   It is found in most cases that satisfactory optical-computer performance can be achieved only by compensating for thickness variations by mounting the material on which the signal is recorded in a "liquid gate."   The liquid gate consists of two optically flat glass plates between which the emulsion and substrate and a liquid medium are sandwiched.   When the emulsion is on a flexible plastic substrate, both plates are required and liquid is in contact with the substrate on one side and with the emulsion on the other.   If the emulsion is already mounted on an optically flat substrate, then only one plate is required, with the liquid on the emulsion side only.   Since the effect of thickness variations is to produce spatial phase modulation of the coherent light passing through the substrate and emulsion, the effect of the liquid gate, when the optical index of the liquid matches those of the substrate and the emulsion, is to remove the spatial phase modulation.   In general, however, the optical indices of the substrate and emulsion are unequal so that the following expression must be evaluated:

$$\Phi_n(x,y) = \frac{2\pi}{\lambda_L} \left[(n_s - n_l)\Delta t_s(x,y) + (n_e - n_l)\Delta t_e(x,y) \right] \tag{5.20}$$

where $\Phi_n(x,y)$ is the spatial-phase-modulation noise function due to thickness variations, $\Delta t_s(x,y)$ and $\Delta t_e(x,y)$, in the substrate and emulsion, respectively.   Since the optical indices of the substrate, emulsion, and liquid (n_s, n_e, n_l, respectively) may not be equal, a knowledge of the rms value of Δt_s and Δt_e is required before n_l can be selected so that the rms value of $\Phi_n(x,y)$ is minimized.

The reader should finally be cautioned that, in choosing a silver halide emulsion for use as a spatial light modulator in a coherent optical computer, spatial optical polarization modulation in the substrate must also be considered.   Certain of the newer substrates, such as Mylar, exhibit this effect, whereas some of the older cellulose acetate substrates do not.   In short, the effective use of silver halide emulsions for spatial light modulation requires a thorough knowledge and analysis of all pertinent parameters.

5.20 Photochromic Materials

In addition to the essentially irreversible photochemical signal-recording media such as silver halide emulsions, there exist a variety of spatial light amplitude modulators, both inorganic and organic, which are reversible and, hence, are reusable.   The term *photochromic* is usually applied to these recording and light-modulating materials.

Photochromic materials may be changed reversibly between two states at least one of which is characterized by the absorption of visible light. (The more general term *phototropism* refers to materials having two or more states which can be detected by the absorption of some form of electromagnetic energy, but not necessarily in the visible-wavelength region.) Typically, photochromics, when in their equilibrium or "bleached" state, absorb in the ultraviolet and/or in the short-wavelength region of the visible spectrum.   When they are illuminated at these absorbing wavelengths, chemical changes occur which produce new absorption bands in the medium- to long-wavelength region of the visible spectrum.   Absorption of light energy at these longer wavelengths and/or thermal decay returns the photochromic material to its original state.

There are a great variety of photochromic materials.   The reader is referred to Refs. [5.11] and [5.12] for general surveys.   In this text photochromic materials are divided into organics, inorganics, and glasses.

5.21   Organic Photochromics   Windsor [5.13] categorizes organic photochromics as belonging to three basic types:

1. *Organic dyes,* which are photochromic due to the positive ions formed (reversibly) by oxidation by means of visible light of sufficient intensity

2. *Stereoisomers,* such as the spirans, where the absorption of short-wavelength light breaks chemical bonds in their ring-type molecules, producing a change in their molecular geometry and, hence, a change in absorption

3. *Triplet-state materials,* such as the polynuclear aromatic hydrocarbons, where short-wavelength light excites ground-state molecules to a triplet state which absorbs longer-wavelength light in the triplet–triplet transition

Many types of organic photochromic films are available from a number of manufacturers.   An abbreviated listing including some typical parameters is provided in Table 5.1.   Typical transmission plots are shown in Fig. 5.11.   Research on these materials continues, and modifications are constantly being made.   The prime goal of this research is to tailor the material to the wavelengths and energies available for

TABLE 5.1

Manufacturer	Material type	Activating wavelengths, nm	Absorbing wavelength, nm	Intensity transmission range, %
American Cyanamid	43-540	300–400	560–580	0.1–90
	43–540A	300–400	425	10–90
	51-142	300–400	590	0.1–90
	63-071	480	600	1–90
Vari-Light	VL-204A	400–500	425–550	30–70
	VL-316A	475–600	475–625	45–92
	VL-200B	320–400	600–700	60–85%
Nuclear Research Associates ..	41-1	400–530	200–530	20–60
	11	400–550	200–530	20–60

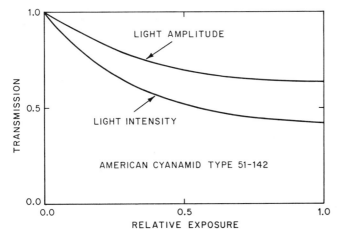

Fig. 5.11　Transmission characteristic of American Cyanamid type 51-142 photochromic material.

activation and for bleaching. Another goal is to eliminate one of the detrimental features of the organic photochromics, namely, that they fatigue with prolonged cycling. It is characteristic of most organic photochromics that upon repeated cycling both the maximum achievable long-wavelength absorption and the rate of bleaching decrease.

Laser-beam recording devices are frequently used for signal recording on organic photochromics. Because of the difficulty of obtaining laser energy in the short-wavelength region, and because of the relatively large number of laser wavelengths available at longer visible wavelengths, organic photochromic material is most frequently used in a mode wherein activation is produced by a noncoherent ultraviolet source, and signal recording is accomplished by selective area bleaching with a longer wavelength.

It is important, therefore, to analyze the bleaching characteristics of photochromic systems. Let

n_{c0} = total number of activation sites or "color centers" per unit area

n_{c1} = total number of deactivated (i.e., bleached) centers per unit area

n_{c2} = total number of activated (i.e., darkened) centers per unit area

Clearly,

$$n_{c1} + n_{c2} = n_{c0}$$

and, if it is assumed that the absorption by bleached centers is small at the recording wavelength and that darkened centers are strongly absorbing at the same wavelength and that they form a continuous molecular sheet, the optical intensity transmission at the recording wavelength is given by

$$t_i = \frac{n_{c0} - n_{c2}}{n_{c0}} = \frac{n_{c1}}{n_{c1} + n_{c2}} \tag{5.21}$$

Let $k_{12}(\lambda_L)$ and $k_{21}(\lambda_L)$ be the spectral rate constants for darkening and bleaching, respectively. Their dimensions are the fraction of centers darkened (or bleached) per unit of light intensity (as a function of irradiating wavelength). The rate constants are directly proportional to quantum efficiency. Let $k_{21}(T)$ be the thermal rate constant, i.e., the rate of conversion of activated centers back to their deactivated state as a function of temperature. Assuming that both $k_{12}(\lambda_L)$ and $k_{21}(\lambda_L)$ are linear with light intensity and that temperature changes in the film due to the optical irradiation are negligible in comparison with the absolute temperature, the time rate change of n_{c2} can be expressed as follows:

$$\frac{dn_{c2}}{dt} = -[k_{21}(\lambda_L)I_r + k_{21}(T)]n_{c2} + k_{12}(\lambda_L)I_r n_{c1} \tag{5.22}$$

where I_r is the recording light intensity. Note that, even if I_r is monochromatic, a significant number of centers may be becoming activated per unit time because of the typical broadness of the $k_{12}(\lambda_L)$ spectrum. Independent of the starting conditions, and dependent only upon I_r and T, an equilibrium condition will be reached where

$$\frac{dn_{c2}}{dt} = 0 \tag{5.23}$$

By combining eqs. (5.22) and (5.23) the ratio of bleached to darkened center in equilibrium is given by

$$\frac{n_{c2}}{n_{c1}} = \frac{k_{12}(\lambda_L)I_r}{k_{21}(\lambda_L)I_r + k_{21}(T)} \tag{5.24}$$

This reduces to the ratio of the darkening and bleaching rate constants if thermal bleaching is negligible. Equations (5.21) and (5.24) may be combined to yield the equilibrium light intensity transmission as follows:

$$t_i = \frac{1}{1 + k_{12}(\lambda_L)/[k_{21}(\lambda_L)I_r + k_{21}(\lambda_L)]} \tag{5.25}$$

The complete solution of eq. (5.22) can be obtained by first substituting the quantity $n_{c0} - n_{c2}$ for n_{c1} and rearranging the terms as follows:

$$\frac{dn_{c2}}{dt} = -\{[k_{12}(\lambda_L) + k_{21}(\lambda_L)]I_r + k_{21}(T)\}n_{c2} + k_{12}(\lambda_L)I_r n_{c0} \tag{5.26}$$

Integration yields

$$n_{c2} = \frac{k_{12}(\lambda_L)I_r n_{c0}}{[k_{12}(\lambda_L)+k_{21}(\lambda_L)]I_r + k_{21}(T)}$$

$$+ n'_{c2} - \frac{k_{12}(\lambda_L)I_r n_{c0}}{[k_{12}(\lambda_L)+k_{21}(\lambda_L)]I_r + k_{21}(T)}\ e^{-\{[k_{12}(\lambda_L)+k_{21}(\lambda_L)]I_r + k_{21}(T)\}t} \quad (5.27)$$

where n'_{c2} is the initial concentration of color centers. For the frequently encountered case where both thermal bleaching and activation of color centers by the irradiating wavelength can be neglected, the above reduces to

$$n_{c2} = n'_{c2}e^{-k_{21}(\lambda_L)I_r t} \quad (5.28)$$

Since the light intensity transmission is given by $(n_{c0}-n_{c2})/n_{c0}$, eq. (5.28) can be revised to yield

$$t_i = 1 - \frac{n'_{c2}}{n_{c0}}e^{-k_{21}(\lambda_L)I_r t} \quad (5.29)$$

Equation (5.29) predicts an exponential increase of t_i with time from an initial value of $(n_{c0}-n'_{c2})/n_{c0}$ to a final value of unity within the scope of the above simplifying assumptions.

Another useful relationship is obtained from eq. (5.29) by changing from light intensity transmission to light intensity absorption, a_i or $1-t_i$. Taking the natural logarithm of a_i yields

$$\ln a_i = \ln a'_i - k_{21}(\lambda_L)I_r t \quad (5.30)$$

where $a'_i = n'_{c2}/n_{c0}$.

Equation (5.30) states that a logarithmic plot of bleaching starting from an initial absorption a'_i plotted against $I_r t$ will have a negative slope proportional to the bleaching rate constant. An example of three such

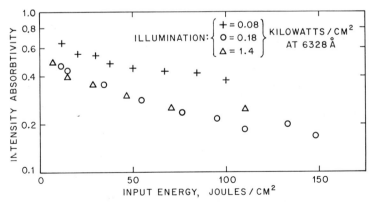

Fig. 5.12 Bleaching characteristic obtained for American Cyanamid type 43-540 photochromic material.

plots made for a typical organic-dye photochromic (American Cyanamid type 43–540) is shown in Fig. 5.12. These plots were obtained for recording light intensity levels having a range of values of more than 10 to 1. The fact that a more negative slope is obtained for the highest value of recording light intensity may be due to thermal bleaching effects. Since lower final absorption values are achieved at higher values of recording light intensity, it is evident that, in the case illustrated, activation of color centers by the irradiating wavelength is playing no part.

5.22   Inorganic Photochromics   Included among the inorganic photochromics are the alkali halides, alkaline-earth titanates and sulfides, certain compounds containing zinc sulfide, many compounds of mercury, etc. The reader is referred to Brown and Shaw [5.11] for listings of many of these materials.

This section will treat the alkali halide photochromics as a case in point because they are one of the best understood of the inorganic photochromic systems. As with the silver halide system described in Sec. 5.10, the alkali halides are ionic crystals which usually have a face-centered cubic lattice structure. Thin films or thin slices of these crystals may be used as spatial light modulators in coherent optical computers. Most alkali halides such as the chlorides of sodium or potassium, potassium bromide, etc., have optical absorption bands only in the ultraviolet when in their equilibrium or "bleached" state. In the visible they are essentially transparent. As is described below, special versions of the alkali halides may be made to exhibit equilibrium-state absorption bands in many regions of the visible and near-infrared spectra. As with other photochromics nonequilibrium absorption bands may be created or destroyed by the action of photons of the appropriate wavelength(s), thus spatially altering the transmission of the alkali halide film at will. In this way, spatial signals may be recorded and erased as desired. Furthermore, there exist other optical wavelengths which may be used for nondestructive interrogation of the recorded signals, i.e., wavelengths which are absorbed by the spatially recorded signals but which do not themselves produce changes in the transmission of the crystal.

The physics of the above processes is reasonably well understood and, as with silver halide emulsions, depends upon deliberately introduced crystallographic defects. For example, heating a stoichiometric alkali halide crystal at several hundred degrees centigrade in an atmosphere of alkali vapor at reduced pressure causes halide ions to leave their lattice sites, diffuse to the surface, and combine with alkali atoms. The electron given up during this combination may enter the conduction band and diffuse back into the crystal. If this occurs, the electron may be attracted to a halogen-ion vacancy or "α center" and may combine with it. If this takes place, what is called an "F center" is formed at the site of the halogen-ion vacancy. (The F centers themselves may diffuse to the surface and furnish electrons to alkali ions which can then evaporate, so that for any given temperature and pressure there is some equilibrium concentration of F centers within the crystal.) Under the conditions mentioned, equilibrium concentrations of between 10^{16} to 10^{17} F centers per cubic centimeter may be created.

The existence of F centers in an alkali halide crystal creates an absorption band in the visible. Bands are found to occur at 4580 Å for NaCl, 5560 Å for KCl, and 6250 Å for KBr. These bands are called the "F bands." When photons are absorbed by these bands, the resultant effect depends to a large extent upon the temperature of the crystal. When an F center absorbs a photon, the associated electron is raised to an excited level, again leaving an α center or vacancy. At cryogenic temperatures the probability that the photoelectron will enter the conduction band is low, and it usually, therefore, recombines with the α center, with the emission of a photon (luminescence). At higher temperatures, such as room temperature, the probability of thermal excitation of photoelectrons into the conduction band becomes high. The probability of trapping such conduction photoelectrons at un-ionized F centers is large. New centers are, therefore, formed; called "F' centers," they contain two electrons at a halide-ion vacancy in the crystal. The result is the formation of new absorption bands, called "F' bands," when the crystal is illuminated at a wavelength absorbed in the F band. The peak absorption wavelengths of these bands as well as absorption at certain other bands are listed below for NaCl, KCl, and KBr:

Band	NaCl	KCl	KBr
F'	5100 Å	7500 Å	9500 Å
M	9180 Å	8250 Å	7250 Å
R_1	5450 Å	6580 Å	7350 Å
R_2	5960 Å	7270 Å	7900 Å
U	1920 Å	2140 Å	2280 Å

The M, R_1, and R_2 bands form when the thermal holes or vacancies migrate to F' centers. When a single hole arrives at an F' center, one of the electrons in the F' is given up to the hole and two adjacent F centers are created. Double F centers cause M-band absorption. This interaction is summarized below:

$$F \xrightarrow{h\nu_F} \alpha + e$$
$$F + e \rightarrow F'$$
$$F' + \alpha \rightarrow M$$

(5.31)

where e indicates an electron.

Combinations of three or more F centers produce the R_1 and R_2 absorption bands.   All such multiple F centers are referred to as "complex" centers.   Unlike the F' centers, which have a finite lifetime at room temperature, the complex centers are stable at this temperature. Complex centers can be thermally dissociated into isolated F centers by heating the crystal to a few hundred degrees centigrade.   Furthermore, although F-band illumination at room temperature creates a condition of absorption at the M and other bands (while decreasing absorption of the F band to illumination at F band), illumination with photons absorbed by bands related to the existence of complex centers produces no further changes in absorption.   Thus optical spatial light modulation may be produced at wavelengths absorbed by the complex bands by means of incident radiation in the F band.

Absorption in the U-band region occurs when alkali halide crystals containing F centers are prepared by heating at several hundred degrees centigrade at several hundred pounds per square inch in hydrogen. These "hydrogenated" alkali halides (NaCl:H, KCl:H, KBr:H, etc.) show no F-band absorptivity.   The F centers have been filled by hydrogen ions to form U centers with the result that a new absorption band, or U band, is produced.   In addition to the hydrogen contained in the F centers, there is excess hydrogen trapped in the crystal; NaCl:H exhibits this effect the least and KBr:H, the most.   When a photon at the U band wavelength is absorbed by the crystal, the net result is to transfer a hydrogen atom to an interstitial position in the lattice and thus recreate an F center.   In this manner ultraviolet radiation of the appropriate U-band wavelength will convert a hydrogenated alkali halide crystal from a condition where it is transparent in the visible to one which is strongly absorbing in the F band.   When such a crystal is illuminated in the F band, there are two possible results:

1. Creation of complex centers and their associated absorption bands, as in the unhydrogenated crystal

2. Creation of U centers by the recombination of hydrogen atoms with F centers

Action in KCl:H in response to illumination in its F band is characteristic of the first process, with the interesting result that the complex bands so created can be removed by U-band irradiation as well as by heat.   Thus optical erasure of stored information is possible as well as nondestructive readout using illumination in certain of the complex bands.   (The M-band in KCl:H is bleached by M-band illumination, but the R-band absorptivity remains stable under R-band illumination.) KBr:H shows a performance typical of the second process mentioned above where no complex bands are formed under F-band illumination but instead there is a return to the initial state of the crystal.   Figure 5.13

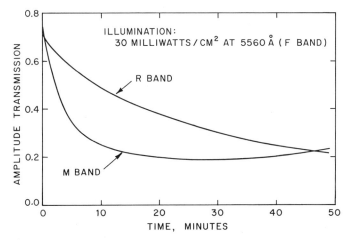

Fig. 5.13 Amplitude-transmission characteristics at R band and M band of hydrogenated potassium chloride illuminated in the F band.

shows M- and R-band activation curves for KCl:H. The reader is referred to Schulman and Compton [5.14] for further information on the details of the above photochromic reactions.

The general mathematical relationships which govern most of the above processes have already been discussed in Sec. 5.21. For example, if we assume thermal stability for F centers, as is usually the case at room temperature, the rate of bleaching under the effect of F-band illumination is described by the equation

$$\frac{dn_F}{dt} = -k_{F\alpha}(\lambda_L)n_F I_r + k_{\alpha F}(T)n_\alpha n_e \tag{5.32}$$

where $k_{F\alpha}(\lambda_L)$ is the spectral rate constant for conversion of F centers into α centers, $k_{\alpha F}(T)$ is the recombination rate constant of α centers with conduction electrons, and n_F, n_α, and n_e are the instantaneous F-center, α-center, and electron concentrations, respectively. Since the instantaneous number of electrons is directly proportional to the number of α centers, eq. (5.32) can be written

$$\frac{dn_F}{dt} = -k_{F\alpha}(\lambda_L)n_F I_r + C_0 k_{\alpha F}(T)n_e^2 \tag{5.33}$$

The constant C_0 turns out to be very small at most temperatures of interest since the lifetime of a conduction electron is much shorter than the lifetime of an α center. In fact, if it is assumed that most α centers combine with F' centers to form complex centers, the final term of eq. (5.33) may be neglected and the equation integrated to yield

$$n_F = n_F' e^{-k_{Fa}(\lambda_L)I_r t} \tag{5.34}$$

where n_F' is the initial F-center concentration. Equation (5.34) is directly analogous to eq. (5.28) and indicates an exponential decay in the F-center concentration with time for constant illumination. As the F-center concentration decays, the absorptivity of the F band will fall and transmission will increase. Simultaneously the transmission of the complex bands will rise.

5.23 Photochromic Glasses Photochromic glasses are treated here primarily because they can be fabricated in such a fashion that they do not exhibit the fatigue that is characteristic of the organic photochromics. Furthermore, being glasses, they can be polished to the high optical quality necessary to preserve phase coherence in coherent optical computers. The chief disadvantage of photochromic glasses at present is the fact that large optical density changes can be obtained only in relatively thick films or slabs of such material (5 to 10 mm, for example). However, in many applications where low-contrast signal recording at high bias levels can be used, this disadvantage is not severe and is more than compensated for by the infinite reusability of these materials.

Smith [5.15] mentions three general classes of photochromic glass:

1. Glasses obtained from melts of the mineral hackmanite (soda alumina silicate-sodalite) with the addition of a B_2O_3 flux to the glass melt as well as the addition of suitable halogens (fluorides, bromides, and/or iodides)

2. Heavy metal borosilicates, again with the addition of halogens

3. Silicates and sodium silicates containing carefully controlled traces of cerium or europium

The second in the above series is of most interest because of the lack of fatigue of this material. Such glasses are usually made with 0.5 to 1.0 percent silver content by weight and with two to three times that amount of one or more of the halogens. Sometimes a small amount of copper is added (0.02 percent by weight) to increase sensitivity.

Apparently small crystals of silver halide form in the glass matrix. The size of these crystals runs from 50 to 300 Å, depending upon heat treatment. It has been found that for crystals smaller than 50 Å photochromic action is not displayed, whereas at 300 Å and over, the crystals are large enough to scatter sufficient light for the glass to lose its optical quality. The performance of silver halide photochromic glasses is strongly related to that of silver halide emulsions (see Sec. 5.10). An incident photon may oxidize a halogen ion, and the resultant photoelectron may be captured by a silver ion, thereby reducing it to metallic silver.   Copper ions act as effective traps of the photoholes which are simultaneously created, preventing hole-electron recombination.   Unlike silver halide emulsions where the halogen is removed by the developer, thus leaving a residue of silver "grains," the halogen in photochromic glass remains and may once again recombine with the silver.   Halide recombination is triggered by ordinary thermal agitation or by light of a wavelength which is absorbed by the new absorption bands created by the existence of reduced silver.   Typically, the activating wavelengths, i.e., those at which incident light causes darkening of the photochromic glass, are in the short-wavelength region of the visible and near-ultraviolet spectrum (3000 to 4000 Å).   The absorption bands created by activation exist across the entire visible spectrum.

Rate constants for the photochromic glasses vary considerably. Typical darkening and bleaching curves are shown in Figs. 5.14 and 5.15. As can be seen, approximately 1.0 J/cm² is required during darkening to produce a change from transmission near unity to a value of 0.2, using 4000 Å illumination.   For the same glass, illumination of approximately ten times this energy is required at 6000 Å to cause bleaching.   A comparison between glass types which clearly illustrates this effect is shown in Fig. 5.16.   Here all three photochromic glasses were exposed to the same level of illumination for a 2-minute exposure time.   All were then

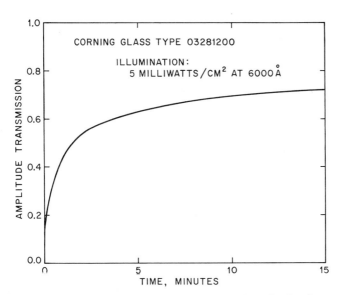

Fig. 5.14 Amplitude-transmission characteristic of Corning photochromic glass type 03281200 when illuminated at 6000 Å. (*After G. P. Smith.*)

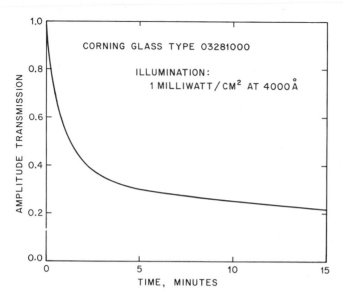

Fig. 5.15 Darkening characteristic of Corning photochromic glass type 03281000 when illuminated at 4000 Å. (*After G. P. Smith.*)

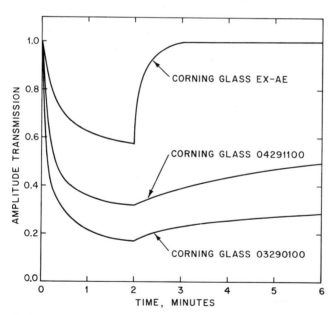

Fig. 5.16 Darkening and bleaching rates of various Corning photochromic glasses. (*After G. P. Smith.*)

allowed to thermally bleach at room temperature. The same experiment was carried out at an elevated temperature (46°C) with the results expected; i.e., equilibrium absorption was lower and thermal bleaching after energization was more rapid [5.15].

In some cases the performance of photochromic glasses may be analyzed by the same method as that already developed in Sec. 5.21. In certain cases, however, the monolayer model upon which the analysis in Sec. 5.21 is based is inadequate to describe the photochromic bleaching process. This is due to the fact that the monolayer model assumes that interactions are primarily of the nature of a surface effect rather than a volume effect. In thick photochromic glass slabs this assumption may not be valid. For bulk photochromism the previous analysis should be extended as follows.* Assume as before that the total color centers per unit volume are constant so that the equation $n_{c0} = n_{c1} + n_{c2}$ is valid. Let the activating photon flux propagate in the z direction through the photochromic material. Assume that the distribution of photons in planes perpendicular to the z axis is always uniform but gradually decreasing in concentration as photons are captured in interactions with both bleached and unbleached centers. Thus the decrease in photon concentration from plane to plane must be equal to the number of centers activated or inactivated at the photon wavelength. The following equation describes such an interaction:

$$\frac{\partial n_p(z,t)}{\partial z} = -n_p(z,t)[k_{12}n_{c1}(z,t) + k_{21}n_{c2}(z,t)] \tag{5.35}$$

Integration of eq. (5.35) with respect to z yields

$$n_p(z,t) = n_p(0,t)e^{-[k_{12}\int_0^z n_{c1}(z,t)\,dz + k_{21}\int_0^z n_{c2}(z,t)\,dz]} \tag{5.36}$$

where $n_p(0,t)$ is the incident photon concentration. For a slab of depth D, the instantaneous light intensity transmission is given by

$$t_i = \frac{n_p(D,t)}{n_p(0,t)} = e^{-[k_{12}\int_0^D n_{c1}(z,t)\,dz + k_{21}\int_0^D n_{c2}(z,t)\,dz]} \tag{5.37}$$

In order to determine the light intensity transmission as a function of time, i.e., as a function of exposure, it should be noted that the increase in the number of bleached color centers per plane is just equal to the instantaneous conversion of activated to bleached centers minus the

---

*Portions of the following analysis were originally developed in an unpublished memorandum by J. L. Kreuzer of the Perkin-Elmer Corporation.

instantaneous conversion of bleached to activated centers, namely,

$$\frac{\partial n_{c1}(z,t)}{\partial t} = n_p(z,t)[k_{21}n_{c2}(z,t) - k_{12}n_{c1}(z,t)]$$

and   (5.38)

$$\frac{\partial n_{c2}(z,t)}{\partial t} = n_p(z,t)[k_{12}n_{c1}(z,t) - k_{21}n_{c2}(z,t)]$$

Solution of the above equations is possible only when the initial spatial distribution of the populations of both bleached and unbleached centers within the volume is known. Since these distributions are, in general, nonuniform, each situation must be solved in terms of the actual starting conditions. However, when it is assumed that k_{12} is zero for the bleaching wavelength, then a useful specific analytic solution may be obtained. First note that under these assumptions eqs. (5.35), (5.36), and (5.38) reduce to

$$\frac{\partial n_p(z,t)}{\partial z} = \frac{\partial n_{c2}(z,t)}{\partial t} = n_p(z,t)[k_{21}n_{c2}(z,t)]$$

$$t_i(t) = e^{-k_{21} \int_0^D n_{c2}(z,t)\,dz} \tag{5.39}$$

In order to determine the relationship between light intensity transmission and exposure, consider first the rate of change of light intensity transmission with time as given below:

$$\frac{\partial t_i}{\partial t} = e^{-k_{21} \int_0^D n_{c2}(z,t)\,dz}\, \frac{\partial}{\partial t}\left[-k_{21}\int_0^D n_{c2}(z,t)\,dz\right]$$

$$= -k_{21}t_i \int_0^D \frac{\partial n_{c2}(z,t)}{\partial t}\,dz \tag{5.40}$$

When eq. (5.39) is combined with eq. (5.40), the following simplification results:

$$\frac{\partial t_i}{\partial t} = -k_{21}t_i \int_0^D [-k_{21}n_p(z,t)n_{c2}(z,t)]\,dz$$

$$= -k_{21}t_i \int_0^D [-k_{21}n_p(0,t)n_{c2}(x,t)e^{-k_{21}\int n_{c2}(z,t)\,dz}]\,dz$$

$$= -k_{21}n_p(0,t)t_i[e^{-k_{21}\int n_{c2}(z,t)\,dz} \,|_0^D]$$

$$= k_{21}n_p(0,t)t_i(1-t_i) \tag{5.41}$$

The physical interpretation of the above is that when $t_i = 0$, that is, when the material is totally opaque, infinite incident illumination $n_p(0,t)$ is required to produce a finite rate of change of transmission. Clearly the other extreme is when $t_i = 1$, when no further change in transmission can occur. Remembering that $n_p(0,t)$ is the incident photon flux, an expression may be derived from eq. (5.41) which relates intensity transmission to the exposure E, namely,

$$\int_0^T \frac{dt_i}{t_i(1-t_i)} = k_{21} \int_0^T n_p(0,t)\, dt = k_{21}E \tag{5.42}$$

where E is the exposure in total incident photons per unit area defined by

$$E = \int_0^T n_p(0,t)\, dt \tag{5.43}$$

Integration of eq. (5.42) by expansion in partial fractions yields

$$\frac{t_i}{1-t_i} = \frac{t_{i0}}{1-t_{i0}} e^E \tag{5.44}$$

where t_{i0} is the initial light intensity transmission. Rearranging terms, the following expressions are obtained:

$$t_i = \frac{[t_{i0}/(1-t_{i0})]e^E}{1 + [t_{i0}/(1-t_{i0})]e^E}$$

or

$$t_i = \frac{t_{i0}}{(1-t_{i0})e^{-E} + t_{i0}} \tag{5.45}$$

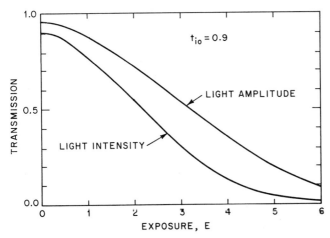

Fig. 5.17 Theoretical transmission characteristics for bulk photochromic materials.

In comparing the above results with that for the monolayer case note that formerly the maximum sensitivity, i.e., maximum change of transmission with exposure, was found at $t_i = 0$. This was also the nearest approach to linearity. Now, for the bulk photochromic, maximum sensitivity and the most linear portion of the characteristic occur when $t_i = 0.5$. Figure 5.17 illustrates this fact and provides as well the curve for amplitude transmission, $t_a = \sqrt{t_i}$. Taking the square root in eq. (5.45) and setting the second derivative of the result with respect to the exposure E equal to zero yield $e^E = 0.5$, $t_i = 0.33$, and $t_a = 1/\sqrt{3}$ for the point of maximum sensitivity in terms of amplitude transmission.

5.24 Noise and Dynamic Range in Photochromic Materials

An advantage of thin photochromic films for use as spatial light modulators is their essentially infinite resolution at the optical wavelength. The grain characteristic of silver halide emulsions is completely absent. This is, of course, because the light-modulating effect is a molecular phenomenon. Conversely this is the reason that such great energies are required for signal recording. For example, Knapp [5.16] reports that even with room-temperature quantum efficiencies of 25 percent the U-band to F-band conversion in KBr:H (to optical densities in the range of 2 to 3) requires about 10^{20} photons/cm². The F-band to U-band conversion in KBr:H proceeds at a quantum efficiency of less than 1 percent, implying that of the order of 10^{22} photons/cm² are required for complete bleaching. Either bleaching or formation of the complex bands of KCl:H has been found to require approximately 10^{19} photons/cm². Similar high-input-energy requirements are characteristic of the organic photochromics and photochromic glasses (see Figs. 5.12 to 5.15). In fact, from an information-theory point of view, the photochromic film is being used with gross inefficiency. Its capacity for information storage is probably thousands of bits per optical resolution element. It is unfortunate that astronomical numbers of photons must be poured into one element of such a film merely for the purpose of what is frequently a single bit recording.

In short, there appears, theoretically at least, to be more dynamic range in photochromic spatial light modulators that can sensibly be utilized in the coherent optical computer. Practical and repeatable confirmation of this fact is not yet available although some early, and as yet inconclusive, measurements have been reported [5.17].

As far as sources of noise are concerned, the organic photochromics in the form of films on plastic substrates exhibit almost all the mechanical distortion problems that are present in similarly mounted silver halide emulsions (Sec. 5.12). Thus a liquid gate is usually required, and careful control of the environment is necessary to avoid mechanical strain. This is less true of the inorganic photochromic crystals. The main source of noise in these materials is spatial-phase-modulation noise due to optical index nonuniformities. Quantitative data on such noise are lacking but it is understood that some such crystals are available with good optical quality over areas of a few square centimeters.

The optical quality of certain photochromic glasses is excellent and a liquid gate is unnecessary. The resolution of signals recorded in bulk material may, however, present quite different problems than do signal recordings on thin films. Interferometric recording, such as in Bragg-angle holography, may present one possible solution. The other course of action is the use of a thin film of photochromic glass, low-contrast recording, and carefully devised methods to remove the deleterious effects of the large amount of undiffracted (zero-order) light thus introduced into the optical system of the computer. When such thin photochromic glass films are utilized, recordings may be made at frequencies up to a few thousands of cycles per millimeter if desired. This is possible because of the 100 Å size of the embedded silver halide crystals. The low contrast of the recording in this case occurs because the distance between crystals is of the order of 10 times their diameter and because the concentration of the light-absorbing silver atoms within each crystal is low. This is quite different from high-resolution silver halide emulsions where crystals may be obtained in densely packed monolayers.

5.30 Thermoplastic Films

The spatial light modulators described in the preceding sections of this chapter are primarily spatial light amplitude modulators. This section and the two ensuing sections discuss spatial light modulators which are spatial phase modulators.

This section treats thermoplastic film which, like some of the photo-chromic materials, is a reusable medium for use in signal introduction into coherent optical computers. Thermoplastic film consists of a substrate (frequently Mylar) coated with a thin transparent conducting layer which in turn is overlaid with a thin film of low-melting-temperature plastic. The latter is the thermoplastic film which typically softens at approximately 100°C. Initially, during the erasure cycle, the thermo-plastic layer is heated above its softening temperature. The effect of surface tension is to pull the surface flat. Also, since the thermoplastic is relatively electrically conductive when heated, any residual electric charge is removed and the entire film is discharged to the potential of the transparent conductive underlayer.

After cooling to room temperature, the thermoplastic layer is recorded upon (usually in vacuum) by means of a scanning electron beam. Alternatively, when the thermoplastic film is made in a photo-conductive form, the film is first flooded with electrons which are then selectively removed during recording by means of exposure to light. The signal charge pattern recorded remains in place because of the high resistivity of the thermoplastic film when at room temperature.   Next, a second heating cycle is performed.   Now the softened thermoplastic film is under electrostatic pressure due to the recorded surface charge pattern.   The film deforms in accordance with the recorded pattern. The thermoplastic film, carrying the recorded signal in the form of thickness modulation, may be used in a coherent optical computer as an optical spatial phase modulator.

Assume, for example, that a sinusoidal signal is to be recorded on the thermoplastic film using an electron-beam current i_b given by

$$i_b(t) = \frac{i_{b0}}{2}(1 + m \sin \omega t) \tag{5.46}$$

where $i_{b0}/2$ is the average current, m is the modulation index, and ω is the radian temporal frequency.   If the velocity of the beam is v_b and the secondary electron emission ratio is negligible, then the recorded charge density is given by

$$q(x) = \frac{i_b}{v_b d_b} = \frac{q_0}{2}(1 + m \sin \omega_x x) \tag{5.47}$$

where $q_0 = i_{b0}/v_b d_b$, d_b is the beam diameter, x is a distance variable in the direction of scan, and ω_x is the radian spatial frequency ω/v_b.   The recorded charge pattern creates an electric field given in electrostatic units by $4\pi q/\epsilon$, where ϵ is the dielectric constant of the thermoplastic. When the thermoplastic is heated, the electrostatic force acting on the surface of the film is given by

$$F_E(x) = \frac{4\pi q^2(x)}{\epsilon} = \frac{\pi q_0^2}{\epsilon}(1 + m \sin \omega_x)^2 \tag{5.48}$$

In the special case where $m \ll 1$, $F_E(x)$ may be written as

$$F_E(x) \approx \frac{\pi q_0^2}{\epsilon}(1 + 2m \sin \omega_x x) \tag{5.49}$$

The differential equation which covers the deflection of an ideal liquid surface when a pressure function $p(x)$ is exerted upon it can be shown to be given by [5.18]

$$T_0 \frac{d^2 z}{dx^2} = p(x) + C_0 \tag{5.50}$$

where T_0 is the undisturbed surface tension of the liquid and z is in the direction of the deformation, i.e., perpendicular to x. Substituting eq. (5.49) in eq. (5.50) and solving for z as a function of x while using the boundary conditions that $z(0) = 0$ and assuming that the medium is incompressible over a full cycle, i.e., that

$$\int_{n/\omega_x}^{(n+2\pi)/\omega_x} z(x)\, dx = 0 \tag{5.51}$$

where $n = 0, 2\pi, 4\pi, \ldots$, yield

$$z(x) = -\frac{2\pi q_0^2}{\epsilon T_0 \omega_x^2} m \sin \omega_x x \tag{5.52}$$

Equation (5.52) demonstrates that (for small values of m) the amplitude deformation falls off as the square of the spatial frequency. This may be compensated for by means of a 12 dB/octave electronic filter in the input amplifier which controls the electron beam. By this mechanism,

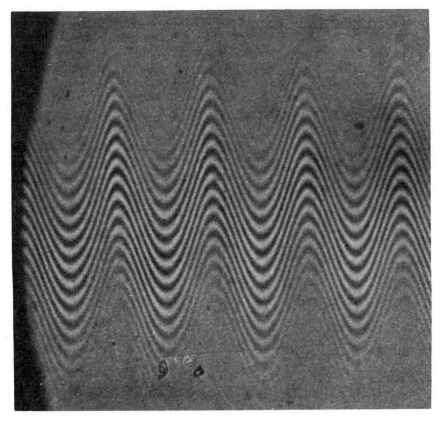

Fig. 5.18   Interferomicrogram of a sinusoidal recording made on thermoplastic film.

it would be possible to preserve signal fidelity in the recording over the frequency band of interest.

Deformation of the thermoplastic film takes place in a time related to the viscosity of the liquefied thermoplastic.   The time constant τ is given by

$$\tau = \frac{2\xi}{\omega_x T_0} \tag{5.53}$$

where ξ is the viscosity.

Glenn and Wolfe [5.19] report that τ is found to be of the order of tenths of a second, whereas the $\rho\epsilon$ time constant for charge decay is

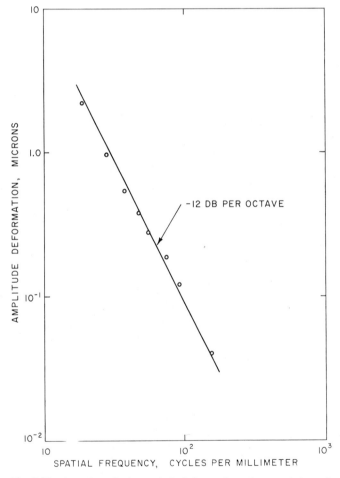

Fig. 5.19 Actual and theoretical deformation characteristics of thermoplastic film.

hundreds of times longer because of the relatively high resistivity ρ of typical thermoplastic materials even when heated.

Figure 5.18 is a microinterferogram due to Tobin [5.20] made of the deformed surface of a 25-μm-thick thermoplastic film. The film was deformed by heating after a sinusoidally varying charge pattern had been recorded. The area shown is approximately 0.2 mm square, and the spatial frequency of the recording is 20 cycles/mm. The corresponding deformation versus spatial frequency curve is shown in Fig. 5.19 and, although charge modulation was not measured, it is of interest to note the close correspondence of measured values to the theoretical 12 dB/octave falloff over the range of 20 to 160 cycles/mm.

5.31 Noise and Dynamic Range in Thermoplastic Films Besides noise due to both lateral and longitudinal mechanical distortion (see Sec. 5.12), thermoplastic-film spatial light modulators are subject to certain other noise problems when used in coherent optical computers. First, there is the practical problem that, even in the cleanest environment, the surface of the thermoplastic film gradually picks up foreign material during the repeated heating cycles which are necessary for erasure and surface deformation. Two problems ensue:

1. The amount of light scattered randomly by the thermoplastic film into the coherent optical computer increases, thus decreasing dynamic range and the output signal-to-noise ratio.

2. Dead spots appear in the thermoplastic film where the surface, stiffened by accumulated foreign material, fails to deform in response to the recorded charge pattern.

These problems may be combated by careful design to exclude all contaminants from the system or by merely limiting the use of the thermoplastic material to a finite number of record-erase cycles.

Another source of noise is the creation of intermodulation distortion. Equation (5.48) indicates that, in general, the square of the applied signal is recorded. If, for example, the signal is composed of two sinusoidal components, the recorded charge density becomes

$$q(x) = \frac{q_0}{2}(1 + m_1 \sin \omega_{x1} x + m_2 \sin \omega_{x2} x) \tag{5.54}$$

where m_1 and m_2 are the modulation indices associated with the recorded spatial frequencies ω_{x1} and ω_{x2}, respectively. Substitution of eq. (5.54) in eq. (5.48) yields the distortion terms $m_1^2 \cos 2\omega_{x1}$, $m_2^2 \cos 2\omega_{x2}$, $m_1 m_2 \cos(\omega_{x1} + \omega_{x2})$, and $m_1 m_2 \cos(\omega_{x1} - \omega_{x2})$. Thus spurious signals are created which, unless the bandwidth is limited to a narrow region about some carrier frequency, will fall within the bandwidth of interest. In general, all Fourier components of any recorded signal will be intermodulated in the thermoplastic recording process. Intermodulation distortion in the recording may be combated, as already discussed, by means of recording with a low modulation index at the expense of less efficient use of the deposited charge. Another alternative, of course, is to modulate the recording electron beam with the square root of the signal to be recorded. However, this strategy coupled with the requirement of a 12 dB/octave filter in the electronics of the recording system may at times be difficult to instrument, especially for broadband video signals.

There is another source of noise which is inherent to optical spatial phase modulation. Once a sinusoidal thermoplastic recording has been produced and introduced in the input aperture of a coherent optical computer, it will spatially phase-modulate the incident illumination. Using the notation developed in Chapter Four, the resultant electric field distribution may be written as

$$E(x_1, y_1) = E_m e^{j[-\omega_L t + \phi(x_1, y_1)]} \tag{5.55}$$

Neglecting the temporal frequency term, limiting the discussion to a simple one-dimensional sinusoidal recording as expressed by eq. (5.52), and assuming an incident wave propagating in the positive z direction, eq. (5.55) becomes

$$E(x_1) = E_m e^{j\phi_m \sin \omega_x x_1} \tag{5.56}$$

where $\phi_m = 2\pi q_0^2 m (n_t - 1)/\epsilon T_0 \omega_x^2 \lambda_L$. Here λ_L is the optical wavelength and n_t is the optical index of the thermoplastic. Using eq. (4.92), eq. (5.56) may be expressed in a Bessel expansion as

$$E(x_1) = \sum_{n=-\infty}^{n=+\infty} J_n(\phi_m) e^{jn\omega_x x_1} \tag{5.57}$$

for the normalized case where $E_m = 1$. An equivalent form of eq. (5.57) which is more useful for the purpose of this discussion is given by

$$E(x_1) = J_0(\phi_m) + 2 \int_{n=1}^{n=+\infty} J_{2n}(\phi_m) \cos 2n\omega_x x_1$$

$$+ 2j \int_{n=1}^{n=+\infty} J_{2n-1}(\phi_m) \sin (2n-1)\omega_x x_1 \tag{5.58}$$

Equation (5.58) makes it clear that the electric field distribution produced by the interaction of an incident plane wave of light with an ideal sinusoidal thermoplastic recording is composed of an infinity of sinusoidal terms whose amplitude coefficients are given by Bessel functions of the first kind and of all positive integral orders. By the diffraction theorem (Sec. 4.20) it can be said that the result of this interaction is the production of an infinity of new plane waves of light propagating in the space beyond the thermoplastic recording. An optical computer using a thermoplastic spatial light modulator must, therefore, have a lens system which accepts all these new plane waves which have significant energy. For example, for the recording shown in Fig. 5.18 where the peak-to-peak phase modulation in reflection is 5 wavelengths, ϕ_m in transmission would be approximately 0.7 wavelength or 1.4π rad. Using $\phi_m = 1.4\pi$ as the argument of the Bessel function, it is easy to determine that significant energy occurs in the resultant new plane waves out to $n = 6$. Thus, although the recording shown in Fig. 5.18 is at 20 cycles/min, the associated optical system would have to handle coherently all spatial frequencies out to 120 cycles/mm.

When the lens system of the optical computer cannot handle the plane waves created by the interaction of the illuminating light wave with the thermoplastic input recording at all significant spatial frequencies, the resultant distortion of the input signal within the optical system is similar to the effect which occurs when significant terms are omitted from a series expansion of the input signal. Thus, this effect is called *truncation noise* and is equivalent to what is called *vignetting* in optical parlance. Truncation noise may, of course, be combated by keeping the value of ϕ_m small at the expense of increasing the zero-order term $J_0(\phi_m)$ in eq. (5.58). Large relative values of $J_0(\phi_m)$ cause an increase in output noise due to zero-order side lobes in the computer output plane. This condition also results in a less efficient use of coherent optical power in the computer. Therefore, in using an optical spatial phase modulator such as thermoplastic film, the coherent-optical-computer designer must balance the cost of complexity in the lens system against the benefit of increased dynamic range and low optical-power requirements.

5.40   Deflectable Membrane Mirrors

The membrane light modulator, or MLM, initially described by Preston [5.21] is an optical spatial phase modulator which phase-modulates light reflected from its surface. Phase modulation is accomplished by electrostatic surface deformation of discrete phase-modulating surface elements. Two types of membrane light modulators exist:

1. The wired membrane light modulator in which surface deformations are produced by means of signals applied to stripe electrodes underlying the mirror surface

2. The photosensitive-membrane light modulator where surface deformations occur on the mirror side of the device in response to the local light intensity level present on the opposite side of the device,

Figure 5.20 shows a sectional view of a portion of a wired MLM. The device is formed by depositing stripe electrodes on an optically flat glass substrate over which a thin dielectric layer is deposited. Microscopic perforations are formed in the dielectric layer, using standard photolithographic techniques. The perforation diameter may be 5 to 100 μm with a depth of the order of 1 μm. Overlying the perforated layer is the membrane mirror. It is usually made of a polymer, such as collodion, 0.1 μm thick and metallized to enhance reflectivity. The metallized surface must also be sufficiently conductive so that it can be held at a fixed electric potential.

Voltages impressed on the stripe electrodes produce an electrostatic attraction between the membrane metallization and the electrode, causing all unsupported regions of the membrane mirror associated with the electrode to deform. For circular perforations the deformation is paraboloidal. Signal voltages of the order of a few tens of volts are sufficient to produce a half-wavelength deformation at the center of each paraboloid, thus causing a full 360° phase reversal of the reflected light at this point.

As discussed later in this section, the resonant frequency of the membrane elements of a wired MLM is in the 1 to 10 MHz range, and the time response is from 0.1 to 1 μs. In using the wired MLM certain problems arise because of oscillatory vibrations of the membrane elements when excited at resonance. These problems can usually be solved by either mechanical or electrical damping, as discussed in Sec. 5.41.

The wired MLM, when used as the input transducer in a coherent

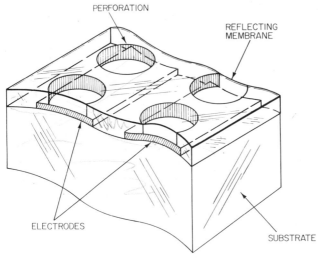

PERFORATION

REFLECTING MEMBRANE

ELECTRODES

SUBSTRATE

Fig. 5.20   Direct-wired membrane light modulator.

optical computer, is capable of handling only one-dimensional signals. This is true because the phase modulation is identical along the entire length of each stripe electrode and varies only from electrode to electrode.   In order to produce an MLM which is a two-dimensional optical spatial phase modulator, the photosensitive-membrane light modulator, or photo-MLM, has been devised as reported by Reizman [5.22].   Figure 5.21 shows a sectional view of this device.   It is constructed from a semiconductor crystal, such as n-type silicon, sliced and polished to a thickness of 50 to 100 μm.   An array of p-n-junction diodes is diffused into the mirror side of the device, with one diode for each membrane element.   Next, a perforated layer of a highly resistive material, such as a semi-insulating glass, is deposited.   The resistivity of this layer is chosen to be intermediate between the effective dark resistivity of the p-n-junction diodes and their effective resistivity when fully illuminated. A perforated collecting electrode is next deposited so as to make ohmic contact with the resistive layer.   The metallized polymer membrane is then applied over the entire structure.   Finally, the side of the photosensitive MLM opposite to the membrane mirror surface is heavily doped in a shallow diffusion.   This diffusion forms an electrode which is transparent in the long-wavelength region of the visible and in the near infrared.

To use the photo-MLM a potential of a few tens of volts is applied between the collecting electrode and the transparent electrode of a polarity such as to back-bias all members of the p-n-junction diode array.   The metallization on the membrane mirror is usually held at the same potential as the collecting electrode.   When the input side of the photo-MLM, i.e., the side opposite the mirror surface, is not illuminated, most of the applied voltage appears across the p-n junctions.   Thus there is little or no potential to deflect the elements of the membrane

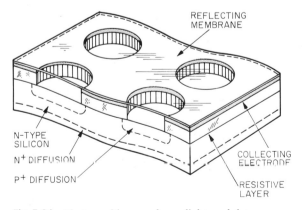

Fig. 5.21   Photosensitive-membrane light modulator.

mirror and essentially no surface deformation occurs. When light is allowed to impinge at a point on the input side of the photo-MLM, hole-electron pairs are created. Holes diffuse toward the p regions, are collected by the nearest p-n junction, and are swept through its depletion layer. The current so created flows through the associated portion of the resistive layer and produces a potential difference between the p region of the p-n-junction diode and the metallization on the membrane. This causes the associated membrane element to deflect.

In general, the deformation D_{ij} of the ijth membrane element will be a function of the input light intensity distribution $I(x_1, y_1)$ at the input side of the device, namely,

$$D_{ij} \propto \iint_{R_{ij}} I(x_1, y_1) \, dx_1 \, dy_1 \tag{5.59}$$

where R_{ij} is the region over which the ijth p-n-junction diode collects holes generated by $I(x_1, y_1)$. The proportionality (5.59) is nonlinear as, for example, R_{ij} is dependent upon $I(x_1, y_1)$. The phase modulation of light reflected from the mirror surface is given by

$$\phi(x_1, y_1) = \sum_{ij} D_{ij} f_d(x, y) * \delta(x - x_i, y - y_j) \tag{5.60}$$

where $f_d(x, y)$ is the deformation function, the asterisk indicates convolution, and δ is the Dirac delta function.

In order to determine the deformation function for the membrane light modulator, the classic membrane equation must be solved with the appropriate boundary conditions. Letting T_0 be the initial surface tension of the membrane and F_E the electrostatic force acting upon it, the membrane equation in polar coordinates is given by

$$T_0 \left(\frac{d^2 z}{dr^2} + \frac{1}{r} \frac{dz}{dr} \right) = F_E \tag{5.61}$$

The electrostatic force F_E is given by $4\pi q^2/\epsilon$, where q is the charge density in esu and ϵ is the dielectric constant. The charge density is in turn given by $\epsilon V/4\pi d$, where V is the voltage in esu and d is the depth of the perforation in centimeters. Assuming that the medium between the metallization on the membrane element and the associated electrode is almost entirely air or vacuum, $\epsilon \approx 1$ and eq. (5.61) becomes

$$\frac{d^2 z}{dr^2} + \frac{1}{r} \frac{dz}{dr} = \frac{V^2}{4\pi T_0 d^2} \tag{5.62}$$

Assuming that the increase in tension due to strain of the membrane during deformation is negligible and applying the boundary condition

$$z|_{r = \pm(D/2)} = 0 \tag{5.63}$$

where D is the diameter of the membrane element, lead to a solution of eq. (5.62) given by

$$z = \frac{V^2 r^2}{16\pi T_0 d^2} - z_m \qquad (5.64)$$

where z_m is the maximum deflection and is given by

$$z_m = \frac{V^2 D^2}{64\pi T_0 d^2} \qquad (5.65)$$

The dynamic response of a membrane element is also of interest in order to predict resonant frequency and calculate response time. In order to determine the dynamic response, the electrostatic force F_E in eq. (5.61) is replaced by the dynamic force F_D given by

$$F_D = (m_c t_c + m_m t_m)\frac{d^2 z}{dt^2} \qquad (5.66)$$

where m_c is the density of the metallization, t_c is the thickness of the metallization, m_m is the density of the membrane, and t_m is the thickness of the membrane. Combining eqs. (5.61) and (5.66) yields the membrane equation in its dynamic form, namely,

$$T_0 \left(\frac{\partial^2 t}{\partial r^2} + \frac{1}{r}\frac{\partial^2 z}{\partial r}\right) = m_T \frac{\partial^2 z}{\partial t^2} \qquad (5.67)$$

where $m_T = m_c t_c + m_m t_m$ and has the units of mass per unit area. The general solution which satisfies the boundary condition given by eq. (5.63) may be written as

$$z(r,t) = \sum_{k=1}^{k=\infty} A_k J_0\left(\sqrt{\frac{m_T}{T_0}}\,\omega_n r\right)\cos \omega_n t \qquad (5.68)$$

where the A_k are the coefficients of the Bessel series expansion of the initial deflection, $z(r,0)$, and ω_n is given by

$$\omega_n = \frac{2n}{D}\sqrt{\frac{T_0}{m_T}} \qquad (5.69)$$

and n is derived from the equation $J_0(n) = 0$, where J_0 is the Bessel function of the first kind of order zero.

5.41 Noise and Dynamic Range in Deflectable Membrane Mirrors

The membrane light modulator, like thermoplastic film, is a strong-effect optical spatial phase modulator. It is therefore subject to truncation noise (see Sec. 5.31) as is discussed below. Also described in this section is membrane-light-modulator noise due to surface irregularities, undamped mechanical oscillations, hysteresis, and intermodulation.

In order to analyze truncation noise, it is necessary to calculate the electric field distribution produced by the membrane light modulator. Note that MLM is a discrete phase modulator rather than a continuous phase modulator like thermoplastic film. Each membrane element deflects as a paraboloid producing an electric field in reflection given in polar coordinates:

$$E(r_1) = E_m e^{j[-\omega_L t + \phi(r_1)]} \tag{5.70}$$

$$\phi(r_1) = \begin{cases} \phi_m \left(1 - \dfrac{r_1^2}{R^2}\right) & 0 \leqslant r_1 \leqslant R \\[2ex] 0 & r_1 > R \end{cases} \tag{5.71}$$

where $\phi_m = 4\pi z_m/\lambda_L$ and R is the radius of the membrane element. Using the diffraction theorem (Sec. 4.20), the electric field distribution given by eqs. (5.70) and (5.71) may be decomposed into an infinity of new plane waves propagating in the space beyond the MLM by the use of eq. (4.34). Expressing eq. (4.33) in polar coordinates yields

$$E(\cos \alpha, \cos \beta) = \frac{E_m}{2\pi} \int\limits_0^R \int\limits_0^{2\pi} e^{j[\phi_m(1 - r_1^2/R^2) - \omega_x r_1 \cos \theta_1 - \omega_y r_1 \sin \theta_1]} r_1 \, dr_1 \, d\theta_1$$

$$+ \frac{E_m}{2\pi} \int\limits_R^\infty \int\limits_0^{2\pi} e^{-j(\omega_x r_1 \cos \theta_1 + \omega_y r_1 \sin \theta_1)} r_1 \, dr_1 \, d\theta_1 \tag{5.72}$$

where $\omega_x = (2\pi \cos \alpha)/\lambda_L$ and $\omega_y = (2\pi \cos \beta)/\lambda_L$. Because of the angular symmetry of $E(r_1)$ either of the direction cosines may arbitrarily be set equal to zero in solving eq. (5.72). Letting $\cos \beta = 0$, replacing $\cos \alpha$ with $\sin \gamma$, and rearranging, the limits of integration yield

$$E(\omega_r) = \frac{E_m}{2\pi} \int\limits_0^\infty \int\limits_0^{2\pi} e^{-j\omega_r r_1 \cos \theta_r} r_1 \, dr_1 \, d\theta_1$$

$$+ \frac{E_m}{2\pi} \int\limits_0^R \int\limits_0^{2\pi} (e^{j[\phi_m(1 - r_1^2/R^2) - \omega_r r_1 \cos \theta]} - 1) r_1 \, dr_1 \, d\theta_1 \tag{5.73}$$

where $\omega_r = (2\pi \sin \gamma)/\lambda_L$. Noting that the first term in eq. (5.73) is merely a delta function at $\omega_r = 0$ and recalling that

$$\int_0^\pi e^{j\xi\cos\eta}\,d\eta = 2\pi J_0(\xi) \qquad (5.74)$$

allow eq. (5.73) to be simplified as follows:

$$E(\omega_r) = \delta(\omega_r - 0) + E_m \int_0^R (e^{j\phi_m(1-r^2/R^2)} - 1) J_0(\omega_r r_1) r_1 \, dr_1 \qquad (5.75)$$

Normalizing to unit field and unit diameter, that is, $E_m = 1$ and $2R = 1$, and defining the P functions $P(n, \phi_m)$ by

$$P(n, \phi_m) = \frac{1}{2\pi} \int_0^{0\cdot 5} (e^{j\phi_m(1-4r^2)} - 1) J_0(2\pi n r) r \, dr \, d\theta \qquad (5.76)$$

yields

$$E(\omega_r) = \delta(\omega_r - 0) + 2\pi P\left(\frac{\omega_r}{2\pi}, \phi_m\right) \qquad (5.77)$$

The P functions for certain values of ϕ_m and n are tabulated in the Appendix. The latter quantity is the normalized spatial frequency in cycles across one membrane element of unit diameter. The square of the modulus of the P function is graphed in Fig. 5.22 as a function of n with ϕ_m as a parameter. From Fig. 5.22 it is possible to determine the effect of truncation noise for any particular MLM design. For example, if an MLM is to be used with peak deflections which yield a peak phase modulation of $360°$ ($\phi_m = 2\pi$), then significant energy appears out to $n \approx 3$. Thus, if the diameter of the MLM is D (in millimeters), the associated lens system must handle coherently all spatial frequencies out to approximately $3/D$ (in cycles per millimeter). Only by so doing is it possible to reproduce faithfully the phase of the electric field distribution produced by the MLM at image planes within the optical system of the optical computer.

In addition to truncation noise, mechanical oscillations of the light-modulating elements of the MLM can degrade computer performance if it is desired to perform calculations at a rate near the resonant frequency of the MLM. Figure 5.23 illustrates the temporal step response of an MLM computer with the associated MLM operating in vacuum as well as with air damping. It is apparent that air damping is desirable in order to prevent oscillations. However, when the membrane light modulator operates in an air ambient, deflection of a membrane element compresses the air molecules which are trapped in the perforation between the membrane and the underlying electrode. Since the membrane is porous, some of the air molecules diffuse through it and, for extended deflection times, the pressure on either side of the deflected membrane is equalized. Now, when the input signal is removed,

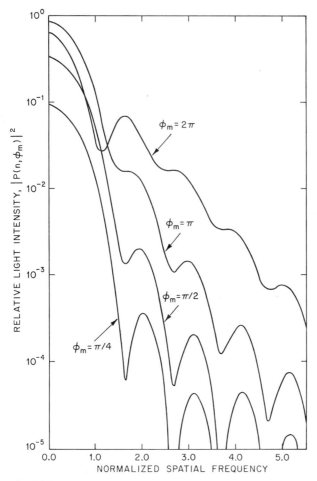

Fig. 5.22 Modulus of the P function plotted against normalized spatial frequency (cycles across the aperture).

the membrane does not return to its initial undeformed state until a number of air molecules equal to those which originally diffused out of the perforation have returned. Diffusion times of many seconds have been observed.

Since the membrane light modulator responds to the square of the applied voltage in a manner essentially similar to thermoplastic film, intermodulation noise may be created unless (1) a large bias term is added to the input signal or (2) the square root of the input signal is used. Since one of the advantages of the MLM is that it can be used as a strong-effect phase modulator operating over a range of many radians, it is usual in most coherent optical computers using the MLM to create

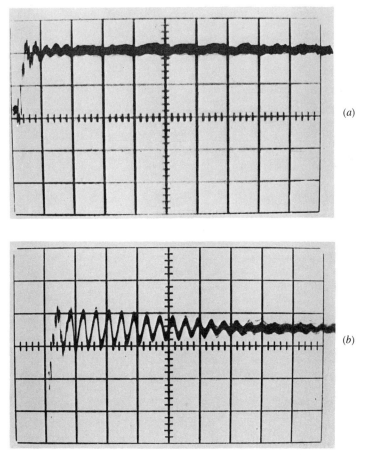

Fig. 5.23 Time-response characteristic of the membrane light modulator: (a) in air; (b) in vacuum.

an energizing voltage proportional to the square root of the input signal in order to avoid intermodulation noise.

Finally, it should be mentioned that the optical quality of the surface of the membrane light modulator is equivalent to that of a good optical flat; i.e., in its undeflected state the MLM surface may be fabricated flat to one-tenth of an optical wavelength or better.   A microinterferogram of a small portion of the surface of an MLM showing both deflected and undeflected elements is shown in Fig. 5.24 for reference.   Measurements indicate that only 1 or 2 percent of the incident light energy is diffracted by surface irregularities, with the balance of the diffracted energy being accounted for either by the action of the applied signal or by aperture effects as discussed in Sec. 5.31.

Fig. 5.24 Interferomicrogram of the surface of a membrane light modulator having rows of 38-μm-diameter elements on 50-μm centers.

5.50   Elastooptic Delay Lines

The optical spatial phase modulator which has been used most frequently as an input transducer in coherent optical computers is the transparent acoustic-delay-line light modulator.   In this device the input signal appears in the form of a traveling acoustic wave in either a liquid or solid medium.   By illuminating the delay-line medium appropriately, spatial phase modulation of the incident light wave is produced.   This interaction between light and sound is due to the elastooptic coupling which exists between strains produced in the medium by the sound wave and the dielectric constants of the medium.   Alternatively, this effect can be regarded from the quantum-mechanical point of view as a phonon-photon interaction.

The interaction of light and sound has been extensively investigated. Historically it was first predicted by Brillouin [5.23] in 1921.   In the early 1930s Debye and Sears [5.24] as well as Lucas and Biquard [5.25] made initial experimental demonstrations.   Later in the 1930s, applications of the effect to television signal processing, of which Okolicsanyi's [5.26] is typical, were devised.   It was not until the 1950s that thought was given to the application of this effect in coherent optical computation.   At that time Rosenthal [5.27], for example, described an application to radar signal processing.   Since that time the effect has been extensively exploited by Lambert [5.28], Preston [5.29], Slobodin and Reich [5.30], and a host of other workers (see Sec. 9.30).   The interested reader is referred at this point to an analytical treatise by Gill [5.31] which reviews this subject rigorously.

It is beyond the scope of this book to do more than present to the reader the fundamental concepts of elastooptic spatial light modulators, with particular emphasis on their use in coherent optical computation. Although both liquid, solid, and crystalline elastooptic-delay-line light modulators have been investigated as input signal transducers for coherent optical computers, this section concentrates on such devices using homogeneous isotropic solids as being of greatest importance at the present time. The use of water as well as certain simple crystalline materials is briefly mentioned.

In general, the interaction of any electromagnetic radiation with a sound wave is described by the so-called "optical index ellipsoid" [5.32]. In a crystalline material the axes of this ellipsoid are chosen in the direction of the principal axes of the crystal. In a homogeneous solid the index ellipsoid can be shown to degenerate into a sphere in the absence of an acoustic disturbance. In this case the choice of the directions of the principal axes is arbitrary. Usually, however, it is useful to select one axis in the direction of acoustic propagation.

The equation which defines the index ellipsoid is

$$\sum_{j=1}^{j=3} \sum_{i=1}^{i=3} B_{ij} x_i x_j = 1 \tag{5.78}$$

where B_{ij} is the so-called "impermeability tensor" and may be expressed in terms of the elastooptic constants p_{ijkl} and the strains s_{kl} as follows:

$$B_{ij} - \frac{\delta_{ij}}{n_i^2} = \sum_{k=1}^{k=3} \sum_{l=1}^{l=3} p_{ijkl} s_{kl} \tag{5.79}$$

where δ_{ij} is the Kronecker delta function and the n_i are the optical indices in the direction of the principal axes. Note that strains having $k = l$ are customarily taken as longitudinal strains, with the situation where $k \neq l$ referring to transverse or shear strains. The convention is that s_{23} is the shear strain about the x_1 axis; s_{13}, about the x_2 axis; and s_{12}, about the x_3 axis. Finally, symmetry considerations lead to the equations

$$\begin{aligned} B_{ij} &= B_{ji} \\ s_{kl} &= s_{lk} \\ p_{ijkl} &= p_{jilk} \end{aligned} \tag{5.80}$$

As is discussed in some detail by Bernstein et al. [5.33], the effect of strains produced in a solid by an acoustic wave upon a plane wave of light passing through the solid may be evaluated by an analysis of the so-called "index ellipse." This ellipse is formed by the intersection with the index ellipsoid of a plane through the origin normal to the direction of optical propagation. In general, the light wave leaving the solid will be found to be divided into two linearly polarized waves having their directions of polarization along the major and minor axes of the index ellipse. Furthermore, the velocities of optical propagation in the solid will be inversely proportional to the lengths of the major and minor axes of the ellipse. This, of course, is the phenomenon called *birefringence*.

In this section, two special cases of interest are treated, both of which are related to homogeneous solids. The interested reader is referred to Spencer et al. [5.34] and Maloney and Carleton [5.35] for information on spatial-light-modulating effects in certain crystalline materials. In the case of a homogeneous, isotropic solid, many of the elastooptic constants p_{ijkl} are zero, and the nonzero constants are abbreviated as follows:

$$
\begin{aligned}
p_{11} &= p_{1111} = p_{2222} = p_{3333} \\
p_{12} &= p_{1122} = p_{1133} = p_{2211} = p_{2233} = p_{3311} = p_{3322} \\
p_{44} &= 2p_{2323} = 2p_{1313} = 2p_{1212}
\end{aligned}
\tag{5.81}
$$

The matrix of elastooptic constants may then be represented in what is called the "reduced form" by

$$
\mathbf{P} =
\begin{bmatrix}
p_{11} & p_{12} & p_{12} & 0 & 0 & 0 \\
p_{12} & p_{11} & p_{12} & 0 & 0 & 0 \\
p_{12} & p_{12} & p_{11} & 0 & 0 & 0 \\
0 & 0 & 0 & p_{44} & 0 & 0 \\
0 & 0 & 0 & 0 & p_{44} & 0 \\
0 & 0 & 0 & 0 & 0 & p_{44}
\end{bmatrix}
\tag{5.82}
$$

First consider a longitudinal acoustic wave propagating along the x_1 axis. All strains are zero except for s_{11}, and the B_{ij} are therefore given by eq. (5.79) as follows:

$$
B_{11} = \frac{1}{n_0^2} + p_{11}s_{11}
$$

$$
B_{22} = \frac{1}{n_0^2} + p_{12}s_{11}
\tag{5.83}
$$

$$
B_{33} = \frac{1}{n_0^2} + p_{12}s_{11}
$$

where n_0 is the optical index of the undisturbed medium. The equation of the optical index ellipsoid is

$$\left(\frac{1}{n_0^2}+p_{11}s_{11}\right)x_1^2+\left(\frac{1}{n_0^2}+p_{12}s_{11}\right)x_2^2+\left(\frac{1}{n_0^2}+p_{12}s_{11}\right)x_3^2=1 \qquad (5.84)$$

If it is assumed that the direction of optical propagation is along the x_3 axis, then the optical index ellipse of interest is given by

$$\left(\frac{1}{n_0^2}+p_{11}s_{11}\right)x_1^2+\left(\frac{1}{n_0^2}+p_{12}s_{11}\right)x_2^2=1 \qquad (5.85)$$

If it is assumed that, for typical strains, $n_0^2 p_{11}s_{11} \ll 1$, the optical indices along the principal axes of this ellipse are given by

$$n_1 = \left(\frac{1}{n_0^2}+p_{11}s_{11}\right)^{-1/2} \approx n_0 - \tfrac{1}{2}n_0^3 p_{11}s_{11}$$

$$n_2 = \left(\frac{1}{n_0^2}+p_{12}s_{11}\right)^{-1/2} \approx n_0 - \tfrac{1}{2}n_0^3 p_{12}s_{11} \qquad (5.86)$$

Thus the effect of a longitudinal wave in a homogeneous solid is to change the optical index by $-n_0^3 p_{11}s_{11}/2$ for light incident along the x_3 axis and polarized in the direction of acoustic propagation and by $-n_0^3 p_{12}s_{11}/2$ for polarization perpendicular to the direction of acoustic propagation. For an incident light wave of any general polarization, the interaction is described by a Jones matrix which is given by

$$\mathbf{L} = \begin{bmatrix} e^{-j(\pi n_0^3 p_{11}s_{11}L/\lambda_L)} & 0 \\ 0 & e^{-j(\pi n_0^3 p_{12}s_{11}L/\lambda_L)} \end{bmatrix} \qquad (5.87)$$

where L is the path length through the medium in the x_3 direction.

Next consider a shear wave about the x_3 axis where all strains are zero except s_{12} so that the only nonzero B_{ij} is B_{12} which is equal to the quantity $p_{44}s_{12}$. The equation of the optical index ellipsoid becomes

$$\frac{x_1^2}{n_0^2}+\frac{x_2^2}{n_0^2}+\frac{x_3^2}{n_0^2}+2p_{44}s_{12}x_2x_2=1 \qquad (5.88)$$

Again assuming that the direction of optical propagation is along the x_3 axis, the equation of the optical index ellipse is given by

$$\frac{x_1^2}{n_0^2}+\frac{x_2^2}{n_0^2}+2p_{44}s_{12}x_1x_2=1 \qquad (5.89)$$

That principal axis of this ellipse lies along an axis inclined at 45° to the x_1 axis may be demonstrated by a rotation of the coordinate system by 45°, using the coordinate transformation

$$x_1 = \frac{x_1'}{2} - \frac{x_2'}{2} \qquad x_2 = \frac{x_1'}{2} + \frac{x_2'}{2} \qquad (5.90)$$

It is useful to note at this point that this coordinate transformation in matrix notation is expressed by $\mathbf{X} = \mathbf{T}\mathbf{X}'$, where the transformation matrix $\mathbf{T}$ is given by

$$\mathbf{T} = \begin{bmatrix} \cos\theta & -\sin\theta \\ \sin\theta & \cos\theta \end{bmatrix} \tag{5.91}$$

and $\sin\theta = \cos\theta = 1/\sqrt{2}$. Substitution of eq. (5.90) in eq. (5.89) yields

$$\left(\frac{1}{n_0^2} + p_{44}s_{12}\right)x_1'^2 + \left(\frac{1}{n_0^2} - p_{44}s_{12}\right)x_2'^2 = 1 \tag{5.92}$$

from which it can be seen that the optical indices along the principal axes are given by

$$n_1' = \left(\frac{1}{n_0^2} + p_{44}s_{12}\right)^{-1/2} \approx n_0 - \tfrac{1}{2}n_0^3 p_{44}s_{12}$$

$$n_2' = \left(\frac{1}{n_0^2} - p_{44}s_{12}\right)^{-1/2} \approx n_0 + \tfrac{1}{2}n_0^3 p_{44}s_{12} \tag{5.93}$$

if it is assumed that $n_0^2 p_{44}s_{12} \ll 1$. Therefore, the Jones matrix for light incident in the x_3 direction upon a shear-mode acoustic wave sheared about the x_3 axis and traveling in the x_1 direction in a homogeneous isotropic solid as related to the transformed coordinates is

$$\mathbf{L}' = \begin{bmatrix} e^{-j(\pi n_0^3 p_{44}s_{12}L/\lambda_L)} & 0 \\ 0 & e^{j(\pi n_0^3 p_{44}s_{12}L/\lambda_L)} \end{bmatrix} \tag{5.94}$$

The Jones matrix in the original coordinate system is obtained as follows:

$$\mathbf{L} = \mathbf{T}^{-1}\mathbf{L}'\mathbf{T} = \begin{bmatrix} \cos\dfrac{\pi n_0^3 p_{44}s_{12}L}{\lambda_L} & j\sin\dfrac{\pi n_0^3 p_{44}s_{12}L}{\lambda_L} \\ j\sin\dfrac{\pi n_0^3 p_{44}s_{12}L}{\lambda_L} & \cos\dfrac{\pi n_0^3 p_{44}s_{12}L}{\lambda_L} \end{bmatrix} \tag{5.95}$$

where $\mathbf{T}^{-1}$ is the inverse of the coordinate transformation matrix.

Figure 5.25 compares the deformation of the optical index ellipse for the case of both longitudinal and shear-mode acoustic waves traveling in a homogeneous solid. The direction of optical propagation is assumed perpendicular to the plane of the page. In the case of a longitudinal acoustic wave the ellipse shrinks for positive strain and enlarges for negative strain. It is worth mentioning at this point that for a longitudinal wave in a liquid $p_{11} = p_{12}$. In this case, the optical index ellipse degenerates into a circle whose radius decreases with

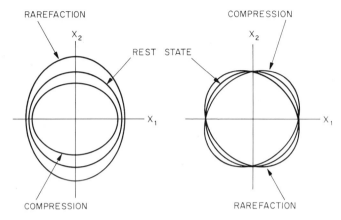

Fig. 5.25   Deformation of the index ellipsoid for both longitudinal (left) and shear (right) excitation.

positive strain and increases with negative strain.   In the case of a shear acoustic wave the expansion and contraction of the principal axes of the optical index ellipse are out of phase so that as one shrinks the other expands.

5.51   Bulk Diffraction Effects in Elastooptic Delay Lines   When an elastooptic delay line is used as an input transducer in a coherent optical computer, the incident light interacts with a traveling acoustic wave which is modulated by some input signal $s(t)$.   The strains which are produced, therefore, take the form given by

$$s_{ij}(x_1, t) = C_{ij}s(x_1 - v_s t) \tag{5.96}$$

where the C_{ij} are the appropriate proportionality constants and v_s is the velocity of sound.   (Note that, since longitudinal and shear-mode acoustic velocities are in general not equal, it is possible to generate two signal waves simultaneously.   This condition is, of course, usually avoided.)   Unlike the thin-film light modulators considered elsewhere in this chapter, the delay-line light modulator modulates light by a bulk effect which takes place over a large region in the body of the elastooptic medium.   The elastooptic interaction between the incident light and the acoustic wave is exceedingly complex.   The general case for arbitrarily large strains and arbitrarily long interaction distances has never been completely calculated.   Because of the fact that the inter-action is typically a weak effect, many simplifying assumptions may be made which lead to a reasonably tractable analysis.

The analysis in this section makes the assumption that only a small amount of the light is diffracted, i.e., that only weak optical phase modulation occurs. Based on this assumption, it is shown how the amount of light diffracted depends upon certain variables, namely:

1. The distance in the medium over which the elastooptic interaction takes place

2. The bandwidth of the input signal

3. Departure of the direction of incident light from a condition parallel to the x_3 axis

4. The physical parameters of the acoustic medium

The interested reader is referred to Klein and Cook [5.36], Dixon [5.37], and Born and Wolf [5.38] for various treatments of this problem.

The traveling acoustic wave given by eq. (5.96) may be expanded in a Fourier series; i.e., it may be thought of as a linear superposition of simple sinusoidal components. Consider at first the light-modulating action of only one of the sinusoidal components of the acoustic wave. This component is pictured in Fig. 5.26 traveling in the x_1 direction. The region of the acoustic medium which is occupied by the acoustic wave can be considered to be divided into a plurality of slabs perpendicular to the x_3 axis and each of width Δx_3. Each slab acts to spatially phase-modulate the incident light as described in Sec. 5.50. Since it has been assumed that the phase-modulating action of all slabs collectively

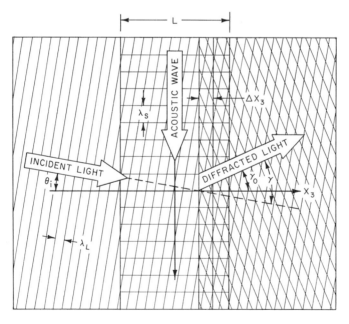

Fig. 5.26 Schematic diagram of the interaction between light and sound.

is small, it can be stated that the action of each individual slab is independent of the action of all other slabs.

Sinsuoidal phase modulation is discussed in Sec. 4.60. When weak phase modulation occurs, the quantity ϕ_m in eq. (4.96) is much less than unity; i.e., only two new plane waves having significant energy are created, so that only the sinc functions at $f_x = \pm f_0$ are important. Because the normals to these plane waves lie in the $x_1 x_3$ plane, their direction cosines with respect to the x_2 axis are zero and, from the definition of f_x, it can be written that $\sin \gamma = \lambda_L f_x / n_0$, where n_0 is the optical index of the acoustic medium. Since $f_0 = 1/\lambda_s$, where λ_s is the acoustic wavelength, and since for small diffraction angles $\sin \gamma = \gamma$, it is possible to write that the diffraction angle γ_0 corresponding to f_0 is approximately equal to $\lambda_L / n_0 \lambda_s$.

Now assume, for reasons made clear in the analysis below, that the incident light wave may arrive at some small angle θ_i with respect to the x_3 axis. The new plane wave of light produced by diffraction and corresponding to $f_x = f_0$ will make an angle with respect to the x_3 axis given by $\gamma_0 - \theta_i$, where γ_0 is now taken relative to the normal to the incident light wave rather than to the x_3 direction.

The phase velocity of the incident wave with respect to the x_3 axis is given in terms of the group velocity c/n_0 by

$$c_{\phi_i} = \frac{c}{n_0} \frac{1}{\cos \theta_i} \tag{5.97}$$

Letting $\theta_0 = \gamma_0 - \theta_i$ the phase velocity of the light wave diffracted at this angle with respect to the x_3 axis is given by

$$c_{\phi_0} = \frac{c}{n_0} \frac{1}{\cos \theta_0} \tag{5.98}$$

For small diffraction angles such as are characteristic of most elastooptic-delay-line light modulators, the cosine can be replaced by the first two terms in its Maclaurin series expansion and the approximation $(1 - \alpha)^{-1} \approx 1 + \alpha$ utilized to obtain

$$c_{\phi_i} = \frac{c}{n_0} \left(1 + \frac{\theta_i^2}{2} \right)$$

$$c_{\phi_d} = \frac{c}{n_0} \left(1 + \frac{\theta_0^2}{2} \right) \tag{5.99}$$

The phase difference $\Delta \phi$ between the light wave diffracted in the θ_0 direction at x_3 and the light wave diffracted at $x_3 + \Delta x_3$ is given in radians by

$$\Delta \phi = \frac{2 \pi n_0}{\lambda_L} \frac{\Delta x_3}{c_{\phi_i}} (c_{\phi_d} - c_{\phi_i}) \tag{5.100}$$

which, when combined with eqs. (5.99), yields

$$\Delta\phi = \frac{2\pi n_0 \Delta x_3}{\lambda_L} \frac{\theta_0^2/2 - \theta_i^2/2}{1 + \theta_i^2/2}$$

$$= \frac{\pi n_0 \Delta x_3}{\lambda_L} \left(\theta_0^2 - \theta_i^2 + \frac{\theta_0^2 \theta_i^2}{2} - \frac{\theta_i^4}{2} \right) \tag{5.101}$$

The fourth-order terms in the parentheses in eq. (5.101) can be neglected for small diffraction angles so that the equation becomes

$$\Delta\phi \approx \frac{\pi n_0 \Delta x_3}{\lambda_L} (\theta_0^2 - \theta_i^2) \tag{5.102}$$

Utilizing the relationship $\theta_0 = \gamma_0 - \theta_i$ and integrating eq. (5.102) over x_3 lead to a general expression for the phase of the diffracted light as a function of x_3, namely,

$$\phi(x_3) \approx \frac{\pi n_0 \Delta x_3}{\lambda_L} (\gamma_0^2 - 2\gamma_0 \theta_i) x_3 \tag{5.103}$$

Since $\gamma_0 \approx \lambda_L/n_0\lambda_s$, eq. (5.103) may be rewritten as

$$\phi(x_3) \approx \frac{\pi}{\lambda_s} \left(\frac{\lambda_L}{n_0\lambda_s} - 2\theta_i \right) x_3 \tag{5.104}$$

Finally, in order to determine the amplitude E_m of the light diffracted, an integration is taken over the interaction distance in the acoustic medium as follows:

$$E_m = \int_{-L/2}^{+L/2} e^{j\phi(x_3)} \, dx_3$$

$$= \frac{C \sin\left[(\pi/2)(L/\lambda_s)(\lambda_L/n_0\lambda_s - 2\theta_i) \right]}{(\pi/2)(L/\lambda_s)(\lambda_L/n_0\lambda_s - 2\theta_i)}$$

$$= C \operatorname{sinc}\left[\frac{1}{2}\left(\frac{L}{\lambda_s}\right)\left(\frac{\lambda_L}{n_0\lambda_s} - 2\theta_i\right) \right] \tag{5.105}$$

where C is a constant of proportionality which depends on the product of the appropriate elastooptic constant and the strain. For normal incidence between the optical and acoustic waves, $\theta_i = 0$, and eq. (5.105) becomes the Raman-Nath equation of Ref. [5.39]. When $\theta_i = \lambda_L/2n_0\lambda_s = \gamma_0/2$, one obtains the Bragg condition where the diffracted waves from all slabs are in phase. Equation (5.105) also shows that the light diffracted behaves as a sinc function in $(1/\lambda_s)^2$ for a constant interaction length L and at constant λ_s behaves as a sinc function in L, if it is assumed that the total light diffracted is held constant. When, instead, it is assumed that the total light diffracted per unit length in the x_3 direction is held constant, then E_m varies sinusoidally with L.

The value of the intensity of the light diffracted, that is, $|E_m|^2$, is plotted in Fig. 5.27. Normalized coordinates are utilized in this plot as given by

$$\kappa = \theta_i \sqrt{\frac{2\pi n_0 L}{\lambda_L}}$$

$$\xi = \frac{1}{\lambda_s} \sqrt{\frac{\pi L \lambda_L}{2n_0}}$$

(5.106)

so that the expression for the light intensity becomes

$$I(\kappa, \xi) = \left| \frac{\sin (\xi^2 - \kappa\xi)}{\xi^2 - \kappa\xi} \right|^2$$

(5.107)

Note that when $\kappa = 0$, that is, for normal incidence, the familiar sinc function is obtained. For $\kappa = \sqrt{\pi}$ there is a Bragg peak close to the origin and for $\kappa = 2\sqrt{\pi}$ the Bragg peak becomes clearly separated from the origin. Figure 5.27 permits a ready evaluation of the weighting

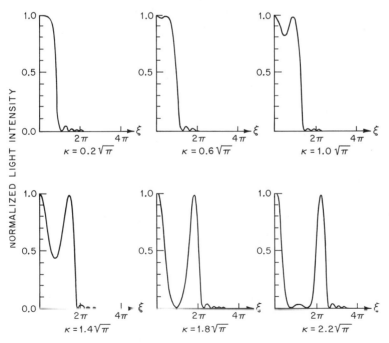

Fig. 5.27 Plots of light diffracted as a function of normalized acoustic frequency (ξ) for various values of normalized angle of incidence (κ).

function which is applied to the Wiener spectrum of an input signal when it is introduced into a coherent optical computer by means of an elastooptic spatial light modulator. The reader should note that this weighting function applies only to waves produced by diffraction in the direction $\theta_0 = \gamma_0 - \theta_i$. In order to determine the weighting function for the conjugate of these waves, the quantity $\theta_0 = \gamma_0 + \theta_i$ may be substituted in eq. (5.102) and an integration carried out as in eq. (5.105). In this case there is no Bragg effect, as would be expected, since, as $\theta_i \geqslant 0$, the light intensity function $I(\kappa, \xi)$ is always positive. There is an evident asymmetry in the Weiner spectrum, with the light intensity at positive and negative spatial frequencies being unequal except for the case where $\theta_i = 0$. The advantage of using the portion of the Wiener spectrum where a Bragg peak occurs is discussed in the next section as it relates to the maximization of the space-bandwidth product of the coherent optical computer.

5.52 Acoustic Bandwidth Limitations   The space-band width product of a coherent optical computer using an acoustic-delay-line light modulator as its input transducer is limited by the electronic bandwidth of the acoustic transducer which transforms the input signal into a traveling acoustic wave.   Such transducers are fabricated of piezoelectric or piezomagnetic crystals, ceramics, or metals and are affixed to the acoustic delay line by a variety of methods.   The reader is referred to Mason [5.40] for a general treatment of acoustic transducers and to Konig et al. [5.41] for a specific discussion of their use in elastooptic light modulators.   It is shown that the greatest efficiency in the conversion of electronic input signal power to acoustic power over the widest bandwidth occurs when (1) the transducer is half-wave resonant at a frequency selected in the bandwidth of interest, (2) the transducer face which is toward the acoustic medium is acoustically impedance-matched to the medium, and (3) the opposite transducer face is backed by an acoustically matched material which completely absorbs energy transmitted into it. For this case of optimum energy conversion the frequency dependence of the strain produced by the acoustic wave is given in terms of the normalized acoustic frequency defined by eq. (5.106) as

$$s_{ij} = C_{ij} \sin a\xi \qquad 0 < \xi < \frac{\pi}{a} \tag{5.108}$$

where $a = \pi/2\xi$ defines the resonant frequency of the transducer. Equation (5.108) places another limitation on the bandwidth of the elastooptic light modulator. Combining eq. (5.108) with eq. (5.107) yields the relationship

$$I(\kappa,\xi) = C \left| \sin a\xi \, \frac{\sin(\xi^2 - \kappa\xi)}{\xi^2 - \kappa\xi} \right|^2 \tag{5.109}$$

Equation (5.109) has been solved on a digital computer for the maximum 1-dB and 3-dB light intensity bandwidth as a function of the variables a, κ, and ξ. Graphs of light intensity versus normalized acoustic frequency are shown in Fig. 5.28 for several cases of interest.

Further insight into the elastooptic interaction and into the results expressed by eqs. (5.107) and (5.109) may be obtained from recognizing that, just as there is a diffraction theorem for optics, there is also one for acoustics. Diffraction by the aperture, L, as defined by the transducer will create new plane waves according to the Fourier transform of the aperture function. Equations (4.76) and (4.77) give the angular energy distribution of these plane waves. Since these plane waves are infinite in extent, a plane wave of light incident upon them at the angle θ_i (see Fig. 5.26) will be transmitted only at the Bragg angle, $\lambda_L/2n_0\lambda_s$. The direction angle of the particular diffracted sound wave with which the

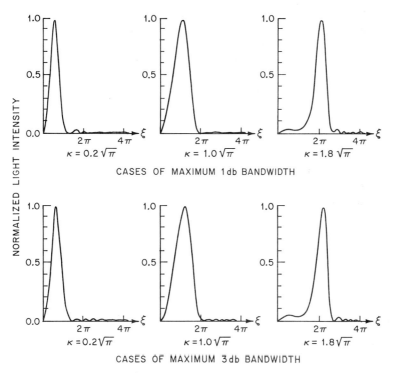

Fig. 5.28 Plots of light diffracted as a function of normalized acoustic frequency (ξ) for various values of normalized angle of incidence (κ) when a matched half-wave resonant acoustic transducer is utilized.

incident light wave satisfies the Bragg condition is, therefore,

$$\gamma_s = \frac{\lambda_L}{2n_0\lambda_s} - \theta_i \tag{5.110}$$

Substituting $f_x = (\cos\alpha_s)/\lambda_s = (\sin\gamma_s)/\lambda_s$ and $A_x = L$ in eq. (4.77) and making the small-angle approximation, it is found that the variation in the diffracted sound intensity and therefore of the light intensity is proportional in the one-dimensional case to the quantity $\mathrm{sinc}^2\,[(L/\lambda_s)$ $(\lambda_L/2n_0\lambda_s - \theta_i)]$.   This result is identical to that expressed in eq. (5.105).

Another consequence of acoustic diffraction is that the acoustic wave is dispersed.   There will be a lateral displacement of the sound wave equal to $\gamma_s x_1$, as predicted by eq. (4.51).   From Fig. 4.5 and eq. (4.77) it is evident that most of the energy is contained within the angular range given by $-\lambda_s/L \leqslant \gamma_s \leqslant +\lambda_s/L$.   Clearly, in order to keep the size of the acoustic medium within bounds, expansion of the acoustic beam by diffraction must be controlled by placing a lower bound on the size of the transducer aperture L.   This size is customarily (and somewhat arbitrarily) set so as to keep most of the energy of the acoustic beam within a region equal to twice the size of the transducer aperture. Thus it can be written that

$$v_s T \approx \frac{L^2}{\lambda_s}$$

$$\tag{5.111}$$

$$L^2 \approx \frac{v_s^2 T}{f_{s\,\mathrm{min}}}$$

where $f_{s\,\mathrm{min}}$ is the lowest temporal acoustic frequency in the input signal bandwidth and T is the input signal duration.

The above constraint on the transducer dimension L may be combined with the above constraints on bandwidth in a final optimization.   Define the normalized bandwidth $\Delta\xi$ by means of the relationship

$$\Delta\xi = \frac{W}{v_s}\sqrt{\frac{\pi L\lambda_L}{2n_0}} \tag{5.112}$$

and rewrite eq. (5.111) as follows:

$$L^2 = \frac{v_s^2 T\Delta\xi}{\xi_{\mathrm{min}}W} \tag{5.113}$$

Taking the fourth power of eq. (5.112) and combining with eq. (5.113) so as to eliminate the quantity L yield

$$T(W)^3 = \xi_{\mathrm{min}}(\Delta\xi)^3\left(\frac{2n_0 v_s}{\pi\lambda_L}\right)^2 \tag{5.114}$$

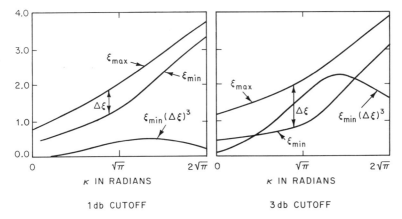

Fig. 5.29 Normalized time-bandwidth plots for the optoacoustic interaction for both 1- and 3-dB acoustic bandwidths.

Figure 5.29 plots the maximum normalized frequency ξ_{max} as well as ξ_{min} and $\xi_{min}(\Delta\xi)^3$ as a function of κ for optimum values of the variable a for both the 1- and the 3-dB bandwidth cases. Optimum performance is at $\kappa = 1.4 \sqrt{\pi}$. Combining this result with eqs. (5.106) yields the optimum angle of incidence as given by

$$\theta_{i_{opt}} = 1.4 \sqrt{\frac{\lambda_L}{2n_0 L}} \tag{5.115}$$

The fundamental time-bandwidth equation for an elastooptic-delay-line light modulator then becomes

$$T(W)^3 = C \left(\frac{n_0 v_s}{\lambda_L}\right)^2 \tag{5.116}$$

where $\quad C = \begin{cases} 0.19 & 1\text{ dB} \\ 1.01 & 3\text{ dB} \end{cases}$

The significance of eq. (5.116) is illustrated in Fig. 5.30 for both longitudinal and shear waves in fused silica which is one of the most commonly used homogeneous elastooptic light-modulating media. For comparison the results for two crystalline media are shown, namely, the slow shear mode in bismuth germanium oxide and the longitudinal mode in aluminium oxide (sapphire). As can be seen, time-bandwidths are increased for high values of acoustic velocity and optical index.

The interested reader is referred at this point for comparison to a figure of merit based upon an optimization which uses elastooptical efficiency but ignores acoustic bandwidth as proposed by Gordon

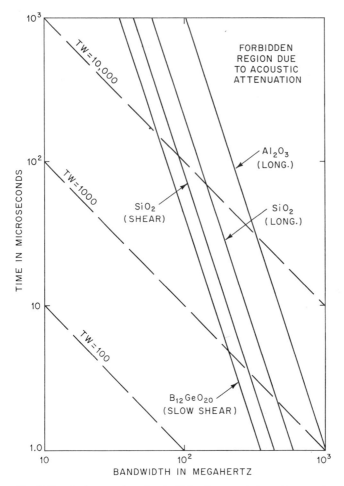

Fig. 5.30 Optimum time-bandwidth characteristics of several materials used in delay-line light modulators for 3-dB bandwidths.

[5.42]. This figure of merit is proportional to n_0^7/v_s and thus strongly favors a high optical index but, in contrast to eq. (5.116), favors a low optical velocity. This is true because larger strains are produced per unit power for low-velocity materials. It is evident, therefore, that the designer who desires to maximize the time-bandwidth product will select a high-velocity medium; to maximize diffraction efficiency, a low-velocity medium. In all cases a high optical index is preferred. High velocity implies a long acoustic path. This presents the practical problems of size which may be solved by folding the acoustic path within the acoustic medium as is illustrated in Fig. 9.20.

5.53   Noise and Dynamic Range in Elastooptic Light Modulators

Because the elastooptic interaction produces weak phase modulation, truncation noise is not a problem in acoustic-delay-line light modulators. The field angle over which the optical system must function is directly determined by the signal bandwidth.   No higher-order diffraction terms are generated as they are in strong-effect optical spatial phase modulators such as thermoplastic films and membrane light modulators. However, there are several other sources of noise which must be considered when designing an optical computer which uses an elastooptic spatial light modulator as an input transducer.

First, there is the phenomenon of acoustic attenuation.   As the acoustic waves travel through the elastooptic medium their energy is absorbed.   This causes eq. (5.96) to be modified as follows:

$$s_{ij}(x_1, t) = C_{ij}s(x_1 - v_s t)e^{-\zeta x} \tag{5.117}$$

where ζ is the acoustic attenuation constant (in units of nepers per unit length).   Attenuation causes the lobes of the Wiener spectrum to broaden and the nulls to vanish, thus decreasing the accuracy of the computations being made.   A normalized plot of the result is shown in Fig. 5.31 calculated for a square (or rectangular) aperture for various values of quantity ζ, which shows the main lobe and the first two side lobes.   For example, for $\zeta = 1$ nP, there is a 20 per cent broadening of

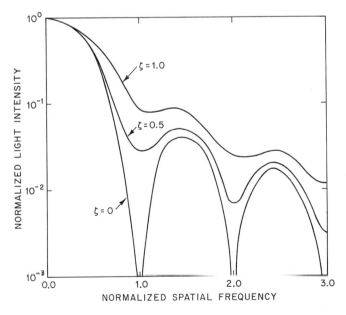

Fig. 5.31   Effect of acoustic attenuation on the Wiener spectrum.

the main lobe and, at the location of the first aperture null, the light level rises to about 10 dB below the peak of the main lobe. The degree to which attenuation degrades performance depends entirely upon the purpose for which the optical computer is utilized and therefore differs with each application.

Note that acoustic attenuation varies with the elastooptic material utilized as well as with temperature and frequency. In fused silica, for example, the attenuation is essentially linear with frequency below 10 MHz ($\approx 3 \times 10^{-9} f_s$ in decibels per centimeter) but is quadratic above 100 MHz ($\approx 2 \times 10^{-17} f_s^2$ in decibels per centimeter). At room temperature many workers have reported attenuation measurements in elasto-optic solids, both homogeneous and crystalline, and the reader is referred to Refs. [5.43] to [5.49]. It should be noted that, although fused silica becomes extremely lossy and essentially useless at microwave acoustic frequencies, certain crystalline materials such as aluminum oxide, lithium niobate, etc., may be utilized in this region with relatively low losses ($\approx 3 \times 10^{-19} f_s^2$ at room temperature). This fact is important in that it may imply the feasibility of microwave optical computers. Some early results of Quate et al. [5.50] in this area should be of interest to the reader.

The reader who desires a more fundamental grasp of the basic physics of attenuation should review Mason [5.51] and Temple [5.52]. Finally it is of interest to note that in some cases acoustic attenuation may be combated by inserting piezoelectric semiconductor amplifiers in the system as initially reported by Hutson et al. [5.53].

A second source of noise in acoustic-delay-line light modulators is the variation of phase with frequency which is produced by the acoustic transducer. Even when the acoustic transducer is properly matched and backed, the acoustic wave entering the acoustic medium is a summation of two waves, one produced at each face of the transducer. The composite wave which enters the acoustic medium is given at each radian acoustic frequency ω_s by the expression

$$s(x_1,t) = C\left(e^{j[(\omega_s/v_s)(x_1-v_st)]} + e^{j[\pi+(\omega_s/v_s)(x_1-v_st-\lambda_{s0}/2)]}\right) \qquad (5.118)$$

where λ_{s0} is the acoustic wavelength in the transducer medium at the resonant frequency of the transducer. When ω_s is the resonant frequency, that is, $\omega_s = 2\pi v_s/\lambda_{s0} = \omega_{s0}$, the two vectors represented by eq. (5.118) are in phase. At all other frequencies there is a phase difference between them so that the composite wave which enters the acoustic medium experiences a phase shift ϕ_Δ with respect to that at the resonant frequency given by

$$\phi_\Delta = \frac{\pi}{2}\left(1 - \frac{\omega_s}{\omega_{s0}}\right) \qquad (5.119)$$

For a system operating with 3-dB bandwidth, $-\pi/4 < \phi_\Delta < +\pi/4$. This causes phase distortion of the signal traveling in the acoustic delay line. Such distortion is most easily corrected by designing an electronic signal amplifier having a compensating linearly increasing phase characteristic.

A third source of noise is caused by spatial distortion of the traveling wave in the acoustic medium, due to temperature gradients. Heat is generated in the backing of the acoustic transducer and near the end of the acoustic delay where an acoustic absorber is usually placed so as to prevent echoes. An extreme example of thermal gradients in a case where a few watts were being dissipated is shown in Fig. 5.32 for a fused-silica delay-line light modulator. As discussed by Fraser et al. [5.54] the temperature coefficient of acoustic velocity is of the order of 10^{-5} per degree centigrade at room temperature. If one-tenth wave fidelity is desired in the optical computer, then thermal control within a temperature range $\Delta T \approx 10^4/SW$ is required, where SW is the space-bandwidth product of the computer. In practice this may be accomplished by Peltier cooling or even by water cooling the transducer backing and the absorber. Alternatively, the entire delay line may be operated in an oven which is temperature-stabilized. Operation at elevated temperature may in some cases have the additional advantage that acoustic attenuation is decreased.

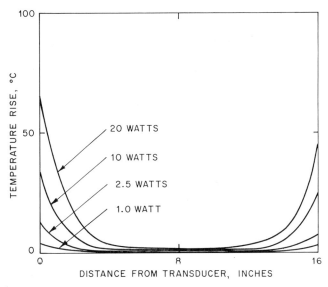

Fig. 5.32 Delay-line temperature measurements as a function of electric input power for a line with both a matched transducer and termination.

A fourth source of noise occurs when the designer assumes that the weak phase modulation produced by an elastooptic modulator can be treated analytically as amplitude modulation with a strong bias.   It can be written that

$$e^{jCs(x_1 - v_s t)} \approx 1 + jCs(x_1 - v_s t) \tag{5.120}$$

where $C \ll 1$.   This permits amplitude reference masks to be used in the optical computer when its function is to perform spatial plane correlation.   The question often arises, when operation is in this mode, as to what phenomenon now limits dynamic range.   To answer this question, the approximation expressed by (5.120) must be scrutinized.   Using eq. (4.92), consider the problem of intermodulation noise and its limiting effect on dynamic range by assuming that two sinusoidal components of equal amplitude are present simultaneously in the input signal.   Let

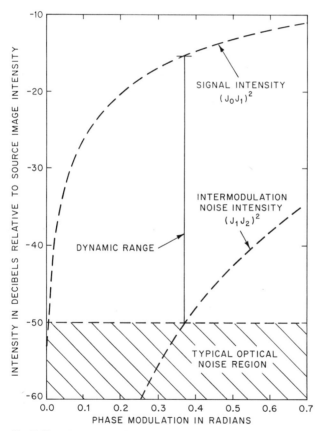

Fig. 5.33 Signal- and intermodulation-noise-intensity characteristics as a function of phase modulation.

the spatial frequencies ω_{x1} and ω_{x2} correspond to the two frequency components and assume $\omega_{x2} > \omega_{x1}$, so that

$$e^{j\phi_m(\sin\omega_{x1}x_1 + \sin\omega_{x2}x_2)} = \sum_{k=-\infty}^{k=+\infty} J_k(\phi_m)e^{jk\omega_{x1}x_1} \sum_{l=-\infty}^{l=+\infty} J_l(\phi_m)e^{jl\omega_{x2}x_1}$$

$$(5.121)$$

The desired terms in eq. (5.121) are, of course, $J_1(\phi_m)J_0(\phi_m)e^{j\omega_{x1}x_1}$ and $J_0(\phi_m)J_1(\phi_m)e^{j\omega_{x2}x_1}$, which correspond to the (k,l) pairs $(1,0)$ and $(0,1)$. The intermodulation terms corresponding to $(k,l) = (\pm 1, \pm 1)$ lie either near zero frequency or outside the bandpass of the usual half-wave resonant transducer. However, for $(k,l) = (\pm 1, \pm 2)$ or $(\pm 2, \pm 1)$, the intermodulation products lie in the band of interest at $2\omega_{x1} - \omega_{x2}$ and $2\omega_{x2} - \omega_{x1}$. Plots of the light intensity of the desired signal, that is, $|J_0(\phi_m)J_1(\phi_m)|^2$, and of the largest intermodulation terms within the bandwidth, that is, $|J_1(\phi_m)J_2(\phi_m)|^2$, are shown in Fig. 5.33 as a function of ϕ_m. The dynamic range which results, assuming a 50-dB optical noise level at the maximum signal-to-intermodulation noise ratio, is 35 dB at a value of $\phi_m = 0.35$ rad.

A fifth source of noise which is sometimes mentioned in regard to electrooptic light modulators has to do with refraction of the diffracted light within the acoustic beam. Lucas and Biquard [5.25] traced rays through a medium having a sinusoidal index variation. Their results are illustrated in Fig. 5.34 which is a plot of certain ray paths against a

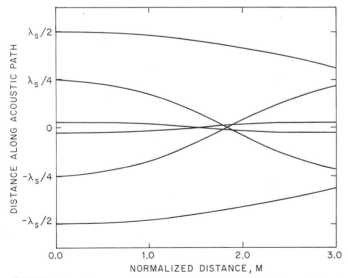

Fig. 5.34 Optical ray-trace geometry through a sinusoidally modulated acoustic beam.

normalized distance M, as defined by

$$M = 2\pi \frac{L}{\lambda_s} \sqrt{\frac{\Delta n_0}{n_0}} = \sqrt{2\pi\phi_m \left(\frac{\lambda_L}{n_0\lambda_s}\right)\left(\frac{L}{\lambda_s}\right)} \tag{5.122}$$

where $\phi_m = 2\pi\Delta n_0 L/\lambda_L$ and $2\Delta n_0$ is the peak-to-peak change in the optical index. Note that M may be related to the normalized bandwidth ξ as $M = 2\xi\sqrt{\pi\phi_m}$. Since optimum values of ξ are in the vicinity of unity for most cases of interest and ϕ_m is usually a few tenths of a radian, M values in the range of 1 to 3 would *appear* to be typical. Figure 5.34 would therefore indicate a severe amount of internal refraction. However, diffraction theory states that ray tracing is a valid method of determining optical energy flow *only* for distances much greater than $\lambda_L f_{no}^2$ from a point of focus. Here $f_{no} = L/\lambda_s$ so that this criterion leads to a requirement that $\xi \ll \pi/2$. Thus refraction of light within the sound beam need be considered only for small values of ξ and thus large values of ϕ_m. From a quantum-mechanical point of view this is equivalent to the case where multiple scattering (of photons by phonons) is very likely. Such a situation is usually not encountered in most elastooptic light modulators.

Finally it should be mentioned in this discussion of noise that, since the acoustic medium is either a vitreous or crystalline solid, it may scatter light because of both surface or bulk imperfections. Such scattered light constitutes noise in the optical computer and decreases dynamic range. Noise of this type for vitreous materials will be discussed in Chapter Six. For crystals there is such a variety of material as well as of methods of growth and preparation that each must be treated separately and measured individually before use. It can be said, however, that owing to extensive work with such materials as aluminum oxide (because of application in crystal lasers) this material and certain similar crystals may be obtained in large sizes having excellent optical quality.

5.60   Comparison of Spatial Light Modulators

This section compares the spatial light modulators which have been discussed in detail in the preceding sections. The comparison is made in Table 5.2 and is self-explanatory. Table 5.2 includes data on information storage density, dynamic range, noise, energy requirements, exposure, development, decay and erasure times, reusability, and both linear and area space-bandwidth products where applicable. The reader should remember that the data listed in the table represent the current state of the art at this writing and do not pretend to extrapolate to future potential in any case. Where data are conflicting or not available no entry is shown. In other cases the symbol n/a is entered to

TABLE 5.2

	Silver halide	10^{-8} J/ϵ Photochromic	10^{-4} J/ϵ Thermoplastic	10^{-8} J/ϵ Deformable membrane	Elastooptic
Maximum linear storage density, cycles/mm	10^3	$> 10^3$	$3 \cdot 10^2$	10^2	50 (isotropic) $2 \cdot 10^3$ (crystal)
Energy required, J/cm²........	10^{-8}–10^{-6}	10^{-2}–10^{-1}	10^{-4}	10^{-4}	10^{-7}–10^{-5} (J/cm³)
Minimum record time, s	$< 10^{-9}$	$< 10^{-9}$	10^{-8}	10^{-8}	10^{-8} (isotropic) 10^{-10} (crystal)
Development time, s............	1.0–10.0	n/a	1.0–10.0	n/a	n/a
Decay time, s	∞	10^{-3}–10^7	∞	n/a	n/a
Minimum erasure time, s......	n/a*	10	10^{-2}	n/a	n/a
Life..........................	Indefinite	Finite number of cycles	Finite number of cycles	$> 10^{12}$	Indefinite
Maximum linear space-bandwidth product	10^5	$> 10^5$	$\approx 10^3$	$\approx 10^3$	10^3
Maximum area space-bandwidth product........	10^{10}	$> 10^{10}$	$\approx 10^6$	$\approx 10^6$	10^4

*Not applicable

169

indicate "not applicable." It should be noted that energy requirements and the square of the information storage density may be combined to yield data on energy required per resolution element.

The ensuing sections briefly describe several types of spatial light modulators whose development is not as advanced as those discussed in detail in the preceding sections. This is not to imply that the spatial light modulators described next are less important than those treated earlier, but only that these particular spatial light modulators and/or light-modulating effects are not yet widely developed and/or utilized. Some may show great promise for the future; therefore it is felt that the reader should be informed of their existence.

5.61 Faraday- and Kerr-effect Spatial Light Modulators   Certain transparent magnetic materials have the property that, according to their state of magnetization, they may produce a rotation in the polarization of light passing through them. This is called Faraday rotation. Typical materials exhibiting this effect are yttrium iron garnet and gadolinium iron garnet. These materials may now be produced in thin layers much like thin-film magnetic memories. Magnetic domains in the thin layers may be switched from one direction of magnetization to another. Polarized light passing through the layer is rotated in a direction which depends upon the state of magnetization and may be sensed by an analyzer beyond the layer. The result is a two-dimensional light modulator. Work on such light modulators is reported in Ref. [5.55].

The magnetooptic Kerr effect is observed in reflection from magneto-optic materials. The longitudinal Kerr effect occurs when the direction of magnetization is parallel to the reflecting surface. There is no rotation of the reflected light when the angle of incidence is normal but the effect reaches a maximum at an angle of incidence of about 60°. The polar Kerr effect occurs when the magnetization is normal to the plane of the reflecting surface. In this case rotation does occur with normal incidence. Furthermore, the polar Kerr effect is about five times stronger than the longitudinal Kerr effect. Finally, the transverse Kerr effect occurs when the magnetization is in the plane of the reflecting surface but is at a right angle to the polarization. There is no rotation of the plane of polarization. There is, however, a small change in reflectance, depending upon the amount of magnetization.

Besides the magnetooptic spatial light modulator mentioned above, there are also electrooptic systems wherein the direction of polarization is changed either in transmission or reflection by an amount dependent upon the intensity of the electric field. For example, spatial light modulators have been made from thin layers of potassium dihydrogen phosphate (KDP) deposited so as to form the target in an electrostatic storage tube. KDP is an insulator so that regions of its surface may be charged or discharged by means of an electron beam, using controlled secondary electron emission in what is called an Ardenne tube [5.56]. Polarized light passing through the target in the Ardenne tube yields spatial amplitude modulation when transmitted through an analyzer.

5.62 Liquid-Crystal Spatial Light Modulators It has been found that certain organic solids, for example, the esters of cholesterols, exist in the so-called "mesomorphic" state which is intermediate between that of the crystalline state and the liquid state [5.57]. Thin layers of these materials have been found to rotate the plane of polarization of transmitted light much as the electrooptic materials mentioned above. Work in the application of this effect to electrooptical light modulators is described in Ref. [5.58].

5.63 Absorption Edge Spatial Light Modulators It is known [5.59] that strong electric fields can shift the absorption bands of certain materials by changing the energy levels of atoms or collections of atoms within the crystal structure. Many materials show this effect. For some, such as cadmium sulfide, the effect is observed in the visible region of the electromagnetic spectrum. For others, such as silicon or germanium, the effect is observed in the near infrared. It has been proposed that the large changes of absorptivity which take place on the steep portion of the absorption lines or bands be utilized for spatial light modulation [5.60]. Reference [5.61] suggests that similar results may be accomplished by using a layer of semiconductor material as the target of an electrostatic storage tube. It should be mentioned that not only do inorganic elements and compounds exhibit this phenomenon but also the same effect may be found in organics such as the polymers discussed in Ref. [5.62].

5.64 Space-charge-layer Spatial Light Modulators Both the reflectivity and transmissivity of certain semiconductors are affected by the density of charge carriers. Both amplitude and/or phase modulation of reflected or transmitted light may be obtained by modulating the carrier density. A description of such an application appears in Ref. [5.63]. In another configuration semiconductor spatial light modulators take advantage of the change in dimensions of the space-charge layer which exists at a *p-n* junction. The effective width of the space-charge layer may be modulated by an applied electric field. Several configurations for accomplishing this type of modulation are discussed in Ref. [5.64]. Studies of spatial reflectivity modulation by semiconductors have also been made; results are given in Ref. [5.65].   Here data on both silicon and germanium as well as certain III-V and II-VI compounds are reported.   This effect unfortunately is a weak one and requires extremely intense electric fields.

5.65 Acoustic-surface-wave Spatial Light Modulators   Besides phase-modulating light in transmission by means of traveling bulk acoustic waves as discussed in Sec. 5.50, it is possible to spatially modulate light by means of surface waves.   Since light incident on the surface is modulated in reflection, phase modulation of a few tenths of a radian may be produced for surface motions of only a few tens of angstroms. Unlike bulk acoustic waves, a low acoustic velocity is preferred because it permits an increased space-bandwidth product.   Surface waves are also of interest because they may be guided in a zig-zag fashion which contributes to an effective match between such a light modulator and the two-dimensional aperture of the associated coherent optical computer. References [5.66 to 5.68] report on investigations of this phenomenon.

5.66 Deformable-film Spatial Light Modulators   Section 5.40 has already discussed spatial light modulation using deformable membrane mirrors.   Other types of spatial light modulators using a deformable surface are also under study.   Paralleling the development of the Eidophor [5.69] where an oil film is deformed by means of charge deposited by an electron beam, work has proceeded in the development of cathode-ray tubes having deformable faceplates.   A typical example is discussed in Ref. [5.70] where the faceplate is constructed of a matrix of wire pins hermetically embedded in glass.   Over the surface of the faceplate is a fluid film which is deformed electrostatically much as with the oil film in the Eidophor.   In this way a spatial phase modulator operating in reflection is created.

5.67 Colloidal-suspension Spatial Light Modulators   It has been found that the transmissivity of a colloidal suspension of asymmetrical particles may be varied by changing the orientation of these particles by an electric field.   Reference [5.71] describes such a system wherein the liquid is a thermoplastic containing opaque particles.   When the thermoplastic film is softened the particles rotate so that their long dimension is parallel to the applied electric field.   In the case discussed the field was produced by selectively discharging precharged photothermoplastic film containing a colloidal suspension of particles.   When heat is applied, a transmission pattern is recorded which is a function of the residual charge pattern.

5.68 Electroplating Spatial Light Modulators   Finally, various types of thin electrolytic cells have been studied for use as spatial light modulators.   Typically the cell consists of two plates of glass coated on the surfaces in contact with the electrolyte with a transparent conductor such as stannous oxide.   Reference [5.72] describes the use of an electrolyte consisting of a solution of silver iodide in sodium hydroxide. Upon the application of local electric fields the metallic silver is reversibly plated out on one of the stannous oxide surfaces.   A further modification is described in Ref. [5.73] where the anode is stannous oxide but the cathode is made of cadmium sulfide selenide deposited on stannous oxide.   In this case the metallic ion in the electrolyte (again a solution of silver iodide and sodium hydroxide) is deposited in accordance with the illumination pattern on the cathode.

REFERENCES

5.1 James, T. H., and G. C. Higgins: "Fundamentals of Photographic Theory," Morgan & Morgan, New York, 1960.

5.2 Hautot, A.: "Photographic Theory," Focal Press, London, 1962.

5.3 Mees, C. E. K., and T. H. James : "The Theory of the Photographic Process," Macmillan, New York, 1965.

5.4 James, T. H., and J. F. Hamilton: The Photographic Process, *Int. Sci. Tech.*, 38 (June 1965).

5.5 O'Neill, E. L.: "Introduction to Statistical Optics," Addison-Wesley, Reading, Mass., 1963.

5.6 Stark, H.: Power Spectral Measurements by the Diffraction of Coherent Light, *Riverside Res. Inst. Tech. Rep.* T-1/006-1-11 (October, 1968).

5.7 Linfoot, E. H.: "Fourier Methods in Optical Image Evaluation," Focal Press, London, 1964.

5.8 Altman, J. H., and R. C. Ball: On the Stability of Photographic Plates, Eastman Kodak Co. (Unpublished.)

5.9 Calhoun, J. M., et al.: A Method of Studying Possible Local Distortions in Aerial Films, *Photogr. Eng.*, **6**:661 (1960).

5.10 Ingalls, A. L.: The Effect of Film Thickness Variations on Coherent Light, *Photogr. Sci. Eng.*, **4**(3):135 (1960).

5.11 Brown, G. H., and W. G. Shaw: Phototropism (Photochromism), *Rev. Pure Appl. Chem.*, **11**(2):2 (1961).

5.12 Exelby, R., and R. Crinter: Phototropy (or Photochromism), *Chem. Rev.*, **65**(2):247 (1965).

5.13 Windsor, M. W.: Photochromism, "Encyclopedia of Chemistry," p. 816, Reinhold, New York, 1966.

5.14 Schulman, J. H., and W. D. Compton: "Color Centers in Solids," Pergamon, New York, 1962.

5.15 Smith, G. P.: Photochromic Glass, *IEEE Spectrum*, **39**· (December, 1965)

5.16 Knapp, R. A.: Techniques for Optical Analogue Multiplication, U.S. Dept. of Commerce Clearinghouse Document AD617961, 1965.

5.17 Herman, S.: Dynamic Range of Photochromic Memories, *Proc. IEEE (Corresp.)*, 330 (1968).

5.18 Dissauer, J. H., and H. E. Clark: "Xerography and Related Processes," Focal Press, London, 1965.

5.19 Glenn, W. E., and J. E. Wolfe: Thermoplastic Recording, *Int. Sci. Tech.*, **8**: (June, 1962).

5.20 Tobin, E.: Image Structure Characteristic of a Photoplastic Film, *Photogr. Sci. Eng.* (Submitted.)

5.21 Preston, K., Jr.: An Array Optical Spatial Phase Modulator, *Proc. ISSCC*, 100 (1968).

5.22 Reizman, F.: Optical Spatial Phase Modulator Array, *Proc. Electro-opt. Syst. Design Conf., New York* (September, 1969).

5.23 Brillouin, L.: Diffusion de la lumière et des rayons X par un corps transparent homogénie, *Ann. Phys.,***7** (9th ser.): 88 (1922).

5.24 Debye, P., and F. W. Sears: On the Scattering of Light by Supersonic Waves, *Proc. Nat. Acad. Sci. U.S.*, **18**: 209 (1932).

5.25 Lucas, R., and P. Biquard: Propriété's optiques des milieux solides et liquides soumis aux vibrations élastiques ultrasonores, *J. Phys. Radium*, **3**(7): 464 (1942).

5.26 Okolicsanyi, F. V.: Television System, U.S. Patent 2,158,990, 1939.

5.27 Rosenthal, A. H.: Correlation System for Radar and the Like, U.S. Patent 3,088,113, 1963.

5.28 Lambert, L.: Advanced Radar Resolution Techniques Development of a Two-dimensional Filter, *Columbia Univ. Electron. Res. Lab., Tech. Rep.* P. 2, p. 153 (January, 1960).

5.29 Preston, K., Jr.: Optical Correlator Modulating Light Twice in Ultrasonic Light Modulator, U.S. Patent 3,457,425, 1969.

5.30 Slobodin, L., and A. Reich: Expansion and Compression of Electronic Pulses by Optical Correlation, U.S. Patent 3,189,746, 1965.

5.31 Gill, S. P.: The Diffraction of Light by Sound, U.S. Dept. of Commerce Clearing-house Document AD603745, 1964.

5.32 Coker, E. G., and L. N. G. Filon: "Photoelasticity," Cambridge University Press, London, 1957.

5.33 Bernstein, S., et al.: Birefringence in Amorphous Solids with Application to Solid Light Modulators, *Columbia Univ. Electron. Res. Lab., Tech. Rep.* T-3/321 (January, 1967).

5.34 Spencer, E. G., et al.: Dielectric Materials for Electrooptic, Elastooptic and Ultra-sonic Device Applications, *Proc. IEEE*, **55**(12): 2074 (1967).

5.35 Maloney, W. T., and H. R. Carleton: Light Diffraction by Transverse Ultrasonic Waves in Hexagonal Crystals, *IEEE Trans. Sonics and Ultrasonics*, **SV-14**(3): 135 (1967).

5.36 Klein, W. R., and B. D. Cook: Unified Approach to Ultrasonic Light diffraction, *IEEE Trans. Sonics and Ultrasonics*, **SV-14**: 123 (1967).

5.37 Dixon, R. W.: Acoustic Diffraction of Light in Anisotropic Media, *IEEE J. Quantum Electron.*, **QE-3**(2): 85 (1967).

5.38 Born, M., and E. Wolf: "Principles of Optics," Pergamon, New York, 1959.

5.39 Raman, C. V., and N. S. Nath: Diffraction of Light by High Frequency Sound Waves, *Proc. Indian Acad. Sci.*, **2(A)**: 406 (1935), **2(A)**: 413 (1935), **3(A)**: 75 (1936), **3(A)**: 119 (1936), **3(A)**: 459 (1936), and **4(A)**: 222 (1936).

5.40 Mason, W. P.: "Electro-Mechanical Transducers and Wave Filters," Van Nostrand, New York, 1948.

5.41 Konig, W. L., et al.: The Bandwidth, Insertion Loss, and Reflection Coefficient of Ultrasonic Delay Lines for Backing Materials and Finite Thickness Bonds, *IRE Int. Conv. Rec.*, (6): 285 (1961).

5.42 Gordon, E. I.: Figure of Merit for Acousto-optical Deflection and Modulation Devices, *IEEE Trans. Quantum Electron. (Corresp.)*, **QE-2**: 104 (May, 1966).

5.43 Lamb, J., et al.: Absorption of Compressional Waves in Solids from 100 to 1000 Mc, *Phys. Rev. Lett.*, **3**(1):28 (July 1, 1959).

5.44 Bommel, H. E., and K. Dransfield: Excitation and Attenuation of Hypersonic Waves in Quartz, *Phys. Rev.*, **117**:1244 (1960).

5.45 Woodruff, T. O., and H. Ehrenreich: Absorption of Sound in Insulators, *Phys. Rev.*, **123**:1553 (1961).

5.46 McSkimin, H. J.: Measurements of Ultrasonic Wave Velocities for Solids in the Frequency Range of 100 to 500 Mc, *J. Acoustic Soc. Amer.*, **34**(4):404 (1962).

5.47 Fitzgerald, T., and J. Truell: Ultrasonic Attenuation in Quartz, U.S. Dept. of Commerce Clearinghouse Document AD257086, 1961.

5.48 Shaw, H. J., et al.: Attenuation of Hypersound in Sapphire and Rutile at Room Temperature, *Appl. Phys. Lett.*, **4**:28 (January, 1964).

5.49 McMahon, D. H.: A Comparison of Brillouin Scattering Techniques for Measuring Microwave Acoustic Attenuation, *IEEE Trans. Sonics and Ultrasonics*, **SV-14**(3):103 (July, 1967).

5.50 Quate, C. F., et al.: Interaction of Light and Microwave Sound, *Proc. IEEE*, **53**:1604 (1965).

5.51 Mason, W. P.: "Physical Acoustics and the Properties of Solids," Van Nostrand, New York, 1958.

5.52 Temple, K. A.: Coherent Microwave Memory Techniques, U.S. Dept. of Commerce Clearinghouse Document AD359987, 1965.

5.53 Hutson, A. R., et al.: Ultrasonic Amplification in CdS, *Phys. Rev. Lett.*, **7**:237 (1961).

5.54 Fraser, D. B., et al.: Dominant Factors Influencing the Properties of Vitreous Silica for Ultrasonic Amplifications, *Proc. IEEE Sonics and Ultrasonics Symp.* (1967).

5.55 Cattani, J.: Univac Memory Has High Bit Density, *Electron. News*, 46 (March 27, 1967).

5.56 Ardenne, M. V.: Tabellen der Elektronenphysik, Ionenphysik, and Ubermikroskopic, *Deut. Verlag der Wiss.*, **1**:202 (1956).

5.57 Gray, G. W.: "Molecular Structure and the Properties of Liquid Crystals," Academic, New York, 1962.

5.58 Williams, R.: Electro Optical Elements Utilizing an Organic Nematic Compound, U.S. Patent 3,322,485, 1967.

5.59 Williams, R.: Electric Field Induced Light Absorption in CdS, *Phys. Rev.*, **117**(6):1487 (1960).

5.60 Heller, W. R.: Electro Optical Devices Utilizing the Stark Shift Phenomenon, U.S. Patent 3,238,843, 1966.

5.61 Bramley, J.: Optical System for the Utilization of Coherent Light, U.S. Patent 3,218,390, 1965.

5.62 Heller, W. R.: Electrochromic Light Valve, U.S. Patent 3,317,266, 1967.

5.63 Lehovec, K.: Light Modulation in a Semi-conductor Body, U.S. Patent 3,158,746, 1964.

5.64 Briggs, H. B.: Semi-conductive Light Valve, U.S. Patent 2,692,952, 1954.

5.65 Birnbaum, N., and T. L. Stockler: Effect of Electron-Hole Recombination Processes on Semiconductor Reflectivity Modulation, *Aerospace Corp. Rep.* TDR-469(9230-02)-4 (1965).

5.66 Krokstad, J., and L. O. Svaasand: Scattering of Light by Ultrasonic Surface Waves in Quartz, *Appl. Phys. Lett.*, **1**:155 (1967).

5.67 Ippon, E. P.: Diffraction of Light by Surface Acoustic Waves, *Proc. IEEE (Corresp.)*, **55**:249 (1967).

5.68 Lean, E. G. H., and C. G. Powell: Optical Probing of Surface Acoustic Waves, *Proc. IEEE*, **58**:1939 (1970).

5.69   Mol, J. C.: The Eidophor System of Larger Screen Television Projection, *Photogr. J.*, **102** : 128 (1968).

5.70   Hamann, O. F.: Random Access Light Valve Study, Rome Air Development Center, *Tech. Rep.* RADC-TR-65-451 (1966).

5.71   Kazan, B., et al.: Image Recording by Particle Orientation, *Proc. IEEE (Corresp.)*, 338 (1968).

5.72   Zarcomb, S.: Light Modulating Means Employing a Self-erasing Plating Solution, U.S. Patent 3,245,313, 1966.

5.73   Hoffman, A. S.: Electrolytic Cell for Use as a Real Time Spatial Filter, *J. Opt. Soc. Amer.*, **56**(6) : 828 (1966).

Chapter Six

Lens-system Fabrication and Test

6.00 Introduction

The fabrication of the optical system of a coherent optical computer combines the sophistication of modern lens-system design with the glass-working lore and craftsmanship still characteristic of high-quality lens manufacture. Starting with the raw glass stock from which each lens element is made, it is necessary to grind and polish the surfaces of each element to their design radii while holding the desired axial thickness. All elements of the lens system are then assembled in lens cells with the proper interelement spacings. Preliminary tests are performed on subassemblies and finally upon the optical system as a whole. This chapter reviews the methods of fabrication, assembly, and test of the optical-computer lens system.

6.10 Glass Physics

Glass, of course, is the basic raw material from which the optical-computer lens system is made. There is an almost infinite variety of glasses available from the major glass manufacturers. Only a few of these glasses are suitable for use in coherent optical computers for which rather stringent quality requirements must be met.

The exact physical and chemical structure of glass is still not completely understood. The major component of glass is silica(SiO_2). The glassy or vitreous state implies a noncrystalline structure which can be likened to a supercooled liquid. It further appears that the SiO_2 molecules in glass form long polymer chains interspersed with the other oxides which compose the particular glass structure. Besides silicon, certain other inorganic oxides are individually glass forming. These include the oxides of boron and phosphorus as well as of germanium, arsenic, and antimony. Other oxides which do not individually form glasses may be included in the glass composition in order to produce particular chemical and physical properties of interest. Excellent reviews of glass composition and glass physics are available in the literature [6.1 to 6.4].

Frequently used by the optical industry are the crown glasses which are composed of silica plus barium oxide and the borosilicate crowns which contain boric oxide as well. Also there are the flint glasses consisting of silica plus lead oxide which are used chiefly because of their high optical index. Typical of the crown glasses are SK16, which is a dense barium crown, and BK7 which is a borosilicate crown. There are also F4, which is a silicate flint, and SF6 which is a heavy silicate flint. Typical values of the optical index for these glasses are given in Table 6.1.

TABLE 6.1

Glass type	Optical index (typical)
Fused silica	1.45842
Borosilicate crown (BK7)	1.51673
Barium crown (SK16)	1.62032
Silicate flint (F4)	1.61644
Heavy silicate flint (SF6)	1.80491

Glass which is entirely SiO_2 is called *fused silica* in the trade and is frequently used as a high-quality, low-optical-index material. Fused silica and BK7 are probably the most frequently used glasses in optical-computer fabrication at the present time. This is true not only because of the values of their optical indices but also because of the extreme uniformity which is achieved in the raw material as now manufactured. In selecting a glass for use in the optical computer, as much consideration is given to homogeneity, workability, and structural qualities as to the optical index.

6.20   Initial Inspection

When raw glass is drawn from stock, it is usually found precut into blocks or "blanks" of relatively standard sizes and thickness.   Only in the case of large lens elements having diameters of, say, 20 to 30 cm and larger must raw glass be made to order.   The first step in selection of the raw stock to be used is to pick several candidate blanks and polish a pair of opposite surfaces on each.   For labor-saving reasons, this polishing is usually not carried to a condition of flatness comparable to a fraction of wavelength but only to the point where optically flat test plates may be applied to both polished surfaces of the blank.   These test plates are affixed with an oil which is selected to have an optical index close to that of the blank.   The test plates and the blank form a sandwich whose optical quality is determined primarily by the blank itself.   This sandwich is placed in an interferometer, and the blank is examined for uniformity.   A typical interferometer test setup used for this purpose is shown in Fig. 6.1.   Here a point source of light is made parallel by a lens L_1 and passes through a beam splitter which directs equal amounts of energy through the blank under test to one mirror,

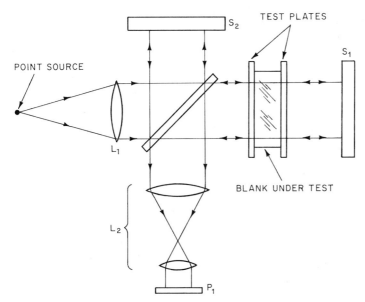

Fig. 6.1   Optical interferometer setup for measuring optical index variations in a glass blank.

S_1, and directly to another mirror, S_2. The mirror S_2 is called the *reference mirror*. Both mirrors are of high optical quality with surfaces which are flat to one-twentieth of a wavelength or better. The beams are reflected from the mirrors, return, are combined by the beam splitter, and exit through lens L_2 to form an interference pattern on the photographic plate P_1. If the reference mirror is adjusted so as to provide a slight angle between the two combined beams, interference fringes will appear as shown in the interferogram of Fig. 6.2. Since the interferometer shown in Fig. 6.1 causes the beam to make a double pass through the blank, the spacing between fringes represents an optical path increment of one-half of a wavelength. Figure 6.2 was made from a blank having approximately one wavelength of curvature in the interference fringes. In this case the blank was 5 cm thick, which corresponds to about 10^5 wavelengths. Here, therefore, fringe curvature of one wavelength represents a variation in optical index of only 0.001 percent which is representative of good uniformity in the raw-glass stock. Clearly, when a lens element is made from the blank, this

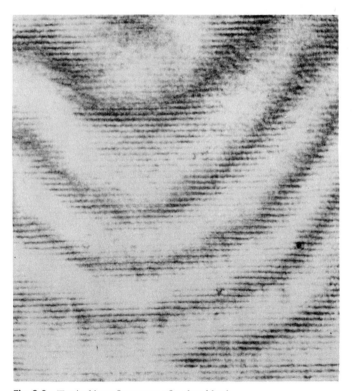

Fig. 6.2   Typical interferogram of a glass blank.

variation in optical index is scaled down by the ratio of the thickness of the element to the thickness of the blank.   In general, variations which are gradual across the blank and are indicative of 0.0001 to 0.001 percent uniformity are considered to be acceptable.   Uniformity in the optical index of the raw-glass stock which is equivalent to the overall quality desired of the finished optical system is not insisted upon.   The optician who does the final polishing of the surfaces of the lens system is expected to correct for residual optical index nonuniformities as required.

After the raw-glass stock has been examined for optical index uniformity it is also examined for bubble content.   Any glass stock, no matter how carefully made, will exhibit small bubbles in the bulk material.   Some of these bubbles will occur near the surfaces and, therefore, will be removed during the fabrication of the lens element.   Other bubbles, however, which are located well into the body of the glass will remain and be present in the lens element itself.   In a coherent-optical-computer lens system any bubble will act as a scattering center and, depending upon its size as a function of the optical wavelength utilized, will produce a certain amount of forward scatter.   This scattered light

TABLE 6.2

Bundle diameter, mm	Central 50 percent of lens		Outer 50 percent of lens	
	Scratch length, $10^2 \mu m$	Bubble/dig diameter, $10^2 \mu m$	Scratch length, $10^2 \mu m$	Bubble/dig diameter, $10^2 \mu m$
0.2–0.4	10	1	15	3
0.4–0.6	10	2	20	5
0.6–1.0	15	3	30	10
1.0–1.6	20	5	40	15
1.6–2.1	30	10	40	20
2.1–2.5	40	15	60	30
2.5–3.2	40	20	60	40
3.2–4.0	60	30	60	40
4.0–5.0	60	40	60	40
5.0–∞	80	50	80	50

Grade	Total bubble cross section (mm^2) per 100 cm^3 of glass volume
1	0.03–0.10
2	0.11–0.25
3	0.26–0.50
4	0.51–1.00
5	1.00–2.00

will decrease the signal-to-noise performance of the system. It is desirable, therefore, to insist on a quality of glass stock which will produce lens elements free of bubbles over the clear aperture, i.e., over the working portion of the optical system. In selecting the glass stock which is to be used in the optical computer one should therefore examine the manufacturer's estimate of the bubble content of the particular glass type chosen. Permissible bubble content is usually specified in accordance with Table 6.2. This table also applies to the size of any scratches or digs which may be created in the surface of the glass during lens-element fabrication. For further information on such specifications the interested reader is referred to the appropriate U.S. Government Standard [6.5].

6.30 Lens-element Fabrication

After the blanks of glass have been selected, they must then be cut, ground, and polished in order to produce the lens elements required. A diamond wheel is used to cut each blank to the approximate axial thickness and to edge it to the approximate diameter necessary for insertion in the lens cell. In these operations, some excess material is left in order to give the optician leeway in the processes of grinding and polishing.

Grinding the two lens surfaces to their proper radii usually requires a pair of grinding tools per surface. Each pair of tools (both convex and concave) are made to the required radius. They are usually iron castings machined to a tolerance of the order of 0.01 percent. Note that it is the radius of the grinding tool, not of the polishing tool, which determines the radius of the lens surface. A typical setup for lens grinding is shown in Fig. 6.3. The grinding tool is placed on a rotating member called a *spindle*. The lens blank, now cut to the proper diameter and thickness, rests upon the upper surface of the tool, is pressed down in the manner shown, and is moved back and forth as the spindle rotates over a distance called the *stroke*.

Grinding takes place in two steps which are rather qualitatively called "rough grinding" and "fine grinding." The distinguishing features of each of these phases of the grinding operation are (1) the particle size of the grinding compound utilized and (2) the associated rate of glass removal. The grinding compound used in lens grinding is usually made of silicon carbide (Carborundum) or aluminum oxide (Corundum). The average particle size for rough grinding lies between a few hundred and several hundred microns, whereas for fine grinding the range is approximately 50 to 100 μm. During the process of

Fig. 6.3 Grinding setup for a concave glass surface, showing the grinding tool attached to the rotating spindle and the glass workpiece attached to the oscillating, weighted arm.

grinding, glass is removed by the shear stresses developed in the glass surface because of the high pressures produced when the sharp particles of abrasive are pinned between the moving grinding tool and the rotating glass surface. The surface of the glass is torn or splintered away. The small particles of glass thus created are constantly flushed away by a stream of water which also acts, to a certain extent, as both lubricant and coolant.

Because of the drastic action of the grinding process, fissures are created which penetrate several hundred microns into the glass surface. These fissures are deep enough to remain after polishing. When used in a coherent optical computer, fissured surfaces produce scatter and cause deterioration of the output signal-to-noise ratio. Therefore in the manufacture of lens elements for use in coherent optical computers it is customary to remove fissures (insofar as possible) by a method called *control grinding*. Control grinding is a grinding method by which, in each sequential stage of the rough- and fine-grinding procedure, grinding is carried to a point where fissures produced by the large abrasive particles of the previous stage are eliminated by removing sufficient glass to go beyond their level of penetration.   Control grinding requires considerably more time to perform than ordinary grinding but it is useful in the creation of lenses for low-noise optical computer systems.

At the same time that the optician is grinding the surface of the lens element itself, he also grinds a second blank to a curvature of opposite polarity, using the other of the pair of grinding tools made for that particular surface.   This blank later serves as a "test plate" in the process of optical polishing.   In general, two test plates are made for each lens element.

After grinding, both the lens and its test plates are polished.   Again the lens is placed on a rotating spindle, and the appropriate tools are utilized for polishing.   In current practice polishing tools are machined from aluminum.   Radii are held to loose tolerances of the order of a few millimeters.   One of the pair of polishing tools is used for polishing the lens element; the other, for the corresponding test plate.   Before use, the polishing tool is coated with a layer of pitch.   The pitch is scored into segments as shown in Fig. 6.4.   In order to be sure that the pitch-coated surface has the shape required for polishing, the pitch-coated polishing tool is pressed hard against the mating grinding tool and heated so that the pitch softens and takes on the shape of the surface to be polished.

Polishing is now commenced and is done on a spindle in a manner similar to the grinding operation.   A slurry of water and polishing compound is spread between the tool and the lens element.   The traditional polishing compound is rouge, or ferric oxide.   Many other finely divided metal oxides or combinations of metal oxides are in current use.   Particle sizes in most polishing compounds range from less than $1\,\mu$m to 5 or $10\,\mu$m.   The physics of polishing is still not under-

Fig. 6.4   Surface of a polishing tool coated with pitch which has been scored in a square pattern.

stood in complete detail although many investigations of this process have been made.   The interested reader is referred to Holland [6.6] for a discussion of the methodology used in working glass surfaces.

It can be said in summary that, during initial polishing, the ragged surface left by the fine-grinding operation is worn down by the abrasive action of the polishing compound.   There also may be a certain chemical erosion due to the resinic acids of the pitch used on the polishing tool.   It appears evident that during final polishing, at sufficiently high pressure, there is a certain amount of thermoplastic flow of the glass at the surface of the lens element.   As pointed out by Holland [6.6], calculations made of the frictional energy produced at the glass surface predict a surface temperature equal to the melting point of the glass itself.   Since the softening or melting temperatures of the particles used in typical polishing compounds are well above that of glass, polishing can continue even at these temperatures.   Thus the effect of initial polishing is to abrasively remove the ragged top surface left by fine grinding.   A point is reached where only a small number of crevices remain in the surface.   Under heavy polishing pressure, the final polishing operation may be able to fill these crevices by plastic flow. Photomicrographs of glass surfaces taken at various stages of polishing give ample evidence of this interpretation of the polishing operation.

Besides pitch polishing, both vegetable-fiber laps, such as cotton, cellulose, etc., as well as animal-fiber laps, such as felt, may be used instead of a pitch lap in the polishing process.   Fiber laps seem to be characterized by a more rapid rate of removal of glass for a given polishing pressure but they are more difficult to control in their operation than the pitch lap.   Typical removal rates for either pitch or fiber laps run between 1 to 10 μm/h at a polishing pressure of a few hundred grams per square centimeter and typical spindle speeds of 50 to 100 r/min (with a corresponding number of strokes per minute).

When polishing lens elements for use in coherent optical computers, two requirements are kept in mind.   First, departures from the desired spherical shape which are due to gradual fluctuations in the surface of the lens element will cause a loss of accuracy in the functions calculated by the computer.   This is due to the fact that integrations, such as those required in calculating Fourier transforms, will be weighted by different spatial phase functions, depending upon what portion of the computer lens system is being utilized.   In a multichannel computer, this will cause a channel-to-channel fluctuation in the value calculated for a given function.   Degradations of this kind are similar to those due to departures from an ideal spherical wavefront in lens-system design and are discussed in Sec. 2.20.

Second, rapid lens-element surface fluctuations due to residual random fissures and scratches left by the grinding process will cause scattering of the light passing through the lens element.   The level of scattered light in the optical computer will determine the dynamic range over which the computer can operate.   With proper selection of the raw glass, control grinding, and careful polishing, this dynamic range may be as large as 60 dB.   When these precautions are not taken, the dynamic range may be degraded to approximately 40 dB.   Illustrations of dynamic-range measurements are given in Sec. 6.50.   Further information on lens-element fabrication may be obtained from Ref. [6.7].

6.40   Lens Assembly and Test

In fabricating the lens element the optician polishes the surfaces of both the test plate and the lens element itself.   By forming interference fringes between the surfaces of the lens element and the test plates, it is possible for the optician to observe both the accuracy and the smoothness of the lens-element surface.   These characteristics are often called the "figure" and "quality" of the surfaces, respectively.

Polishing is continued until the desired results are obtained.   At this point only the figure and the quality of each surface of the lens element may be observed.   No compensation can be or has been made for the effect of internal gradients in the refractive index upon the passage of light through the glass.   This additional compensation (if necessary) is made during the final working of the lens-system surfaces as described below.

After the various elements of a lens system have been completed, the next step is assembly.   Before assembly, the axial thickness and radii of curvature of all surfaces are measured.   These measurements and measurements of the optical index are given to the optical designer so that he may calculate the optimum spacings of all elements of the lens system.   Upon completion of these calculations, the spacers for use within the lens cell are fabricated.

Figure 6.5 shows a typical optical-computer lens cell (disassembled) with all its spacers (unthreaded members) and retainers (threaded members).   The cell shown was designed for a six-element lens and uses six spacers and four retainers.   Four spacers and two retainers are used to position the inner four lens elements, whereas each outer element has its own spacer and retainer.   In some cases a lens cell may be constructed of several subcells each of which holds individual lens elements. Radial positioning of the lens element is determined by accurately turning the cell on a lathe and machining each lens seat in the cell to the required tolerance.   If certain lens elements are closely spaced, a

Fig. 6.5 Interior view of a lens cell with associated spacers and retaining rings for a six-element lens.

retainer may be used to hold two or more elements in place with spacers located between each pair of elements. When distances between the lens elements are large, individual subcells may be used for each lens element. Designs requiring the cementing together of lens elements are usually avoided in optical-computer lens design because of the scatter generated by cemented surfaces.

Figure 6.6 shows a completed optical-computer lens. When all spacings have been checked against those called for by the recalculated optical design, the completed lens is subjected to tests by means of interferometry. Since optical-computer lenses are frequently designed

Fig. 6.6 Completed six-element lens.

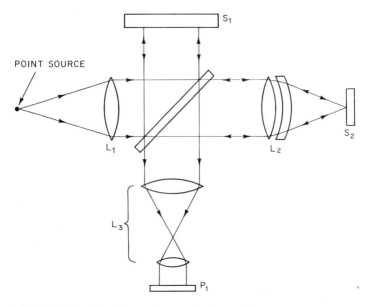

Fig. 6.7 Optical interferometer setup for lens testing.

for use in parallel light, interferometric tests with the lens itself in one arm of the interferometer are particularly simple. A typical interferometer setup for this kind of lens is shown in Fig. 6.7. Spatially coherent light having the wavelength for which the computer lens is designed is made parallel by the collimating lens L_1 and passes through a beam splitter. Equal amounts of light energy are then directed to the reference mirror S_1 and to the lens under test L_2. The lens L_2 is arranged with a mirror S_2 in its back focal plane. The interference pattern which is produced by a recombination of the beams returning from the reference mirror and through the lens is imaged by a lens L_3, onto a viewing screen or photographic plate in the output plane of the interferometer. The wavefront makes a double pass through the lens under test and, in this interferometer, each ray passes through two separate regions of the lens system. Aberrations which are symmetric about the optical axis have a double effect in the output plane so that the fringe separations in the interferogram represent an interval of one-half a wavelength. Aberrations which are not angularly symmetric, however, produce an ambiguous interference pattern which is not exactly interpretable. Fortunately the process of polishing the lens elements usually produces angularly symmetric variations in the lens which cause the wavefront passing through the lens to be either retarded or advanced by essentially the same small fraction of a wavelength during each of the two passes through the lens. This type of aberra-

Fig. 6.8 Interferogram of a completed coherent-optical-computer lens.

tion may readily be evaluated by the interferometric method described here. Other interferometric test methods, such as those described next, may be necessary to remove ambiguities in the case of asymmetric aberrations.

Figure 6.8 shows the interferogram resulting from an interferometric examination of the lens shown in Fig. 6.6. The fringes in the interferogram indicate a peak-to-peak accuracy, over the clear aperture, of approximately one-twentieth of a wavelength (recall that single-path aberrations are doubled by the interferometric system used in this case). The interferogram shown in Fig. 6.8 is typical of that produced when testing a high-quality optical-computer lens.

To attain still further measuring accuracy and obtain an ambiguity-free presentation of lens aberrations, the interferometric system shown in Fig. 6.9 may be utilized. This interferometer is similar to the one shown in Fig. 6.7 with the exception that the plane mirror in the back focal plane of the lens under test has been replaced by a spherical mirror having a virtual focus confocal with the back focus of the lens being tested. This causes a ray entering the lens to be returned upon itself; i.e., the ray makes two passes through the same region of the lens before reaching the output plane. In this type of interferometer the effect of aberrations is again doubled but there is no ambiguity as in the interferometer shown in Fig. 6.7.

When still further precision is required in the examination of the optical-computer lens, the arm of the interferometer in which the lens is placed may be made a resonant cavity. This may be accomplished by inserting a partially silvered mirror (dotted lines in Fig. 6.9) in the arm of the interferometer containing the lens. The effect of this mirror is to cause multiple traverses of the wavefront within the resonant arm of the interferometer which now acts as a Fabry-Perot system [6.8]. The

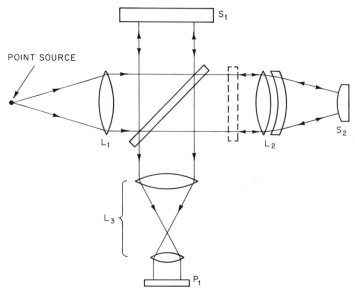

Fig. 6.9 Optical interferogram setup using an auxiliary optical flat (dashed lines) for making Fabry-Perot interferograms.

principle of the Fabry-Perot interferometer is that constructive interference takes place in the cavity only where corresponding points on the walls of the cavity are an integral number of half-wavelengths apart. This causes fine interference fringes to be produced which contour the wavefront at half-wavelength intervals. Figure 6.10 shows an interferogram of an optical-computer lens system which was measured by this technique.

Automatic methods of interferogram interpretation are often employed in order to determine the characteristics of the wavefront which exits from the lens system under test. An interferogram is scanned using an automatic x-y microdensitometer which records measurements of transmission in computer-compatible format. For an interferogram such as that shown in Fig. 6.10, where the fringe width is approximately one one-hundreth of the width of the interferogram, many scans are made in a direction perpendicular to the fringes. Several hundred data points are taken per scan. When all scans are complete, the data recorded are used as an input to a computer program which finds the coordinates of the center of each fringe for each scan across it and prints out a table of fringe locations such as that shown in Table 6.3. In Table 6.3 each column gives the intercept coordinates for all scans of a single fringe to an accuracy of about one part in a thousand. Each column in the table defines points of equal phase on a

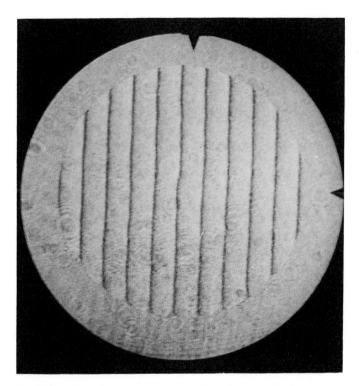

Fig. 6.10 Fabry-Perot interferogram of a coherent-optical-computer lens.

three-dimensional wavefront. In order to determine lens performance, it is desired to determine to what degree of accuracy this wavefront is planar. In the more general case it is desirable to measure the degree to which the wavefront may be approximated by a sphere rather than by a plane. However, in adjusting the interferometer from which the original interferogram is obtained, it is usually possible to remove the spherical component.

Consider, therefore, the specific example of fitting the measured wavefront to the nearest plane. The fringe locations given in Table 6.3 may be used to describe a sampled position function as defined by the equation

$$D_{ijk} = D(x_i, y_j, z_k) \tag{6.1}$$

where the x direction is taken as the scan direction, and the z direction is parallel to the direction taken by the reference wavefront in producing the interferogram. The measure of x and y is continuous distance but the measure of z is quantized in half-wavelengths. The index k takes

TABLE 6.3

j \ k	1	2	3	4	5	6	7	8	9	10	11
1	0.000	0.000	0.000	0.000	3.944	4.087	4.228	0.000	0.000	0.000	0.000
2	0.000	0.000	0.000	3.806	3.945	4.088	4.228	4.372	0.000	0.000	0.000
3	0.000	0.000	3.668	3.804	3.946	4.088	4.227	4.370	4.508	0.000	0.000
4	0.000	0.000	3.670	3.805	3.947	4.087	4.224	4.374	4.513	0.000	0.000
5	0.000	3.523	3.667	3.807	3.944	4.088	4.227	4.370	4.516	4.651	0.000
6	0.000	3.525	3.664	3.806	3.944	4.085	4.229	4.369	4.514	4.650	0.000
7	0.000	3.526	3.661	3.799	3.943	4.086	4.229	4.370	4.512	4.651	0.000
8	3.383	3.523	3.660	3.799	3.944	4.088	4.226	4.365	4.508	4.650	4.783
9	3.383	3.521	3.660	3.801	3.942	4.086	4.223	4.362	4.507	4.647	4.789
10	3.381	3.518	3.659	3.800	3.943	4.091	4.220	4.361	4.507	4.651	4.788
11	3.379	3.518	3.658	3.799	3.939	4.086	4.219	4.363	4.508	4.650	4.786
12	3.378	3.518	3.658	3.798	3.937	4.075	4.219	4.365	4.507	4.650	4.786
13	3.382	3.519	3.653	3.795	3.934	4.072	4.216	4.366	4.504	4.653	0.000
14	0.000	3.517	3.655	3.801	3.934	4.073	4.220	4.367	4.507	4.644	0.000
15	0.000	3.518	3.657	3.799	3.939	4.075	4.221	4.364	4.507	4.646	0.000
16	0.000	3.517	3.658	3.801	3.937	4.078	4.220	4.364	4.505	4.644	0.000
17	0.000	0.000	3.658	3.800	3.939	4.079	4.222	4.363	4.502	0.000	0.000
18	0.000	0.000	3.658	3.798	3.941	4.080	4.226	4.361	0.000	0.000	0.000
19	0.000	0.000	0.000	3.799	3.942	4.078	4.218	4.360	0.000	0.000	0.000
20	0.000	0.000	0.000	0.000	3.941	4.081	0.000	0.000	0.000	0.000	0.000

on as many values as there are fringes in the interferogram.   The index j takes on a new value for each scan across the interferogram.   Finally for each k there is a set of values of i corresponding to the positional intercepts of the kth fringe for the jth scan.

A plane, which is the best approximation (on an rms basis) to the measured wavefront may be determined.   The equation for any plane is represented by

$$lx + my + nz - C_0 = 0 \tag{6.2}$$

where l, m, n are the direction cosines of the normal to the plane and C_0 is the perpendicular distance from the plane to the origin.   The distance from a point (x_i, y_j, z_k) to this plane is given by

$$\Delta_{ijk} = lx_i + my_j + nz_k - C_0 \tag{6.3}$$

The rms value of these aberrations is given by the equation

$$\Delta_{rms} = \sqrt{\frac{1}{N} \sum_j \sum_k \Delta_{ijk}^2} \tag{6.4}$$

where N is the product of the number of scans and the number of fringes, that is, $j_{max}k_{max}$.   The quantity Δ_{rms} is a function of the direction cosines of the plane and its perpendicular distance to the origin.   When Δ_{rms} is minimized with respect to these variables, the best rms approximation of a plane wave to the measured wavefront is obtained.

The Δ_{ijk} (given in fractions of a wavelength) to the best-fitting plane are shown in Table 6.4 for the interferogram in Fig. 6.10.   The value of Δ_{rms} in this case was found to be 0.01 wavelength.   It is also of interest to note that the peak-to-peak variation of the measured wavefront to the best-fitting plane was found to be 0.06 wavelength.   A contour map of the measured wavefront in question is shown in Fig. 6.11 with a contour interval of 0.005 wavelength.

The optician may utilize this contour map to perform what is called *final figuring* of the lens.   This operation is used to compensate for the small residual errors which remain because of internal gradients in refractive index, as discussed in Sec. 6.30.   Final figuring also corrects for cumulative errors due to other imperfections such as small amounts of decentering, poor figure, etc.   Frequently the lens cell is designed so that the outer elements may remain locked in the cell by their retainers during final figuring.   Final figuring is frequently done by hand rather than by means of the polishing tools.   Using either the interferogram of the wavefront contour map as a reference, the optician makes small corrections to the outer surface of the lens by spreading a slurry of fine polishing compound over the surface, placing the entire lens assembly

TABLE 6.4

j \ k	1	2	3	4	5	6	7	8	9	10	11
1	0.000	0.000	0.000	0.000	0.014	0.007	0.007	0.000	0.000	0.000	0.000
2	0.000	0.000	0.000	0.001	0.007	0.001	0.003	-0.005	0.000	0.000	0.000
3	0.000	0.000	-0.012	0.006	0.002	-0.003	0.005	-0.004	0.011	0.000	0.000
4	0.000	0.000	-0.020	0.001	-0.002	-0.001	0.013	-0.017	-0.009	0.000	0.000
5	0.000	0.003	-0.013	-0.009	0.003	-0.005	0.001	-0.008	0.023	-0.001	0.000
6	0.000	-0.011	-0.003	-0.006	0.002	0.004	-0.007	-0.004	-0.017	0.001	0.000
7	0.000	-0.017	0.004	0.015	0.004	-0.002	-0.009	-0.008	-0.012	-0.005	0.000
8	-0.013	-0.008	0.005	0.013	-0.000	-0.011	-0.001	0.007	0.000	-0.005	0.023
9	0.014	-0.002	0.005	0.004	0.003	-0.006	0.009	0.014	-0.000	0.002	0.000
10	0.008	0.005	0.006	0.007	-0.002	-0.027	0.017	0.016	-0.002	0.011	0.004
11	-0.005	0.004	0.006	0.009	0.009	-0.029	-0.018	0.007	-0.006	-0.009	0.008
12	-0.001	0.000	0.006	0.009	0.014	0.026	0.016	-0.003	-0.004	-0.014	0.006
13	-0.018	-0.003	0.020	0.018	0.025	0.024	0.025	-0.009	0.003	-0.025	0.000
14	0.000	0.002	0.012	-0.007	0.023	0.029	0.010	-0.013	-0.011	0.004	0.000
15	0.000	-0.005	0.001	-0.002	0.001	0.019	0.004	-0.005	-0.012	-0.003	0.000
16	0.000	-0.003	-0.002	-0.009	0.007	0.009	0.003	-0.008	-0.007	-0.000	0.000
17	0.000	0.000	-0.005	-0.008	-0.000	0.002	-0.005	-0.006	0.001	0.000	0.000
18	0.000	0.000	-0.006	-0.003	-0.010	-0.005	-0.019	-0.000	0.000	0.000	0.000
19	0.000	0.000	0.000	-0.008	-0.014	0.002	0.007	0.001	0.000	0.000	0.000
20	0.000	0.000	0.000	0.000	-0.015	-0.010	0.000	0.000	0.000	0.000	0.000

Fig. 6.11   Wavefront contours determined from Fig. 6.10 (contour interval 1/200 wavelength).

on the spindle, and using his thumb as the lap.   Once a correction has been made in this manner the lens is retested.   Final figuring continues until the requirements of the optical computer are met.   The time expended in this rather painstaking process may run to several weeks.

6.50   Final Test of the Optical-computer Lens System

Three of the most important criteria on which acceptance of the optical computer is based are (1) the departure of the zero spatial-frequency lobe (central lobe) from theoretical, (2) the rate of falloff of the side lobes in the proximity of the central lobe as a function of distance from the central lobe, and (3) the background noise level.   Using the tabulation of Δ_{ijk} given in Table 6.4 it is possible to calculate the central and side-lobe structure in the output plane of the lens for uniform input illumination. As explained in Chapter Four, the square of the modulus of the Fourier transform taken over the input aperture of the lens system yields the light intensity distribution in the output plane. This light intensity distribution is the Wiener spectrum and, in the particular case of uniform illumination over a circular aperture in the input plane, is the well-known Airy pattern. For example, when the Wiener spectrum is taken of the spatial phase function represented by the wavefront contour map in Fig. 6.11, the results are as shown in Fig. 6.12. In Fig. 6.12 the contour lines are lines of constant light intensity (isophotes) in the output plane. A detailed examination of the accompanying computer calculations shows that there is approximately a $\frac{1}{2}$ percent drop in the peak of the central lobe with respect to theoretical. The peaks

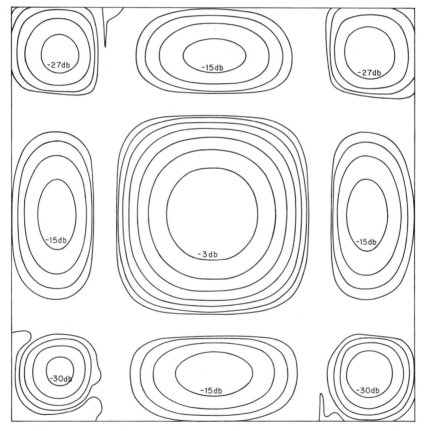

Fig. 6.12 Focal-plane light intensity contours for the wavefront shown in Fig. 6.11 (contour interval 3 dB).

of the primary side lobes adjacent to the central lobe range from 0.2 dB above to 0.4 dB below theoretical. Note how aberrations in the wavefront contribute to an asymmetry in the secondary side-lobe structure.

Side lobes which are considerably above theoretical will produce spurious output signals from the optical computer whereas departures of the height and width of the central lobe from theoretical will decrease the accuracy of the calculations performed. For accuracies of the order of 1 percent, it is necessary to maintain rms wavefront aberrations to 0.02 wavelength. For 10 percent accuracy this requirement may be relaxed to 0.08 wavelength. Figure 6.13 plots permissible rms phase aberrations versus departure of the height of the central lobe from the ideal, i.e., when there are no aberrations. This graph assumes that the phase aberrations are essentially random. These results make it clear why the absolute accuracy of the coherent optical computer is limited to the range of 1 to 10 percent. Relative accuracy may be considerably better, with the exact value being dependent upon the particular optical-computer design.

In order to confirm the computer analysis of optical-system performance, further tests are frequently made. One of the most useful tests is a direct measurement of the light-intensity distribution in the output plane. For this purpose various measuring instruments have been built. One such instrument is shown in Fig. 6.14. This instrument is called a diffraction pattern scanner (DPS). It consists of a

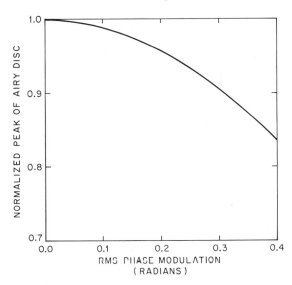

Fig. 6.13 Falloff in focal-point light intensity as a function of rms phase modulation.

Fig. 6.14   Precision photometric measuring instrument for diffraction pattern scanning.

photomultiplier mounted vertically on an elevated precision x-y mechanical stage.   A folding mirror below the stage causes the focal plane of the lens under test on the optical bench to appear in a horizontal plane beneath the stage.   The light intensity distribution in the plane is enlarged and imaged by means of a microscope objective onto a circular aperture in front of the photomultiplier.   At the same time, it is possible to observe the light intensity distribution visually through an eyepiece for purposes of focusing and centering.   As the DPS is scanned across the output plane, the output of the photomultiplier may be recorded by means of an oscilloscope or oscillograph.   Potentiometers on the x and y hand wheels of the DPS permit signals to be delivered to a recorder which are proportional to the coordinates of the points at which the light intensity distribution is being observed.   A typical graph taken by means of such an instrument when performing a single scan through the central lobe in the output plane of an optical computer is shown in Fig. 6.15.   This figure shows the falloff in the side lobes of the Airy pattern over a range of 100 or more side lobes. The sampling theorem would not permit a calculation of the structure

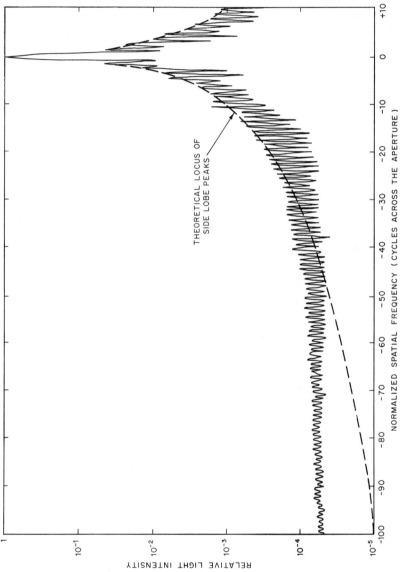

Fig. 6.15 Typical graph made by a diffraction pattern scanner when used to trace the light intensity pattern in the output plane of a coherent optical computer.

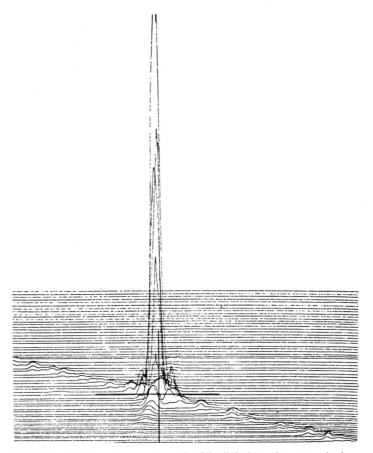

Fig. 6.16 Multitrace, isometric graph of the light intensity pattern in the computer output plane made with the diffraction pattern scanner shown in Fig. 6.14.

of this many side lobes from the quantized tabulation of wavefront aberrations given in Table 6.4.   Thus, one advantage of a direct scan of the output-plane light intensity distribution is the ability to examine as many side lobes as is desired.   Another type of output-plane graph which may be produced by using a DPS is shown in Fig. 6.16.   This graph is an isometric composite of many scans across the output plane.

Neither of the graphs shown in Figs. 6.15 and 6.16 can replace interferometric analysis.   Because phase information is lost in the Wiener spectrum, it is impossible from measurements of this kind to compute the information required by the optician to correct aberrations in the optical system.   Thus, interferometric measurements and direct output-plane light-intensity-distribution measurements complement each other.

6.60   Noise Evaluation

Another valuable result which is obtained by output plane scanning is a
determination of the background noise level in the optical computer.
As has been mentioned above, noise is produced by scatter from surface
dust and surface irregularities, from discontinuities of refractive index,
and from bubbles in the glass of which the lens elements are made.
Another source of noise is multiple reflection of optical energy within
the lens system. Especially significant are those reflections which
produce "ghost" images of the illuminating source.   Figure 6.17 shows
a single-element lens, which is designed to perform a Fourier transform
between its front and back focal planes. The central lobe of the
Wiener spectrum ideally appears at the back focus as shown.   However, at each air-to-glass and glass-to-air passage there will ordinarily
be only partial transmission of the optical energy traveling through the
lens system.   Light striking the first surface of the lens is partially reflected. As is well known, the ratio of transmitted to reflected light
depends upon both polarization and the optical indices of both air and
glass.   The following equations apply:

$$R_{is} = \left[\frac{\sin{(I_i' - I_i)}}{\sin{(I_i' + I_i)}}\right]^2$$

$$R_{ip} = \left[\frac{\tan{(I_i' - I_i)}}{\tan{(I_i' + I_i)}}\right]^2$$

(6.5)

where R_{is} and R_{ip} are the reflectances (with respect to intensity) for
components of the electric field in the plane of the surface and in the

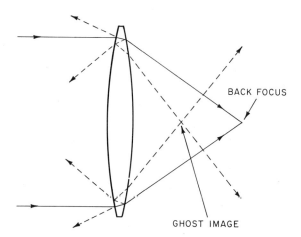

BACK FOCUS

GHOST IMAGE

Fig. 6.17 Optical schematic showing how ghost images
contribute to back-focal-plane noise.

plane of incidence, respectively; I_i is the angle of incidence; and I_i' is the angle of refraction.

In the case illustrated in Fig. 6.17 it is evident that light reflected by the first surface is reflected out of the lens system. Unless it strikes reflecting surfaces which cause this light to be returned into the optical system, it will have no further effect on system performance. This, of course, is the primary reason for blackening all portions of the lens cell as well as other mountings or supports of the optical system upon which spuriously reflected light may impinge. As the rays which have been transmitted through the first surface arrive at the second surface and exit once more into air, there is again a partial reflection as shown. The rays for this second reflection are returned to the first surface of the lens where once more some light is transmitted and some reflected. Transmitted light is returned toward the upstream side of the optical system, and it will be assumed that it is absorbed by a nonreflecting surface. However, light reflected from the first surface is once more returned to the second surface where most of it is transmitted in accordance with eqs. (6.5). This light forms an image or quasi-image of the optical-power source in the downstream portion of the optical computer. This image is the so-called "ghost" image mentioned above. This ghost image contributes a certain amount of defocused optical energy in the computer output plane, which contributes to background noise.

In a typical situation where the index of glass is in the range of 1.60 to 1.70, the total amount of energy contained in the ghost image due to the single lens element shown in Fig. 6.16 may be as great as 1 percent of the total light arriving in the output plane. Usually this energy is spread over a far greater area than the energy which forms the central lobe of the Wiener spectrum. The exact ratio of the height of the central lobe to the background noise level depends upon three quantities: (1) the cone angle of light normally brought to a focus in the output plane, (2) the distance from the ghost image to the output plane, and (3) the cone angle of the light which is brought to a focus in producing the ghost image itself. In general, the signal-to-noise ratio which relates the intensity of the central lobe to the background noise level due to a ghost image a distance d from the output plane is given by the equation

$$\frac{S}{N} = \frac{1}{\delta}\left(\frac{d}{\lambda_L f_{\mathrm{no}_s} f_{\mathrm{no}_n}}\right)^2 \tag{6.6}$$

where δ is the ratio of the total energy in the ghost image to the total energy in the central lobe, f_{no_s} is the f-number of the cone which forms the central lobe, and f_{no_n} is the f-number of the cone which forms the ghost image.

In order to increase the ratio of signal energy to background noise produced by ghost images, the usual technique is to improve the impedance match at all air-to-glass passages. If it were possible to obtain and vapor-deposit materials of arbitrary optical index, it would be possible to prevent essentially all reflected light by merely applying a half-wave coating of the appropriate material to all glass surfaces with an optical index n_c, given by

$$n_c = \sqrt{n_0 n_g} \tag{6.7}$$

where n_0 is the optical index of air and n_g is the optical index of glass. This equation implies that the material for the half-wave coating lies in the range of approximately 1.20 to 1.30.   Unfortunately, materials of this optical index which are suitable for coatings are unobtainable and compromises must, therefore, be made.

A frequently used coating material which is an effective compromise is magnesium fluoride (MgF_2) having an optical index of 1.38. MgF_2 is readily deposited by vapor deposition and presents a uniform and durable surface.   Figure 6.18 plots reflectivity against angle of incidence of a typical air-to-glass interface where the glass is coated with a half-wavelength layer of MgF_2.   As can be seen, the reflected light is reduced considerably over that reflected in the situation where the glass is un-

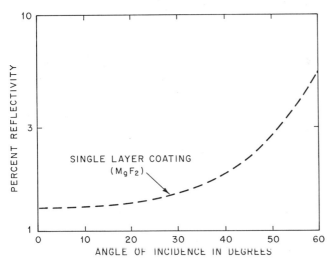

Fig. 6.18 Reflectivity as a function of angle of incidence at an air-to-glass interface coated with a single layer of magnesium fluoride.

coated. Still further improvements may be achieved by using multi-layer coatings on the glass surfaces [6.9]. Such coatings are arranged so that the amplitudes of light reflected from the various boundaries of the multilayer coating produce a vector sum which is essentially zero at the required angle of incidence. Many combinations of metal oxides may be utilized in these multilayer coatings. For example, bismuth oxide with an optical index of 2.40 may be layered with magnesium fluoride in order to produce reflectivities of a small fraction of a percent. These low reflectivities are obtained, of course, only for a limited range of the angle of incidence and must be designed for the specific requirements of the optical-computer lens system in question.

One danger in the use of multilayer coatings is that either bulk or surface nonuniformities in these coatings may produce random phase modulation in the transmitted wavefront and cause scatter of the transmitted light. Thus the coating which is so carefully designed and applied for the purpose of removing background noise due to ghost images may increase background scatter. An extreme example of

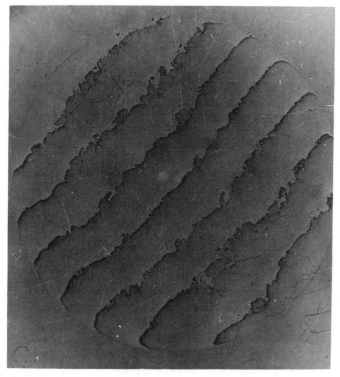

Fig. 6.19 Fabry-Perot interferogram of a glass surface coated with a multilayer antireflection coating, showing severe irregularities.

irregularities which may be found in the wavefront transmitted through a multilayer coating is interferometrically shown in Fig. 6.19.   At the present writing, the best compromise between the multilayer antireflection coating, which can essentially eliminate ghost images but which may contribute to scatter, and the simpler, scatter-free single-layer coating is not completely resolved.   In general, it may be said that the single- or double-layer coatings are presently preferred to multilayer coatings.   However, this preference may change with the rapid advances which are being made in the art of coating optical-computer lens elements.   Of course, whatever coatings are used must be durable. Periodic cleaning of the lens system must not scratch or remove the lens coatings or else catastrophic increases in the output noise level will occur.

Finally, referring to Fig. 6.15 it is seen that, for the computer lens system measured, the background noise level is approximately 45 dB below the level of the central lobe.   Signals in the input plane of this computer having an amplitude modulation of less than 1 percent or a phase modulation less than 1/100 rad (0.6°) would produce a corresponding component in the Wiener spectrum having the same level as noise in the output plane.   The noise level in the particular system whose measurements are shown in Fig. 6.15 is higher than normal because of ghost images due to uncoated lens elements.   Other optical-computer lens systems having coated lens elements have been made which have achieved a 60-dB central lobe-to-background noise ratio.

REFERENCES

6.1   MacKenzie, J. D.: "Modern Aspects of the Vitreous State," Butterworth, London, 1960.
6.2   Morey, W.: "The Properties of Glass," Reinhold, New York, 1964.
6.3   Stamworth, J. E.: "Physical Properties of Glass," Clarendon Press, Oxford, 1950.
6.4   Stevels, J. M.: "Progress in the Theory of the Physical Properties of Glass," Elsevier, Amsterdam, 1948.
6.5   U.S. Government Military Standard MIL-0-13830 (Ord).
6.6   Holland, L.: "The Properties of Glass Surfaces," Wiley, New York, 1964.
6.7   Tyman, F.: "Prism and Lens Making," University of Glasgow Press, Glasgow, 1957.
6.8   Tolansky, S.: "Multiple Beam Interferometry," Oxford University Press, London, 1948.
6.9   Holland, L.: "Vacuum Deposition of Thin Films," Wiley, New York, 1956.

Chapter Seven

Methods of Output Detection

7.00 Introduction

The output of the coherent optical computer is the changing light intensity distribution in its output plane. This light intensity distribution expresses the results of the calculations being performed by the computer. In order to translate these results into useful output signals, a transducer or array of transducers must be supplied. The output transducer(s) converts photon arrivals into electrical signals. The choice of output transducer determines, to a certain extent, the efficiency and accuracy with which the optical computer is utilized.

The general problem of real-time output detection is treated in this chapter. After reviewing the primary physical effects which are now in use for light detection, a number of devices for output detection are discussed. Finally, a comparison is made between the use of these devices for direct detection of the computer output and for heterodyne detection.

For other than real-time output detection such materials as silver halide emulsions, photochromic layers, photothermoplastic films, etc., may be used for making output-plane recordings.   For a discussion of these materials and methods of utilization the reader is referred to the appropriate sections of Chapter Five.

7.10   Physical Means for Photodetection

Basically, two physical effects are used in the optical computer today to convert optical energy into electric energy.   One of these effects is vacuum photoemission and the other is photoconduction in semiconductors.   Photoemission is the effect which is utilized in vacuum photomultipliers and phototubes, including imaging tubes such as the image orthicon and the image dissector.   Photoconduction is used in both bulk and p-n-junction semiconductor detectors as well as in the Vidicon, Plumbicon, and other related imaging tubes.

In selecting the particular computer readout method, the optical-computer engineer must consider available devices as related to computer output requirements for:

1. Photosensitivity
2. Bandwidth and time response
3. Spatial and temporal noise
4. Spatial coverage

Because of the enormous variety of uses of the coherent optical computer, no general statements can be made as to which method of output detection is preferred.   Therefore, this chapter does not attempt to treat the many possible combinations of computer output requirements and output detection devices.   Instead, each of the most important output detectors which are in current use for the purpose of converting optical to electric energy is considered individually.   Basic operating regions are outlined for each device with the hope that the individual computer engineer will thereby be aided in selecting the one which is the most useful for his particular application.

7.20   Vacuum Photomultipliers

For light detection in the visible region of the optical spectrum, the vacuum photomultiplier is probably the most useful detector now in existence.   This is true because of its high-gain, low-noise, wide bandwidth and wide dynamic range.   Although its quantum efficiency does not quite approach that achievable in the semiconductor light-sensitive devices, this disadvantage is more than offset by the other advantages of the vacuum photomultiplier.

In the vacuum photomultiplier, photoelectrons are created by the interaction between arriving photons and a photoemissive surface.

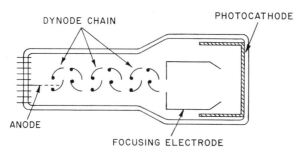

Fig. 7.1   Internal structure of a vacuum photomultiplier.

Electrically the photoemissive surface forms the cathode of the device, as shown in Fig. 7.1.   The photocathode current which is produced is generally small.   It is amplified by causing the photoelectrons to interact sequentially with a chain of secondary-emissive surfaces, or *dynodes*, with the resultant current being collected at the anode to produce the output signal.

Most photocathodes are made from low-work-function semiconductors.   The photoemissive surface is selected for its stability, spectral response, and quantum efficiency.   Of the various elements available, compounds using the alkali metals have found the greatest use as efficient photoemitters.   In order to increase quantum efficiency, certain composite photoemitting surfaces have been developed.   Typical photocathode materials are cesium antimonide (Cs_3Sb), cesium iodide (CsI), and cesium oxide (CsO).

Typical spectral-response curves for several photoemissive surfaces are shown in Fig. 7.2.   The curves are given in terms of microamperes per watt as well as in terms of quantum efficiency.   Both scales are important in that, although the quantum efficiency is relatively constant with wavelength throughout the visible, the emission in terms of microamperes per watt drops in the shorter-wavelength region because of the decrease in the number of quanta (electrons) per second which are produced at constant light flux for these wavelengths.   The S-4 surface is Cs_3Sb.   The S-1 surface is obtained by using a compound of silver–cesium oxide and cesium designed to extend performance into the near-infrared region.   Finally the S-20 surface is another compound photoemissive material containing other metals as well as cesium.

Photons penetrate the surface of the photocathode and excite valence electrons into states above the vacuum level.   The quantum efficiency of the photocathode depends upon the total absorption coefficient α_T, the absorption coefficient of photoemissivity α_{PE}, and the mean escape depth l_0.   Using the notation employed by Spicer and Wooten [7.1], the escape probability for an excited electron is given by

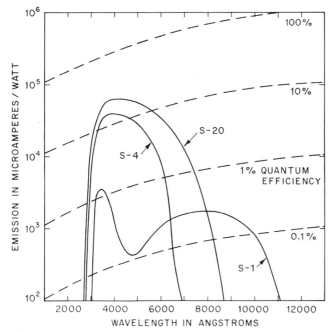

Fig. 7.2 Emission characteristics of several types of photosurfaces.

$$P(x) = Ae^{-x/l_0} \tag{7.1}$$

where A is the escape probability for a surface electron and x is the distance from the surface along a perpendicular to the surface. Note that the absorption coefficients have the dimension of reciprocal length.

The rate of excitation of electrons in a slab of width dx in a plane parallel to the photocathode surface may be expressed as

$$(I_0 e^{-\alpha_T x})(\alpha_{PE}\, dx) \tag{7.2}$$

where I_0 is the incident light intensity in photons per second per unit area. The number of electrons which escape from this slab per second per unit area is given by the equation

$$de_{PE} = \alpha_{PE} I_0 e^{-(\alpha_T + 1/l_0)x}\, dx \tag{7.3}$$

When integrated, eq. (7.3) yields the quantum efficiency of the photocathode. For typical photoemissive materials α_T is of the order of 10^6 per centimeter and the escape depth is of the order of a few hundred angstroms.

The response time of the photoemissive reaction may be calculated from the velocity of the electron, the energy loss per lattice collision, and the mean distance between collisions. Spicer and Wooten [7.1] quote an order of magnitude of 10^{-12} s for this process. Similar considerations hold for the time response of the secondary-emission multiplication process in the dynode structure.

If the response time of the photomultiplier were limited only by the response time of the photocathode and secondary-electron-emitting surface, the device would respond within picoseconds. The fact that this is not true is due to velocity dispersion as electrons travel from dynode to dynode in the photomultiplier structure. Between the photocathode and the first dynode there may be an electron lens system. Whether this electron lens system is present depends primarily on the use for which the photomultiplier is designed, as discussed later in this section. Again for reasons mentioned later in this section, the voltage between the photocathode and the first dynode is frequently considerably larger than the dynode-to-dynode potential along the multiplier chain. The specific voltage selected depends upon the signal levels to be detected by the photocathode and upon the material used for secondary-electron multiplication at the dynode.

Typical plots showing how the secondary-emission ratio (δ) varies as a function of the energy of incident electrons are shown in Fig. 7.3. Although cesium antimonide has one of the highest secondary-emission ratio values available, other secondary emitters are frequently preferred because of their greater stability under electron bombardment and their higher values of δ in the lower electron-energy ranges. The shape of the secondary-emission curve is explained as follows: As the energy of incident electrons increases, the ratio of emitted secondary electrons to incident electrons rapidly rises. As the energy of the primary electrons increases still further, these electrons penetrate farther and farther into

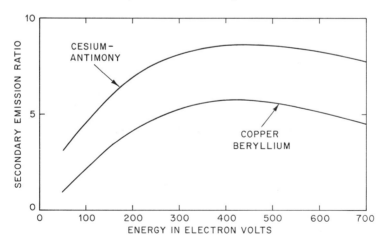

Fig. 7.3 Secondary-electron-emission characteristics of cesium antimony and copper beryllium.

the material. Some secondary electrons are now produced so far beneath the surface of the material that they are unable to escape. For sufficiently high primary-electron energies the secondary-emission ratio begins to drop. For most materials the maximum value of secondary-emission ratio occurs in a primary-electron energy range corresponding to 200 to 1,000 V.

For primary-electron energies corresponding to approximately 100 V or less, the value of the secondary-emission ratio is relatively independent of the angle of incidence of the primary electrons. However, for higher primary-electron energy levels, the value of the secondary-emission ratio is found to be dependent on the angle of incidence. The ratio is found to increase when the angle of primary-electron incidence decreases. The angular distribution of the secondary electrons as well as their energy distribution is important in the design of electron multipliers.

Fig. 7.4 shows the energy-distribution histogram for secondary electrons emitted in response to primary electrons at 150 V. The peak at 150 V is due to primary electrons which are merely reflected from the surface. Electrons lying in the range of 0 to 50 V are the true secondaries. Electrons lying between 50 and 150 V are primaries reflected from the surface with a loss of energy. Over a wide range of primary-electron energies the secondary-electron energy distribution has been found to exhibit a maximum which occurs in the range of a few volts to several volts. These secondary electrons are emitted with an angular distribution which is generally independent of the angle of incidence of the primary electrons and which is found to be proportional to the cosine

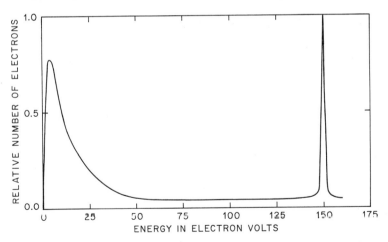

Fig. 7.4 Typical energy distribution for both secondary electrons and reflected primary electrons.

of the angle between the direction of the emission and the normal to the emitting surface.   Interestingly it has been found that the energy distribution of the true secondaries is independent of the energy of the primaries except at very low levels where the primary electrons have an energy corresponding to less than 10 V.   At this point little or no secondary-electron emission occurs.

All the above considerations are important in selecting materials for the photoemitting and secondary-electron multiplying surfaces, in designing the physical structure of the photomultiplier, and in selecting the voltage at which it will operate.   In turn, these considerations are controlled by the exact use of the photomultiplier in the optical computer.   The goal of the optical computer engineer is to select or to design a photomultiplier which optimizes signal-to-noise ratio in the configuration for which it is intended.   The photoelectron multiplication required, and hence the number of dynodes furnished, is determined by the signal bandwidth and by the light level expected in the computer output plane.   As will be discussed in Sec. 7.22, electron multiplication must be sufficient to amplify the photomultiplier signal to the point where it is above the thermal noise level of whatever external electronic device is used to accept the photomultiplier output.   The fewer the number of dynodes, the less is the electron velocity dispersion, and the wider is the available bandwidth.   For very high light levels, as is characterized by optical heterodyne detection (see Sec. 7.40), it is possible to operate at unity gain and omit the dynode chain completely. In this case, when broad bandwidths are also required, a traveling-wave structure may be employed.

The configuration of a traveling-wave phototube is shown in Fig. 7.5. Light arrives at the photocathode and emitted photoelectrons produce the electron stream which is focused into the helix.   The helix in the traveling-wave phototube acts as a series of resonant-cavity couplers

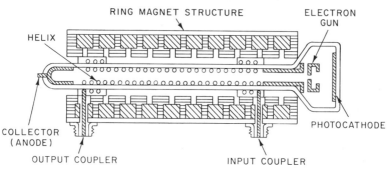

Fig. 7.5   Internal structure of a traveling-wave phototube.

whose output signals are added in phase.   Electron velocity dispersion is negligible, and extremely broadband operation is possible.   Discussions by McMurtry and Siegman [7.2] and by Caddes [7.3] provide additional information on this type of detector.

When gain is required in conjunction with broad-bandwidth performance, it is possible to combine a dynode structure with the traveling-wave phototube configuration as described by Blattner et al. [7.4]. Also, the so-called "cross-field" photomultiplier configuration, as described by Gaddy and Holshouser [7.5] and by Miller and Wittner [7.6], may be applicable.   When light levels are low and single-point detection in the optical-computer output plane is permissible, the photomultiplier for this situation should have an extremely small photoemitting surface in order to minimize thermionic emission, should electronically focus the emitting area on the first dynode, should utilize as high a potential as possible between the photocathode and the first dynode, and should have a multiplication ratio as high as is required to overcome thermal noise in the associated electronics.   Eberhardt [7.7] discusses design problems in photomultipliers of this type.

7.21 Multichannel Output Detection   So far this chapter has discussed vacuum photoemission devices which provide a single output channel.   When the coherent optical computer requires multiple outputs, two possible choices are available.   One choice is to use an array of photodetectors.   This is, of course, a cumbersome approach because of the relatively large size of most phototubes and photomultipliers.   The other choice is to time-multiplex the outputs of the computer, i.e., to use a scanned photoemissive surface or to physically move a single photodetector over the output plane.   Both of these approaches are discussed below.   The image orthicon and image dissector are taken as examples of electronically scanned devices and then a mechanical scanner is examined.

The general structure of an image orthicon is shown in Fig. 7.6.   Incident photons cause photoelectrons to be transferred from a large photoemissive surface to corresponding points on the target.   As each point on the target is scanned by the electron beam, it is returned to cathode potential.   The number of electrons landing upon each point on the target depends upon the surface potential.   Thus in regions where the input light intensity is high the surface will have a relatively large positive charge, whereas where the input has been dark the potential will be less positive.   Returning electrons which are reflected from the surface are multiplied in a standard photomultiplier-dynode chain.   All the considerations discussed above with relation to photomultiplier tubes apply here.   Except for the high cost, large size, and

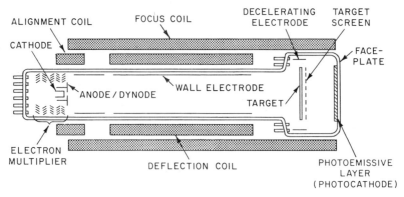

Fig. 7.6 Internal structure of the image orthicon.

relative complexity of the image orthicon, it is a useful device for high-speed computer-output-plane scanning where the "memory" of the photoemissive surface is used to permit wideband operation with a basically narrowband output.   Dwell times of the order of 100 ns per resolution element are possible with satisfactory signal-to-noise ratio performance.

Another electronically scanned photoemissive device is the image dissector which has the sensitivity and dynamic range of the orthicon without its memory capacity.   This imaging tube differs from the image orthicon only in that its photoemissive surface is held at a fixed potential. Photoelectrons emitted from each region of the photoemissive surface are sequentially focused on the first dynode of the electron multiplier chain by means of a system of deflection coils.   The location of the selected photoemitting region is determined by the field impressed by the deflection coils in the space between the photoemissive surface and the first dynode and is controlled by the current in the deflection coils themselves.

Both the image orthicon and the image dissector suffer from point-to-point variability in the photoemissivity of the input surface.   Variation may be as great as 50 percent about the mean value of photoemissivity. Thus these electronically scanned output-plane detectors are of use primarily in optical computers where the presence or absence of signal must be detected in many output channels with only a marginal requirement on accuracy in determining the signal level.   Where the computer output signals are continuous over the time period required to scan the output plane, the image dissector is useful.   If the duration of the output signals is short with respect to the time required for a complete scan, then the image orthicon must be employed.

When output-signal accuracy is required in multiple-output optical computers, mechanical scanners may be used. One of the most accurate and convenient output-plane scanners is the oscillating-mirror scanner which is shown in Fig. 7.7. The oscillatory motion of two orthogonal mirrors causes an image of the entire output plane of the computer to be scanned over a small aperture in front of the input face of a single photomultiplier tube. This scanner has all the characteristics of an image dissector except for the fact that output selection is done optomechanically rather than by electronic means. There is therefore no modulation of the output signals due to variations in photoemission, as the same region of the photomultiplier's photosurface is used at all times. Thus this output-plane scanner takes full advantage of the dynamic range of the photomultiplier in precision output detection. Its primary defect is that it is relatively slow, with a minimum dwell time of the order of a microsecond.

Even more complex optomechanical scanners using photomultipliers as detectors find frequent use in the static testing of the coherent optical computer. In this application the relatively slow speed of mechanical scanning is unimportant since the purpose of static testing is to examine output-plane performance on a point-by-point basis as various patterns of input test signals are applied to the optical computer in a predetermined manner. Certain rather elaborate scanners have been built for

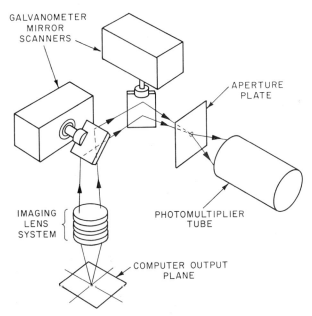

Fig. 7.7 Output-plane scanner using two orthogonal oscillating mirrors.

this purpose.   A typical example is the diffraction pattern scanner, or DPS, discussed in Chapter Six (see Sec. 6.50).   Here the scanning motion is obtained by means of a machinist's microscope stage (see Fig. 6.14).   The total travel of the stage is of the order of a few centimeters in both x and y to a precision of 1 or 2 μm.

In use the DPS is positioned on the test bench with the optical computer as shown in a typical setup illustrated by Fig. 7.8.   The 45° folding mirror shown is used to image the output plane of the optical computer in a horizontal plane beneath the microscope stage.   The DPS is then driven in a programmed fashion across the output plane. Its exact position is monitored by precision rotary potentiometers on both the x and y drives.   Signals from these potentiometers are used to control the x and y deflections of a recording system while the photomultiplier output is mixed with the y deflection so as to produce an isometric output.   The reader is referred to Fig. 6.16 for an illustration of a typical isometric plot which is an example of an actual opticalcomputer output-plane light intensity distribution.   Up to several

Fig. 7.8 Typical optical-computer test bench setup showing (1) the diffraction pattern scanner in the background, (2) the optical computer system, (3) the spatial light modulator, (4) the electronic input-signal synthesizer, and (5) the laser light source.

million output channels may be accurately monitored and recorded with such a DPS system.

7.22 Signal and Noise Considerations in Photomultipliers Shot noise and dark current are the primary sources of noise in photoemissive devices. With sufficient electron multiplication, thermal noise in the associated electronic amplifier may be made negligible. Define I_T as the total light flux reaching the photoemissive surface of the photomultiplier. Part of this light flux will be due to the desired output signal and part will be background light which is always present. Thus I_T may be decomposed into signal and background as given by the following equation:

$$I_T = I_s + I_b \tag{7.4}$$

The units of I_s are intensity in power per unit area for the signal, and, similarly, I_b is the intensity of the background illumination. As explained in Sec. 7.40, I_b is generally noise in the case of direct detection of the output but includes a desired reference background in the case of heterodyne detection. It is often the purpose of the computer and the threshold circuitry which follows the photomultiplier to determine the probability of a signal being present in any given interval of time. It may also be the purpose of the computer to determine as accurately as possible the value of a signal which is known to exist at the particular time interval.

The current reaching the first dynode due to I_s is given by

$$i_s = \int \frac{q \eta I_s}{h \nu} dA \tag{7.5}$$

where q is the charge of the electron, η is the quantum efficiency of the photocathode, h is Planck's contant, ν is the optical frequency, and dA is the differential area of the photoemissive surface. Similarly, the current reaching the first dynode due to I_b is given by

$$i_b = \int \frac{q \eta I_b}{h \nu} dA \tag{7.6}$$

The total current arriving at the first dynode, i_T, is given by

$$i_T = i_s + i_b + i_d \tag{7.7}$$

where i_d is the dark current or thermionic emission of the photocathode. At the output of the dynode chain, the available signal power output P_s is usually expressed by the equation

$$P_s = M^2 i_s^2 R_{eq} \tag{7.8}$$

where the symbol M represents the current multiplication of the dynode structure and R_{eq} is the so-called "equivalent resistance" of the photomultiplier. This equivalent resistance has the dimensions of impedance; is, in general, frequency-dependent; and is a conversion factor relating the multiplied photocurrent to the maximum available power output of the photomultiplier.

In order to calculate the output signal-to-noise ratio, both shot noise and thermal noise should be considered. In general, thermal noise as represented by dark current is negligible in photomultipliers. Dark-current levels vary over wide ranges but are usually quoted in the range of 10^{-9} to 10^{-12} W of equivalent input power. At the input to the first dynode, there will be an rms shot-noise current given by

$$i_{n_{rms}} = \sqrt{2qi_TB} \tag{7.9}$$

where B is the bandwidth of the system. Like the signal current, this noise current will be multiplied by the dynode structure to yield an rms noise at the output as follows:

$$i'_{n_{rms}} = M\sqrt{2qi_TF_xB} \tag{7.10}$$

where F_x is the excess noise factor contributed by the multiplication process itself. A plot of F_x, as given by Anderson and McMurtry [7.8], is shown in Fig. 7.9. The equation for F_x is given in Ref. [7.8] as follows:

$$F_x = \frac{\delta^{N+1} - 1}{\delta^N(\delta - 1)} \tag{7.11}$$

Figure 7.9 makes it clear why it is important to operate with a high secondary-emission ratio per dynode, especially for the first few dynodes. Thus for low photocathode current levels it is usually the practice to operate with a potential difference between the first dynode and the photocathode at a higher value than is typical for the dynode-to-dynode potential in the rest of the photomultiplier chain. This minimizes the shot-noise contribution of the dynode structure itself.

The total noise power output including thermal noise is given by the following expression:

$$P_n = 2M^2qi_TF_xBR_{eq} + kTB \tag{7.12}$$

Combining eq. (7.12) with eq. (7.8) yields the resultant equation for output signal-to-noise ratio as follows:

$$\frac{S}{N} = \frac{M^2i_s^2R_{eq}}{2M^2qi_TF_xBR_{eq} + kTB} \tag{7.13}$$

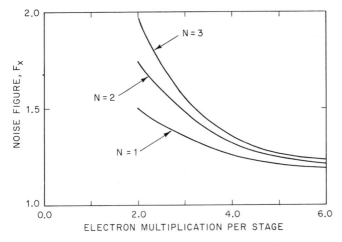

Fig. 7.9 Photomultiplication noise figure. (*After McMurtry.*)

where T is the absolute temperature.   It is now clear that for high values of $M^2 R_{eq}$ thermal noise can be made negligible and shot-noise-limited performance can be achieved.   This requirement is expressed by the inequality

$$M^2 R_{eq} \gg \frac{kT}{2q F_x i_T} \tag{7.14}$$

In Table 7.1, taken from Ref. [7.8], values for both M and $M^2 R_{eq}$ of three basically different types of photomultipliers are given.

7.30   Semiconductor Photoconductive Detectors

Solid-state photodetectors have the advantage of small size.   Also, their quantum efficiency is high in comparison with photoemissive light

TABLE 7.1*

Photodetector	Current multiplication M	$M^2 R_{eq}$, ohms
Vacuum phototube	1	50
Traveling-wave phototube	1	10^5–10^7
Photomultiplier	10^5–10^6	10^{12}–10^{14}
Static crossed-field photomultiplier	10^5	10^{11}–10^{12}
Germanium p-i-n diode	1	≈ 100
Germanium avalanche diode.....................	25	≈ 100
Silicon avalanche diode	100	10^5–10^6

*Adapted from Anderson and McMurtry [7.8].

detectors, especially in the near infrared. However, the bandwidth of these devices is inherently narrower than that of phototubes and photomultipliers. Also, thermal noise may present serious problems at low light levels. Thus the use of solid-state photodetectors is restricted to relatively narrow-bandwidth optical-computer applications where the incident flux is high.

Quantum efficiency as a function of wavelength is plotted in Fig. 7.10 for both silicon and germanium. Values of $M^2 R_{eq}$ are given in Table 7.1 and can be seen to be lower than corresponding values for photoemissive light detectors. This explains why these devices are usually thermal-noise limited [see eq. (7.14)].

Most solid-state photodetectors are activated by light flux incident on a shallow back-biased *p-n* junction. Diffusion depths are designed so that hole-electron pairs are generated in the depletion layer by the intense field which is present, thus producing the photocurrent. If the depletion layer is too wide, transit-time effects will limit frequency response. If the depletion layer is too thin, photons will penetrate it and fail to produce hole-electron pairs where desired. A thin depletion layer will also have excessive capacitance which limits the speed of response of the device. Saturated drift velocities in the depletion layer in the region of 10^6 cm/s are typical for silicon and germanium with α_T values in the vicinity of 10^3 per centimeter. Thus transit times near 10^{-9} s may be predicted. The equivalent series resistance of the junction usually is between 10 and 100 Ω with junction capacitance running from a few to several hundred picofarads, depending upon the size of the active area. Anderson and McMurtry [7.8] give an upper

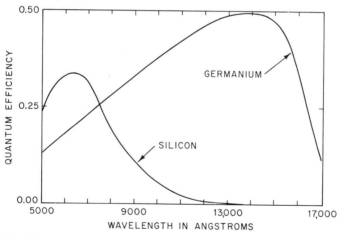

Fig. 7.10   Quantum efficiency of silicon and germanium detectors as a function of wavelength.

bound for R_{eq} in these devices as

$$R_{\mathrm{eq}} \leqslant \frac{1}{4BC} \tag{7.15}$$

where C is the capacitance of the junction. For example, with $B = 10^7$ Hz and $C = 1\,\mathrm{pF}$, the maximum value of R_{eq} is of the order of 10^4. Thus, as already stated, the solid-state photodetector is almost always thermal-noise-limited at room temperature except for the case of narrow-bandwidth signals and/or large signal currents.

By increasing the field in the depletion layer and properly designing the characteristics of the device, it is possible to produce electron multiplication in solid-state photodetectors. With sufficient voltage across the p-n junction, carriers reach velocities high enough to ionize neutral atoms in the lattice. In this manner a situation equivalent to an avalanche discharge in gases may result. Work on the avalanche photodiode, as reported by Johnson [7.9], Miller [7.10], and Goetzberger et al. [7.11], has led to multiplication ratios which in some cases are high enough to permit shot-noise-limited performance. However, large-area, plasma-free, and structurally perfect junctions are still difficult to produce, and values of M greater than about 100 are not yet readily achievable. With careful design, video bandwidths from 10 to as high as 100 MHz have been attained. Finally, it should be noted that the avalanche photodiode produces excess noise due to the statistical nature of the avalanche process and that response times are lengthened by the time required by the cumulative process by which the avalanche builds up and/or subsides.

Despite these deficiencies, no photodetectors other than p-n-junction detectors are available for the detection of energy at optical wavelengths greater than about $1\,\mu\mathrm{m}$. Although optical computers almost invariably are designed to operate at wavelengths in the visible, the optical-computer engineer should keep in mind that excellent optical-power sources are available which emit in the near infrared and which could be used to advantage with silicon or germanium p-n-junction output detectors in certain special cases.

7.31 Arrays for Multiple-output Detection Semiconductor light detectors are sufficiently small in size that arrays of these devices may be constructed for use as detectors in multiple-output optical computers. Where output signal levels are high enough to permit the use of either standard p-n-junction or avalanche photodiodes, it is possible to take advantage of the convenience of arrays of these devices. A typical photodiode has an active area which is only a few thousandths of an inch square. The high-yield diffusion and vapor-deposition processes developed by the integrated-circuit industry permit large arrays of these diodes to be fabricated with reasonable uniformity and at low cost. With them it is possible to observe simultaneously a multiplicity of points in the output plane of the optical computer. When functions being calculated by the optical computer must be monitored individually at many points at once, data may be sensed at all output points in the photodiode array. In this case the number of outputs is limited primarily by the mechanical problems involved in producing multilead device packages. Photodiode arrays with hundreds of outputs have been produced, as, for example, in the array used for reading simultaneously all elements in all rows and columns of a punched card. In certain cases, however, when the output light energy of the computer is momentarily concentrated in only one of many points in the output plane, it is possible to take advantage of certain combinatorial methods of arranging the output leads to make signal processing less cumbersome. Figure 7.11 shows an *x-y* photodiode array designed so that the *x* and *y* coordinates of an output light pulse are read out instantaneously as it is received. Although this system may give ambiguous outputs when three or more light pulses appear simultaneously in the computer output plane, its simplicity of construction is extremely useful in the situation where the likelihood of such occurrences is small.

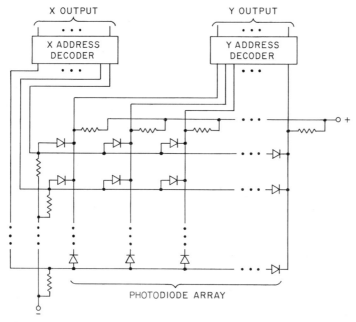

Fig. 7.11   Electrical schematic for decoding the output of a photodiode array for use in optical-computer readout.

As the size of the output detector array increases, a point is reached, especially in the case where simultaneous monitoring of many outputs is necessary, when it is impossible to solve the mechanical problem of providing individual connections to all the photodetectors. A solution to this problem has been provided by Gordon [7.12] who reported the development of an array of p-n junctions which are sequentially addressed by an electron beam. Junctions are formed in a thin slice of n-type silicon with the p regions facing toward the electron gun. As the beam scans the array, each p region is brought to cathode potential. Holding the body of the material at a slight negative potential back-biases the junctions. Light impinging on the side of the slice which is opposite the junctions produces carriers which travel through the depletion layer and discharge the nearest p region. When the p region is again charged by the electron beam, a time-multiplexed output is generated, as in the image orthicon. Another semiconductor output time-multiplexer is the Plumbicon tube where the p-n-junction layer is continuous rather than discrete. This device uses a lead oxide–tin oxide interface to form the junction. The Plumbicon's performance is very similar to a discrete p-n-junction device and is described in detail by De Haan et al. [7.13].

Both the above devices are variations of the well-known Vidicon and, as with the Vidicon, owe their appeal to their low cost and simplicity. The Vidicon (see Fig. 7.12) incorporates a photosensitive layer of intrinsic semiconductor material such as antimony trisulfide. One side of this layer is scanned by an electron beam which keeps it at cathode potential. The other side is connected to a transparent electrode held at a potential which is 10 to 20 V above the cathode potential. Hole-electron pairs, created by incident light striking the photoconductor, diffuse through the photoconductor, thus causing a change in surface

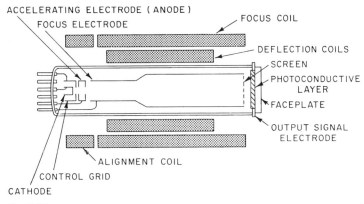

Fig. 7.12 Internal structure of the Vidicon.

potential.   When the scanning electron beam impinges on a point on the surface which has a slight positive charge, electrons are deposited so as to return the surface to cathode potential.   These electrons capacitatively induce current in the transparent electrode on the opposite face of the photoconductive layer, causing a current flow which is allowed to pass through an external resistor.   Signal current through this so-called "target resistor" permits the detection of the desired time-multiplexed output-signal-voltage waveform.

Although the standard Vidicon has the advantage of simplicity in its target construction, it must operate at higher input light levels than the Plumbicon or the electron-beam-scanned silicon diode array because of the existence of a relatively large amount of dark current.   Dark current is suppressed in the p-n-junction output devices because of the high impedance of the back-biased junction(s).

7.40   Direct Versus Heterodyne Detection

In all coherent optical computers the output may be obtained by either direct or heterodyne detection.   In heterodyne detection some of the optical energy which is used to power the computer is diverted to the output plane in an appropriate fashion.   In the output plane this energy is used to provide a background light level which is constant in phase and intensity.   By applying this background appropriately the output signals generated by the computer may be amplified.   In this manner the thermal noise associated with the output detectors may be overcome.

The maximum signal-to-noise ratio which may be achieved by direct detection has already been derived in Sec. 7.22.   When the amplification of the output detector is sufficient to overcome thermal noise, eqs. (7.13) and (7.14) may be combined to yield

$$\frac{S}{N} = \frac{i_s}{2qF_xB} \qquad (7.16)$$

Equation (7.16) is based on the assumption that dark current and background are vanishingly small, that is, $i_d \ll i_s$ and $i_b \ll i_s$.   Using eq. (7.5) this expression for signal-to-noise ratio may be rewritten as

$$\frac{S}{N} = \frac{\eta P_s}{2h\nu F_xB} \qquad (7.17)$$

where P_s is the total signal power and is given by

$$P_s = \int I_s \, dA \qquad (7.18)$$

In the case of heterodyne detection let the output light amplitude distribution due to the signal be given by

$$E_s(x,y,t) = E_s(x,y)e^{-j\omega_L t} \tag{7.19}$$

where ω_L is the radian temporal frequency of the light and is assumed to be constant over the output plane. Next, let the background light amplitude distribution be given by

$$E_b(x\ y,t) = E_b(x,y)e^{-j(\omega_L + \Delta\omega_L)t} \tag{7.20}$$

where $\Delta\omega_L$ is the intermediate frequency (IF) to be used in heterodyning. Methods for introducing this IF will be reviewed in Sec. 7.41.

Wherever $E_s(x,y,t)$ and $E_b(x,y,t)$ are spatially coincident the output detector will produce a signal current given by

$$i_s(x,y) = C_0 \frac{\eta q}{h\nu} \left[E_s^2(x,y) + E_b^2(x,y) + 2E_s(x,y)E_b(x,y) \cos \Delta\omega_L t\right] \tag{7.21}$$

where C_0 is a constant and it is assumed that $E_s(x,y)$ and $E_b(x,y)$ are real, that is $E_s(x,y) = E_s^*(x,y)$ and $E_b(x,y) = E_b^*(x,y)$.

In heterodyne detection it is customary to make the background illumination far stronger than that due to the output signal. The signal from the output detector is passed through an IF filter to remove the dc background term. Thus the only source of noise in the output signal is background shot noise.

After multiplication in the detector and IF filtering, the output current is

$$i_s'(x,y) = \frac{2C_0 M\eta q}{h\nu} E_s(x,y)E_b(x,y) \cos \Delta\omega_L t \tag{7.22}$$

The rms value of this output current is, of course,

$$i_{s_{\text{rms}}}'(x,y) = \frac{\sqrt{2}C_0 M\eta q}{h\nu} E_s(x,y)E_b(x,y) \tag{7.23}$$

Finally, the maximum signal power available is given by

$$P_s(x,y) = \tfrac{1}{2}\left[i_{s_{\text{rms}}}'(x,y)\right]^2 R_{\text{eq}} = \left[\frac{C_0 M\eta q}{h\nu} E_s(x,y)E_b(x,y)\right]^2 R_{\text{eq}} \tag{7.24}$$

The output shot-noise current due to the background illumination is

$$i_{n_{\text{rms}}}'(x,y) = M\sqrt{\frac{2\eta q^2 C_0 E_b^2(x,y)F_x B}{h\nu}} \tag{7.25}$$

with a corresponding available output noise power of

$$P_n(x,y) = \frac{C_0 M^2 \eta q^2 E_b^2(x,y)F_x B R_{\text{eq}}}{h\nu} \tag{7.26}$$

Combining eqs. (7.23) and (7.26) and integrating yield an output signal-to-noise ratio of

$$\frac{S}{N} = C_0 \int \frac{E_s^2(x,y)\eta}{h\nu F_x B}\, dA = \frac{\eta P_s}{h\nu F_x B} \tag{7.27}$$

where

$$P_s = C_0 \int E_s^2(x,y)\, dA \tag{7.28}$$

A comparison of eq. (7.26) with eq. (7.17) shows the expected 3-dB improvement in signal-to-noise ratio which is characteristic of heterodyne detection.

In order that thermal noise in the output detection process be negligible, it is necessary that the integral of eq. (7.26) be considerably greater than kTB, that is

$$P_b \gg \frac{kTh\nu}{\eta q^2 F_x M^2 R_{eq}} \tag{7.29}$$

where the background power P_b is given by

$$P_b = C_0 \int E_b^2(x,y)\, dA \tag{7.30}$$

The above equations make it clear how thermal-noise problems may be combated by heterodyne detection even when the value of $M^2 R_{eq}$ is low.

The drawbacks of heterodyne detection are:

1. The high level of background energy required may cause over-heating and thermal damage to the output detector.

2. Additional noise may be introduced into the computer output because of the self-noise of the background illumination (see Chap. Three).

3. It may be difficult to make the required background illumination both spatially coincident and coherent in both polarization and phase over the signal output region in the computer output plane.

4. It may be difficult to provide the $\Delta\omega_L$ frequency translation of the background light so as to achieve the desired IF output.

Several of the above problems have been discussed by DeLange [7.14].

7.41   Practical Aspects of Direct and Heterodyne Detection   An appreciation of when to employ either direct or heterodyne detection is essential in optimizing optical-computer performance and in understanding the trade-offs which exist between sources of optical power, optical-system configurations, and means of output detection.   This

section treats some of the practical aspects of the output detection problem by means of a few illustrative examples.

Consider, for example, a coherent optical computer of the configuration shown in Fig. 1.17. Assume that the signal which is introduced in the input plane is

$$s(x_1) = B_1 + \cos \omega_{x0}(x_1 - v_T t)$$
$$= B_1 + \tfrac{1}{2}e^{j\omega_{x0}(x_1 - v_T t)} + \tfrac{1}{2}e^{-j\omega_{x0}(x_1 - v_T t)} \quad (7.31)$$

where B_1 is a bias term and v_T is the transport velocity. For reasons of simplicity the y dimension is neglected in the following analysis. Also, the input aperture is assumed to be infinite.

When the signal $s(x_1)$ is illuminated by light of unit amplitude and of radian temporal frequency ω_L, the light amplitude distribution in the spatial frequency plane is given by

$$E_2(\omega_x) = B_1\delta(\omega_x - 0)e^{-j\omega_L t} + \tfrac{1}{2}\delta(\omega_x - \omega_{x0})e^{-j(\omega_L + \Delta\omega_L)t}$$
$$+ \tfrac{1}{2}\delta(\omega_x + \omega_{x0})e^{-j(\omega_L - \Delta\omega_L)t} \quad (7.32)$$

where $\Delta\omega_L = \omega_{x0}v_T$ and represents a temporal frequency translation.

Assume that a single reference function occupies the reference plane and that it is a stationary replica of the input signal, namely,

$$r(x_3) = B_3 + \cos \omega_{x0}x_3$$
$$= B_3 + \tfrac{1}{2}e^{j\omega_{x0}x_3} + \tfrac{1}{2}e^{-j\omega_{x0}x_3} \quad (7.33)$$

If the zero order is not removed in the spatial frequency plane, the light amplitude distribution in the reference plane is given by

$$E_3(x_3) = (B_1 e^{-j\omega_L t} + \tfrac{1}{2}e^{-j\omega_{x0}x_3}e^{-j(\omega_L + \Delta\omega_L)t} + \tfrac{1}{2}e^{j\omega_{x0}x_3}e^{-j(\omega_L - \Delta\omega_L)t})$$
$$\times (B_3 + \tfrac{1}{2}e^{j\omega_{x0}x_3} + \tfrac{1}{2}e^{-j\omega_{x0}x_3}) \quad (7.34)$$

If the zero order is removed in the spatial frequency plane, then the term B_1 is omitted from eq. (7.34). Equation (7.34) contains nine cross-product terms which lead to the following delta functions in the output plane:

$$E_4(\omega_x) = \tfrac{1}{4}e^{-j(\omega_L - \Delta\omega_L)t}\delta(\omega_x - 2\omega_{x0})$$
$$+ \left(\frac{B_3}{2}e^{-j(\omega_L - \Delta\omega_L)t} + \frac{B_1}{2}e^{-j\omega_L t}\right)\delta(\omega_x - \omega_{x0})$$
$$+ (B_1 B_3 e^{-j\omega_L t} + \tfrac{1}{4}e^{-j(\omega_L + \Delta\omega_L)t} + \tfrac{1}{4}e^{-j(\omega_L - \Delta\omega_L)t})\delta(\omega_x - 0)$$
$$+ \left(\frac{B_3}{2}e^{-j(\omega_L + \Delta\omega_L)t} + \frac{B_1}{2}e^{-j\omega_L t}\right)\delta(\omega_x + \omega_{x0})$$
$$+ \tfrac{1}{4}e^{-j(\omega_L + \Delta\omega_L)t}\delta(\omega_x + 2\omega_{x0}) \quad (7.35)$$

The reader should first note the spatial separation of light energy in the output plane. Outputs occur not only on the optical axis ($\omega_x = 0$) but also at $\omega_x = \pm\omega_{x0}$ and $\omega_x = \pm 2\omega_{x0}$. Note also that the translated optical frequency occurs at both $\omega_x = 0$ and $\omega_x = \pm\omega_{x0}$ with the original (untranslated) frequency. This makes heterodyne detection possible at these points if desired without the necessity of an auxiliary system for frequency translation.

Before continuing the analysis, note that biases are added in an optical computer of necessity and carry no information. In the above example the desired output correlation function is given by

$$C(t) = \int s(x_3, t) r(x_3)\, dx_3 = \int \cos \omega_{x0}(x_3 - v_T t) \cos \omega_{x0} x_3\, dx_3 \tag{7.36}$$

which by simple trigonometry may be written

$$C(t) = \tfrac{1}{2} \cos \Delta\omega_L t \tag{7.37}$$

Returning to the above example, consider the case of direct detection when B_1 is set equal to zero. (This may be accomplished by means of a zero stop in the spatial frequency plane.) The light intensity at $\omega_x = \pm 2\omega_{x0}$ and $\omega_x = \pm\omega_{x0}$ is constant and yields no signal. On the optical axis at $\omega_x = 0$ the detected signal is given by

$$I_4(0) = E_4(0) E_4^*(0) = \tfrac{1}{8}(1 + \cos 2\Delta\omega_L t) \tag{7.38}$$

which is the square of the modulus of the desired signal as expected. Detection at $\omega_x = 0$ with removal of the bias term B_1 is analogous to double-sideband detection with the carrier suppressed, when one considers the term $e^{-j\omega_L t}$ as the carrier term at the optical temporal frequency.

When the carrier is not suppressed, that is, $B_1 \neq 0$, then the IF signal at $\omega_x = 0$ is given by

$$I_{4_{IF}}(0) = \frac{B_1 B_3}{2} \cos \Delta\omega_L t \tag{7.39}$$

This is the desired correlation function multiplied by the product of the biases. It appears with a dc term given by $(B_1 B_3)^2$. There is also a much smaller term at twice the IF, as may be readily derived from eq. (7.35). This type of detection is analogous to ordinary double-sideband detection, when the carrier is not suppressed.

At the point $\omega_x = \pm\omega_{x0}$ the detected IF signals are both equal to

$$I_{4_{IF}}(\pm\omega_{x0}) = \frac{B_1 B_3}{2} \cos \Delta\omega_L t \tag{7.40}$$

which is the same as at $\omega_x = 0$ except that the associated dc term is given by $(B_1^2 + B_3^2)/4$. There is no signal at twice the IF. Finally at

$\omega_x = \pm 2\omega_{x0}$ the signal level is constant and small and carries no information.

Detection of the correlation function at $\omega_x = 0$ is called *axial detection*; at $\omega_x = \pm\omega_{x0}$, it is called *offset detection*.   Axial detection may be performed with or without the carrier suppressed, whereas offset detection requires that the carrier be present.   Axial detection may also be performed on a single-sideband basis with or without carrier suppression. Offset detection forms the basis of the "homodyne correlator" which will be further discussed in Chapter Nine (Sec. 9.31).   In offset detection the output light energy is spread over a spatial bandwidth proportional to the signal bandwidth whereas in axial detection all the output light energy of interest arrives at a point on the optical axis.   Thus offset detection requires an area photodetector; axial detection requires a point photodetector.

Figures 7.13 to 7.15 are furnished for the purpose of illustrating some of the above methods of output detection.   Figure 7.13 is from Izzo

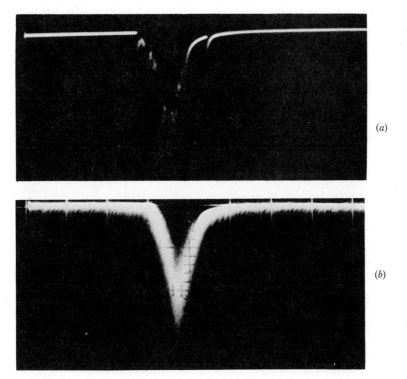

(a)

(b)

Fig. 7.13   Photomultiplier output of a single-sideband, suppressed-carrier, direct-axial-detection optical computer showing (a) a single trace and (b) superimposed multiple traces.   The time scale is 10 μs per major division. (*After Izzo.*)

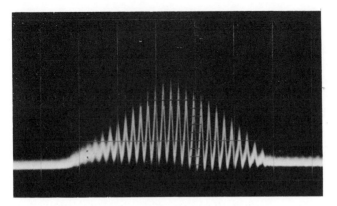

Fig. 7.14 Photodetector output for a double-sideband, suppressed-carrier, direct-axial-detection optical computer. The time scale is 0.5 μs per major division. (*United States Navy.*)

[7.15] and shows single-sideband, suppressed-carrier, direct axial detection of the output signal when a 10-μs RF pulse was correlated against an identical reference, using ultrasonic-delay-line light modulators to introduce both signal and reference. Figure 7.13a illustrates a single output detection of the triangular correlation signal where shot noise due to the arrival of individual packets of photoelectrons is clearly shown. Figure 7.13b is a time average of many sequential output detections and shows the average signal spread owing to shot noise. Figure 7.14 is due to Jernigan [7.16] and illustrates double-sideband, suppressed-carrier, direct axial detection of an RF pulse using an ultrasonic-delay-line light modulator to introduce the signal and a fixed reference mask. Figure 7.15, which was furnished by the Rome Air

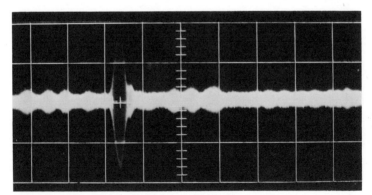

Fig. 7.15 Photodetector output for a coherent optical computer using offset detection. The time scale is 0·5 μs per major division. (*United States Air Force.*)

Development Center,* illustrates the performance of the optical computer shown in Fig. 1.5 with offset detection using delay-line light modulators for both the signal and the reference.   Both the bias level and IF signal envelope are visible.

The reader is referred to Carleton et al. [7.17] for further information on heterodyne detection and to Atzeni and Pantani [7.18] who provide additional examples of interest.

REFERENCES

7.1   Spicer, W. E., and F. Wooten: Photoemission and Photomultipliers, *Proc. IEEE*, **51**:1119 (1963).

7.2   McMurtry, B. J., and A. E. Siegman: Photo-mixing Experiments with Ruby Optical Maser and a Traveling Wave Microwave Phototube, *Appl. Opt.*, **1**:51 (1962).

7.3   Caddes, P. E.: A Ku-band Traveling-wave Phototube, *Microwave J.*, **8**:3 (1965).

7.4   Blattner, D., et al.: Microwave Photomultipliers Using Transmission Dynodes, *RCA Rev.*, **26**:22 (1965).

7.5   Gaddy, O. L., and D. F. Holshouser: A Microwave Frequency Dynamic Crossed-field Photomultiplier, *Proc. IEEE*, **51**:153 (1952).

7.6   Miller, R. C., and N. C. Wittner: Secondary-electron-emission Amplification at Microwave Frequencies, *IEEE J. Quantum Electron.*, **QE-1**:49 (1965).

7.7   Eberhardt, E. H.: Multiplier Phototubes for Single Electron Counting, *IEEE Trans. Nucl. Sci.*, **NS-11**:48 (1964).

7.8   Anderson, L. K., and B. J. McMurtry: High Speed Photodetectors, *Proc. IEEE*, **54**:1335 (1966).

7.9   Johnson, K. M.: High Speed Photo-Diode Signal Enhancement at Avalanche Breakdown Voltage, *IEEE Trans. Electron Devices*, **ED-12**:55 (1965).

7.10   Miller, S. L.: Avalanche Breakdown in Germanium, *Phys. Rev.*, **99**:1234 (1955).

7.11   Goetzberger, A., et al.: Avalanche in Silicon *p-n* Junctions-II. Structurally Perfect Junctions, *J. Appl. Phys.*, **34**:1591 (1963).

7.12   Gordon, E. I., and M. H. Crowell: A Charge Storage Target for Electron Image Sensing, *Bell Syst. Tech. J.*, **47**:1855 (1968).

7.13   De Haan, E. F., et al.: The "Plumbicon," A New Television Camera Tube, *Philips Tech. Rev.*, **25**(6/7):133 (1963/1964).

7.14   DeLange, O. E.: Optical Heterodyne Detection, *IEEE Spectrum*, 77 (October 1968).

7.15   Izzo, N. F.: Optical Correlation Technique Using a Variable Reference Function, *Proc. IEEE (Corresp.)*, **53**:1740 (1965).

7.16   Jernigan, J. L.: Correlation Technique Using Microwaves, *Proc. IEEE (Corresp.)*, **56**:374 (1968).

7.17   Carleton, et al.: Collinear Heterodyning in Optical Processors, *Proc. IEEE*, **57**:769 (1969).

7.18   Atzeni, C., and L. Pantani: A Simplified Optical Correlator for Radar Signal Processing, *Proc. IEEE (Corresp.)*, **57**:344 (1969).

*The author is indebted to M. H. Bickelhaupt and R. R. Menard of the USAF Rome Air Development Center for this photograph.

Chapter Eight

Digital Techniques

8.00 Introduction

Other chapters of this book deal with coherent optical computation by analog methods, i.e., computation wherein the values of variables delivered to the computer as well as the values of the computed output variables are continuous, not discrete. Such methods of coherent optical computation have the advantage of speed and simplicity but, as with electronic analog computers, they have the disadvantage of lacking accuracy and precision. In fact, whereas today electronic analog computers readily achieve accuracies of one part in a thousand, the coherent optical analog computer is usually limited in its accuracy to from 1 to 10 parts in 100. It is the enormous parallel-processing capability of the coherent optical analog computer that gives it an advantage over alternative technology. Applications of coherent optical analog computers are limited to those areas where accuracy requirements are not severe.

It is the purpose of this chapter to outline an advance in the technology of coherent optical computation which permits the realization of calculation by digital methods. Although no complete coherent-optical-digital-computer systems based on this technology have yet been brought into being, it is felt that, nevertheless, a review of the principles of the technology should be presented.

Coherent optical digital computation can be performed by a chain (or chains) of light-sensitive optical phase modulators (such as the photosensitive-membrane light modulator, the photothermoplastic light modulator, etc.) interleaved with lens systems and light-redirecting holograms. One stage in such a computer is shown in Fig. 8.1. The input light detector and modulator for the stage lie in the x_1y_1 plane; a Fourier hologram is in the x_2y_2 plane; and the output light detector and modulator are in the x_3y_3 plane. The digital inputs to the system occur at discrete points in the x_1y_1 plane where coherent optical power is caused to have zero phase to represent a binary zero and π phase (180°) to represent a binary 1. In the output plane a binary 0 at a particular point is represented by the absence of optical power at that point and a binary 1 by the presence of optical power. The notation

$$(x_1 = x_i, y_1 = y_i), \angle\theta, E \tag{8.1}$$

is used to represent the existence of an electric field of strength E and phase angle θ at the point (x_i, y_i) in the x_1y_1 plane. Thus an input binary 0 of unity strength on axis is represented by

$$(x_1 = 0, y_1 = 0), \angle 0, 1$$

and an input binary 1 of unit strength by

$$(x_1 = 0, y_1 = 0), \angle\pi, 1$$

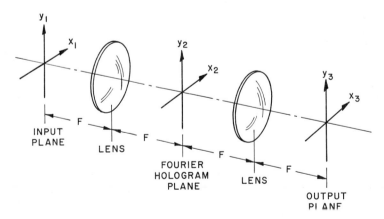

Fig. 8.1 Optical schematic of the basic stage of a coherent optical digital computer using holographic logic.

In the $x_3 y_3$ plane an output 0 or 1 on axis is given by

$$(x_3 = 0, y_3 = 0), \angle\theta, 0$$

or

$$(x_3 = 0, y_3 = 0), \angle\theta, E$$

respectively, where both θ and E may take on arbitrary values.

8.10   Principles of Holography

In this section holographic methodology typical of that utilized in coherent optical digital computation is described.   The formation and use of certain simple holograms are discussed in order to demonstrate fundamental principles.   The ensuing discussion treats the formation and use of holograms of single-input variables.   Later sections discuss holograms of multiple-input variables.

In order to form a hologram of a binary zero of strength α located on the optical axis, the illumination or "source" in the $x_1 y_1$ plane is made equal to

$$S(x_1, y_1) = \alpha\delta(x_1 - 0_1, y_1 - 0) + \delta(x_1 - x_r, y_1 - 0) \tag{8.2}$$

where δ is the Dirac delta function.   The part of the source $S(x_1, y_1)$ given by $\alpha\delta(x_1 - 0, y_1 - 0)$ is the binary zero, and $\delta(x_1 - x_r, y_1 - 0)$ is the reference part of the source having a field strength of unity and located a distance x_r from the optical axis.   The hologram is recorded in the $x_2 y_2$ plane by exposing an area square-law detector (such as photographic film) to the electric field in that plane given by

$$E(\omega_{x_2}, \omega_{y_2}) = \int\int [\alpha\delta(x_1 - 0, y_1 - 0) + \delta(x_1 - x_r, y_1 - 0)]$$
$$\times e^{-j(\omega_{x_2}x_1 + \omega_{y_2}y_1)} dx_1\, dy_1$$

$$= \alpha + e^{-j\omega_{x_2}x_r} \tag{8.3}$$

(Note that, for reasons of simplicity, the multiplier $j\sqrt{2\pi}/\lambda F$ is not applied to the integral.)

Assuming a positive-recording, area square-law detector, the hologram transmission is proportional to the intensity I_A, given by

$$I_A = EE^* = (\alpha + e^{-j\omega_{x_2}x_r})(\alpha + e^{j\omega_{x_2}x_r}) = (1 + \alpha^2) + 2\alpha\cos\omega_{x_2}x_r \tag{8.4}$$

Similarly, the hologram of a binary 1 of strength α located on axis in the input plane is produced by exposing an area square-law detector to the resultant field in the $x_2 y_2$ plane given by

$$E(\omega_{x_2}, \omega_{y_2}) = \alpha e^{j\pi} + e^{-j\omega_{x_2}\omega_r} \tag{8.5}$$

yielding a hologram with transmission proportional to the intensity

I_B, given by

$$I_B = EE^* = (\alpha e^{j\pi} + e^{-j\omega_{x_2}x_r})(\alpha e^{-j\pi} + e^{j\omega_{x_2}x_r})$$

$$= (1 + \alpha^2) + 2\alpha \cos(\omega_{x_2}x_r + \pi)$$

$$= (1 + \alpha^2) - 2\alpha \cos \omega_{x_2}x_r \qquad (8.6)$$

The intensity function I_B might be called the "negative" of I_A because its value is minimum where the other is maximum and vice versa.

If a binary zero is moved off axis to the point $(x_d, 0)$ where $x_d \ll x_r$, the electric field distribution in the hologram plane is then given by

$$E(\omega_{x_2}, \omega_{y_2}) = \alpha e^{-j\omega_{x_2}x_d} + e^{-j\omega_{x_2}x_r} \qquad (8.7)$$

and the corresponding hologram transmission is proportional to

$$I_C = EE^* = (1 + \alpha^2) + 2\alpha \cos \omega_{x_2}(x_r - x_d) \qquad (8.8)$$

which is also a cosinusoidal hologram but with a lower spatial frequency than those given by eqs. (8.4) and (8.6), that is, $\omega_{x_2}(x_r - x_d) < \omega_{x_2}x_r$, and has a maximum at $\omega_{x_2} = 0$.

Similarly for the case of a binary 1 moved off axis by the amount x_d, the hologram transmission is proportional to

$$I_D = (1 + \alpha^2) - 2\alpha \cos \omega_{x_2}(x_r - x_d) \qquad (8.9)$$

which has the same spatial frequency as that given by eq. (8.8) but, like eq. (8.6), has a minimum at $\omega_{x_2} = 0$.

Using a source consisting of a binary 0 of unit strength on axis in the x_1y_1 plane and with the hologram of eq. (8.4) in the x_2y_2 plane, the electric field distribution in the x_2y_2 plane is given by

$$E(\omega_{x_2}, \omega_{x_2}) = I_A(\alpha^4 + 4\alpha^2 + 1)^{-1/2} = (\alpha + e^{-j\omega_{x_2}x_r})(\alpha + e^{j\omega_{x_2}x_r})$$

$$\times (\alpha^4 + 4\alpha^2 + 1)^{-1/2} \quad (8.10)$$

where $(\alpha^4 + 4\alpha^2 + 1)^{-1/2}$ is a normalizing factor. Note that this assumes that the light *amplitude* transmission of the hologram is equal to I_A $(\alpha^4 + 4\alpha^2 + 1)^{-1/2}$. This is strictly true only when the hologram records the *square* of the light intensity distribution I_A. This is because of the square-root relationship between light amplitude transmission t_a and light intensity transmission t_i. It is interesting to note that, if $\alpha \ll 1$, and if the hologram records the light intensity *directly* (not the square), then for eq. (8.5)

$$t_i = (1 + \alpha^2) + 2\alpha \cos \omega_{x_2}x_r$$

$$t_a = \sqrt{t_i} \approx 1 + \alpha \cos \omega_{x_2}x_r \qquad (8.11)$$

Therefore, except for a factor of about 50 percent in the amplitude of the cosinusoidal term, the desired light amplitude transmission t_a is obtained.

The resultant output in the $x_3 y_3$ plane is given by the electric field distribution

$$E(\omega_{x_3}\omega_{y_3}) = (1+\alpha^2)(\alpha^4+4\alpha^2+1)^{-1/2} \int e^{-j(\omega_{x_3}x_2 + \omega_{y_3}y_2)}\, dx_2\, dy_2$$

$$+ \alpha(\alpha^4+4\alpha^2+1)^{-1/2} \int e^{-j(\omega_{x_2}x_r + \omega_{x_3}x_2 + \omega_{y_3}y_2)}\, dx_2\, dy_2$$

$$+ \alpha(\alpha^4+4\alpha^2+1)^{-1/2} \int e^{-j(\omega_{x_2}x_r + \omega_{x_3}x_2 + \omega_{y_3}y_2)}\, dx_2\, dy_2 \quad (8.12)$$

Noting that

$$(\omega_{x_2}x_r + \omega_{x_3}x_2) = \left(\frac{2\pi}{\lambda F}x_r + \omega_{x_3}\right)x_2$$

$$\omega_{x_3} = \frac{2\pi}{\lambda F}x_3 \quad (8.13)$$

and assuming that all focal lengths are equal, eq. (8.12) may be solved to yield the following output delta functions in the $x_3 y_3$ plane:

Location	Phase	Electric field strength
$x_3 = -x_r, y_3 = 0$	$0°$	$\alpha(\alpha^4+4\alpha^2+1)^{-1/2}$
$x_3 = 0, y_3 = 0$	$0°$	$(1+\alpha^2)(\alpha^4+4\alpha^2+1)^{-1/2}$
$x_3 = +x_r, y_3 = 0$	$0°$	$\alpha(\alpha^4+4\alpha^2+1)^{-1/2}$

Using the hologram made from a binary 1 on axis, i.e., as given by eq. (8.6), in the $x_2 y_2$ plane with an on-axis source in the $x_1 y_1$ plane consisting of a binary 0 of strength unity, the electric field distribution in the $x_2 y_2$ plane is given by

$$E(\omega_{x_2}, \omega_{y_2}) = I_B(\alpha^4+4\alpha^2+1)^{-1/2}$$

$$= (\alpha e^{j\pi} + e^{-j\omega_x x_r})(\alpha e^{-j\pi} + e^{j\omega_{x_2} x_r})(\alpha^4+4\alpha^2+1)^{-1/2} \quad (8.14)$$

which yields outputs in the $x_3 y_3$ plane as follows:

Location	Phase	Electric field strength
$x_3 = -x_r, y_3 = 0$	$-180°$	$\alpha(\alpha^4+4\alpha^2+1)^{-1/2}$
$x_3 = 0, y_3 = 0$	$0°$	$(1+\alpha^2)(\alpha^4+4\alpha^2+1)^{-1/2}$
$x_3 = +x_r, y_3 = 0$	$+180°$	$\alpha(\alpha^4+4\alpha^2+1)^{-1/2}$

When the hologram of a binary 1 on axis is used with a source in the $x_1 y_1$ plane consisting of a binary 1 of strength unity on axis, the electric field distribution in the $x_2 y_2$ plane is

$$E(\omega_{x_2}, \omega_{y_2}) = I_B e^{j\pi}(\alpha^4+4\alpha^2+1)^{-1/2}$$

$$= e^{j\pi}(\alpha e^{j\pi} + e^{-j\omega_{x_2} x_r})(\alpha e^{-j\pi} + e^{j\omega_{x_2} x_r})(\alpha^4+4\alpha^2+1)^{-1/2} \quad (8.15)$$

This yields outputs in the x_3y_3 plane as follows:

Location	Phase	Electric field strength
$x_3 = -x_r, y_3 = 0$	$0°$	$\alpha(\alpha^4 + 4\alpha^2 + 1)^{-1/2}$
$x_3 = 0, y_3 = 0$	$+180°$	$(1 + \alpha^2)(\alpha^4 + 4\alpha^2 + 1)^{-1/2}$
$x_3 = +x_r \ \ y_3 = 0$	$+360°$	$\alpha(\alpha^4 + 4\alpha^2 + 1)^{-1/2}$

Finally, when the hologram of a binary 0 on axis is used with a source equal to a binary 1 on axis, it can easily be shown that the outputs in the x_3y_3 plane are:

Location	Phase	Electric field strength
$x_3 = -x_r, y_3 = 0$	$+180°$	$\alpha(\alpha^4 + 4\alpha^2 + 1)^{-1/2}$
$x_3 = 0, y_3 = 0$	$+180°$	$(1 + \alpha^2)(\alpha^4 + 4\alpha^2 + 1)^{-1/2}$
$x_3 = +x_r, y_3 = 0$	$+180°$	$\alpha(\alpha^4 + 4\alpha^2 + 1)^{-1/2}$

8.20 Tabulation of Results

Table 8.1 summarizes the results obtained so far with holograms of single binary inputs on axis illuminated by single binary sources on axis. Table 8.1 assumes, for simplicity, that α is much less than unity. As can be seen, the hologram creates additional images of the input source which appear at $(-x_r, 0)$ and $(+x_r, 0)$ in the x_3y_3 plane. The hologram retards the phase in the source image at $(-x_r, 0)$ and advances the phase at $(+x_r, 0)$ by the phase angle of the input which was used to create the hologram.

If the hologram of a binary zero on axis as given by eq. (8.8) is used with a source consisting of a binary zero of unity strength at $(x_d, 0)$ in the

TABLE 8.1 Input-Output Relationships for Single Binary Inputs on Axis

Input	Hologram	Output
$(x_1 = 0, y_1 = 0), \angle 0, 1$	$(x_1 = 0, y_1 = 0), \angle 0, \alpha$	$(x_1 = x_r, y_1 = 0), \angle 0, \alpha$ $(x_1 = 0, y_1 = 0), \angle 0, 1$ $(x_1 = -x_r, y_1 = 0), \angle 0, \alpha$
$(x_1 = 0, y_1 = 0), \angle \pi, 1$	$(x_1 = 0, y_1 = 0), \angle \pi, \alpha$	$(x_1 = x_r, y_1 = 0), \angle 2\pi, \alpha$ $(x_1 = 0, y_1 = 0), \angle \pi, 1$ $(x_1 = -x_r, y_1 = 0), \angle 0, \alpha$
$(x_1 = 0, y_1 = 0), \angle \pi, 1$	$(x_1 = 0, y_1 = 0), \angle 0, \alpha$	$(x_1 = x_r, y_1 = 0), \angle \pi, \alpha$ $(x_1 = 0, y_1 = 0), \angle \pi, 1$ $(x_1 = -x_r, y_1 = 0), \angle \pi, \alpha$
$(x_1 = 0, y_1 = 0), \angle 0, 1$	$(x_1 = 0, y_1 = 0), \angle \pi, \alpha$	$(x_1 = x_r, y_1 = 0), \angle \pi, \alpha$ $(x_1 = 0, y_1 = 0), \angle 0, 1$ $(x_1 = -x_r, y_1 = 0), \angle -\pi, \alpha$

input plane, the electric field in the x_2y_2 plane is

$$E(\omega_{x_2}, \omega_{y_2}) = e^{-j\omega_{x_2}x}dI_C(\alpha^4 + 4\alpha^2 + 1)^{-1/2}$$

$$= e^{-j\omega_{x_2}x}d(\alpha e^{-j\omega_{x_2}x}d + e^{-j\omega_{x_2}x}r)(\alpha e^{j\omega_{x_2}x}d + e^{j\omega_{x_2}x}r)$$

$$\times (\alpha^4 + 4\alpha^2 + 1)^{-1/2}$$

$$= [(1+\alpha^2)e^{-j\omega_{x_2}x}d + \alpha(e^{j\omega_{x_2}(x_r - 2xd)} + e^{-j\omega_{x_2}x}r)]$$

$$\times (\alpha^4 + 4\alpha^2 + 1)^{-1/2} \qquad (8.16)$$

which produces in the x_3y_3 plane the distribution

$$E(\omega_{x_3}, \omega_{y_3}) = (1+\alpha^2)(\alpha^4 + 4\alpha^2 + 1)^{-1/2} \int e^{-j(\omega_{x_2}x}d + \omega_{x_3}x_2 + \omega_{y_3}y_2)} dx_2\, dy_2$$

$$+ \alpha(\alpha^4 + 4\alpha^2 + 1)^{-1/2} \int e^{-j(\omega_{x_2}x}r + \omega_{x_2}x_2 + \omega_{y_3}y_2)} dx_2\, dy_2$$

$$+ \alpha(\alpha^4 + 4\alpha^2 + 1)^{-1/2} \int e^{j(\omega_{x_2}x}r - 2\omega_{x_2}x}d - \omega_{x_3}x_2 - \omega_{y_3}y_2)} dx_2\, d_2$$

$$\qquad (8.17)$$

Thus the outputs in the x_3y_3 plane are:

Location	Phase	Electric field strength
$x_3 = -x_r, y_3 = 0$	$0°$	$\alpha(\alpha^4 + 4\alpha^2 + 1)^{-1/2}$
$x_3 = -x_d, y_3 = 0$	$0°$	$(1+\alpha^2)(\alpha^4 + 4\alpha^2 + 1)^{-1/2}$
$x_3 = x_r - 2x_d, y_3 = 0$	$0°$	$\alpha(\alpha^4 + 4\alpha^2 + 1)^{-1/2}$

With the hologram given by eq. (8.6) in the x_2y_2 plane and a source x_1y_1 plane at $(x_1 = x_d, y_1 = 0)$ of field strength unity and $180°$ phase, the electric field distribution in the x_2y_2 plane is given by

$$E(\omega_{x_2}, \omega_{y_2}) = e^{j\pi}e^{-j\omega_{x_2}x}dI_D(\alpha^4 + 4\alpha^2 + 1)^{-1/2}$$

$$= e^{j\pi}e^{-j\omega_{x_2}x}d(\alpha e^{j\pi}e^{-j\pi x_2 x}d + e^{-j\omega_{x_2}x}r)$$

$$\times (\alpha e^{-j\pi}e^{j\omega_{x_2}x}d + e^{j\omega_{x_2}x}r)(\alpha^4 + 4\alpha^2 + 1)^{-1/2}$$

$$= [(1+\alpha^2)e^{j\pi}e^{-j\omega_{x_2}x}d + \alpha e^{j2\pi}e^{j\omega_{x_2}(x_r - 2xd)} - j\omega_{x_2}x}r]$$

$$\times (\alpha^4 + 4\alpha^2 + 1)^{-1/2} \qquad (8.18)$$

which yields source images in the x_3y_3 plane as given below:

Location	Phase	Electric field strength
$(x_3 = -x_r, y_3 = 0)$	$0°$	$\alpha(\alpha^4 + 4\alpha^2 + 1)^{-1/2}$
$(x_3 = -x_d, y_3 = 0)$	$180°$	$(1+\alpha^2)(\alpha^4 + 4\alpha^2 + 1)^{-1/2}$
$(x_3 = x_r - 2x_d, y_3 = 0)$	$360°$	$\alpha(\alpha^4 + 4\alpha^2 + 1)^{-1/2}$

TABLE 8.2   Outputs for Single Input Sources Off Axis

Input	Hologram	Output
$(x_3 = x_d, y_3 = 0), \angle 0, 1$	$(x_3 = x_d, y_3 = 0), \angle 0, \alpha$	$(x_3 = -x_r, y_3 = 0), \angle 0, \alpha$
		$(x_3 = -x_d, y_3 = 0), \angle 0, 1$
		$(x_3 = x_r - 2x_d, y_3 = 0), \angle 0, \alpha$
$(x_3 = x_d, y_3 = 0), \angle \pi, 1$	$(x_3 = x_d, y_3 = 0), \angle \pi, \alpha$	$(x_3 = -x_r, y_3 = 0), \angle 0, \alpha$
		$(x_3 = -x_d, y_3 = 0), \angle \pi, 1$
		$(x_3 = x_r - 2x_d, y_3 = 0), \angle 2\pi, \alpha$

Table 8.2 summarizes the last two results given above.

At this point it should be evident that, when the hologram of a single input of either 0 or 180° phase is used in the $x_2 y_2$ plane with that input in the $x_1 y_1$ plane as a source, a source image, always of zero phase, is created in the output $x_3 y_3$ plane at $(x_3 = -x_r, y_3 = 0)$, where x_r is the x_1 coordinate of the reference input used in creating the hologram.

This conclusion can be broadened by considering a generalized input as follows:

$$\delta_k = \sum_k (x_1 = x_k, y_1 = y_k), \angle \phi_k, \alpha_k \tag{8.19}$$

The hologram of this input is proportional to

$$I = EE^* = \left(e^{-j\omega x_2 x_r} + \sum_k \alpha_k e^{j\phi_k} e^{-j(\omega x_2 x_k + \omega y_2 y_k)} \right)$$
$$\times \left(e^{j\omega x_2 x_r} + \sum_k \alpha_k e^{-j\phi_k} e^{j(\omega x_2 x_k + \omega y_2 y_k)} \right) \tag{8.20}$$

When this hologram is placed in the $x_2 y_2$ plane and is illuminated by a source in the x_1, y_1 plane given by

$$S_k = \sum_k (x_1 - x_k, y_1 - y_k), \angle \phi_k, 1 \tag{8.21}$$

then the electric field distribution in the $x_2 y_2$ plane is

$$E(\omega_{x_2}, \omega_{y_2}) = \sum_k e^{j\phi_k} e^{-j(\omega x_2 x_k + \omega y_2 y_k)} \left(e^{-j\omega x_2 x_r} + \sum_k \alpha_k e^{j\phi_k} \right.$$
$$\left. \times e^{-j(\omega x_2 x_k + \omega y_2 y_k)} \right) \left(e^{j\omega x_2 x_r} + \sum_k \alpha_k e^{-j\phi_k} e^{j(\omega x_2 x_k + \omega y_2 y_k)} \right) \tag{8.22}$$

Assuming that $x_r \gg x_k$, the output in the $x_3 y_3$ plane at the point $(x_3 = -x_r, y_3 = 0)$ is thus given by

$$\delta'_k = (x_3 = -x_r, y_3 = 0), \angle 0, \sum_k \alpha_k \tag{8.23}$$

This shows that, in general, there is a coherent summation of images of the individual points in the source S_k, all at zero phase at the location $(x_3 = -x_r, y_3 = 0)$ in the output plane.

8.30 Illustrative Example

In this section coherent optical computation by digital techniques is demonstrated by realization of the identity function. The identity function is a function of two input variables, A and B, whose truth table is given in Table 8.3.

TABLE 8.3

A	B	$f(A,B)$
0	0	1
0	1	0
1	0	0
1	1	1

With reference to the input variables A and B recall that light of $0°$ phase represents a binary 0; of $180°$ phase, a binary 1. Also recall that the output is a binary 1 when light energy reaches $(x_3 = -x_r, y_3 = 0)$ and 0 when no light reaches that same point. To perform the identity function, a hologram is made of the input S_{AB}, given by

$$S_{AB} = \begin{cases} (x_1 = x_A, y_1 = 0), \angle 0, \alpha \\ (x_1 = x_B, y_1 = 0), \angle 0, \alpha \end{cases} \tag{8.24}$$

This hologram has a transmission proportional to the intensity I_{AB}, given by

$$I_{AB} = EE^* = (\alpha e^{-j\omega x_2 x_A} + \alpha e^{-j\omega x_2 x_B} + e^{-j\omega x_2 x_r})(\alpha e^{j\omega x_2 x_A}$$
$$+ \alpha e^{j\omega x_2 x_B} + e^{j\omega x_2 x_r})$$
$$= (1 + 2\alpha^2) + 2\alpha[\cos \omega_{x_2}(x_r - x_A) + \cos \omega_{x_2}(x_r - x_B)]$$
$$+ 2\alpha^2 \cos \omega_{x_2}(x_B - x_A) \tag{8.25}$$

When this hologram is illuminated by the source S'_{AB} given by

$$S'_{AB} = \begin{cases} (x_1 = x_A, y_1 = 0), \angle 0, 1 \\ (x_1 = x_A, y_1 = 0), \angle 0, 1 \end{cases} \tag{8.26}$$

the electric field distribution in the $x_2 y_2$ plane is

$$E(\omega_{x_2}, \omega_{y_2}) = I_{AB}(e^{-j\omega x_2 x_A} + e^{-j\omega x_2 x_B})(10\alpha^4 + 12\alpha^2 + 1)^{-1/2} \tag{8.27}$$

where the final term is a normalizing factor. Combining eqs. (8.27) and (8.25) yields several terms, namely,

$$E(\omega_{x_2}, \omega_{y_2}) = (1+2\alpha^2)(e^{-j\omega x_2 x_A} + e^{-j\omega x_2 x_B})$$

$$+ \alpha(e^{j\omega x_2(x_r - 2x_A)} + e^{j\omega x_2(x_r - 2x_B)} + 2e^{j\omega x_2(x_r - x_A - x_B)})$$

$$+ \alpha(e^{-j\omega x_2(x_r + x_A - x_B)} + e^{-j\omega x_2(x_r + x_B - x_A)}) + 2\alpha e^{-j\omega x_2 x_r}$$

$$+ \alpha^2(e^{-j\omega x_2 x_A} + e^{-j\omega x_2 x_B}) + \alpha^2[e^{-j\omega x_2(2x_A - x_B)} + e^{-j\omega x_2(2x_B - x_A)}) \quad (8.28)$$

This yields the following source images in the $x_3 y_3$ plane:

Location	Phase	Electric field strength
$(x_3 = -x_A, y_3 = 0)$	$0°$	$(1+3\alpha^2)(10\alpha^4 + 12\alpha^2 + 1)^{-1/2}$
$(x_3 = -x_B, y_3 = 0)$	$0°$	$(1+3\alpha^2)(10\alpha^4 + 12\alpha^2 + 1)^{-1/2}$
$(x_3 = x_B - 2x_A, y_3 = 0)$	$0°$	$\alpha^2(10\alpha^4 + 12\alpha^2 + 1)^{-1/2}$
$(x_3 = x_A - 2x_B, y_3 = 0)$	$0°$	$\alpha^2(10\alpha^4 + 12\alpha^2 + 1)^{-1/2}$
$(x_3 = -x_r, y_3 = 0)$	$0°$	$2\alpha(10\alpha^4 + 12\alpha^2 + 1)^{-1/2}$
$(x_3 = -x_r - (x_B - x_A), y_3 = 0)$	$0°$	$\alpha(10\alpha^4 + 12\alpha^2 + 1)^{-1/2}$
$(x_3 = -x_r + (x_B - x_A), y_3 = 0)$	$0°$	$\alpha(10\alpha^4 + 12\alpha^2 + 1)^{-1/2}$
$(x_3 = x_r - 2x_A, y_3 = 0)$	$0°$	$\alpha(10\alpha^4 + 12\alpha^2 + 1)^{-1/2}$
$(x_3 = x_r - 2x_B, y_3 = 0)$	$0°$	$\alpha(10\alpha^4 + 12\alpha^2 + 1)^{-1/2}$
$(x_3 = x_r - (x_A + x_B), y_3 = 0)$	$0°$	$2\alpha(10\alpha^4 + 12\alpha^2 + 1)^{-1/2}$

The outputs in the $x_3 y_3$ plane for this case are represented pictorially in Fig. 8.2 for the situation when the input is symmetric, for example, $x_A = -x_B = 1$. Figure 8.3 shows an asymmetric case, for example, $x_A = 1$, $x_B = 3$. Note the downward translation of the terms near the origin and near the point $(x_3 = x_r, y_3 = 0)$ whereas the light distribution near $(x_3 = -x_r, y_3 = 0)$ remains unchanged.

When the same hologram is illuminated by the source S''_{AB} given by

$$S''_{AB} = \begin{cases} (x_1 = x_A, y_1 = 0), \angle 0, 1 \\ (x_1 = x_B, y_3 = 0), \angle \pi, 1 \end{cases} \quad (8.29)$$

it is not difficult to show that the following source images are produced

Location	Phase	Electric field strength
$(x_3 = -x_A, y_3 = 0)$	$0°$	$(1+2\alpha^2)(2\alpha^4 + 3\alpha^2 + 1)^{-1/2}$
$(x_3 = -x_A, y_3 = 0)$	$180°$	$\alpha^2(2\alpha^4 + 3\alpha^2 + 1)^{-1/2}$
$(x_3 = -x_B, y_3 = 0)$	$180°$	$(1+2\alpha^2)(2\alpha^4 + 3\alpha^2 + 1)^{-1/2}$
$(x_3 = -x_B, y_3 = 0)$	$0°$	$\alpha^2(2\alpha^4 + 3\alpha^2 + 1)^{-1/2}$
$(x_3 = x_B - 2x_A, y_3 = 0)$	$0°$	$\alpha^2(2\alpha^4 + 3\alpha^2 + 1)^{-1/2}$
$(x_3 = x_A - 2x_B, y_3 = 0)$	$180°$	$\alpha^2(2\alpha^4 + 3\alpha^2 + 1)^{-1/2}$
$(x_3 = -x_r, y_3 = 0)$	$0°$	$\alpha(2\alpha^4 + 3\alpha^2 + 1)^{-1/2}$
$(x_3 = -x_r, y_3 = 0)$	$180°$	$\alpha(2\alpha^4 + 3\alpha^2 + 1)^{-1/2}$
$(x_3 = -x_r - (x_B - x_A), y_3 = 0)$	$180°$	$\alpha(2\alpha^4 + 3\alpha^2 + 1)^{-1/2}$
$(x_3 = -x_r + (x_B - x_A), y_3 = 0)$	$0°$	$\alpha(2\alpha^4 + 3\alpha^2 + 1)^{-1/2}$
$(x_3 = x_r - 2x_A, y_3 = 0)$	$0°$	$\alpha(2\alpha^4 + 3\alpha^2 + 1)^{-1/2}$
$(x_3 = x_r - 2x_B, y_3 = 0)$	$180°$	$\alpha(2\alpha^4 + 3\alpha^2 + 1)^{-1/2}$
$(x_3 = x_r - (x_A + x_B), y_3 = 0)$	$0°$	$\alpha(2\alpha^4 + 3\alpha^2 + 1)^{-1/2}$
$(x_3 = x_r - (x_A + x_B), y_3 = 0)$	$180°$	$\alpha(2\alpha^4 + 3\alpha^2 + 1)^{-1/2}$

- $(x_3 = x_r+2), \angle 0, a$

- $(x_3 = x_r), \angle 0, 2a$

- $(x_3 = x_r-2), \angle 0, a$

- $(x_3 = 3), \angle 0, a^2$

- $(x_3 = 1), \angle 0, (1+3a^2)$
+
- $(x_3 = -1), \angle 0, (1+3a^2)$

- $(x_3 = -3), \angle 0, a^2$

- $(x_3 = -x_r+2), \angle 0, a$

- $(x_3 = -x_r), \angle 0, 2a$

- $(x_3 = -x_r-2), \angle 0, a$

- $(x_3 = x_r-2), \angle 0, a$

- $(x_3 = x_r-4), \angle 0, 2a$

- $(x_3 = x_r-6), \angle 0, a$

- $(x_3 = 1), \angle 0, a^2$
+
- $(x_3 = -1), \angle 0, (1+3a^2)$

- $(x_3 = -2), \angle 0, (1+3a^2)$

- $(x_3 = -5), \angle 0, a^2$

- $(x_3 = -x_r+2), \angle 0, a$

- $(x_3 = -x_r), \angle 0, 2a$

- $(x_3 = -x_r-2), \angle 0, a$

- $(x_3 = x_r+2), \angle \pi, a$

− $(x_3 = x_r), \angle 0, 0$

- $(x_3 = -x_r), \angle 0, a$

- $(x_3 = 3), \angle \pi, a^2$

- $(x_3 = 1), \angle \pi, (1+a^2)$
+
- $(x_3 = -1), \angle 0, (1+a^2)$

- $(x_3 = -2), \angle 0, a^2$

- $(x_3 = -x_r+2), \angle \pi, a$

− $(x_3 = -x_r), \angle 0, 0$

- $(x_3 = -x_r-2), \angle 0, a$

Fig. 8.2 Entire output light amplitude distribution for a symmetrical input where $x_A = -x_B = 1$.

Fig. 8.3 Entire output light amplitude distribution for the asymmetrical case where $x_A = 1, x_B = 3$.

Fig. 8.4 Entire output light amplitude distribution for the symmetrical case when x_A is phase-shifted by 180°.

Taking the vector sums at the above points causes the electric field to be zero at $(x_3 = -x_r, y_3 = 0)$ and $1+\alpha^2$ at both $(x_3 = -x_A, y_3 = 0)$ and $(x_3 = -x_B, y_3 = 0)$. The result is diagramed in Fig. 8.4 for the case where $x_A = -x_B = 1$. The important point to note is the cancellation of the electric field by destructive interference at $(x_3 = -x_r, y_3 = 0)$.

When the phases of the inputs at $(x_1 = x_A, y_1 = 0)$ and $(x_1 = x_B, y_3 = 0)$ are reversed from that given in eq. (8.29) to π and 0, respectively, destructive interference again occurs, with the distribution of light being the mirror image about the $x_3 = 0$ axis of that shown in Fig. 8.4. Finally, when the inputs A and B are both π, the same electric field strengths occur as in the initial case except that all phases reverse by 180°.

The identity function over these two input variables is, therefore, generated by the hologram given by eq. (8.25). The results of the above discussion are given in Table 8.4.

It should also be noted that a binary input variable may be complemented or negated using the identity-function hologram. The input is introduced at $(x_1 = x_A, y_1 = 0)$ with a binary 0 always at $(x_1 = x_B, y_1 = 0)$. A binary 0 at the input yields light at the output point $(x_3 = -x_r, y_3 = 0)$,

TABLE 8.4

Input	Output
$(x_1 = x_A, y_1 = 0), \angle 0, 1$	
$(x_1 = x_B, y_1 = 0), \angle 0, 1$	$(x_3 = -x_r, y_3 = 0), \angle 0, 2\alpha$
$(x_1 = x_A, y_1 = 0), \angle 0, 1$	
$(x_1 = x_B, y_1 = 0), \angle \pi, 1$	$(x_3 = -x_r, y_3 = 0), \angle 0, 0$
$(x_1 = x_A, y_1 = 0), \angle \pi, 1$	
$(x_1 = x_B, y_1 = 0), \angle 0, 1$	$(x_3 = -x_r, y_3 = 0), \angle 0, 0$
$(x_1 = x_A, y_1 = 0), \angle \pi, 1$	
$(x_1 = x_B, y_1 = 0), \angle \pi, 1$	$(x_3 = -x_r, y_3 = 0), \angle \pi, 2\alpha$

that is, an output binary 1, whereas a binary 1 input yields no light at the output, i.e., a binary 0.

8.40   Experimental Demonstration

This section discusses the results of laboratory experiments conducted to illustrate the performance of the identity function by means of holographic logic.   A drawing of the experimental setup for constructing the hologram is shown in Fig. 8.5.   A helium-neon laser operating

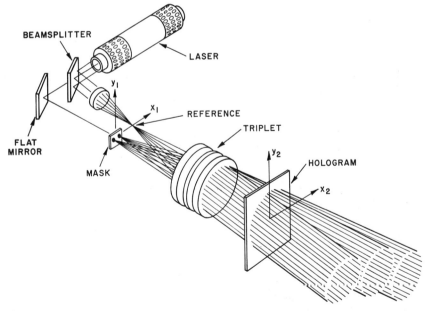

Fig. 8.5 Experimental coherent-optical-computer configuration for use in demonstrating holographic digital logic.

at 6328 Å was utilized as the light source.   In order to make a hologram of the source S_{AB}, as given in eq. (8.24), a mask consisting of two 10-μm-diameter pinholes on 100-μm centers was placed on axis in the x_1y_1 plane.   The pinholes were directly illuminated by the laser while part of the beam was split off and focused by a microscope objective to form the reference input.   A 600-mm f/8 triplet was used to form the Fourier transform in the x_2y_2 plane, i.e., the plane of the hologram.   The lens used was a three-element system designed specifically for use in optical computers (see Chap. Two, Fig. 2.15).   At the 6328 Å wavelength the space-bandwidth product of the lens system was approximately 5,000 with less than 1/20 wavelength of optical phase aberration across a $\pm 1.3°$ field.

A photographic plate having Eastman 649-type emulsion was exposed in the hologram plane.   A photograph of the resultant hologram is shown in Fig. 8.6.   The dark central spot in the hologram is spurious and is due to the finite amount of light transmitted through the supposedly opaque region surrounding the two pinholes.   The low-contrast vertical bars are due to the low-spatial-frequency terms in eq. (8.25) which are proportional to the pinhole separation.   In this case the spatial frequency was approximately 0.3 cycle/mm.   Figure 8.7 shows an enlarged region of the hologram where the high spatial frequencies corresponding to the distance x_r are displayed.   As shown by a micro-densitometer trace across the hologram in Fig. 8.8, the carrier spatial frequency is approximately 50 cycles/mm.   Its contrast is approximately 20 percent, indicating a value of $\alpha = 0.1$.

Coherent optical digital computation of the identity function was demonstrated by using four binary input combinations simultaneously. A binary phase modulator was synthesized by depositing approximately 1 μm of thorium fluoride on an optically flat fused-silica substrate in the pattern shown in Fig. 8.9.   This photomicrograph shows four circular

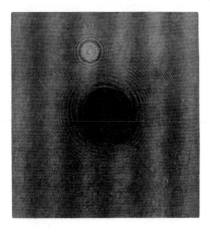

Fig. 8.6   Hologram formed from two   10-μm-diameter   pinholes on 100-μm centers.

Fig. 8.7 Enlargement of the hologram in Fig. 8.6 to show the high spatial frequencies.

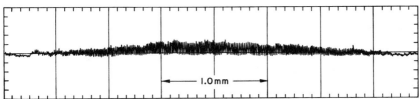

Fig. 8.8 Microdensitometer trace across the hologram in Fig. 8.6, showing both carrier spatial frequency (50 cycles/mm) and low-spatial-frequency modulation (0.25 cycle/mm).

pockets in the coating, each 50 μm in diameter.   A microinterferogram of a single pocket taken by reflection in white light is shown in Fig. 8.10. As can be seen, there is a 720° phase shift in reflection which implies a 180° phase shift in transmission as the optical index of thorium fluoride is approximately 1.5.   Thus the input pattern shown caused the optical phase in transmission to be retarded by 180° wherever a pocket appeared.   The pockets were spaced on 100-μm centers corresponding to the 100-μm spacing of the original pinholes from which the hologram was made.   Thus the inputs produced by the pattern shown in Fig. 8.9 correspond (from top to bottom) to 00, 01, 10, and 11, respectively.

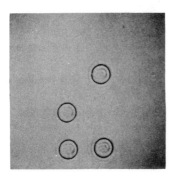

Fig. 8.9 Photomicrograph of a binary phase modulator consisting of four 50-μm-diameter modulating elements.

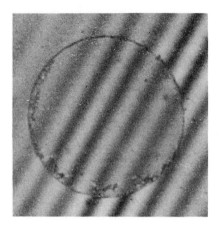

Fig. 8.10   Interferomicrogram of a single phase-modulating element.

The input pattern described above was used as a source in the computer configuration shown in Fig. 8.11 in order to demonstrate the identity function.   (Note that the scale of the input and output planes of Fig. 8.11 are deliberately exaggerated for clarity.)   Light from a helium-neon laser (6328 Å) was used to illuminate the input pattern, and

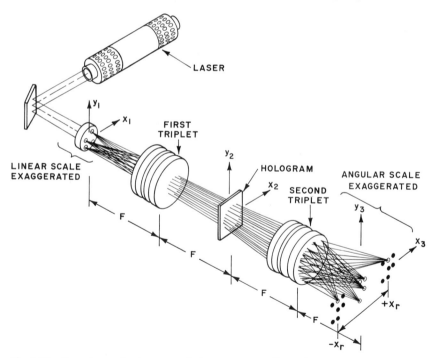

Fig. 8.11   Experimental coherent-optical-computer configuration used in calculating the binary identity function, using holographic logic.

the Fourier transform of the resultant illumination function was produced in the back focal plane of the first triplet. The hologram shown in Fig. 8.6 was placed in the transform plane and a second identical 600-mm f/8 triplet was used to take the inverse Fourier transform. The direct image of the optical phase modulator could be observed in the output plane on the optical axis. At the point ($x_3 = -x_r, y_3 = 0$) in the x_3y_3 plane the function given in Table 8.3 was produced. A photograph of the result is shown in Fig. 8.12. The center column represents the binary identity function. It consists of a binary 1 at the top (bright background) below which are two binary 0s followed by a fourth binary 1. To the left and right of this column are other binary 0s produced by destructive interference between the 180° light from the binary 1s in the input pattern and the background illumination which has equal amplitude but opposite phase.

An important variation is produced by translation of the hologram in the x_2 direction. Translation causes a relative phase shift of the light arriving in various parts of the output plane. Referring again to eq. (8.25), it is noted that, if the hologram is moved by one-half cycle of the low spatial frequency $\omega_{x_2}(x_B - x_A)$, then the change in the argument of the third term is given by

$$\Delta\omega_{x_2} = \frac{\pi}{x_A - x_B} \tag{8.30}$$

Making a corresponding change in the arguments of the expressions in the second term of eq. (8.25), it is noted that the relative phase, $\Delta\phi$, between the two expressions is given by

$$\Delta\phi = \frac{\pi(x_r - x_B)}{x_A - x_B} - \frac{\pi(x_r - x_A)}{x_A - x_B} = \pi \tag{8.31}$$

Thus, there is a relative phase shift of 180° in the light arriving at the point ($x_3 = -x_r, y_3 = 0$) from the input at ($x_1 = x_A, y_1 = 0$) with respect to that arriving from ($x_1 = x_B, y_1 = 0$). This causes previous in-phase

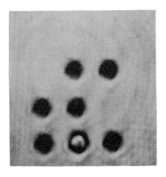

Fig. 8.12 Photomicrograph of the computer output plane when used to calculate the binary identity function.

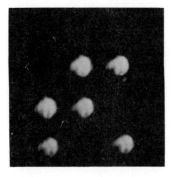

Fig. 8.13 Photomicrograph of the optical-computer output plane, showing the result when the hologram is translated by one-half cycle of the low spatial frequency to permit calculation of the binary exclusive OR function.

conditions (constructive interference) to become out of phase (destructive interference) and vice versa. By the same token the in- and out-of-phase conditions of all other points in the $x_3 y_3$ plane reverse. The result is shown in Fig. 8.13 which is the negate of the binary identity function or the "exclusive OR." The truth table for this function is given in Table 8.5.

TABLE 8.5

A	B	$f(A, B)$
0	0	0
0	1	1
1	0	1
1	1	0

The hologram for the exclusive OR could, of course, be produced by making a hologram of the source:

$$S''_{AB} = \begin{cases} (x_1 = x_A, y_1 = 0), \angle 0, \alpha \\ (x_1 = x_B, y_1 = 0), \angle \pi, \alpha \end{cases} \tag{8.32}$$

This hologram would have a transmission proportional to

$$I''_{AB} = EE^* = (\alpha e^{j\pi} e^{-j\omega_{x_2} x_A} + \alpha e^{-j\omega_{x_2} x_B} + e^{-j\omega_{x_2} x_r})$$

$$\times (\alpha e^{-j\pi} e^{j\omega_{x_2} x_A} + \alpha e^{j\omega_{x_2} x_B} + e^{j\omega_{x_2} x_r})$$

$$= (1 + 2\alpha^2) + 2\alpha[\cos \omega_{x_2}(x_r - x_A) - \cos \omega_{x_2}(x_r - x_B)]$$

$$- 2\alpha \cos \omega_{x_2}(x_B - x_A) \tag{8.33}$$

8.50 Propositional Logic

Unfortunately all propositional logic may not be performed by means of the identity function and the exclusive OR. It is necessary to add the

AND, OR, NAND, or NOR operator.   This chapter will close with a final example demonstrating a multiple-input OR.

At this point it is obvious that the output functional is taken at the point $(x_3 = -x_r, y_3 = 0)$.   Therefore in the following analysis all terms which represent outputs elsewhere in the $x_3 y_3$ plane will be dropped. Consider a multiplicity of inputs in the $x_1 y_1$ plane at $x_A, x_B, x_C, \ldots$.   It is desired to perform the OR function on these variables; i.e., we wish to form an output function $f(A, B, C, \ldots)$ as follows:

$$f(A, B, C, \ldots) = A + B + C + \cdots \qquad (8.34)$$

To accomplish this, form the hologram of the following source:

$$S_{A,B,C,\ldots} = \begin{cases} (x_1 = x_0, y_1 = 0), \angle 0, \alpha \\ (x_1 = x_A, y_1 = 0), \angle 2\pi/(n+1), \alpha \\ (x_1 = x_B, y_1 = 0), \angle 4\pi/(n+1), \alpha \\ \cdots\cdots\cdots\cdots\cdots\cdots \end{cases} \qquad (8.35)$$

where n is the total number of input variables.   The transmission of this hologram is proportional to

$$I_{A,B,C,\ldots} = (\alpha e^{-j\omega_{x_2} x_0} + \alpha e^{j2\pi/(n+1)} e^{-j\omega_{x_2} x_A} + \alpha e^{j4\pi/(n+1)} e^{-j\omega_{x_2} x_B}$$
$$+ \cdots e^{-j\omega_{x_2} x_r}) + (\alpha e^{j\omega_{x_2} x_0} + \alpha e^{-j2\pi/(n+1)} e^{j\omega_{x_2} x_A}$$
$$+ \alpha e^{-j4\pi/(n+1)} e^{j\omega_{x_2} x_B} + \cdots e^{j\omega_{x_2} x_r}) \beta \qquad (8.36)$$

where β is a normalizing factor.

If this hologram is illuminated by the source $S'_{A,B,C,\ldots}$ given by

$$S'_{A,B,C,\ldots} = \begin{cases} (x_1 = x_0, y_1 = 0), \angle 0, 1 \\ (x_1 = x_A, y_1 = 0), \angle 0, 1 \\ (x_1 = x_B, y_1 = 0), \angle 0, 1 \\ \cdots\cdots\cdots\cdots\cdots\cdots \end{cases} \qquad (8.37)$$

the light distribution in the $x_2 y_2$ plane is given by

$$E(\omega_{x_2}, \omega_{y_2}) = I_{A,B,C,\ldots}(e^{-j\omega_{x_2} x_0} + e^{-j\omega_{x_2} x_A} + e^{-j\omega_{x_2} x_B} + \cdots) \qquad (8.38)$$

in which expression the cross-product terms of interest are

$$\alpha\beta e^{-j\omega_{x_2} x_r}, \; \alpha\beta e^{j2\pi/(n+1)} e^{-j\omega_{x_2} x_r}, \; \alpha\beta e^{j4\pi/(n+1)} e^{-j\omega_{x_2} x_r}, \ldots \qquad (8.39)$$

All these terms lead to outputs at $(x_3 = -x_r, y_3 = 0)$.   Each output has an electric field strength $\alpha\beta$.   The phase of the outputs are $0, 2\pi/(n+1)$, $4\pi/(n+1), \ldots$.   This situation is diagramed in Fig. 8.14 for the case where $n = 4$.   Since the vectors shown, when summed, form a closed $(n+1)$-sided polygon, the electric field is zero for the input given by eq. (8.37).   Note that it is required either that the number of inputs n

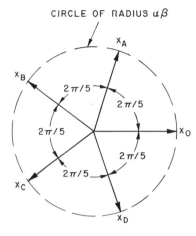

CIRCLE OF RADIUS $\alpha\beta$

Fig. 8.14   Digital-holographic-logic electric field vector configuration for use in instrumenting a four-input binary AND function.

be even or, when n is odd, that a second fixed vector x_0' be added to the set shown in Fig. 8.14.   This assumes a polygon with an odd number of sides, i.e., a polygon which does not possess mirror symmetry.

When one or more of the input variables is changed from an input phase of 0° (binary 0) to 180° (binary 1) the polygon is unbalanced and an output results.   As long as this output is large enough to activate the associated light detector, the desired result is obtained, and it can be written that

Input	*Output*
$(x_1 = x_A, y_3 = 0), \angle 0,1$	
$(x_1 = x_B, y_3 = 0), \angle 0,1$	
$(x_1 = x_C, y_3 = 0), \angle 0,1$	0
....	
One or more inputs, $\angle \pi$	1

This is the required binary OR.   With this and the 1s complement demonstrated in Sec. 8.30 all propositional logic may be performed.

Chapter Nine

Applications

9.00 Introduction

This chapter describes several of the most important applications of coherent optical computers. Most of these applications take advantage of the Fourier-transformable property of optics. Some of them combine this property with the ability of the optical system to calculate either two-dimensional or multichannel correlation functions. In most cases both multiplication and integration are done by the optical system. The role of the output signal transducer(s) is primarily the square-law detection of the electromagnetic field in the output plane. In one important exception to this rule the output detector itself performs both multiplication and integration whereas the purpose of the associated lens system is primarily the uniform illumination of the input transducer(s) and the direction of light diffracted by the input signal(s) to the output detector(s). This exception is the homodyne correlator discussed in Sec. 9.31.

It is not possible within the scope of this chapter to cover all applications of the coherent optical computer. In choosing the applications which are described, every attempt has been made to demonstrate breadth of application. Care is taken to avoid presenting a mass of detailed information about specific features of individual computers. In fact, in most cases, this chapter avoids discussion of specific design characteristics but rather refers the reader to one of the standard optical-computer configurations which are used as illustrations in Chapter One.

9.10 Antenna Pattern Analysis

As discussed in Chapter Four, (Sec. 4.30), the relationship between the light amplitude distribution in the front and back focal planes of a lens is given by the equation

$$E_2(\omega_x, \omega_y) = C_0 \iint E_1(x_1 y_1) e^{-j(\omega_x x_1 + \omega_y y_1)}\, dx_1\, dy_1 \tag{9.1}$$

where x_1 and y_1 are the spatial coordinates of the front focal plane and ω_x and ω_y are the spatial frequency coordinates in the back focal plane. The spatial frequency coordinates are related to the spatial coordinates of the back focal plane by the relationships

$$x_2 = \frac{\lambda_L F}{2\pi}\, \omega_x \qquad y_2 = \frac{\lambda_L F}{2\pi}\, \omega_y \tag{9.2}$$

where F is the back focal length and λ_L is the optical wavelength.

Equation (9.1) is the Fourier integral which relates the near-field amplitude distribution (the kernel function of the integral) to the far-field amplitude distribution of a radiation system. Thus, one of the most natural applications of the coherent optical computer is in studying near-field, far-field problems in radiation pattern analysis.

One example occurs in the study of antenna radiation patterns. In this application the kernel function in eq. (9.1) represents the instantaneous two-dimensional distribution of the electromagnetic field produced by the antenna to be analyzed. If this function is introduced into the front focal plane of the optical-computer lens system by means of an appropriate spatial light modulator, then in the back focal plane of the lens system an area spatial square-law detector (such as an imaging tube or scanned photomultiplier) may be used to detect and/or record the far-field distribution as related to the particular antenna configuration.

It should be noted that in utilizing the coherent optical computer for antenna pattern analysis it is not necessary to scale the dimensions of the spatial light modulator which is used to introduce the near-field radiation pattern at optical frequencies to the electromagnetic wavelength

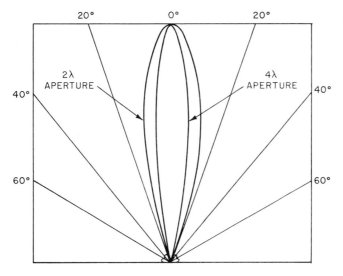

Fig. 9.1 Polar radiation patterns of a uniformly illuminated circular antenna.

utilized in the actual antenna. Take, for example, the radiation pattern of a uniformly illuminated circular antenna whose far-field radiation pattern is given in Chapter Four, by eq. (4.74), as

$$W(\omega_r) = \left| \frac{2\pi R^2 J_1(\omega_r R)}{\omega_r R} \right|^2 \tag{9.3}$$

where ω_r is the radian spatial frequency in the output plane. The radiation pattern associated with this antenna is shown in polar coordinates in Fig. 9.1 for two cases: one where the aperture is 2 wavelengths in diameter; the other 4 wavelengths in diameter. Assume that this antenna pattern is analyzed optically by placing a circular aperture in the front focal plane of a coherently illuminated lens system wherein, for reasons of mechanical simplicity, the aperture of the circle is several thousand optical wavelengths. The output light intensity pattern which results is given in Chapter Four in Fig. 4.3. As can be seen, many antenna pattern lobes are shown. However, only those lobes which would occur over an angle corresponding to π rad are recognized as being physically meaningful for the problem at hand. This does not detract from the utility of optical computation of antenna patterns without scaling. In fact, two of the advantages of antenna pattern analysis by optical computation are:

1. Highly complicated antenna radiation patterns may be computed with ease.

2. There is the possibility of direct visual observation of the antenna radiation pattern itself.

A particularly dramatic example is given in the case of the heliograph antenna.   The heliograph antenna is a 3-km-diameter array of ninety-six-m-diameter radar subantennas whose outputs are combined to yield images of the sun at 80 MHz.   Several workers have utilized coherent optical computation to study the far-field radiation pattern of this antenna system.   To do this, a circular array of 96 apertures may be placed in the front focal plane of the computer lens system and the light intensity distribution in the back focal plane recorded by exposing photographic film to the light arriving in that plane.   One example of the heliograph far-field antenna pattern calculated in this manner is shown in Fig. 9.2.   This particular result is due to Ramsey at the Commonwealth Scientific and Industrial Research Organization (CSIRO) in Australia.

Fig. 9.2   Result of calculating the far-field radiation pattern of the heliograph antenna, using a coherent optical computer. *(Commonwealth Scientific and Industrial Research Organization, Australia.)*

Far-field antenna radiation patterns of this type could be computed by digital electronic means and displayed on the output cathode-ray tube of a general-purpose digital machine.   However, the lengthy computational procedure required and the limited resolution and dynamic range of available cathode-ray-tube display units make this a difficult task. The simplicity and elegance of the coherent-optical-computer approach to this problem may be appreciated by an analysis of the enormous amount of information available from an analysis of Fig. 9.2.   Furthermore, as has been demonstrated by Cutrona [9.1], not only may the far-field pattern of the heliograph be calculated in this manner but also many intermediate-field patterns may be computed and analyzed just as easily.   Thus coherent-optical-computation techniques are extremely helpful in the design of complex antennas of many varieties.

9.11 Phased-array Beam Forming   If the radiation patterns of antenna arrays may be calculated by coherent optical computation, so also may the optical computer be used to process signals arising from such arrays.   This leads to interesting applications in both radar and sonar systems.   For example, Lambert [9.2] at the Columbia University Electronics Research Laboratory produced a two-dimensional phased-array optical computer as illustrated in Fig. 9.3.   In this system a linear array of many identical acoustic-delay-line light modulators produces multichannel spatial phase modulation of the input to the optical com-

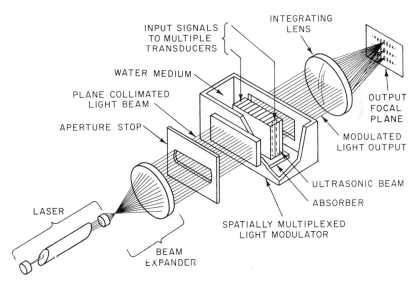

Fig. 9.3 Coherent-optical-computer system for two-dimensional phased-array signal processing. (*Columbia University Electronics Research Laboratory, now Riverside Research Institute.*)

puter.   The signal delivered to the ith acoustic transducer is composed of a temporal multiplex of the signals received from each element in the ith column of the associated phased-array antenna.   Every $1/T$ sec, where T is the transit time of the acoustic signal across the input aperture of the computer, all signals received from all elements in the entire phased-array antenna are momentarily aligned in the optical-computer aperture.   Assuming that the antenna is operating at an electromagnetic wavelength λ_0 and that a point target resides in the far field, then at the appropriate instant of time the input transducer system will produce a spatial phase modulation given by the function

$$\Phi(i,j) = \frac{2\pi d}{\lambda_0} (i \cos \phi + j \cos \theta) \tag{9.4}$$

where d is the interelement spacing of the actual phased array, ϕ is the elevation angle of the target, and θ is the azimuth angle of the target. Assuming a square array with n^2 elements so that $i = j = 1, 2, 3, \ldots, n$, the time-multiplexed input signals will be aligned in the input aperture for $1/nT$ s.   During that instant of time there will occur in the output of the optical computer an image of the target at coordinates given by

$$x_2 = F \cos \phi \qquad y_2 = F \cos \theta \tag{9.5}$$

For a multitarget situation all targets in the range interval cT will appear simultaneously, where c is the velocity of electromagnetic propagation. Thus the optical computer shown in Fig. 9.3 models the far-field phased-array antenna pattern in such a way as to map the angular position of all targets instantaneously into the output plane of the computer.   For further details the reader is referred to Ref. [9.2].

9.12   Synthetic-aperture Techniques   A more complex application of near-field, far-field calculations by a coherent optical computer is found in the "synthetic-aperture" approach to the analysis of radiation fields.   In airborne synthetic-aperture radar the reflectivity of the ground at microwave wavelengths is mapped as shown in Fig. 9.4.   The aircraft shown flies a straight path parallel to the surface of the earth. An airborne antenna is designed to provide a narrow primary-lobe radiation pattern in the azimuth direction (typically 1°) and a relatively wide radiation pattern in elevation (typically 10°).   As the antenna moves along the flight path, short microwave frequency pulses are emitted.   Electromagnetic energy backscattered by the ground is received from a region on the ground which is determined by the radiation pattern of the antenna.   For each emitted pulse many back-scattered pulses are received from a swath along the ground extending from a slant range R_1 to a slant range R_2 as shown in Fig. 9.4.   Each

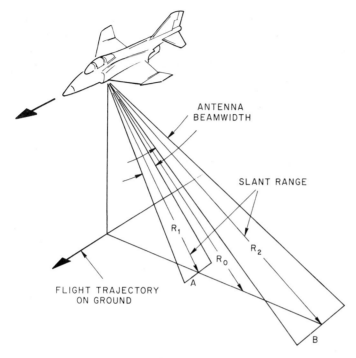

Fig. 9.4   Synthetic-aperture-radar geometry.

backscattered pulse will return at a time which is given by $2R/c$, where c is the velocity of propagation and R is the instantaneous slant range of the scatterer.   In synthetic-aperture radar a record is made of the phase and amplitude of the composite signal formed from all backscattered pulses returned from the ground.   This is usually accomplished by heterodyning the composite signal with the local oscillator which was gated to produce the emitted pulse.

Consider, for example, a point scatterer on the ground which has a broadside slant range of R_0, as shown in Fig. 9.4.   Taking the direction of the flight path as the x axis and its origin as the position of the flight at which the point scatterer is broadside to the aircraft, the instantaneous distance from the aircraft to the point scatterer is given by $\sqrt{R_0^2 + x^2}$ which, when $x \ll R_0$, may be approximated by $R_0 + x^2/2R_0$. Making the assumption that the relative phase is zero at the origin, the phase of a pulse which is received after making a round trip to and from the point scatterer is given by the following function of x:

$$\phi(x) = \frac{2\pi x^2}{R_0 \lambda_0} \tag{9.6}$$

Since $x = v_a t$, where v_a is the aircraft velocity, it is evident that the phase function is quadratic in time and that its rate of change with time is linear. This linear relationship of the rate of change of phase with time is called the *doppler history* of the point of scatterer.

At the instant of time when backscattered pulses are received from the shortest range, R_1, the sweep of a line-scanning cathode-ray-tube (CRT) recorder is started. The cosine of the phase angle of the composite signal multiplied by its amplitude is used for z-axis modulation of the CRT. The output of the CRT is recorded on a sheet of moving photographic film whose motion is perpendicular to the scan direction and is synchronized with the aircraft velocity. A new CRT sweep is started for each of the emitted pulses. A typical recording is shown in Fig. 9.5. In drawing Fig. 9.5 it was assumed that there were only two point scatters on the ground, both of which were broadside simultaneously. The general expression for the recording for each point scatterer is

$$t_a(x,y) = B + \cos \frac{2\pi x_r^2}{C y_r} \tag{9.7}$$

where t_a is the light amplitude transmission in the $x_r y_r$ plane of the film, B is an added bias, and $C = \lambda_0 c v_y^{-1} (v_a/v_T)^{-2}$, where v_y is the sweep velocity of the scanner and v_T is the film transport velocity.

Inspection of eq. (9.7) indicates that it represents the phase contours of a conical wavefront. Thus, if an optical computer is built as shown in Fig. 9.6 with a conical lens of matching power in the reference position, the conical wavefront produced by diffraction of the input illumination by the recording will be collimated, i.e., made parallel. The balance of the lens system shown is astigmatic and brings light collimated by the conical lens to a focus in the output plane while simultaneously focusing

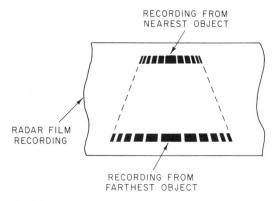

RECORDING FROM
NEAREST OBJECT

RADAR FILM
RECORDING

RECORDING FROM
FARTHEST OBJECT

Fig. 9.5 Schematic of an ideal synthetic-aperture-radar recording.

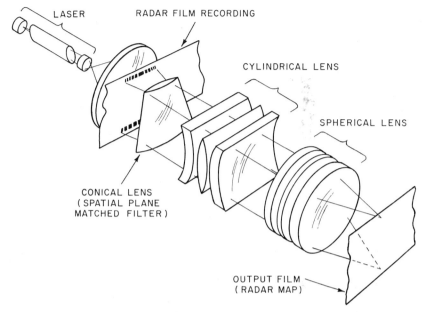

Fig. 9.6 Optical-computer configuration used for synthetic-aperture-radar signal processing.

light diffracted in the y direction.   The optical computer shown in Fig. 9.6 is a multichannel correlator as discussed in Chapter One (Sec. 1.60).   The output function is given by

$$E_4(t, y_i) = \int s_i(x - v_T t) t_i(x) \, dx \qquad (9.8)$$

where $i = 1, 2, \ldots, N$ and N is the number of resolution elements in the range direction.   The set of reference functions $r_i(x)$ are provided by the conical lens.

It is shown by Cutrona et al. [9.3] that, as the recorded radar film moves through the input plane of the optical computer, the images formed in the output plane of point scatterers on the ground will travel at a velocity in the output plane which is a function of range.   To record the synthetic-aperture-radar map without blurring, a slit is placed in the output plane and unexposed photographic film is moved past this slit in synchronism with the input film.   The resultant recording is a map of the microwave reflectivity of the ground.   Thus the optical computer as used in synthetic-aperture radar maps a composite recording of many doppler histories into point images in the output plane.   The reason for using a synthetic-aperture-radar system is that the resultant map has a resolution equivalent to that produced by a very large antenna having an aperture equal to $R_0 \sin \theta$, where θ is the angular subtense of the primary azimuth lobe.

Figure 9.7 shows a portion of a typical synthetic-aperture-radar recording.* Since the x direction is horizontal, the horizontal bands correspond to composite doppler histories of objects on the ground at corresponding slant ranges. A synthetic-aperture-radar map as produced by means of coherent optical computation is shown in Fig. 9.8. This map is of Washington, D.C., and its excellence illustrates the importance of synthetic-aperture-radar mapping systems, especially when it is recalled that these maps may be produced on an all-weather day-or-night basis. It should be noted here that the primary reason for the advanced state of development of coherent optical computers has been the necessity for their use in the synthetic-aperture-radar field.

Although the backscattered radiation field of the earth is actually three-dimensional, the synthetic-aperture radar assumes a flat earth so that, except for certain radar shadows, three-dimensionality is deliberately suppressed. This approach to the problem is usually completely satisfactory as the height of the aircraft above the earth is usually much greater than the vertical height of any object on the ground. Furthermore, the earth is illuminated at a grazing angle where three-dimension-

*The author is indebted to E. N. Leith of the University of Michigan who furnished Figs. 9.7 and 9.8.

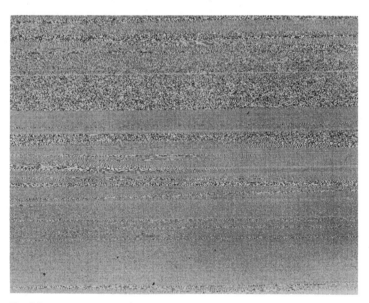

Fig. 9.7 Typical synthetic-aperture-radar signal recording. (*University of Michigan.*)

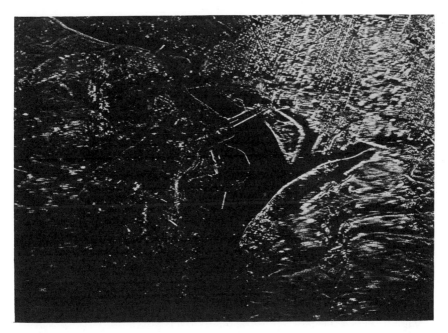

Fig. 9.8 Synthetic-aperture-radar map of Washington, D.C., produced by means of a coherent optical computer. (*University of Michigan.*)

al effects are minimized.   There are, however, other synthetic-aperture systems where the entire backscattered radiation field must be recorded so that a full three-dimensional near-field, far-field analysis may be performed by the associated optical computer.   One example is synthetic-aperture acoustic holography as described by Preston and Kreuzer [9.4].   Here, much as in synthetic-aperture radar, high-frequency pulses are emitted and a detector scans the backscattered radiation field. A photographic recording is made whose transmission is determined by the detected phase and amplitude of the backscattered signals as determined by heterodyning.   In synthetic-aperture acoustic holography, however, a single linear scan of the detector is not sufficient.   Range information, being three-dimensional, may not be read as a function of the time of arrival of backscattered signals.   Instead, the detector is scanned in a raster fashion over a plane.   If it is assumed that the broadside range of a point scatterer is R_1, then the recording has the form

$$t_a(x,y) = B + \cos\left(\frac{4\pi}{\lambda_s}\sqrt{R_i^2 + x^2 + y^2}\right) \tag{9.9}$$

where λ_s is the acoustic wavelength and the origin in the xy plane is taken at the point where the point scatterer is broadside to the scanning detector.   Equation (9.9) is known in optics as a *Fresnel zone plate* [9.5]. It is also the on-axis hologram of the point scatterer [9.6].   When such a recording is placed in the input plane of a coherent optical computer, the resultant electric field distribution is given by

$$E_1(x,y) = E_0(B + \tfrac{1}{2}e^{j(4\pi/\lambda s)\sqrt{R_i^2 + x^2 + y^2}} + \tfrac{1}{2}e^{-j(4\pi/\lambda s)\sqrt{R_i^2 + x^2 + y^2}}) \qquad (9.10)$$

where the first term represents undiffracted light, the second term represents a diverging spherical wave, and the third term represents a converging spherical wave.

A schematic of an optical computer for use in forming images from synthetic-aperture acoustic holograms is shown in Fig. 9.9.   As can be seen, undiffracted light arising from the bias term B is removed in the first Fourier-transform plane by a zero-spatial-frequency suppression, i.e., by means of a zero-order stop.   Both the diverging and converging spherical waves form images of the point scatterer, but in different planes.   Either image may be observed as desired.   The noise produced in one image plane by the background spherical wave from the other image plane is not found to be a problem in practice.   However, improper scaling of the recording may introduce aberrations in the image.   This is discussed in some detail in a report by Kreuzer [9.7].

In general, the recording produced by a system for making synthetic-aperture acoustic holograms will consist of the superposition of a

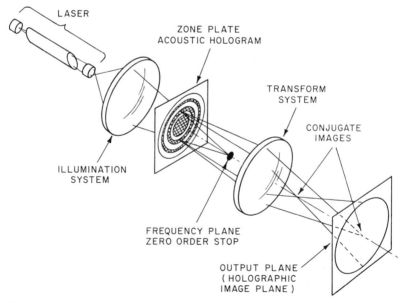

Fig. 9.9 Coherent-optical-computer configuration for use in synthetic-aperture acoustic holography.

multitude of Fresnel zone plates each of which corresponds to an individual point scatterer. When introduced into the optical computer, each zone plate produces both a diverging and a converging spherical wave, one of which will focus near the output plane. There will, in fact, exist in the vicinity of the output plane a three-dimensional holographic image of the object(s) whose backscattered radiation field was mapped by the detector. If the depth of focus is sufficient, it will be possible to observe a recognizable image in the output plane. An example is given in Fig. 9.10 which shows a synthetic-aperture acoustic hologram formed on photographic film by recording the output of a 0.01-in. detector which scanned a 10×10 in. plane in a raster fashion at about 100 scan lines per inch. The object whose radiation field was mapped was an 0.5-in.-diameter bolt threaded at approximately 10 threads per inch. Acoustic radiation at a frequency of 5 MHz was utilized. The synthetic-aperture hologram illustrated in Fig. 9.10 was placed in the front focal plane of a coherent optical computer and the light intensity distribution in a region near the output plane was record-

Fig. 9.10 Typical synthetic-aperture acoustic hologram.

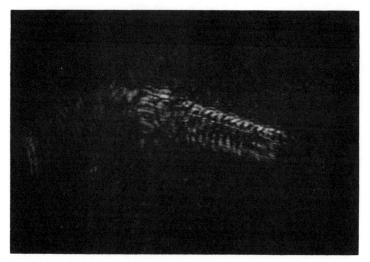

Fig. 9.11 Optical computer output showing a synthetic-aperture acoustic holographic image of an 0.5-in-diameter bolt having 10 threads per inch.

ed.   The resultant recording of the computer output is shown in Fig. 9.11.   Figure 9.11 clearly shows both the shaft and threads of the bolt.   This result illustrates one of the more complex uses of the coherent optical computer in performing the calculations involved in the three-dimensional   near-field,   far-field   light-amplitude-distribution mapping which is required in the field of synthetic-aperture acoustics.

9.20   Signal Spectrum Analysis

Any signal(s) which is a function of one variable may be introduced into the input plane of a coherent optical spectrum analyzer (see Chap. One, Sec. 1.30) so that the Fourier transform is displayed in the output plane.   Many spatial light modulators are available for use in both real-time and delayed-time signal introduction as discussed in Chapter Five.   This type of optical computer provides a facility for the continuous examination of all frequency components of an incoming signal as a function of time.   This type of analysis is particularly useful since it provides wide-open spectrum analysis as required for detailed observation of the signal patterns produced by "frequency-hopping" radars and "spread-spectrum" communication devices.   These complex signal sources are difficult to observe by other means.

A related example, provided by Queen, Grant, and others at the Johns Hopkins University Applied Physics Laboratory, concerns a coherent optical computer for use in real-time frequency-hopping radar signal processing.   The configuration of this computer is shown in Fig. 9.12.   The input transducer is a membrane light modulator (MLM) of the wired type discussed in Sec. 5.40 which has 10,000 circular light-modulating elements arranged in 100 rows containing 100 elements each.   The surface of the MLM is imaged onto an opaque mask containing 10,000 transmitting apertures each of which is half the diameter of the corresponding MLM element.   The purpose of the mask is to permit piston-like phase modulation where only the center of each paraboloidally deflected membrane element contributes to the modulation across the apertures of the mask.   The mask is followed by an optical system which is used for computing the Fourier transform. A one-axis oscillating-mirror output-plane scanner similar to the type described in Sec. 7.21 is used to convert the computer output into an oscillogram for display purposes.

In one mode of operation the computer is used for processing 100 radar echoes obtained by repetitively pulsing at a single transmission frequency.   An electrical signal proportional to the phase of each echo is applied to the corresponding row electrode of the MLM.   The output of the coherent optical computer then represents doppler frequency which, in turn, is proportional to target velocity.   The upper oscillogram in Fig. 9.13 shows the results obtained from such a

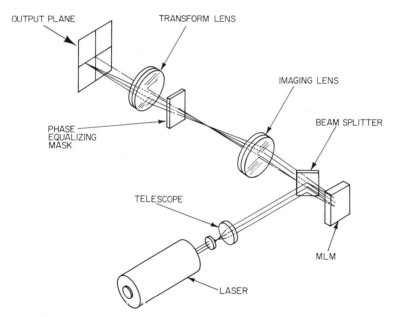

Fig. 9.12 A coherent-optical-computer system for use in radar signal processing to achieve real-time high resolution range/velocity discrimination.

system when six complete sets of 100 echoes each are sequentially analyzed by means of the computer. Each trace shows a separate analysis. The target return shown has a positive doppler of approximately 15 m/s at a resolution of 0.62 m/s.

Johns Hopkins University has also applied this coherent optical computer to a 100-pulse system for determining range resolution rather than doppler. The lower oscillogram in Fig. 9.13 shows the results of analyzing a 100-pulse waveform where each pulse was transmitted at a different frequency. Frequencies were selected to cover a 500-MHz bandwidth at equal spacings of 5 MHz. Doppler-corrected echoes were frequency-ordered and signals corresponding to their phases applied to the rows of the MLM. The light distribution in the output plane of the computer now yields the structure of a target lying within a range-resolution cell whose size corresponds to a single pulse width and whose resolution corresponds to the full 500-MHz bandwidth. In this case the range-resolution cell is 100 ft with a resolution of 1 ft. The vertical scale of the display is logarithmic so that it is possible to observe the fine structure of the target.

Markevitch of the Ampex Corporation has taken advantage of both dimensions of the coherent optical spectrum analyzer in treating signals which are essentially one dimensional. The signal to be analyzed is used to modulate the spot intensity of a CRT recorder in the same manner employed in synthetic-aperture radar (see Sec. 9.22). A continuous recording is made on a roll of photographic film whose movement is perpendicular to the CRT scan direction. If the incoming signal is sinusoidal and has an integral number of cycles per CRT sweep, the recording is similar to the simple sinusoidal recording discussed in Chapter One. (See Fig. 1.9.) Its Wiener spectrum displays both positive and negative frequency components on the ω axis. When the input signal no longer has an integral number of cycles per CRT sweep, the sinusoidal recording is tilted with respect to the direction of film motion and the corresponding components of the Wiener spectrum move off the ω axis in an orthogonal trajectory.

When the incoming signal contains many sinusoidal frequency components, the Wiener spectrum contains corresponding on-axis terms (for components having an integral number of cycles per sweep) as well as a multiplicity of off-axis terms corresponding to the nonintegral components. An example of the Wiener spectrum of such a recording produced by a coherent optical computer is shown in Fig. 9.14a. In this case the original photographic recording was made by using a broadband radio-frequency receiver covering the 0.5–12 MHz band in the San Francisco Bay Area. In addition to the on-axis zero-order term, Fig. 9.14a shows the spectrum of all radio broadcast stations as well as some of the short-wavelength stations.

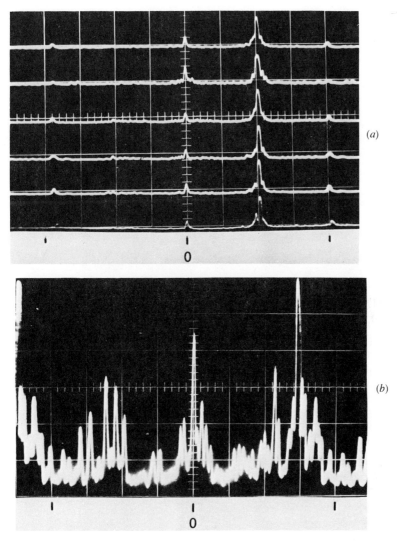

(a)

(b)

Fig. 9.13 Oscillographic output displays taken from the optical computer system shown in Fig. 9.12 showing (*a*) target velocity at 0.62 m/s resolution over a 62 m/s unambigious velocity interval for six 100-pulse transmit cycles and (*b*) target range at 1-ft resolution over a 100-ft unambigious range interval. (*U.S. Navy and Applied Physics Laboratory, The Johns Hopkins University.*)

Another example of this type of spectrum analysis is shown in Fig. 9.14*b* which demonstrates results obtained from an experiment involving vibration analysis. Here the signal developed by an accelerometer mounted on a J57-P37A jet aircraft engine was recorded. The recording was made using a CRT sweep frequency of 42 Hz slaved to the low-

pressure spool of the engine.   The recording was made with a sweep
length of 1 cm on photographic film continuously moving at a velocity of 0.83 cm/s.   This film was introduced into an optical spectrum
analyzer having an input aperture of 1 × 1 cm.   The Wiener spectrum

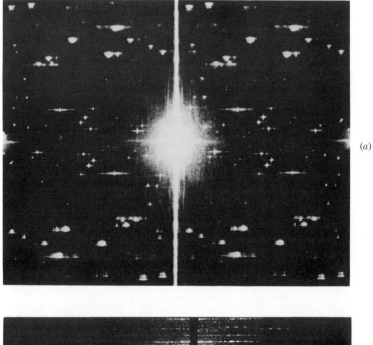

(a)

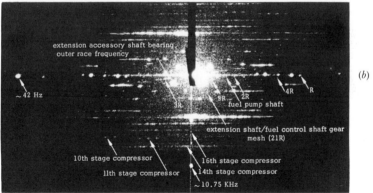

(b)

Fig. 9.14   (*a*) Wiener spectrum of radio frequencies received and recorded
in the San Francisco Bay area.   (*b*) Vibration analysis performed by taking
the Wiener spectrum of a recording of the output of an accelerometer
mounted on a J57-P37A jet aircraft engine.   (*c*) Detail of a portion of a
Wiener spectrum like that in part (*b*) showing two frequency components
having a 0.5 Hz separation. (*U.S. Navy and Ampex Corporation.*)

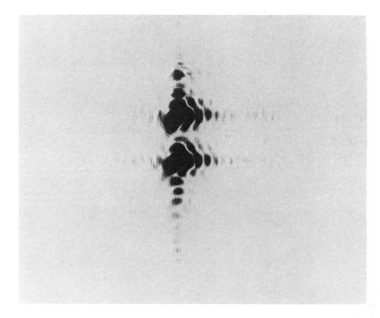

Fig. 9.14 *Continued.*

corresponding to the full 12-s recording was displayed and photographed.   Many frequency components are visible, some correspond to fuel pump shaft vibrations, to vibrations of various compressor stages, and to the fundamental and harmonic frequencies of the high-pressure spool.   Many vibrational modes are displayed which could not be observed readily using traditional electronic spectrum analyzers.   In fact, Markevitch reports that signals from the accelerometer covering a dynamic range of as much as 50 dB could be located.   The frequency resolution corresponding to the full 12-s aperture was obtained.   An illustration of frequency resolution is provided in Fig. 9.14c which shows a portion of the Wiener spectrum indicating two well-resolved components having a separation of only 0.5 Hz.

Spectrum analysis by optical computer is also useful when dealing with signals which are a function of two variables.   Here the optical computer may be used to display both spatial-frequency coordinates in the output plane.   An example of the use of this type of analysis is provided in Fig. 9.15 which shows an aerial reconnaissance photograph with the accompanying Wiener spectrum shown in the insert.   In this case the coherent optical spectrum analyzer is used for screening aerial reconnaissance photography by locating periodic structure in the spectrum which may be indicative of the existence of man-made struc-

Fig. 9.15 Aerial photograph and its Wiener spectrum as calculated by an optical computer.

tures on the ground. Note, for example, the periodic spatial-frequency components in two orthogonal directions due to the rows of parked cars in Fig. 9.15. Once again, the coherent optical computer excels in this operation because of its superiority in data-processing speed over equivalent electronic means for two-dimensional spectrum analysis.

9.21 Frequency-multiplexed Television In certain television systems where electronic imaging tubes of proper sensitivity are unavailable and mechanical scanning is not desired a "frequency-multiplexed" imaging system may be utilized. Such a system was originally described by D'Albe [9.8]. Here the intensity of each point in the image is transmitted by using the value of the intensity to modulate the amplitude of a frequency which is explicitly assigned to that image point. Typical frequency assignments for an $n \times n$ format are shown in Fig. 9.16. To transmit an image having $n \times n$ resolution elements, n^2 frequencies are simultaneously combined with the appropriate amplitude values to form the video signal. The frequency-multiplexed video signal may be expressed by the equation

$$s(t) = \sum_{i=1}^{i=n} \sum_{j=1}^{j=n} I_{ij} \sin \omega_{ij} t \qquad (9.11)$$

where I_{ij} is the instantaneous intensity of the ijth image point and ω_{ij} is the corresponding frequency.

At the receiver this signal may be demultiplexed and converted into the original image by use of a coherent optical spectrum analyzer. To accomplish this goal the signal is recorded on photographic film by means of a line-scanning cathode-ray tube or a scanned laser recorder. The photographic film is moved in a direction perpendicular to that of the scanner. The line-scan frequency is chosen such that one sweep will contain an integral number of cycles of any of the frequencies assigned to the first column of image points. For example, if only the first element in the ith row of the image were illuminated, the recording would take the form given by

$$R(x,y) = B + s(t) = B + I_{i1} \sin \frac{\omega_{i1} x}{v_x} \qquad (9.12)$$

where v_x is the sweep velocity. Since there is no phase shift from line to line, this recording is a spatial sine wave in the x coordinate only. If only the second element in the ith row of the image is illuminated, the resultant recording would be given by

$$R(x,y) = B + s(t) = B + I_{i2} \left(\sin \frac{\omega_{i2} x}{v_x} + l \Delta\phi_{i2} \right) \qquad (9.13)$$

	1ST COLUMN	2ND COLUMN	$\cdots$	nTH COLUMN
1ST ROW	f_0	$f_0 + \Delta f$	$\cdots$	$f_0 + n\Delta f$
2ND ROW	$2f_0$	$2f_0 + \Delta f$	$\cdots$	$2f_0 + n\Delta f$
3RD ROW	$3f_0$	$3f_0 + \Delta f$	$\cdots$	$3f_0 + n\Delta f$
$\vdots$	$\vdots$	$\vdots$		$\vdots$
iTH ROW	if_0	$if_0 + \Delta f$	$\cdots$	$if_0 + n\Delta f$
$\vdots$	$\vdots$	$\vdots$		$\vdots$
nTH ROW	nf_0	$nf_0 + \Delta f$	$\cdots$	$nf_0 + n\Delta f$

Fig. 9.16 Frequency assignments used in frequency-multiplexed television.

where the index l denotes the lth scan line and the term $\Delta\phi_{i2}$ is the phase shift per scan line for the frequency f_{i2}. The phase shift provides a y component to the spectrum of the recorded signal.

When the two-dimensional Fourier transform of the function given by eq. (9.12) is taken in polar coordinates, delta functions appear at $\omega_r = 0$ and at $\omega_r = \pm\omega_{x_{i1}}$, where $\omega_{x_{i1}} = \omega_{i1}v_x^{-1}$. The latter two delta functions lie on the $\theta = 0$ axis. The Fourier transform of the function given in eq. (9.13) again yields the delta function at $\omega_r = 0$ but now the delta functions corresponding to the tilted sine wave are at $(\omega_r, \theta) = (\pm\omega_{x_{i2}}, \Delta\phi_{i2}/2\pi d)$, where d is the scan-line spacing. With appropriate frequency assignments there is a one-to-one mapping of each image point into a corresponding delta function through the mechanism of the Fourier transform.

Figure 9.17a shows a recording of a simple frequency-multiplexed image where only two image points are illuminated. When this recording is placed in the input plane of a coherent optical spectrum analyzer, the Wiener spectrum observed in the output plane is as

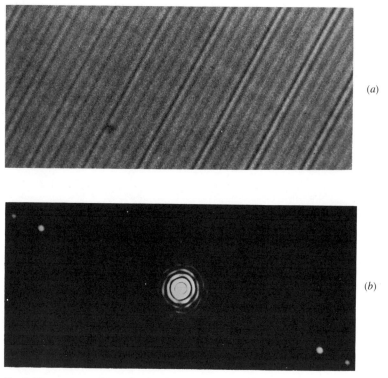

(a)

(b)

Fig. 9.17 (a) Recordings of a simple frequency-multiplexed television and signal and (b) its Wiener spectrum.

shown in Fig. 9.17*b*. The Wiener spectrum shows a strong zero-order delta function at $\omega_r = 0$ because of the bias term plus the two image points and their conjugates.

For the reader who is familiar with holography it is worth noting that the frequency-multiplexed video recording described above is the Fourier hologram of the original image. This of course is a fictive hologram in that it is made from a noncoherently illuminated image through the mechanism of frequency-multiplexed television. However, the result is exactly as if a hologram of the image had been made by optical heterodyning with a reference beam in the Fourier plane. The utility of the optical computer in this instance is in the direct conversion of the recorded frequency-multiplexed television into a visible image by means of the two-dimensional Fourier transform.

9.22 Time-difference Detection Frequently it is desired to measure the time difference of propagation of a signal along two alternative paths without a priori knowledge of the signal waveform and/or its time of occurrence. Assume that the composite received signal is recorded by a suitable spatial light amplitude modulator in the form

$$f(x) = \alpha_1 s(x) + \alpha_2 s(x + \Delta x) \tag{9.14}$$

where $x = v_T t$ and $\Delta x = v_T \Delta t$ and Δt is the time difference between two arrivals of the same signal having amplitudes α_1 and α_2, respectively.

When the recording is introduced in the input plane of a coherent optical spectrum analyzer, the output plane will contain a light amplitude distribution given by

$$F(\omega_x) = E_0 e^{j\omega_L t}[\alpha_1 S(\omega_x) + e^{j\omega_x \Delta x}\alpha_2 S(\omega_x)] \tag{9.15}$$

where E_0 is the amplitude of the illumination in the input plane, ω_L is its radian temporal frequency, and $S(\omega_x)$ is the Fourier transform of $s(x)$. A spatial square-law detector placed in the output plane will record the Wiener spectrum of the composite signal, namely,

$$W(\omega_x) = S(\omega_x)S^*(\omega_x)(\alpha_1^2 + \alpha_2^2 + 2\alpha_1\alpha_2 \cos \Delta x \omega_x) \tag{9.16}$$

As can be seen, the Wiener spectrum contains what might be thought of as a "homodyne" term resulting from the coherent interference or "mixing" of the spectra of the two components of the composite signal. The modulation of this spatially cosinusoidal term is $2\alpha_1\alpha_2/(\alpha_1^2 + \alpha_2^2)$ and it is superimposed upon the usual Wiener spectrum of the signal, namely, $S(\omega_x)S^*(\omega_x)$. The spatial frequency of the modulation is directly related to Δx. If $s(x)$ occupies a spatial bandwidth W in cycles per unit length, then $W(\omega_x)$ will exist over the interval $-2\pi W \leqslant \omega_x \leqslant +2\pi W$ and the argument of the cosinusoidal modulation term will have values between $-2\pi W \Delta x$ and $+2\pi W \Delta x$. Thus for each $\Delta x = 1/2W$ there will be a full cycle of variation across $W(\omega_x)$ at the modulation given above. The total number of cycles is given by $2W \Delta x$, or twice the product of the signal bandwidth and the spatial separation. By measuring the spatial frequency of the modulation, the time difference of propagation may be determined without knowledge of the exact signal waveform. This type of analysis, which is readily instrumented by a coherent optical spectrum analyzer, has been called *cepstrum analysis* and is discussed in detail in Ref. [9.9].

9.30   Correlation Detection

Some of the most important applications of coherent optical computers lie in the field of correlation detection of high time-bandwidth signals. For example, in high-resolution, peak-power-limited radar it is customary to generate relatively long coded signals at a level equal to the peak-power limit. The signal waveform is designed to fill the full bandwidth of the radar transmit-receive system. In such radars it is desired to resolve targets to better than cT, where c is the velocity of electromagnetic propagation and T is the signal duration. In order to do this, a receiver must perform correlation detection by continuously calculating the result of the integration

$$E(t) = \int s(x - v_T t) r(x) \, dx \tag{9.17}$$

where $s(x - v_T t)$ is the incoming signal moving through the input plane at the velocity v_T and $r(x)$ is a reference function which is usually made equal to $s^*(x)$. In this case the output $E(t)$ is, of course, the autocorrelation function.

For an appropriately designed signal, the duration of the output correlation pulse will be of the order of $1/W$, thus yielding resolution of c/W. This implies a resolution improvement equal to the time-bandwidth product TW. This type of operation is called *pulse compression*. Realization of this operation by purely electronic means is difficult when the time-bandwidth product is large. On the other hand, the optical computer is capable of correlation detection for signal waveforms having these large time-bandwidth products. Furthermore the optical computer may be used to perform correlation detection on a multichannel basis when necessary.

For maximum utility the equipment used for pulse compression should also be capable of generating the signal itself. When a delta function is applied to the pulse compressor, the reference function should appear at the output. In the optical pulse compressor the incoming signal spatially modulates the illuminating light in the input plane. A recording of the reference signal is placed in the reference plane, as discussed in Chapter One (Sec. 1.60).   If a pulse is applied to the input spatial light modulator its image travels sequentially across the reference recording.   If the photometry of the system is such that sufficient photons are received per unit time in the output plane to provide a satisfactory signal-to-noise ratio, the pulse compressor will in fact produce the output signal waveform desired.   This operation is called *pulse expansion.*

Pulse expanders and compressors of this type have in fact been built and some are now in production.   For example, Izzo [9.10] has reported on such a system wherein both input signal and reference are introduced by means of delay-line light modulators.   Typical output waveforms are shown in Fig. 7.13, as an illustration of a single-sideband, suppressed-carrier pulse compressor.   Izzo's optical system is of considerable interest and is shown in Fig. 9.18.   Rather than using four separated lenses in the traditional layout shown in Chapter One, only two lenses are used in a cleverly folded system.   Each lens performs two functions simultaneously.   Lens L_1 acts both to illuminate the input-signal delay-line light modulator and to perform the output integration required to calculate the correlation function.   Lens L_2 both calculates the Fourier transform (in order to permit spatial-frequency-plane filtering) and images the input-signal delay-line light modulator upon the reference-delay-line light modulator.   Izzo's folded system is made possible by the utilization of a reflective spatial-frequency-plane filter in the Fourier-transform plane.

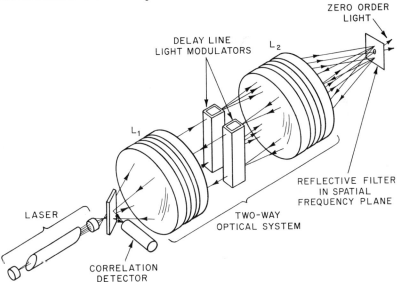

Fig. 9.18 Simplified coherent-optical-computer configuration for use in correlation detection.

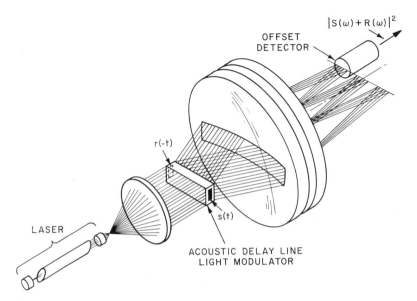

Fig. 9.19   Coherent-optical-computer configuration which uses offset detection for production of the correlation function.

9.31   The Homodyne Correlator   A still more compact optical pulse compressor system is diagramed in Fig. 9.19.   Here both the input and reference signals are entered coaxially in a single-delay-line modulator.   Because the signals travel in opposite directions, a reference must be generated which is the time inverse of the signal to be detected.   The spatial frequency plane is not displayed so that the zero-order term may not be removed by traditional means.   Heterodyne detection may be performed on the optical axis.   If advantage is taken of the polarization modulation of the illuminating light by the delay-line light modulator (see Chap. Five, Sec. 5.50), polarized illumination may be used at the appropriate angle and the zero-order term removed by an analyzer in the output plane, thus permitting direct detection on either a single- or double-sideband suppressed-carrier basis.   However, acoustic-delay-line light modulators usually produce weak modulation and the signal arriving on axis in the output plane is doubly diffracted so that in most cases an analyzer with an extinction of 10^{-5} to 10^{-6} must be used.   This is a difficult requirement.   A high level of input illumination is also required.

An extremely interesting alternative is the so-called "homodyne correlator" where offset detection is used in the spatial frequency plane.   The output detector is placed off axis in the position where the Fourier transforms of the signal and reference appear superimposed.   In this mode of operation the correlation function is calculated by the detector, *not* by the optical system. The detector must form the Wiener spectrum as follows:

$$W(\omega_x) = |S(\omega_x)e^{-j\omega_x v_T t} + R(\omega_x)e^{j\omega_x v_T t}|^2$$

$$= |S(\omega_x)|^2 + |R(\omega_x)|^2$$

$$+ S(\omega_x)R^*(\omega_x)e^{-j2\omega_x v_T t} + S^*(\omega_x)R(\omega_x)e^{j2\omega_x v_T t} \quad (9.18)$$

The first two terms, when integrated over ω_x, yield quantities proportional to the instantaneous power in the signal and the reference. Integration *by the detector* of the second two terms yields the desired correlation function.

There are three advantages of the homodyne correlator:

1. Light is singly diffracted by both acoustic signals in the delay-line light modulator, thus placing 10 to 30 dB more power in the output plane.

2. No analyzer is required because zero-order removal is obtained by spatial separation of the diffracted light and the undiffracted zero order in the output plane. (Note that an analyzer may still be useful in the output plane, in that zero-order side lobes may be removed at the off-axis location of the detector.)

3. The output is the true correlation function which modulates a carrier whose frequency is equal to twice the intermediate frequency at which signal and reference are entered. (Note that the modulus of the correlation function is detected axially when the carrier is suppressed, which is a disadvantage when dealing with phase-shift-keyed signals when a received binary 1 differs from a binary 0 by a phase shift only.)

The disadvantages of the homodyne correlator are:

1. The photodetector must be designed to tolerate the continuous light flux which is received at all times when either signal and/or reference is present.

2. The photodetector must be an area detector since the Fourier transform may be spread over a relatively large region in the output plane.

In general, the region occupied by the Fourier transform will be larger than that required for axial detection by a factor equal to the system TW. Since integration is performed in the photodetector, its transit-time uniformity must be satisfactory to coherently sum all photoelectrons as required. The simplicity of the homodyne correlator permits the use of a folded acoustic path in the delay-line light modulator as shown in Fig. 9.20 when the signal transducer and reference transducer are located on opposite corners of a rectangular delay line. This configuration makes it possible to achieve the full time-bandwidth product

REFERENCE, r(-t)   SIGNAL, s(t)

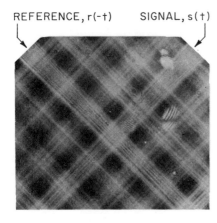

Fig. 9.20 Schlieren image of two superimposed acoustic beams in a folded-path delay-line light modulator.

predicted for acoustic-delay-line light modulators in Chapter Five (Sec. 5.52) in an extremely simple optical-computer system having an aperture size of only a few centimeters.

The results of recent work by Atzeni and Pantani [9.11] using a homodyne correlator are shown in the oscillogram of Fig. 9.21. The lower trace of this oscillogram shows the photodetector output at a scale of 10 μs per division. This signal is the result of autocorrelating the 13-bit Barker code which is shown in the upper trace of the oscillogram. Because of the high signal-to-shot noise ratio the main peak and side-

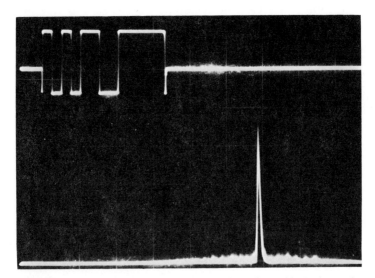

Fig. 9.21 Results of homodyne autocorrelation of a 13-bit Barker code using an optical computer with dual delay-line light modulators (*Instituto di Ricerca Sulle Onde Elettromagnetiche, Italy.*)

lobe structure of the Barker code are clearly evident.   In this particular experiment the acoustic-delay-line light modulators used a water medium with an acoustic center frequency of 15 MHz, a bandwidth of approximately 1 MHz, and an optical aperture of 100 mm.

9.32 Multichannel Correlation Detection

A good example of a useful application of coherent optical computers to multichannel correlation detection is to consider the use of such a computer to provide protection against fading in tropospheric-scatter communications.   In a typical tropospheric-scatter system, multiple paths exist between the transmitter and the receiver.   Correlation detection is thus hampered by synchronization difficulties.   One answer to this problem has been described in a paper by Bitzer et al. [9.12] where use is made of simultaneous multichannel correlation detection.   The reference signal in each channel is delayed with respect to the neighboring channels by a time interval equal to $1/W$.   For reasons of economy, electronics systems used for this purpose are limited to 10 channels corresponding to typical short-term multipath spread over distances of a few hundred kilometers at a bandwidth of 5 MHz.   Clearly, as tropospheric-scatter systems are expanded so as to use wider bandwidths and longer communications distances, the inherently large channel capacity and wide-bandwidth capability of the coherent optical computer could be used to advantage.

9.33 Two-dimensional Correlation Detection

As illustrated in the design example in Chapter Two (Sec. 2.30), one of the fundamental limitations on the maximum space-bandwidth (SW) product of the optical computer is the lens system itself.   Large precision optics may be utilized to yield an area SW product of 10^{10}.   It would seem, however, in systems using single-channel signal introduction that the linear SW of 10^5 places an upper bound on the pulse-compression ratio. However this is not the case, and a particularly advantageous method exists for using the full area SW.   This method, as described by Spann [9.13], uses a two-dimensional reference mask for what is essentially a one-dimensional signal.   The signal must be recorded in a raster fashion on the input spatial light modulator.   Spann's method may be then utilized and requires no synchronization between the incoming signal and the recorder.   A simple example is illustrated in Fig. 9.22 which shows a 15-bit binary code recorded in a three-line raster and the associated reference mask.   As can be seen, no matter when the code is initiated, there will be a position of the reference mask with which it will correlate.   The Spann type of reference mask is therefore particularly useful in taking advantage of the 100 dB of pulse compression which a large optical system could furnish.

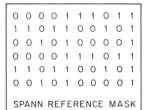

```
0 1 1 0 0
1 0 1 0 0
0 0 1 1 1

INPUT RECORDING
```

```
0 0 0 0 1 1 1 0 1 1
1 1 0 1 1 0 0 1 0 1
0 0 1 0 1 0 0 0 0 1
0 0 0 0 1 1 1 0 1 1
1 1 0 1 1 0 0 1 0 1
0 0 1 0 1 0 0 0 0 1

SPANN REFERENCE MASK
```

Fig. 9.22   Spann code mask for two-dimensional correlation detection.

9.40   Matched Filtering and Pattern Recognition

The two-dimensional processing capability of optical computers may be used to advantage in pattern recognition.   Certain signals are inherently two-dimensional.   One excellent example is the speech spectrogram. This spectrogram is constructed by frequency-analyzing the voice waveform and recording this analysis as a function of time.   Speech spectrograms of the same speaker speaking different but similar-sounding words are shown in Fig. 9.23.   These spectrograms may be readily recorded on photographic film.   By means of the holographic technique described in Chapter Four (Sec. 4.40) it is possible to record the complex conjugate of the Fourier transform of any speech spectrogram. The result is a matched filter of the spectrogram which may be used to perform correlation detection as described in Chapter One (Sec. 1.40).

In order to detect the occurrence of a known word in the speech of a known speaker, a continuous speech spectrogram would be made of the speaker's voice waveform.   This recording would enter the input plane of a coherent optical computer having the above matched filter in the spatial frequency plane.   Such an operation was carried out for the speech spectrograms shown in Fig. 9.23; the resultant cross-correlation and autocorrelation functions of specific interest are shown in Fig. 9.24.[*] The graphs shown in Fig. 9.24 were made by taking photometric scans across the output plane of the computer.   The peak values of the autocorrelation functions obtained are from 30 to 40 dB above the maximum value of the cross correlation.   This example is a simple demonstration of the power of the coherent optical computer in speech analysis and of its potential in word recognition..

[*]The information presented here is taken from an unpublished memorandum by T. W. Barnard of the Perkin-Elmer Corp.

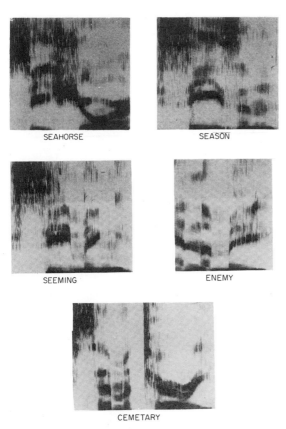

Fig. 9.23 Speech spectrograms of six words containing similar phonemes. (*Voiceprints, Inc.*)

9.41 Frequency-plane Filtering

The insertion of matched filters in the spatial frequency plane for the purpose of signal detection is described in the preceding section.   In closing this chapter two other uses of frequency-plane filtering are mentioned.   In the first case the frequency-plane filter is not used to detect the presence of a known signal in the input plane of the computer, but rather to alter the relative frequency content of the input and to produce an output which is simply a revised version of the input.   This is readily performed in the type of optical computer which is ordinarily used for frequency-plane matched filtering.   Now, however, the light intensity distribution in the entire output plane is recorded.   An example of this process of input alteration and/or modification due to Dobrin [9.14] is shown in Fig. 9.25.   On the left is an original recording of a seismic record made during a seismic geological survey.   The original was made by recording

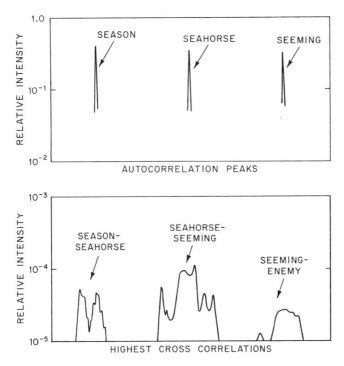

Fig. 9.24 Autocorrelation and cross-correlation functions for the speech spectrogram shown in Fig. 9.19 as calculated by a coherent optical computer.

the outputs of a string of geophones situated on the earth's surface. The outputs occurred in response to an acoustic signal generated on the surface which caused a series of reflections from the subsurface structure. The structure itself is identified on the record as the wave cycles which extended horizontally. These waves are obscured by noise in the left-hand portion of Fig. 9.25. Since the structural detail of interest has both a characteristic frequency and direction it can be extracted from the original record by optical spatial filtering. This has in fact been accomplished with the result shown in the right-hand portion of Fig. 9.25. This portion is a recording of the output light intensity distribution from the optical computer utilized.

The other use of spatial-frequency-plane filtering is in the synthesis of electronic filters. The coherent optical spectrum analyzer exhibits the Fourier transform of the input electric field distribution in the spatial frequency plane without the usual restriction on causality. Thus it is possible to synthesize frequency-domain filters which are otherwise difficult to realize by constructing appropriate masks for

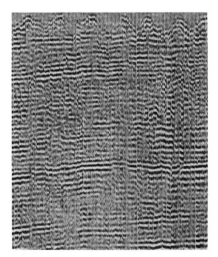

Fig. 9.25 Demonstration of the use of spatial-frequency-plane filtering by a coherent optical computer for the purpose of enhancing pertinent information in seismic recordings. (*After Dobrin.*)

insertion in the spatial frequency plane. "Comb filters," for example, are readily constructed by merely placing a slitlike mask in the spatial frequency plane with the width and spacing of the slits determined by the particular comb required. High-pass, low-pass, and bandpass filters may also be constructed. It is interesting to note that these filters are readily made with constant phase throughout the passband and with attenuation of 30 dB or more outside the passband.

This permits the signal-processing engineer to specify filter design with little regard to the usual realizability restrictions which determined the design of electronic filters. Simple operations such as taking derivatives and performing integration are also possible by means of spatial filtering. Full advantage has not been taken of this possible use of the coherent optical computer, especially when one realizes that a multichannel frequency-plane filter could select many filtered versions of the same input signal simultaneously. The interested reader is referred to Cheatham and Kohlenberg [9.15] and to other pertinent references in Chapter One for further information on this topic.

REFERENCES

9.1 Cutrona, L. J.: Recent Developments in Coherent Optical Technology, "Optical and Electro-optical Information Processing," M.I.T., Cambridge, Mass., 1965.

9.2 Lambert, L. B., et al.: Electro-optical Signal Processors for Phased Array Antennas, "Optical and Electro-optical Information Processing," M.I.T., Cambridge, Mass., 1965.

9.3 Cutrona, L. J., et al.: On the Application of Coherent Optical Processing Techniques to Synthetic Aperture Radar, *Proc. IEEE*, **54**: 1026 (1966).

9.4 Preston, K., Jr., and J. L. Kreuzer: Ultrasonic Imaging Using a Synthetic Holographic Technique, *Appl. Phys. Lett.*, **10**: 150 (1967).

9.5 Stone, J. M.: "Radiation and Optics," McGraw-Hill, New York, 1963.

9.6 Preston, K., Jr.: Fundamentals of Holography, *Photogr. Sci. Eng.*, **11**: 190 (1967).

9.7 Kreuzer, J. L.: Ultrasonic Three-dimensional Imaging Using Holographic Techniques, *Polytech. Inst. Brooklyn, Proc. Symp. Modern Optics,* March, 1967.

9.8 D'Albe, E. E. F.: Telegraphic Transmission of Pictures and Images, British Patent 233, 745, 1925.

9.9 Bogert, B. P., M. J. R. Healy, and J. W. Tukey: The Frequency Analysis of Time Series for Echoes: Cepstrum, Pseudo-Auto-Covariance, Cross-Cepstrum and Saphe Cracking, "Time Series Analysis," Wiley, New York, 1963.

9.10 Izzo, N. F.: Optical Correlation Technique Using a Variable Reference Function, *Proc. IEEE (Corresp.),* **53**: 1740 (1965).

9.11 Atzeni. C., and L. Pantani: Optical Signal-Processing Through Dual-Channel Ultrasonic Light Modulators, *Proc. IEEE (Corresp.),* **58**: 501 (1970).

9.12 Bitzer, D. R., et al.: A Rake System for Tropospheric Scatter, *IEEE Trans. Commun. Theory,* **COM-14**: 499 (1966).

9.13 Spann, R.: A Two-dimensional Correlation Property of Pseudo-random Maximal Length Sequences, *Proc. IEEE (Corresp.),* **53**: 2137 (1965).

9.14 Dobrin, M. B.: Optical Processing in the Earth Sciences, *IEEE Spectrum,* **6**: 59 (September, 1968).

9.15 Cheatham, T. P., Jr., and A. Kohlenberg: Optical Filters: Their Equivalence to and Differences from Electrical Networks, *IRE Conv. Rec.,* (4): 6 (1954).

Glossary of Symbols

$a(x,y)$ Spatial-amplitude-modulation function

a_i Light intensity absorption; aberration weighting factor (Sec. 2.30)

a_0 Constant term in Fourier series

(a.t.) Axial thickness

(**a.t.**) Optical axial thickness, that is, a.t. normalized by the wavelength

A, A_x, A_y Aperture size

A_{ij} ijth element in Meiron matrix

b_{kl} k, lth coefficient of cosine terms in Fourier series expansion

B Bias term; brightness (Sec. 3.10); temporal bandwidth (Secs. 7.22, 7.40)

B_s Brightness of source

B_i Brightness of image

B_{ij} ijth element of impermeability tensor

BFL Back focal length

c	Group velocity of electromagnetic propagation
c_ϕ	Phase velocity of electromagnetic propagation
c_{kl}	k, lth coefficient of sine terms in Fourier series expansion
C, C_0, C_i, C_{ij}	Constant(s) of proportionality
C	Capacitance
C_i	Curvature of ith surface in a lens system (Sec. 2.10)
$c(t), C(T)$	Temporal correlation function
$C(\nu, m)$	Coefficients in gamma-function expansion of nonlinear recording function
C_{t_a}	Autocorrelation function of light amplitude transmission
d	Differential (as in dx, dy, etc.)
d	Diameter of Airy disk (Sec. 1.10); end-mirror spacing in laser cavity (Sec. 3.20); depth (Sec. 5.40); interelement spacing in phased array (Sec. 9.11)
d_i	Distance from $(i-1)$st to ith surface in a lens
$\mathbf{d}_i$	Optical distance from $(i-1)$st surface in a lens system, i.e., distance normalized by wavelength
d_b	Diameter of electron beam
d_{kl}	k, lth complex coefficient in complex Fourier series expansion
$d_x(x,y), d_y(x,y)$	Lateral-spatial-distortion functions
D	Depth (Sec. 5.23); diameter (Sec. 5.40)
D_{ij}	Deformation
D_{ijk}	Interferometer-fringe-position function
e	Charge on the electron
e_{PE}	Photoelectron flux per unit area
$\mathbf{E}, \mathbf{E}(x,y)$	Jones vector
$E_x, E_x(x,y,t)$	Spatial electric field vector distribution parallel to x axis
$E_y, E_y(x,y,t)$	Spatial electric field vector distribution parallel to y axis
$E_m, E_m(x,y)$	Maximum value of spatial electric field vector distribution
$E_s, E_s(x,y,t)$	Spatial electric field distribution due to a signal
$E_b, E_b(x,y,t)$	Spatial electric field distribution due to background
$E_i(x,y)$	Spatial electric field distribution in ith spatial coordinate plane
$E_i(\omega_x, \omega_y)$	Spatial electric field distribution in ith spatial-frequency coordinate plane
$E_0(x,y)$	Incident spatial electric field distribution in input plane
$E^{(1)}, E^{(2)}$	Electric field distribution across laser-cavity end mirrors
E_g	p-n-junction gap energy
EBFL	Equivalent back focal length
EFFL	Equivalent front focal length
f_x	Spatial frequency in the x-coordinate direction
f_y	Spatial frequency in the y-coordinate direction
f_s	Spatial frequency; temporal acoustic frequency (Sec. 5.52)
$f(x,y)$	A real function of the variables x and y

$\mathbf{f}(x,y)$	A complex function of the variables x and y
f_i	ith Meiron aberration
$f_i(x)$	Multichannel spatial recording
$f_d(x,y)$	Deformation function
$\mathbf{f}_{ij}(x,y)$	i,jth component of Jones matrix $(i=j=1,2)$
f_{no}	f-number
$\mathbf{F}$	Fourier-transform operator
$F(\omega_x,\omega_y)$	Fourier transform of the function $f(x,y)$
$F^{-1}(x,y)$	Inverse Fourier transform of $F(\omega_x,\omega_y)$
F, F_i	Focal length
$\mathscr{F}$	Light flux
$\mathscr{F}_l$	Luminous flux
$\mathscr{F}_r$	Radiant flux
$d\mathscr{F}_A$	Light flux across differential area dA
F_x	Dynode noise factor
F_E	Electrostatic force
F_D	Dynamic force
FFL	front focal length
$G(x,y,z)$	Green's function for electromagnetic propagation in free space
h	Planck's constant
h_i	Height of ray with respect to optical axis at ith surface
$H(\omega_x,\omega_y)$	Spatial-frequency-plane filter function
i_b	Electron beam current (Sec. 5.30); photodetector current due to the background (Sec. 7.22)
i_d	Photodetector dark current
$i_{n\mathrm{rms}}$	rms input noise current
$i'_{n\mathrm{rms}}$	rms output noise current
i_s	Photodetector current due to a signal
i_T	Total photodetector current
I_0	Incident light intensity
I_l	Luminous intensity
I_r	Radiant intensity
$I, I(x,y)$	Spatial-light-intensity distribution
$I_s, I_s(x,y)$	Spatial-light-intensity distribution due to a signal
$I_b, I_b(x,y)$	Spatial-light-intensity distribution due to background
I_i	Angle of incidence
I'_i	Angle of refraction
$I_{A,B,C,\dots}$	Digital Fourier hologram function
IF	Intermediate frequency
$J_n(\phi_m)$	Bessel function of order n and argument ϕ_m
k	Boltzmann's constant
$k_{12}(\lambda_L)$	Spectral rate constant for photochromic activation (darkening)

$k_{21}(\lambda_L)$ Spectral rate constant for photochromic deactivation (bleaching)

$k_{21}(T)$ Thermal rate constant for photochromic deactivation (bleaching)

$k_{F\alpha}(\lambda_L)$ Spectral rate constant for conversion of F centers to α centers

$k_{\alpha F}(\lambda_L)$ Spectral rate constant for conversion of α centers to F centers

$k_{\alpha F}(T)$ Thermal rate constant for conversion of α centers to F centers

$k(t,\tau)$ Kernel function for a general linear operation

$K^{(1)}, K^{(2)}$ Kernel functions for laser-cavity electric field equations

l, l_i, l_n Direction cosine

l_0 Mean photoelectron escape depth

L Length of acoustic transducer perpendicular to beam

$\mathbf{L}$ Jones matrix

m Modulation index

m, m_i, m_n Direction cosine

m_c Mass density of membrane coating

m_m Mass density of membrane

m_T Mass of coating plus membrane per unit area

M Merit function; photoelectron multiplication ratio (Sec. 7.22)

n, n_i, n_n Direction cosine

n Optical index; number of spatial cycles across membrane element (Sec. 5.41)

n_α Number of α centers

n_b Storage capacity in bits

$\bar{n}_b$ Average storage capacity in bits

n_c Optical index of coating

n_{c0} Number of activation sites

n_{c1} Number of deactivated (bleached) sites

n_{c2} Number of activated (darkened) sites

n_e Optical index of emulsion (Sec. 5.12); number of electrons (Sec. 5.22)

n_F Number of F centers

n_g Number of silver grains (Sec. 5.11); optical index of glass (Sec. 6.60)

$\bar{n}_g$ Average number of silver grains

n_l Number of detectable levels (Sec. 5.11); optical index of liquid (Sec. 5.12)

n_p Number of photons

n_s Optical index of substrate

n_t Optical index of thermoplastic film

n_0 Optical index of air; optical index of undisturbed electro-optic material (Sec. 5.50)

n_i Optical index to left of ith surface; optical index along the ith principal axis ($i = 1, 2, 3$) (Sec. 5.50)

n_i' Optical index to right of ith surface

Δn_m Maximum change in the optical index

n_x, n_y Integers specifying location of nulls in Wiener spectrum

$n(x, y)$ Spatial-noise function

$N(\omega_x, \omega_y)$ Fourier transform of spatial-noise function

OPD   Optical path difference

$\mathrm{OPD}(x, y, \alpha, \beta)$ Optical-path-difference function

$p(x)$ Linear distribution of electrostatic pressure

$p(r)$ Probability that silver-grain radius is less than r

$p(t_a = 0)$ Probability that the light amplitude transmission is zero

$p(t_i = 0)$ Probability that the light intensity transmission is zero

p_{ijkl} Elastooptic constants

P_i Power of ith surface

$P_b, P_b(x, y)$ Background power distribution

$P_n, P_n(x, y)$ Noise power distribution

$P_0, P_0(x, y)$ Input signal power distribution

$P_s, P_s(x, y)$ Output signal power distribution

$P(n)$ Poisson probability for argument n

$P(n, \phi_m)$ P function of arguments n and ϕ_m

q Charge density; charge on the electron (Sec. 7.22)

$q(x)$ Linear charge density distribution

rms   Root mean square

rep_n Woodward's repetition function of interval n, that is, $\delta(x - nN)$

r_i Multichannel-spatial-reference functions

$r(x, y)$ Spatial-reference function

r_a Light amplitude reflectance

r_g Radius of silver grain

$\bar{r}_g$ Average radius of silver grain

r_i Light intensity reflectance

r_{is}, R_{is} Light intensity reflectance for vector in plane of surface

r_{ip}, R_{ip} Light intensity reflectance for vector in plane of incidence

R Radius of circular aperture

R_i Radius of ith surface in a lens system

R_0 Broadside slant range

R_{ij} Region

R_{eq} Equivalent resistance

$R(x, y)$ Spatial-film-recording function

sinc (x) Woodward's sinc function of argument x, that is, $(\sin \pi x)/\pi x$

$s_i(x)$ Multichannel-spatial-signal functions

$s(x, y)$ Spatial-signal function

$S(\omega_x, \omega_y)$	Fourier transform of spatial-signal function
s_{ij}	i,jth mechanical strain
S	Surface area
S_k	Simple-digital-source function
$S_{A,B,C,\ldots}$	Multiple-digital-source function
SW	Space-bandwidth
t, T	Time
Δt	Time-difference interval
t_a	Light amplitude transmission
t_i	Light intensity transmission
t_{i0}	Initial light intensity transmission
t_c	Thickness of membrane coating
t_m	Thickness of membrane
$\Delta t_s(x,y)$	Spatial-thickness-distortion function of substrate
$\Delta t_e(x,y)$	Spatial-thickness-distortion function of emulsion
T	Transformation matrix
T	Temperature
Δt	Temperature interval
T_0	Surface tension
TW	Time-bandwidth
TEM	Transverse electromagnetic field
TEM_{mn}	Transverse electromagnetic field of mode (m, n)
u_i	Meiron design parameters
v_a	Aircraft velocity
v_b	Electron beam scanning velocity
v_s	Acoustic velocity
v_T	Film transport velocity
v_x, v_y	Cathode-ray-tube sweep velocity
V	Voltage
$V(x_1, y_1, z_1, x_n, y_n, z_n)$	Hamilton's characteristic function
W	Bandwidth (spatial or temporal)
$W(\omega_x, \omega_y)$	Wiener spectrum
x	Spatial coordinate axis, as in x axis
x_i	Coordinates of principal axes, $i = 1, 2, 3$
Δx	Spatial displacement
y	Spatial coordinate axis, as in y axis
z	Spatial coordinate axis, as in z axis (usually taken as direction of optical axis)
z_m	Maximum deflection
α	Direction angle with respect to x axis; electric field strength corresponding to a binary 1 (Sec. 8.10)

α_{PE} Absorption coefficient for photons capable of producing photoelectrons

α_T Coefficient of total photon absorption

β Direction angle with respect to y axis

γ Direction angle with respect to z axis

γ_i Direction angle of ray to left of ith surface

γ_i' Direction angle of ray to right of ith surface

$\boldsymbol{\gamma}_i, \boldsymbol{\gamma}_i'$ Optical direction angle, i.e., normalized by the wavelength

$\gamma^{(1)}, \gamma^{(2)}$ Laser-cavity operator functions

$\gamma(\tau)$ Degree of spatial coherence

$\Gamma(\tau)$ Temporal-coherence function

$\Gamma(\xi, \eta)$ Spatial-coherence function

$\Gamma(n)$ Gamma function of argument n

δ Secondary-emission ratio

$\delta(x - x_i, y - y_i)$ Dirac delta function at the point (x_i, y_i)

δ_{ij} Kronecker delta function

Δ_{rms} rms distance from optical wavefront to reference plane

Δ_{ijk} Distance function relating optical wavefront to reference plane

ϵ Dielectric constant; differential illuminance (Sec. 3.10)

ϵ_m Neumann factor

ζ Coefficient of acoustic attenuation

η Quantum efficiency

$\bar{\eta}$ Average quantum efficiency

θ Angular coordinate; azimuth angle (Sec. 9.21)

θ_i Angle of incident light with respect to acoustic beam

θ_0 Angle of diffracted light with respect to acoustic beam

θ_k, θ_l Field angles of lens

κ Normalized angle of incidence in an acoustic light modulator

λ, λ_L Optical wavelength

λ_0 Radar wavelength

λ_s Acoustic wavelength

λ_{s0} Acoustic wavelength at resonance

ν Electromagnetic frequency; exponent in nonlinear recording function (Sec. 4.70)

ξ Spatial coordinate (Sec. 3.40); viscosity (Sec. 5.30); normalized frequency for acoustic light modulator (Sec. 5.52)

$\Delta\xi$ Normalized bandwidth for acoustic light modulator

ρ Resistivity

σ Standard deviation

Σ Illuminance

τ Time; time constant

ϕ Phase angle; elevation angle (Sec. 9.11)

ϕ_m Peak phase angle

$\Delta\phi$ Phase difference

ϕ_Δ Shift in phase angle due to noise

ϕ_{ijk} Sampled-interferogram-phase function

$\phi(i,j)$ Sampled-radar-phase function

$\phi(\omega,\tau)$ Ambiguity function

$\phi(x,y,\alpha,\beta)$ Angular-optical-path-difference function

$\Phi_n(x,y)$ Spatial-phase-modulation-noise function

ω_x, ω_y Angular spatial frequencies

ω_r Angular spatial frequency for radial coordinate system

ω, ω_L Optical angular temporal frequency

ω_s Acoustic angular temporal frequency

$\Delta\omega_L$ Intermediate frequency

Ω Solid angle

Appendix

This appendix presents a tabulation of the P functions (see Chap. Five, Sec. 5.41) which are necessary in the design of coherent optical computer systems using the membrane light modulator. The specific tabulation given is of the quantity

$$P(N,\phi_m) = \frac{1}{2\pi} \int_0^{0.5} (e^{j\phi_m(1-4r^2)} - 1) J_0(2\pi Nr)r\, dr$$

Each page of the table corresponds to a fixed value of ϕ_m, starting with $\pi/4$ (45°) and extending through 4π (720°). Seven quantities are tabulated; namely, N, $2\pi N$, the real and imaginary parts of $P(N,\phi_m)$, the modulus and modulus squared of $P(N,\phi_m)$, and, finally, the phase angle in degrees.

$\phi = 45.00000$ degrees

N	$2\pi N$	Real part	Imag. part	Modulus	$(\text{Mod})^2$	Arg. in deg.
0.0	0.0000	-0.7829E-01	-0.2929E 00	0.3032E 00	0.9192E-01	255.035
0.1	0.6283	-0.7780E-01	-0.2904E 00	0.3007E 00	0.9041E-01	255.003
0.2	1.2566	-0.7636E-01	-0.2832E 00	0.2933E 00	0.8602E-01	254.909
0.3	1.8850	-0.7400E-01	-0.2714E 00	0.2813E 00	0.7912E-01	254.747
0.4	2.5133	-0.7079E-01	-0.2555E 00	0.2651E 00	0.7027E-01	254.512
0.5	3.1416	-0.6682E-01	-0.2360E 00	0.2453E 00	0.6016E-01	254.190
0.6	3.7699	-0.6222E-01	-0.2137E 00	0.2226E 00	0.4954E-01	253.768
0.7	4.3982	-0.5710E-01	-0.1894E 00	0.1978E 00	0.3912E-01	253.219
0.8	5.0265	-0.5161E-01	-0.1638E 00	0.1717E 00	0.2948E-01	252.507
0.9	5.6549	-0.4589E-01	-0.1377E 00	0.1452E 00	0.2108E-01	251.575
1.0	6.2832	-0.4008E-01	-0.1121E 00	0.1191E 00	0.1418E-01	250.329
1.1	6.9115	-0.3432E-01	-0.8761E-01	0.9410E-01	0.8854E-02	248.607
1.2	7.5398	-0.2874E-01	-0.6487E-01	0.7095E-01	0.5035E-02	246.102
1.3	8.1681	-0.2346E-01	-0.4442E-01	0.5024E-01	0.2524E-02	242.162
1.4	8.7965	-0.1856E-01	-0.2666E-01	0.3248E-01	0.1055E-02	235.147
1.5	9.4248	-0.1413E-01	-0.1182E-01	0.1843E-01	0.3395E-03	219.918
1.6	10.0531	-0.1022E-01	-0.3013E-04	0.1022E-01	0.1044E-03	180.169
1.7	10.6814	-0.6859E-02	0.8756E-02	0.1112E-01	0.1237E-03	128.071
1.8	11.3097	-0.4061E-02	0.1469E-01	0.1524E-01	0.2324E-03	105.449
1.9	11.9381	-0.1817E-02	0.1805E-01	0.1814E-01	0.3289E-03	95.750
2.0	12.5664	-0.1003E-03	0.1916E-01	0.1916E-01	0.3671E-03	90.300
2.1	13.1947	0.1131E-02	0.1844E-01	0.1847E-01	0.3413E-03	86.491
2.2	13.8230	0.1929E-02	0.1632E-01	0.1644E-01	0.2702E-03	83.259
2.3	14.4513	0.2357E-02	0.1325E-01	0.1346E-01	0.1811E-03	79.912
2.4	15.0796	0.2481E-02	0.9645E-02	0.9959E-02	0.9917E-04	75.572
2.5	15.7080	0.2369E-02	0.5886E-02	0.6345E-02	0.4026E-04	68.079

2.7	16.9646	0.1694E-02	−0.8548E-03	0.1897E-02	0.3599E-05	333.218
2.8	17.5929	0.1247E-02	−0.3397E-02	0.3619E-02	0.1310E-04	290.160
2.9	18.2212	0.7932E-03	−0.5220E-02	0.5280E-02	0.2788E-04	278.640
3.0	18.8496	0.3685E-03	−0.6288E-02	0.6298E-02	0.3967E-04	273.354
3.1	19.4779	0.4692E-06	−0.6628E-02	0.6628E-02	0.4394E-04	270.004
3.2	20.1062	−0.2930E-03	−0.6324E-02	0.6331E-02	0.4008E-04	267.347
3.3	20.7345	−0.5032E-03	−0.5496E-02	0.5519E-02	0.3046E-04	264.769
3.4	21.3628	−0.6290E-03	−0.4289E-02	0.4335E-02	0.1879E-04	261.657
3.5	21.9911	−0.6760E-03	−0.2861E-02	0.2940E-02	0.8642E-05	256.705
3.6	22.6195	−0.6549E-03	−0.1365E-02	0.1514E-02	0.2293E-05	244.370
3.7	23.2478	−0.5796E-03	0.5901E-04	0.5826E-03	0.3395E-06	174.187
3.8	23.8761	−0.4659E-08	0.1296E-02	0.1377E-02	0.1897E-05	109.772
3.9	24.5044	−0.3300E-03	0.2261E-02	0.2285E-02	0.5221E-05	98.303
4.0	25.1327	−0.1870E-03	0.2902E-02	0.2908E-02	0.8455E-05	93.687
4.1	25.7611	−0.5036E-04	0.3200E-02	0.3201E-02	0.1025E-04	90.901
4.2	26.3894	0.6927E-04	0.3171E-02	0.3171E-02	0.1006E-04	88.748
4.3	27.0177	0.1642E-03	0.2852E-02	0.2857E-02	0.8162E-05	86.705
4.4	27.6460	0.2301E-03	0.2306E-02	0.2318E-02	0.5371E-05	84.303
4.5	28.2743	0.2654E-03	0.1606E-02	0.1628E-02	0.2650E-05	80.618
4.6	28.9027	0.2716E-03	0.8320E-03	0.8752E-03	0.7659E-06	71.919
4.7	29.5310	0.2524E-03	0.6099E-04	0.2596E-03	0.6740E-07	13.588
4.8	30.1593	0.2128E-03	−0.6373E-03	0.6719E-03	0.4514E-06	288.469
4.9	30.7876	0.1594E-03	−0.1207E-02	0.1217E-02	0.1482E-05	277.523
5.0	31.4159	0.9854E-04	−0.1609E-02	0.1612E-02	0.2598E-05	273.505
5.1	32.0442	0.3668E-04	−0.1822E-02	0.1823E-02	0.3322E-05	271.153
5.2	32.6726	−0.2055E-04	−0.1846E-02	0.1846E-02	0.3409E-05	269.362
5.3	33.3009	−0.6868E-04	−0.1696E-02	0.1697E-02	0.2881E-05	267.681
5.4	33.9292	−0.1045E-03	−0.1401E-02	0.1405E-02	0.1973E-05	265.732
5.5	34.5575	−0.1264E-03	−0.1001E-02	0.1009E-02	0.1018E-05	262.802

$\phi = 90,00000$ degrees

N	$2\pi N$	Real part	Imag. part	Modulus	$(\mathrm{Mod})^2$	Arg. in deg.
0.0	0.0000	-0.2854E 00	-0.5000E 00	0.5757E 00	0.3314E 00	240.282
0.1	0.6283	-0.2836E 00	-0.4955E 00	0.5709E 00	0.3260E 00	240.220
0.2	1.2566	-0.2781E 00	-0.4823E 00	0.5567E 00	0.3100E 00	240.029
0.3	1.8850	-0.2692E 00	-0.4608E 00	0.5337E 00	0.2848E 00	239.702
0.4	2.5133	-0.2572E 00	-0.4319E 00	0.5026E 00	0.2527E 00	239.225
0.5	3.1416	-0.2423E 00	-0.3966E 00	0.4647E 00	0.2160E 00	238.574
0.6	3.7699	-0.2250E 00	-0.3562E 00	0.4213E 00	0.1775E 00	237.716
0.7	4.3982	-0.2059E 00	-0.3122E 00	0.3740E 00	0.1399E 00	236.601
0.8	5.0265	-0.1853E 00	-0.2662E 00	0.3243E 00	0.1052E 00	235.153
0.9	5.6549	-0.1640E 00	-0.2196E 00	0.2740E 00	0.7510E-01	233.253
1.0	6.2832	-0.1423E 00	-0.1739E 00	0.2247E 00	0.5051E-01	230.712
1.1	6.9115	-0.1209E 00	-0.1306E 00	0.1780E 00	0.3167E-01	227.206
1.2	7.5398	-0.1002E 00	-0.9073E-01	0.1352E 00	0.1828E-01	222.150
1.3	8.1681	-0.8073E-01	-0.5529E-01	0.9785E-01	0.9574E-02	214.409
1.4	8.7965	-0.6273E-01	-0.2498E-01	0.6752E-01	0.4559E-02	201.711
1.5	9.4248	-0.4653E-01	-0.2064E-03	0.4653E-01	0.2165E-02	180.254
1.6	10.0531	-0.3233E-01	0.1887E-01	0.3744E-01	0.1402E-02	149.726
1.7	10.6814	-0.2024E-01	0.3238E-01	0.3818E-01	0.1458E-02	122.014
1.8	11.3097	-0.1029E-01	0.4065E-01	0.4193E-01	0.1758E-02	104.212
1.9	11.9381	-0.2445E-02	0.4423E-01	0.4430E-01	0.1962E-02	93.164
2.0	12.5664	0.3418E-02	0.4382E-01	0.4395E-01	0.1932E-02	85.539
2.1	13.1947	0.7464E-02	0.4021E-01	0.4090E-01	0.1673E-02	79.485
2.2	13.8230	0.9903E-02	0.3426E-01	0.3566E-01	0.1272E-02	73.876
2.3	14.4513	0.1098E-01	0.2680E-01	0.2896E-01	0.8388E-03	67.722
2.4	15.0796	0.1095E-01	0.1864E-01	0.2162E-01	0.4676E-03	59.569
2.5	15.7080	0.1008E-01	0.1051E-01	0.1456E-01	0.2121E-03	46.174

2.7	16.9646	0.6821E-02	−0.3460E-02	0.7648E-02	0.5849E-04	333.104
2.8	17.5929	0.4868E-02	−0.8507E-02	0.9802E-02	0.9607E-04	299.780
2.9	18.2212	0.2946E-02	−0.1199E-01	0.1235E-01	0.1525E-03	283.800
3.0	18.8496	0.1190E-02	−0.1389E-01	0.1394E-01	0.1943E-03	274.897
3.1	19.4779	−0.3004E-03	−0.1428E-01	0.1429E-01	0.2041E-03	268.795
3.2	20.1062	−0.1464E-02	−0.1338E-01	0.1346E-01	0.1812E-03	263.756
3.3	20.7345	−0.2274E-02	−0.1144E-01	0.1166E-01	0.1360E-03	258.757
3.4	21.3628	−0.2735E-02	−0.8773E-02	0.9189E-02	0.8445E-04	252.688
3.5	21.9911	−0.2874E-02	−0.5706E-02	0.6389E-02	0.4082E-04	243.266
3.6	22.6195	−0.2740E-02	−0.2553E-02	0.3745E-02	0.1403E-04	222.972
3.7	23.2478	−0.2393E-02	0.4066E-03	0.2427E-02	0.5891E-05	170.357
3.8	23.8761	−0.1897E-02	0.2944E-02	0.3502E-02	0.1227E-04	122.805
3.9	24.5044	−0.1320E-02	0.4893E-02	0.5068E-02	0.2569E-04	105.101
4.0	25.1327	−0.7234E-03	0.6159E-02	0.6201E-02	0.3846E-04	96.699
4.1	25.7611	−0.1597E-03	0.6713E-02	0.6715E-02	0.4509E-04	91.363
4.2	26.3894	0.3283E-03	0.6592E-02	0.6600E-02	0.4356E-04	87.149
4.3	27.0177	0.7112E-03	0.5884E-02	0.5927E-02	0.3513E-04	83.108
4.4	27.6460	0.9723E-03	0.4719E-02	0.4818E-02	0.2321E-04	78.357
4.5	28.2743	0.1107E-02	0.3250E-02	0.3434E-02	0.1179E-04	71.184
4.6	28.9027	0.1124E-02	0.1642E-02	0.1990E-02	0.3959E-05	55.619
4.7	29.5310	0.1036E-02	0.5328E-04	0.1038E-02	0.1077E-05	2.943
4.8	30.1593	0.8682E-03	−0.1376E-02	0.1627E-02	0.2647E-05	302.251
4.9	30.7876	0.6447E-03	−0.2533E-02	0.2614E-02	0.6832E-05	284.278
5.0	31.4159	0.3930E-03	−0.3341E-02	0.3364E-02	0.1132E-04	276.708
5.1	32.0442	0.1390E-03	−0.3761E-02	0.3764E-02	0.1417E-04	272.117
5.2	32.6726	−0.9451E-04	−0.3793E-02	0.3794E-02	0.1439E-04	268.573
5.3	33.3009	−0.2896E-03	−0.3469E-02	0.3481E-02	0.1212E-04	265.227
5.4	33.9292	−0.4339E-03	−0.2853E-02	0.2886E-02	0.8327E-05	261.352
5.5	34.5575	−0.5208E-03	−0.2027E-02	0.2093E-02	0.4380E-05	255.591

$\phi = 180.00000$ degrees

N	$2\pi N$	Real part	Imag. part	Modulus	(Mod)^2	Arg. in deg.
0.0	0.0000	−0.7854E 00	−0.5000E 00	0.9310E 00	0.8669E 00	212.482
0.1	0.6283	−0.7797E 00	−0.4939E 00	0.9229E 00	0.8517E 00	212.351
0.2	1.2566	−0.7626E 00	−0.4757E 00	0.8988E 00	0.8078E 00	211.955
0.3	1.8850	−0.7348E 00	−0.4463E 00	0.8597E 00	0.7391E 00	211.273
0.4	2.5133	−0.6971E 00	−0.4069E 00	0.8072E 00	0.6516E 00	210.274
0.5	3.1416	−0.6508E 00	−0.3593E 00	0.7434E 00	0.5526E 00	208.905
0.6	3.7699	−0.5972E 00	−0.3054E 00	0.6707E 00	0.4499E 00	207.088
0.7	4.3982	−0.5380E 00	−0.2475E 00	0.5922E 00	0.3507E 00	204.705
0.8	5.0265	−0.4750E 00	−0.1879E 00	0.5108E 00	0.2609E 00	201.583
0.9	5.6549	−0.4099E 00	−0.1289E 00	0.4297E 00	0.1847E 00	197.455
1.0	6.2832	−0.3446E 00	−0.7269E-01	0.3522E 00	0.1241E 00	191.909
1.1	6.9115	−0.2808E 00	−0.2122E-01	0.2816E 00	0.7930E-01	184.322
1.2	7.5398	−0.2200E 00	0.2387E-01	0.2213E 00	0.4896E-01	173.806
1.3	8.1681	−0.1635E 00	0.6137E-01	0.1746E 00	0.3050E-01	159.427
1.4	8.7965	−0.1125E 00	0.9045E-01	0.1443E 00	0.2083E-01	141.189
1.5	9.4248	−0.6769E-01	0.1108E 00	0.1298E 00	0.1686E-01	121.426
1.6	10.0531	−0.2974E-01	0.1225E 00	0.1260E 00	0.1588E-01	103.649
1.7	10.6814	0.1165E-02	0.1260E 00	0.1260E 00	0.1587E-01	89.470
1.8	11.3097	0.2504E-01	0.1222E 00	0.1247E 00	0.1555E-01	78.415
1.9	11.9381	0.4219E-01	0.1122E 00	0.1199E 00	0.1437E-01	69.398
2.0	12.5664	0.5310E-01	0.9747E-01	0.1110E 00	0.1232E-01	61.420
2.1	13.1947	0.5846E-01	0.7936E-01	0.9857E-01	0.9715E-02	53.623
2.2	13.8230	0.5909E-01	0.5939E-01	0.8378E-01	0.7019E-02	45.144
2.3	14.4513	0.5589E-01	0.3897E-01	0.6814E-01	0.4643E-02	34.889
2.4	15.0796	0.4980E-01	0.1940E-01	0.5344E-01	0.2856E-02	21.287
2.5	15.7080	0.4172E-01	0.1753E-02	0.4176E-01	0.1744E-02	2.405
2.6	16.3363	0.3954E-01	−0.1313E-01	0.3509E-01	0.1931E-02	338.093

2.7	16.9646	0.2303E-01	−0.2468E-01	0.3376E-01	0.1139E-02	313.011
2.8	17.5929	0.1385E-01	−0.3261E-01	0.3543E-01	0.1255E-02	293.006
2.9	18.2212	0.5532E-02	−0.3690E-01	0.3731E-01	0.1392E-02	278.526
3.0	18.8496	−0.1531E-02	−0.3776E-01	0.3779E-01	0.1428E-02	267.678
3.1	19.4779	−0.7097E-02	−0.3563E-01	0.3633E-01	0.1320E-02	258.734
3.2	20.1062	−0.1106E-01	−0.3106E-01	0.3297E-01	0.1087E-02	250.408
3.3	20.7345	−0.1342E-01	−0.2475E-01	0.2815E-01	0.7925E-03	241.525
3.4	21.3628	−0.1431E-01	−0.1739E-01	0.2252E-01	0.5071E-03	230.546
3.5	21.9911	−0.1392E-01	−0.9687E-02	0.1696E-01	0.2875E-03	214.844
3.6	22.6195	−0.1249E-01	−0.2285E-02	0.1270E-01	0.1612E-03	190.368
3.7	23.2478	−0.1032E-01	0.4280E-02	0.1117E-01	0.1248E-03	157.476
3.8	23.8761	−0.7692E-02	0.9597E-02	0.1230E-01	0.1513E-03	128.714
3.9	24.5044	−0.4886E-02	0.1340E-01	0.1426E-01	0.2034E-03	110.035
4.0	25.1327	−0.2149E-02	0.1557E-01	0.1572E-01	0.2470E-03	97.859
4.1	25.7611	0.3156E-03	0.1613E-01	0.1613E-01	0.2603E-03	88.879
4.2	26.3894	0.2355E-02	0.1523E-01	0.1541E-01	0.2375E-03	81.212
4.3	27.0177	0.3871E-02	0.1312E-01	0.1368E-01	0.1871E-03	73.561
4.4	27.6460	0.4821E-02	0.1012E-01	0.1121E-01	0.1256E-03	64.516
4.5	28.2743	0.5214E-02	0.6576E-02	0.8393E-02	0.7044E-04	51.590
4.6	28.9027	0.5099E-02	0.2863E-02	0.5848E-02	0.3420E-04	29.311
4.7	29.5310	0.4560E-02	−0.6869E-03	0.4611E-02	0.2126E-04	351.433
4.8	30.1593	0.3702E-02	−0.3784E-02	0.5294E-02	0.2802E-04	314.370
4.9	30.7876	0.2642E-02	−0.6208E-02	0.6747E-02	0.4552E-04	293.053
5.0	31.4159	0.1498E-02	−0.7818E-02	0.7960E-02	0.6337E-04	280.846
5.1	32.0442	0.3783E-03	−0.8556E-02	0.8564E-02	0.7335E-04	272.532
5.2	32.6726	−0.6245E-03	−0.8444E-02	0.8468E-02	0.7170E-04	265.771
5.3	33.3009	−0.1439E-02	−0.7578E-02	0.7713E-02	0.5949E-04	259.244
5.4	33.9292	−0.2021E-02	−0.6105E-02	0.6431E-02	0.4136E-04	251.688
5.5	34.5575	−0.2347E-02	−0.4217E-02	0.4826E-02	0.2329E-04	240.901

$\phi = 270.00000$ degrees

N	$2\pi N$	Real part	Imag. part	Modulus	(Mod)^2	Arg. in deg.
0.0	0.0000	−0.9521E 00	−0.1667E 00	0.9665E 00	0.9342E 00	189.929
0.1	0.6283	−0.9433E 00	−0.1617E 00	0.9570E 00	0.9159E 00	189.728
0.2	1.2566	−0.9172E 00	−0.1471E 00	0.9289E 00	0.8629E 00	189.111
0.3	1.8850	−0.8749E 00	−0.1236E 00	0.8835E 00	0.7807E 00	188.044
0.4	2.5133	−0.8177E 00	−0.9263E-01	0.8229E 00	0.6772E 00	186.463
0.5	3.1416	−0.7478E 00	−0.5576E-01	0.7498E 00	0.5622E 00	184.265
0.6	3.7699	−0.6675E 00	−0.1503E-01	0.6677E 00	0.4458E 00	181.290
0.7	4.3982	−0.5797E 00	0.2738E-01	0.5803E 00	0.3368E 00	177.296
0.8	5.0265	−0.4873E 00	0.6922E-01	0.4922E 00	0.2422E 00	171.915
0.9	5.6549	−0.3932E 00	0.1083E 00	0.4079E 00	0.1663E 00	164.598
1.0	6.2832	−0.3004E 00	0.1427E 00	0.3326E 00	0.1106E 00	154.590
1.1	6.9115	−0.2117E 00	0.1708E 00	0.2720E 00	0.7396E-01	141.108
1.2	7.5398	−0.1294E 00	0.1911E 00	0.2308E 00	0.5327E-01	124.090
1.3	8.1681	0.5552E-01	0.2031E 00	0.2105E 00	0.4432E-01	105.292
1.4	8.7965	0.8264E-02	0.2062E 00	0.2064E 00	0.4260E-01	87.705
1.5	9.4248	0.6092E-01	0.2008E 00	0.2098E 00	0.4403E-01	73.122
1.6	10.0531	0.1019E 00	0.1874E 00	0.2133E 00	0.4549E-01	61.465
1.7	10.6814	0.1311E 00	0.1671E 00	0.2124E 00	0.4510E-01	51.873
1.8	11.3097	0.1490E 00	0.1412E 00	0.2053E 00	0.4215E-01	43.454
1.9	11.9381	0.1565E 00	0.1114E 00	0.1921E 00	0.3691E-01	35.454
2.0	12.5664	0.1547E 00	0.7952E-01	0.1739E 00	0.3026E-01	27.205
2.1	13.1947	0.1451E 00	0.4722E-01	0.1526E 00	0.2329E-01	18.027
2.2	13.8230	0.1294E 00	0.1624E-01	0.1304E 00	0.1700E-01	7.153
2.3	14.4513	0.1093E 00	−0.1193E-01	0.1099E 00	0.1208E-01	353.769
2.4	15.0796	0.8644E-01	−0.3603E-01	0.9364E-01	0.8769E-02	337.375

x					
2.7	16.9646	0.1735E-01	−0.7642E-01	0.7837E-01	0.6141E-02	282.789
2.8	17.5929	−0.1765E-02	−0.7858E-01	0.7860E-01	0.6177E-02	268.713
2.9	18.2212	−0.1751E-01	−0.7560E-01	0.7760E-01	0.6021E-02	256.962
3.0	18.8496	−0.2945E-01	−0.6823E-01	0.7432E-01	0.5523E-02	246.651
3.1	19.4779	−0.3747E-01	−0.5743E-01	0.6858E-01	0.4703E-02	236.879
3.2	20.1062	−0.4166E-01	−0.4428E-01	0.6080E-01	0.3696E-02	226.742
3.3	20.7345	−0.4236E-01	−0.2988E-01	0.5184E-01	0.2687E-02	215.204
3.4	21.3628	−0.4005E-01	−0.1535E-01	0.4289E-01	0.1840E-02	200.973
3.5	21.9911	−0.3536E-01	−0.1673E-02	0.3539E-01	0.1253E-02	182.709
3.6	22.6195	−0.2895E-01	0.1032E-01	0.3073E-01	0.9445E-03	160.386
3.7	23.2478	−0.2153E-01	0.1998E-01	0.2937E-01	0.8626E-03	137.140
3.8	23.8761	−0.1376E-01	0.2690E-01	0.3022E-01	0.9130E-03	117.089
3.9	24.5044	−0.6237E-02	0.3091E-01	0.3153E-01	0.9943E-03	101.408
4.0	25.1327	0.5433E-03	0.3205E-01	0.3205E-01	0.1027E-02	89.029
4.1	25.7611	0.6205E-02	0.3057E-01	0.3119E-01	0.9728E-03	78.526
4.2	26.3894	0.1050E-01	0.2688E-01	0.2886E-01	0.8328E-03	68.662
4.3	27.0177	0.1332E-01	0.2152E-01	0.2531E-01	0.6405E-03	58.256
4.4	27.6460	0.1466E-01	0.1510E-01	0.2104E-01	0.4427E-03	45.850
4.5	28.2743	0.1463E-01	0.8223E-02	0.1678E-01	0.2817E-03	29.338
4.6	28.9027	0.1344E-01	0.1495E-02	0.1352E-01	0.1829E-03	6.347
4.7	29.5310	0.1134E-01	−0.4568E-02	0.1223E-03	0.1495E-03	338.061
4.8	30.1593	0.8623E-02	−0.9550E-02	0.1287E-01	0.1656E-03	312.080
4.9	30.7876	0.5588E-02	−0.1316E-01	0.1430E-01	0.2045E-03	293.001
5.0	31.4159	0.2519E-02	−0.1526E-01	0.1546E-01	0.2391E-03	279.377
5.1	32.0442	−0.3308E-03	−0.1582E-01	0.1582E-01	0.2504E-03	268.802
5.2	32.6726	−0.2761E-02	−0.1496E-01	0.1521E-01	0.2314E-03	259.542
5.3	33.3009	−0.4629E-02	−0.1290E-01	0.1370E-01	0.1878E-03	250.258
5.4	33.9292	−0.5854E-02	−0.9931E-02	0.1153E-01	0.1329E-03	239.481
5.5	34.5575	−0.6417E-02	−0.6397E-02	0.9061E-02	0.8210E-04	224.913

$\phi = 360.00000$ degrees

N	$2\pi N$	Real part	Imag. part	Modulus	(Mod)^2	Arg. in deg.
0.0	0.0000	−0.7854E 00	0.1000E-10	0.7854E 00	0.6169E 00	180.000
0.1	0.6283	−0.7757E 00	0.3065E-02	0.7757E 00	0.6018E 00	179.774
0.2	1.2566	−0.7472E 00	0.1204E-01	0.7473E 00	0.5584E 00	179.077
0.3	1.8850	−0.7009E 00	0.2625E-01	0.7014E 00	0.4919E 00	177.855
0.4	2.5133	−0.6388E 00	0.4466E-01	0.6403E 00	0.4100E 00	176.001
0.5	3.1416	−0.5634E 00	0.6589E-01	0.5673E 00	0.3218E 00	173.330
0.6	3.7699	−0.4778E 00	0.8835E-01	0.4859E 00	0.2361E 00	169.524
0.7	4.3982	−0.3854E 00	0.1103E 00	0.4008E 00	0.1607E 00	164.022
0.8	5.0265	−0.2897E 00	0.1302E 00	0.3176E 00	0.1008E 00	155.801
0.9	5.6549	−0.1943E 00	0.1462E 00	0.2432E 00	0.5914E-01	143.031
1.0	6.2832	−0.1027E 00	0.1572E 00	0.1878E 00	0.3527E-01	123.157
1.1	6.9115	−0.1807E-01	0.1621E 00	0.1631E 00	0.2660E-01	96.362
1.2	7.5398	0.5696E-01	0.1602E 00	0.1700E 00	0.2891E-01	70.429
1.3	8.1681	0.1202E 00	0.1514E 00	0.1933E 00	0.3737E-01	51.539
1.4	8.7965	0.1703E 00	0.1358E 00	0.2178E 00	0.4743E-01	38.580
1.5	9.4248	0.2062E 00	0.1142E 00	0.2357E 00	0.5556E-01	28.985
1.6	10.0531	0.2279E 00	0.8764E-01	0.2442E 00	0.5961E-01	21.037
1.7	10.6814	0.2358E 00	0.5745E-01	0.2427E 00	0.5891E-01	13.691
1.8	11.3097	0.2311E 00	0.2523E-01	0.2325E 00	0.5406E-01	6.229
1.9	11.9381	0.2154E 00	−0.7323E-02	0.2155E 00	0.4643E-01	358.052
2.0	12.5664	0.1905E 00	−0.3849E-01	0.1944E 00	0.3778E-01	348.578
2.1	13.1947	0.1588E 00	−0.6667E-01	0.1723E 00	0.2967E-01	337.230
2.2	13.8230	0.1227E 00	−0.9046E-01	0.1524E 00	0.2323E-01	323.595
2.3	14.4513	0.8443E-01	−0.1087E 00	0.1377E 00	0.1895E-01	307.824
2.4	15.0796	0.4634E-01	−0.1208E 00	0.1294E 00	0.1673E-01	290.990
2.5	15.7080	0.1042E-01	−0.1262E 00	0.1266E 00	0.1602E-01	274.723
2.6	16.3363	0.9161E-01	0.1240E 00	0.1568E 01	0.1608E 01	260.122

x						
2.7	16.9646	−0.4844E-01	−0.1175E 00	0.1271E 00	0.1616E-01	247.600
2.8	17.5929	−0.6918E-01	−0.1047E 00	0.1255E 00	0.1575E-01	236.544
2.9	18.2212	−0.8337E-01	−0.8749E-01	0.1209E 00	0.1461E-01	226.382
3.0	18.8496	−0.9096E-01	−0.6717E-01	0.1131E 00	0.1278E-01	216.444
3.1	19.4779	−0.9229E-01	−0.4510E-01	0.1027E 00	0.1055E-01	206.043
3.2	20.1062	−0.8803E-01	−0.2269E-01	0.9091E-01	0.8265E-02	194.452
3.3	20.7345	−0.7911E-01	−0.1274E-02	0.7912E-01	0.6260E-02	180.923
3.4	21.3628	−0.6663E-01	0.1796E-01	0.6900E-01	0.4762E-02	164.918
3.5	21.9911	−0.5177E-01	0.3403E-01	0.6195E-01	0.3838E-02	146.686
3.6	22.6195	−0.3576E-01	0.4623E-01	0.5844E-01	0.3416E-02	127.718
3.7	23.2478	−0.1972E-01	0.5416E-01	0.5764E-01	0.3322E-02	110.003
3.8	23.8761	−0.4669E-02	0.5771E-01	0.5789E-01	0.3352E-02	94.626
3.9	24.5044	0.8549E-02	0.5705E-01	0.5769E-01	0.3328E-02	81.478
4.0	25.1327	0.1932E-01	0.5266E-01	0.5609E-01	0.3146E-02	69.855
4.1	25.7611	0.2724E-01	0.4517E-01	0.5275E-01	0.2782E-02	58.906
4.2	26.3894	0.3216E-01	0.3540E-01	0.4783E-01	0.2288E-02	47.748
4.3	27.0177	0.3413E-01	0.2426E-01	0.4187E-01	0.1753E-02	35.402
4.4	27.6460	0.3340E-01	0.1265E-01	0.3572E-01	0.1276E-02	20.740
4.5	28.2743	0.3038E-01	0.1445E-02	0.3041E-01	0.9250E-03	2.723
4.6	28.9027	0.2557E-01	−0.8593E-02	0.2697E-01	0.7276E-03	341.423
4.7	29.5310	0.1954E-01	−0.1686E-01	0.2581E-01	0.6661E-03	319.225
4.8	30.1593	0.1290E-01	−0.2291E-01	0.2629E-01	0.6914E-03	299.378
4.9	30.7876	0.6197E-02	−0.2654E-01	0.2725E-01	0.7427E-03	283.144
5.0	31.4159	−0.5936E-04	−0.2771E-01	0.2771E-01	0.7676E-03	269.877
5.1	32.0442	−0.5461E-02	−0.2657E-01	0.2713E-01	0.7360E-03	258.387
5.2	32.6726	−0.9710E-02	−0.2346E-01	0.2539E-01	0.6447E-03	247.517
5.3	33.3009	−0.1263E-01	−0.1881E-01	0.2265E-01	0.5131E-03	236.120
5.4	33.9292	−0.1416E-01	−0.1313E-01	0.1931E-01	0.3728E-03	222.844
5.5	34.5575	−0.1435E-01	−0.6982E-02	0.1596E-01	0.2547E-03	205.943

$\phi = 540.00000$ degrees

N	$2\pi N$	Real part	Imag. part	Modulus	(Mod)^2	Arg. in deg.
0.0	0.0000	−0.7854E 00	−0.1667E 00	0.8029E 00	0.6446E 00	191.981
0.1	0.6283	−0.7762E 00	−0.1646E 00	0.7934E 00	0.6296E 00	191.975
0.2	1.2566	−0.7490E 00	−0.1586E 00	0.7656E 00	0.5861E 00	191.959
0.3	1.8850	−0.7051E 00	−0.1491E 00	0.7207E 00	0.5194E 00	191.942
0.4	2.5133	−0.6466E 00	−0.1367E 00	0.6609E 00	0.4368E 00	191.941
0.5	3.1416	−0.5762E 00	−0.1223E 00	0.5891E 00	0.3470E 00	191.987
0.6	3.7699	−0.4972E 00	−0.1069E 00	0.5086E 00	0.2587E 00	192.134
0.7	4.3982	−0.4133E 00	−0.9144E-01	0.4232E 00	0.1791E 00	192.477
0.8	5.0265	−0.3280E 00	−0.7692E-01	0.3369E 00	0.1135E 00	193.201
0.9	5.6549	−0.2450E 00	−0.6423E-01	0.2533E 00	0.6414E-01	194.690
1.0	6.2832	−0.1677E 00	−0.5403E-01	0.1762E 00	0.3104E-01	197.857
1.1	6.9115	−0.9902E-01	−0.4677E-01	0.1095E 00	0.1199E-01	205.282
1.2	7.5398	−0.4127E-01	−0.4263E-01	0.5933E-01	0.3521E-02	225.930
1.3	8.1681	0.3927E-02	−0.4150E-01	0.4169E-01	0.1738E-02	275.405
1.4	8.7965	0.3570E-01	−0.4299E-01	0.5589E-01	0.3123E-02	309.705
1.5	9.4248	0.5397E-01	−0.4649E-01	0.7123E-01	0.5074E-02	319.256
1.6	10.0531	0.5938E-01	−0.5118E-01	0.7839E-01	0.6145E-02	319.245
1.7	10.6814	0.5328E-01	−0.5612E-01	0.7738E-01	0.5988E-02	313.515
1.8	11.3097	0.3756E-01	−0.6034E-01	0.7107E-01	0.5051E-02	301.901
1.9	11.9381	0.1453E-01	−0.6290E-01	0.6456E-01	0.4167E-02	283.011
2.0	12.5664	−0.1321E-01	−0.6298E-01	0.6435E-01	0.4141E-02	258.158
2.1	13.1947	−0.4299E-01	−0.5996E-01	0.7378E-01	0.5443E-02	234.363
2.2	13.8230	−0.7220E-01	−0.5345E-01	0.8983E-01	0.8070E-02	216.510
2.3	14.4513	−0.9848E-01	−0.4334E-01	0.1076E 00	0.1158E-01	203.754
2.4	15.0796	−0.1198E 00	−0.2984E-01	0.1235E 00	0.1525E-01	193.987
2.5	15.7080	−0.1347E-01	−0.1344E-01	0.1353E 00	0.1831E-01	185.699
2.6	16.3363	−0.1420E 00	0.5120E-02	0.1421E 00	0.2019E-01	177.935

2.7	16.9646	−0.1414E 00	0.2488E-01	0.1436E 00	0.2062E-01	170.024
2.8	17.5929	−0.1331E 00	0.4472E-01	0.1404E 00	0.1970E-01	161.422
2.9	18.2212	−0.1176E 00	0.6350E-01	0.1336E 00	0.1786E-01	151.627
3.0	18.8496	−0.9608E-01	0.8006E-01	0.1251E 00	0.1564E-01	140.197
3.1	19.4779	−0.7006E-01	0.9336E-01	0.1167E 00	0.1362E-01	126.883
3.2	20.1062	−0.4121E-01	0.1026E 00	0.1105E 00	0.1222E-01	111.894
3.3	20.7345	−0.1138E-01	0.1070E 00	0.1076E 00	0.1158E-01	96.070
3.4	21.3628	0.1763E-01	0.1064E 00	0.1079E 00	0.1164E-01	80.593
3.5	21.9911	0.4414E-01	0.1008E 00	0.1100E 00	0.1211E-01	66.349
3.6	22.6195	0.6670E-01	0.9041E-01	0.1123E 00	0.1262E-01	53.580
3.7	23.2478	0.8419E-01	0.7589E-01	0.1133E 00	0.1285E-01	42.035
3.8	23.8761	0.9584E-01	0.5811E-01	0.1121E 00	0.1256E-01	31.230
3.9	24.5044	0.1013E 00	0.3813E-01	0.1083E 00	0.1172E-01	20.623
4.0	25.1327	0.1007E 00	0.1714E-01	0.1022E 00	0.1044E-01	9.658
4.1	25.7611	0.9441E-01	−0.3641E-02	0.9448E-01	0.8927E-02	357.791
4.2	26.3894	0.8322E-01	−0.2302E-01	0.8634E-01	0.7455E-02	344.540
4.3	27.0177	0.6815E-01	−0.3991E-01	0.7898E-01	0.6238E-02	329.645
4.4	27.6460	0.5042E-01	−0.5345E-01	0.7347E-01	0.5398E-02	313.330
4.5	28.2743	0.3131E-01	−0.6297E-01	0.7033E-01	0.4946E-02	296.438
4.6	28.9027	0.1212E-01	−0.6813E-01	0.6920E-01	0.4788E-02	280.088
4.7	29.5310	−0.5952E-02	−0.6884E-01	0.6909E-01	0.4774E-02	265.058
4.8	30.1593	−0.2187E-01	−0.6532E-01	0.6888E-01	0.4744E-02	251.491
4.9	30.7876	−0.3480E-01	−0.5805E-01	0.6768E-01	0.4580E-02	227.199
5.0	31.4159	−0.4419E-01	−0.4772E-01	0.6504E-01	0.4231E-02	227.199
5.1	32.0442	−0.4976E-01	−0.3521E-01	0.6096E-01	0.3716E-02	215.287
5.2	32.6726	−0.5148E-01	−0.2148E-01	0.5578E-01	0.3112E-02	202.645
5.3	33.3009	−0.4962E-01	−0.7506E-02	0.5018E-01	0.2518E-02	188.602
5.4	33.9292	−0.4463E-01	0.5759E-02	0.4500E-01	0.2025E-02	172.647
5.5	34.5575	−0.3715E-01	0.1747E-01	0.4105E-01	0.1685E-02	154.810

$\phi = 720.00000$ degrees

N	$2\pi N$	Real part	Imag. part	Modulus	(Mod)²	Arg. in deg.
0.0	0.0000	−0.7854E 00	−0.5002E-11	0.7854E 00	0.6169E 00	180.000
0.1	0.6283	−0.7757E 00	0.1533E-02	0.7757E 00	0.6018E 00	179.887
0.2	1.2566	−0.7472E 00	0.6018E-02	0.7473E 00	0.5584E 00	179.539
0.3	1.8850	−0.7012E 00	0.1313E-01	0.7014E 00	0.4919E 00	178.928
0.4	2.5133	−0.6399E 00	0.2234E-01	0.6403E 00	0.4099E 00	178.001
0.5	3.1416	−0.5660E 00	0.3299E-01	0.5669E 00	0.3214E 00	176.664
0.6	3.7699	−0.4829E 00	0.4430E-01	0.4849E 00	0.2351E 00	174.758
0.7	4.3982	−0.3942E 00	0.5547E-01	0.3981E 00	0.1585E 00	171.991
0.8	5.0265	−0.3039E 00	0.6572E-01	0.3109E 00	0.9665E-01	167.795
0.9	5.6549	−0.2154E 00	0.7435E-01	0.2279E 00	0.5193E-01	160.958
1.0	6.2832	−0.1323E 00	0.8079E-01	0.1550E 00	0.2403E-01	148.590
1.1	6.9115	−0.5744E-01	0.8464E-01	0.1023E 00	0.1046E-01	124.163
1.2	7.5398	0.6840E-02	0.8572E-01	0.8599E-01	0.7394E-02	85.437
1.3	8.1681	0.5895E-01	0.8403E-01	0.1026E 00	0.1054E-01	54.950
1.4	8.7965	0.9805E-01	0.7980E-01	0.1264E 00	0.1598E-01	39.142
1.5	9.4248	0.1241E 00	0.7341E-01	0.1442E 00	0.2078E-01	30.611
1.6	10.0531	0.1377E 00	0.6538E-01	0.1524E 00	0.2323E-01	25.401
1.7	10.6814	0.1402E 00	0.5632E-01	0.1510E 00	0.2282E-01	21.892
1.8	11.3097	0.1333E 00	0.4688E-01	0.1413E 00	0.1997E-01	19.372
1.9	11.9381	0.1194E 00	0.3767E-01	0.1252E 00	0.1556E-01	17.516
2.0	12.5664	0.1006E 00	0.2923E-01	0.1048E 00	0.1098E-01	16.199
2.1	13.1947	0.7951E-01	0.2198E-01	0.8249E-01	0.6805E-02	15.452
2.2	13.8230	0.5831E-01	0.1617E-01	0.6051E-01	0.3661E-02	15.503
2.3	14.4513	0.3899E-01	0.1190E-01	0.4076E-01	0.1662E-02	16.977
2.4	15.0796	0.2314E-01	0.9072E-02	0.2486E-01	0.6179E-03	21.406
2.5	15.7080	0.1188E-01	0.7431E-02	0.1402E-01	0.1964E-03	32.018
2.6	16.3363	0.5800E-02	0.6592E-02	0.8780E-02	0.7709E-04	48.656

2.7	16.9646	0.4953E-02	0.6077E-02	0.7840E-02	0.6146E-04	50.815
2.8	17.5929	0.8914E-02	0.5367E-02	0.1040E-01	0.1083E-03	31.050
2.9	18.2212	0.1683E-01	0.3955E-02	0.1729E-01	0.2988E-03	13.228
3.0	18.8496	0.2751E-01	0.1404E-02	0.2755E-01	0.7589E-03	2.922
3.1	19.4779	0.3957E-01	−0.2611E-02	0.3966E-01	0.1573E-02	356.225
3.2	20.1062	0.5154E-01	−0.8259E-02	0.5220E-01	0.2724E-02	350.896
3.3	20.7345	0.6196E-01	−0.1553E-01	0.6388E-01	0.4081E-02	345.931
3.4	21.3628	0.6958E-01	−0.2422E-01	0.7367E-01	0.5428E-02	340.807
3.5	21.9911	0.7337E-01	−0.3395E-01	0.8084E-01	0.6535E-02	335.165
3.6	22.6195	0.7264E-01	−0.4419E-01	0.8503E-01	0.7229E-02	328.690
3.7	23.2478	0.6712E-01	−0.5426E-01	0.8631E-01	0.7449E-02	321.048
3.8	23.8761	0.5690E-01	−0.6344E-01	0.8522E-01	0.7262E-02	311.888
3.9	24.5044	0.4247E-01	−0.7100E-01	0.8273E-01	0.6845E-02	300.891
4.0	25.1327	0.2468E-01	−0.7624E-01	0.8013E-01	0.6421E-02	287.940
4.1	25.7611	0.4628E-02	−0.7858E-01	0.7872E-01	0.6197E-02	273.370
4.2	26.3894	−0.1640E-01	−0.7762E-01	0.7933E-01	0.6294E-02	258.068
4.3	27.0177	−0.3703E-01	−0.7314E-01	0.8198E-01	0.6721E-02	243.145
4.4	27.6460	−0.5592E-01	−0.6516E-01	0.8586E-01	0.7372E-02	229.366
4.5	28.2743	−0.7182E-01	−0.5394E-01	0.8982E-01	0.8068E-02	216.909
4.6	28.9027	−0.8373E-01	−0.3998E-01	0.9278E-01	0.8608E-02	205.523
4.7	29.5310	−0.9089E-01	−0.2395E-01	0.9400E-01	0.8835E-02	194.764
4.8	30.1593	−0.9291E-01	−0.6730E-02	0.9315E-01	0.8678E-02	184.143
4.9	30.7876	−0.8972E-01	0.1074E-01	0.9036E-01	0.8165E-02	173.172
5.0	31.4159	−0.8161E-01	0.2747E-01	0.8611E-01	0.7415E-02	161.399
5.1	32.0442	−0.6920E-01	0.4248E-01	0.8120E-01	0.6594E-02	148.455
5.2	32.6726	−0.5337E-01	0.5492E-01	0.7658E-01	0.5865E-02	134.180
5.3	33.3009	−0.3520E-01	0.6408E-01	0.7311E-01	0.5345E-02	118.784
5.4	33.9292	−0.1590E-01	0.6945E-01	0.7125E-01	0.5076E-02	102.898
5.5	34.5575	0.3287E-02	0.7078E-01	0.7085E-01	0.5020E-02	87.341

Index

309